Centerville Library
Washington-Centerville Public Library
Centerville, Ohio

Competitive Intelligence, Analysis and Strategy

D0781456

The Holy Grail for most organisations is the successful attainment, and retention, of inimitable competitive advantage. This book addresses the question of how to leverage the unique intangible assets of an organisation: its explicit, implicit, acquired and derived knowledge. The refreshingly innovative concept of *Intelligence-Based Competitive Advantage*© is one which will eclipse the cost-driven and resource-reduction attitudes most prevalent in the first decade of this century. Tomorrow's organisations will need to derive *IBCA*© through the expert execution of bespoke competitive intelligence practice, unique analytical processes, pioneering competitive strategy formulation, and timely execution of all three, if they are to succeed. This volume consists of insights from Competitive Intelligence practices at both country and organisational level, Competitive Analysis processes within the firm and within challenging sector and economic environments and Competitive Strategy formulation in profit, non-profit, real and virtual world contexts. It is essential reading for anybody wishing to gain a formal understanding of the practical and intellectual challenges which will face organisations in the future as they strive to achieve strategic foresight and *Intelligence-Based Competitive Advantage*©.

This book was originally published as two special issues of the *Journal of Strategic Marketing*.

Sheila Wright is Reader in Competitive Intelligence and Marketing Strategy at De Montfort University, UK. She is widely regarded as a thought leader in the Competitive Intelligence and Insight Management field. Previous contributions to the field include numerous Journal articles and conference papers as well as invited addresses to industry bodies and practitioners.

Centerville Library
Washington-Centerville Public Library
Centerville, Ohio

Competitive Intelligence, Analysis and Strategy

Creating Organisational Agility

Edited by
Sheila Wright

Routledge
Taylor & Francis Group

LONDON AND NEW YORK

First published 2013
by Routledge
2 Park Square, Milton Park, Abingdon, Oxfordshire OX14 4RN

Simultaneously published in the USA and Canada
by Routledge
711 Third Avenue, New York, NY 10017

First issued in paperback 2015

Routledge is an imprint of the Taylor & Francis Group, an informa business

© 2013 Taylor & Francis

This book is a compilation of two special issues of the *Journal of Strategic Marketing*: Volume 18, Issue 7 and Volume 20, Issue 1. The Publisher requests to those authors who may be citing this book to state, also, the bibliographical details of the special issues on which the book was based.

All rights reserved. No part of this book may be reprinted or reproduced or utilised in any form or by any electronic, mechanical, or other means, now known or hereafter invented, including photocopying and recording, or in any information storage or retrieval system, without permission in writing from the publishers.

Trademark notice: Product or corporate names may be trademarks or registered trademarks, and are used only for identification and explanation without intent to infringe.

British Library Cataloguing in Publication Data
A catalogue record for this book is available from the British Library

ISBN13: 978-1-138-94394-0 (pbk)
ISBN13: 978-0-415-63128-0 (hbk)

Typeset in Times New Roman
by Taylor & Francis Books

Publisher's Note
The publisher would like to make readers aware that the chapters in this book may be referred to as articles as they are identical to the articles published in the special issue. The publisher accepts responsibility for any inconsistencies that may have arisen in the course of preparing this volume for print.

Contents

CONTENTS

Citation Information

The chapters in this book (with the exception of Chapter 1) were originally published in the *Journal of Strategic Marketing*. When citing this material, please use the original issue information and page numbering for each article, as follows:

Chapter 1
Wright, S. (2013), 'Converting input to insight: Organising for Intelligence-Based Competitive Advantage', pp 1-35 in Wright, S. (Ed), *Competitive Intelligence, Analysis and Strategy: Creating Organisational Agility,* Abingdon, UK, Routledge

Chapter 2
Smith, J.R., Wright, S. & Pickton, D.W. (2012), 'Competitive Intelligence Programmes for SMEs in France: Evidence of Changing Attitudes', *Journal of Strategic Marketing,* 18(7), pp 523-536

Chapter 3
Larivet, S. & Brouard, F. (2010), 'Complaints are a Firm's Best Friend', *Journal of Strategic Marketing,* 18(7), 537-551

Chapter 4
Wright, S., Bisson, C. & Duffy, A.P. (2012), 'Applying a Behavioural and Operational Diagnostic Typology of Competitive Intelligence Practice: Empirical Evidence from the SME Sector in Turkey, *Journal of Strategic Marketing*, 20(1), 19-33

Chapter 5
Larivet, S. & Brouard, F. (2012), 'SMEs' Attitude towards SI Programmes: Evidence from Belgium', *Journal of Strategic Marketing*, 20(1), 5-18

Chapter 6
Simkin, L. & Dibb, S. (2012), 'Leadership Teams Rediscover Market Analysis in Seeking Competitive Advantage and Growth During Economic Uncertainty', *Journal of Strategic Marketing*, 20(1), 45-54

Chapter 7
Patterson, A., Quinn, L. & Baron, S. (2012), 'The Power of Intuitive Thinking: A Devalued Heuristic of Strategic Marketing, *Journal of Strategic Marketing*, 20(1), 35-44

Chapter 8

Fleisher, C.S. & Wright, S. (2010), 'Competitive Intelligence Analysis Failure: Diagnosing Individual Level Causes and Implementing Organisational Level Remedies', *Journal of Strategic Marketing,* 18(7), 553-572

Chapter 9

Bennett, D. & Graham, C. (2010), 'Is Loyalty Driving Growth for the Brand in Front? A Two-Purchase Analysis of Car Category Dynamics in Thailand', *Journal of Strategic Marketing,* 18(7), 573-585

Chapter 10

Tamaddoni Jahromi, A., Sepehri, M.M., Teimourpour, B. & Choobdar, S. (2010), 'Modeling Customer Churn in a Non-Contractual Setting: The Case of Telecommunications Service Providers'. *Journal of Strategic Marketing*, 18(7), 587-598

Chapter 11

Hartland, T. & Williams-Burnett, N. (2012), 'Protecting the Olympic Band: Winners and Losers', *Journal of Strategic Marketing*, 20(1), 69-82

Chapter 12

Mejtoft, T. (2010), 'Moving Closer to the Customers: Effects of Vertical Integration in the Swedish Commercial Printing Industry', *Journal of Strategic Marketing*, 18(7), 599-611

Chapter 13

Modi, P. (2012), 'Market Orientation in Nonprofit Organizations: Innovativeness, Resource Scarcity, and Performance', *Journal of Strategic Marketing*, 20(1), 55-67

Chapter 14

Bretonès, D.D., Quinio, B. & Réveillon, G. (2010), 'Bridging Virtual and Real Worlds: Enhancing Outlying Clustered Value Creations', *Journal of Strategic Marketing*, 18(7), 613-625

Notes on Contributors

Steve Baron is Professor of Marketing at the University of Liverpool Management School, UK. He was Chair of the AMA Servsig International Research Conference, 2008, and Academic Chair of the Academy of Marketing Conference, 2011. He has publications in services, marketing, education and management journals, including *Journal of Service Research, European Journal of Marketing, International Journal of Market Research, Industrial Marketing Management, Higher Education Quarterly, Journal of Business Research* and *Journal of Strategic Marketing*. He is co-author of *Services Marketing: Text and Cases* (2009), and *Relationship Marketing: A Consumer Experience Approach* (2010).

Dr. Dag Bennett is the Director of the Ehrenberg Centre for Research in Marketing and a Reader in Marketing at London South Bank University, UK. Before becoming an academic, he gained extensive international marketing experience with Procter and Gamble in the US. He then worked as a marketing director in Chicago and London for a variety of FMCG and consumer durables companies. His focus is on consumer behaviour and brand growth, especially in rapidly developing markets such as China.

Dr. Christophe Bisson is President of the Internationally Accepted Marketing Standards Board, and Editor-in-Chief of the *International Journal of Marketing Principles and Practices*. He currently lectures at Kadir Has University in Istanbul, Turkey, specialising in the fields of Competitive Intelligence and Strategic Information Systems. Dr. Bisson also has extensive international experience in the corporate world as a senior business leader and consultant.

Daniel Bretonès is Professor of Management at ESCEM Business School (Tours/Poitiers), France. He is Head of ADVISE "ICT Consulting and Management" Masters Program. As a member of the CRESCEM Labs, his research streams focus on industrial clusters development and start-ups, ICT and virtual worlds. He is an Associate Research Fellow with the Paris I Sorbonne University PRISM lab. He is Publishing Manager of *Vie & Sciences de l'Entreprise* (VSE), a French Management journal and President of ANDESE, a PhDs in Management Association.

François Brouard, DBA, FCPA, FCA is a Fellow Chartered Professional Accountant (FCPA) and a Fellow Chartered Accountant (FCA). He is currently an Associate Professor in the accounting group (taxation and financial accounting) at the Sprott School of Business, Carleton University, Canada, and Founding Director of the

Sprott Centre for Social Enterprises (SCSE). He acts as coordinator for Entrepreneurship programmes. He is founding co-editor in chief of the peer reviewed journal, ANSERJ – *Canadian Journal of Non-profit and Social Economy Research/Revue Canadienne de recherche sur les OSBL et l'économie sociale*. His research interests include social entrepreneurship, strategic intelligence, social enterprises, business transfer, SME and governance.

Sarvenaz Choobdar is a PhD candidate in MAP-i Doctoral Program in Computer Science and a researcher at Center for Research in Advanced Computing Systems (CRACS), INESC-Porto, Portugal. She is pursuing her PhD in the field of graph mining. She received her Master degree in Information Technology at Tarbiat Modares University, Iran and received her engineering degree from Alzahra University, Iran. Her research interests are Data Mining for Graphs, Evolving Networks and Evolutionary Data Mining.

Sally Dibb is Professor of Marketing at the Open University Business School, UK, and Director of the Institute for Social Marketing (ISM-Open). Her research focuses on market segmentation, marketing strategy, marketing planning, and consumer behaviour, in which areas she has published extensively in leading European and US academic journals. Sally chairs the Academy of Marketing's special interest group in Market Segmentation and is Associate Editor of the *Journal of Marketing Management*. She is a trustee of the research charity Alcohol Research UK and provides strategic marketing and targeting advice for a mix of organisations.

Dr Alistair Duffy is Reader in Electromagnetics at De Montfort University, Leicester, UK, blending research and teaching interests in technology and the management of technology. He has an interest in technology strategy and in particular the role of knowledge management to such activities as forecasting. He is a member of the Board of Directors of the IEEE EMC Society and is a past Distinguished Lecturer of the Society. He serves on a number of other Boards, standards groups and has a variety of editorial responsibilities including Series Editor for the SciTech (an imprint of the IET) book series on electromagnetic compatibility (EMC).

Dr. Craig S. Fleisher is Chief Learning Officer of Aurora WDC, Wisconsin, USA and a member of the graduate faculties at Tampere University of Technology, Finland and Università della Svizzera italiana (Switzerland). He was President of the Strategic and Competitive Intelligence Professionals (SCIP), Chair of the Competitive Intelligence Foundation, Editor of the *Journal of Competitive Intelligence & Management*, and is a SCIP Meritorious Award winner and Fellow. A former Dean MBA director, and endowed university research chair holder, he has authored over ten books and has been a member of university faculties in Australia, Canada, NZ, South Africa, UK and USA.

Charles Graham is an Associate of the Ehrenberg Centre for Research in Marketing and a Senior Lecturer at London South Bank University, UK. He has had extensive national and international experience of managing entrepreneurial FMCG and service brands. His research examines long-term behavioural loyalty and the determinants and characteristics of brand growth.

Trevor Hartland is Senior Lecturer in Marketing and BA Marketing award leader at the University of Glamorgan in South Wales, UK. He teaches marketing communications, sports marketing and trends. His main research interests lie in sports sponsorship and ambush marketing, with a particular emphasis towards the sponsorship of motor racing, of which Trevor is also an active participant. Prior to taking up his current post, Trevor worked in the motor industry for Volkswagen, Lotus and Toyota. He was also a partner in a strategic marketing design consultancy.

Dr. Sophie Larivet is Professor of Marketing and Strategy at the Ecole Supérieure du Commerce Extérieur (ESCE) in Paris, France. She holds a Master's degree in Marketing and a PhD in Strategy. She has been teaching marketing research and CI in business, engineering and military schools since 2000. She won the French Economic Intelligence Academy award in 2009 for her book on CI in small businesses. Dr. Larivet is a member of the editorial board of several CI academic journals. She is also as a trainer and consultant specialized in SMEs' CI issues.

Dr. Thomas Mejtoft is an Associate Professor of Media Technology and the Programme Director of the MSc in Interaction Technology and Design at Umeå University, Sweden. He holds a PhD from the Royal Institute of Technology (KTH) in Stockholm and has worked as a Senior Research Associate at the Research Institute STFI-Packforsk. His research interests include strategic management, concurrent sourcing and the effects of media technology in small and medium sized firms. His work has been published in the *Journal of Strategic Marketing, Industrial Marketing Management,* and *Journal of Media Business Studies,* and he has presented at numerous international conferences.

Dr. Pratik Modi is an Assistant Professor in Marketing at the Institute of Rural Management Anand (IRMA) in India. His research works have appeared in *Journal of Marketing Management, Journal of Strategic Marketing, Asian Case Research Journal, International Journal of Rural Management* among others. The *Journal of Research Practice* honoured him twice with the Best Reviewer Award. His research interests are market orientation, social and non-profit marketing, and BoP marketing. He is editor of *International Journal of Rural Management.*

Dr. Anthony Patterson is Professor of Marketing at the University of Liverpool Management School, UK. Before joining Liverpool, he taught on faculties at the University of Sheffield and also the University of Ulster where he gained his PhD in consumer behaviour. His research focuses on the cultural issues of social networking and text messaging, exploring how these phenomena impact on consumer behaviour. His other research interests include city branding, nation branding, and book marketing. Anthony is the recipient of the University of Liverpool's Sir Alistair Pilkington Award for Teaching Excellence and his publications have appeared in the *Journal of Business Research, Psychology & Marketing, Journal of Marketing Management* and *Journal of Strategic Marketing,* among others.

David Pickton is Honorary Academic Fellow at De Montfort University, Leicester, UK, having been Head of Marketing. He is Visiting Academic at the Universities of Birmingham, UK, and Vienna, Austria. He is on the Editorial Boards of a number of respected marketing journals and his professional affiliations include Fellow and Chartered Member of the Chartered Institute of Marketing, Fellowships of the Royal Society of Arts and the Higher Education Academy. His research interests include competitive intelligence and integrated marketing communications. He has contributed to various academic texts, written numerous articles and conference papers and is co-author of two highly successful marketing books.

Lee Quinn is a Lecturer in Marketing and Director of Studies for the BA Marketing programme at the University of Liverpool Management School. The primary focus of his research concerns the managerial implementation of market segmentation and customer profiling solutions. This focus also enables him to examine some of the more unusual aspects of managerial behaviour including, for example, the intuitive nature of managerial decision-making, and the communicative impact of story-telling. His work has been published in the *European Journal of Marketing, Journal of Marketing Management, Journal of Strategic Marketing* and *Journal of Customer Behaviour,* among others.

Dr. Bernard Quinio is an engineer in computer science and gained his Doctorate in Management Science. After 10 years as a consultant; he now works at the University of Paris Ouest Nanterre La Défense and is an Affiliate Professor at ESCP Europe. His areas of specialisation are Information Systems and Project Management. He is particularly interested in the evaluation of the economic impact of information systems in the corporate world. Since 2006, he has been studying the impact of Web 2.0 and Virtual Social Network on organisations.

Gilbert Réveillon, MBA is affiliate teacher at IREST Paris 1 Panthéon – Sorbonne, France, and is CEO the Mobile LOOV Ltd. After 10 years at LaSer dealing with loyalty schemes and financial products, he created and chaired the international intr@Verse Awards with 100 case studies of worldwide companies from the 3 regions, North America, Asia and Europe. These dealt with value creation by using virtual social networks technology and ecosystems. He is also President of the ICT and Digital Economic at CNCCEF (French Trade Advisor).

Dr. Mohammad Mehdi Sepehri is an Associate Professor at the Department of Industrial Engineering, Tarbiat Modares University, Tehran, Iran, Head of group of Industrial Engineering, and Editor-in-Chief of *International Journal of Hospital Research (IJHR).* Dr. Sepehri obtained his PhD in Management Science from the University of Tennessee, Knoxville and now teaches MS and PhD level courses at TMU. His teaching interests include network flows, data mining and knowledge discovery, mathematical programming, and business models. His current research focuses on Operations Research in Medicine and Healthcare, Lean Hospital, Healthcare and Medical Decision Making, and Health Information Technology.

Lyndon Simkin is Professor of Strategic Marketing at Oxford Brookes University, UK, Associate Editor of the *Journal of Marketing Management,* on the Academy of Marketing's Research Committee and co-chair of its Segmentation SIG. His work has been published in the *European Journal of Marketing, Industrial Marketing Management, Services Industries Journal, Journal of Marketing Management, OMEGA, Journal of Industrial & Business Marketing, Journal of Strategic Marketing* and the *International Journal of Advertising.* Lyndon has authored nine books, including *Marketing: Concepts and Strategies, Marketing Essentials, Marketing Planning,* and *Market Segmentation Success.* He is a consultant to many corporations, coach to CEOs, and a recognised expert witness in marketing litigation.

Dr. Jamie Smith is a lecturer of Marketing Strategy at ESCEM School of Management in Poitiers, France. During his PhD studies at De Montfort University, he has been an active researcher in the Competitive Intelligence-Management Interface Teaching and Research Initiative (CIMITRI). His research areas include CI as public policy and the role of Competitive Intelligence attitude antecedents for decision-makers in Small and Medium-sized Enterprises. He has twice been a speaker at international SCIP conferences and has presented papers at colloquiums on CI across Europe. He has taught CI at *L'Ecole de Petrole et Moteur* in Paris.

Ali Tamaddoni Jahromi is a PhD candidate in the Department of Marketing at Monash University in Melbourne, Australia. Tamaddoni Jahromi completed his Master's degree in Marketing and e-Commerce at Tarbiat Modares University, Tehran, Iran. His areas of interest are Analytical CRM, Churn Management, and Stochastic Buyer Behavior Models. His current research focus is on investigating consumers' purchase/dropout behaviour in non-contractual settings.

Dr. Babak Teimourpour obtained his PhD in Information Technology Engineering from the Department of Industrial Engineering, Tarbiat Modares University (TMU), Tehran, Iran, having completed an MSc in Socio-Economic Systems Engineering at the Institute for Research on Planning and Development, Tehran, Iran. He currently teaches BS and MS level courses. His research interests include Data Mining, Social Network Analysis, Burst Detection, Mapping Knowledge Domains, Text Mining, Market Segmentation and New Product Development. His team won the Iran Data Mining Cup in 2010.

Nicola Williams-Burnett is a Lecturer in Marketing at Cardiff Metropolitan University, South Wales, UK, where she teaches strategic brand management. Her main areas of interest lie in branding, body image, motivations of consumer behaviour, physical activity (particularly the determinants) and the health and fitness industry where Nicola is a part-time fitness instructor. Nicola worked as a marketer in a number of B2B organisations in the manufacturing and IT industries. She has also written a number of articles on practical marketing for health and fitness professionals before making the transition into academia.

Dr. Sheila Wright is a Reader in Competitive Intelligence & Marketing Strategy at De Montfort University, Leicester. She has served as an elected Board member for both the Strategic Planning Society and the US based Strategic & Competitive Intelligence Professionals. Sheila's research has been published in *European Journal of Marketing, Journal of Marketing Management, Journal of Strategic Marketing, Thunderbird International Business Review,* among others and focuses on securing improvements in CI&IM practice at the individual, organisational and national levels. Sheila draws equally on her practitioner and academic knowledge when teaching, which contributed to her receiving a Vice Chancellor's Distinguished Teaching Award on two occasions.

Introduction

Converting input to insight: organising for *Intelligence-Based Competitive Advantage*

Sheila Wright

Department of Marketing, De Montfort University, Leicester, UK

Introduction

This book represents the culmination of a significant amount of intellectual endeavour put into the subject area of Competitive Intelligence & Insight Management (CI&IM) by a number of highly respected authors in the field. It has been produced as a consequence of two special issues devoted to the topic by the *Journal of Strategic Marketing*.

The Holy Grail for most organisations is the successful attainment, and retention, of inimitable competitive advantage. This collection of peer-reviewed research articles address the question of how to leverage those unique intangible assets of the organisation, its explicit, implicit, acquired, derived knowledge and use these as the foundation for creating organisational agility. The refreshingly innovative concept of *Intelligence-Based Competitive Advantage (IBCA©)*, is poised to eclipse the cost-driven and resource reduction attitudes most prevalent in the first decade of this century (Wright, 2011). Tomorrow's organisations will need to derive *IBCA©* through the expert execution of bespoke competitive intelligence practice, unique analytical processes, pioneering competitive strategy formulation and timely execution of all three if they are to succeed. The panorama for this collection consists of insight from:

- Competitive Intelligence practices at both country and organisational level
- Competitive Analysis processes within firms and their challenging environments
- Competitive Strategy formulation in profit, non-profit, real and virtual world contexts.

This book is the first of its kind in the field, being both academically rigorous , yet accessible to all wishing to understand the practical and intellectual challenges which organisations face as they strive to achieve strategic foresight and *IBCA©*. The individual chapters have already successfully navigated the double-blind peer review process of the *Academy of Marketing*, where they were first presented as limited page conference papers and then the editorial processes for both the special issue format, and finally this text. Before introducing the specific contributions made by these authors and their work, it is worth examining the context of CI and *IBCA©* within the business discipline.

Historical Context

The rich heritage of Competitive Intelligence (CI) has been uniquely documented by Juhari & Stephens (2006) and can be traced back over 5,000 years (Prescott, 1999; Qingjiu & Prescott, 2000; Chen *et al,* 2010). One of the more frequently cited sources is the work of Sun Tzu who, some 2400 years ago, wrote *The Art of War,* a seminal text which provided a detailed description of how to develop intelligence for military applications (Tzu, 1988). Frederick the Great (b. 1712) who ruled as King of Prussia from 1740 until his death in 1786 is commonly attributed as saying *"It is pardonable to be defeated, but never to be surprised".* It is the avoidance of surprise that Competitive Intelligence seeks to address. There is a danger that *"CI is too frequently limited to competitor intelligence which focuses on identifying, monitoring and under-standing specific current competitors"* (Frates & Sharp, 2005, p. 18). The point is well made and this is one of the key reasons that the name has evolved to become Competitive Intelligence & Insight Management (CI&IM) which reflects a broader strategic orientation and use, rather than simple collection, of information. Information becomes intelligence only after it has been filtered, checked, analysed and processed.

Commercial CI&IM has a long history. Wright *et al* (2004) referred to Nathan Rothschild's timely intelligence to make a fortune on the London stock exchange following the Battle of Waterloo in 1815. Among Rothschild's intelligence network was an agent who watched Napoleon's defeat at Waterloo, subsequently sent carrier pigeons to Rothschild, who the following morning sold large volumes of shares. Observers wrongly concluded that the French had won the battle, and shares slumped. Rothschild then bought back and awaited the news, which arrived conventionally that Wellington had won. The market correction helped Rothschild to his fortune (Ferguson, 1998). Historical records point towards commercial intelligence collection activities happening even earlier. The Byzantine emperor Justinian I (483–565) in the 6th century used monks to steal silk worms from the Chinese in an attempt to understand how to make silk (Fraumann, 1997). Although this is more an example of what would now be termed "industrial espionage" than CI, it does demonstrate how long there have been efforts to scan the environment for information that will provide organisations or countries with a competitive advantage.

It is reported that 87 per cent of all large companies, regardless of location, have an intelligence capability (Global Intelligence Alliance, 2006), but as can be seen from the examples above, the commercial application of CI, as we know it, has been around for at least 5000 years, if not longer.

Preparing for Intelligence-Based Competitive Advantage

To achieve *IBCA*© firms need to first evaluate their stock of intellectual capital, understand the potential for knowledge creation from cross-functional activities and strive to prevent organisational forgetting. This is the overarching goal of a Competitive Intelligence & Insight Management (CI&IM) approach to cultivating competitive advantage. There is general agreement among those firms which practice the art of Competitive Intelligence, Competitive Analysis and Competitive Strategy (CIAS), that the process of CI&IM is not just a function in the firm, rather it is a mind-set, a philosophy even, which fosters organisational learning, information sharing, a co-operation driven management culture and a desire by decision makers to capitalise on gathered intelligence (Badr & Wright, 2004a; Badr *et al*, 2006; Heppes, 2006; Williams, 2006; Wright & Calof, 2006; Dishman & Calof, 2008; Spender, J-C, 2008; Qiu, 2008; Argote & Miron-Spektor, 2009; Sánchez et al, 2009; Wong *et al*, 2009; Zangoueinezhad & Moshabaki, 2009; Besanko et al, 2010; Smith *et al*, 2010; Yakhlef 2010; Franco *et al*, 2011; Patterson *et al*, 2012; Simkin & Dibb, 2012). There is also agreement that Competitive Intelligence as the primer for the delivery of *IBCA©* is an important activity for firms of all sizes, strategies or cultures, regardless of whether or not it is formalised as a function or role (APQC, 1998; 2000; 2003; Wright *et al*, 2002; April & Bessa, 2006; Global Intelligence Alliance, 2006; Appelbaum & Gonzalo, 2007; Zhou *et al*, 2007; Carr *et al*, 2008; Adidam *et al*, 2009; Larivet & Brouard, 2009; Smith, 2009; Adidam *et al*, 2012; Larivet & Brouard, 2012; Wright *et al*, 2012).

CI&IM is not just about data is collection. Today's information rich world has made that part of the task easier, albeit harder to value because of the ubiquitous nature of search engines. Effective CI&IM is about how that data is dealt with by the firm, how it is exploited and capitalised upon, how the process is organised and the structures which are put in place to facilitate the execution of a vital decision making tool. In a recent, in-depth discussion of the theory of *intellectual capital generation*, Bratianu *et al*, (2011) suggested that the traditional perspective of data generation can be changed. They demonstrated the value of intellectual capital derived from organisational mechanisms which they called "integrators". These systems have the power to bring together the primary constituents of information and knowledge and can integrate them into the final intellectual capital of the organisation.

The *resource-based view* can also be utilised as a theory to guide the pursuit of sustainable competitive advantage as illustrated in the work of DeNisi *et al* (2009) and Fiol (2009). Of the many theories of organisational management, the resource-based view (RBV) is well suited to align with the human capital view of people within the firm. The RBV theory suggests that the method in which resources are applied within a firm can create a competitive advantage (Barney, 1991; Mata *et al*, 1995; Peteraf, 1993; Wernerfert, 1984), and this is also a key philosophy within CI&IM practice.

Brown (2007) states that the RBV of competitive advantage is based on two main assumptions: *resource diversity* and *resource immobility* (Barney, 1991; Mata *et al*, 1995). An action passes the resource diversity test if it is one which competing firms are unable to imitate. For example, legal protection in the case of trademarks or patents, supplier or distributor contracts in the case of manufacturing firms and R&D teams in the case of scientific or technology driven firms. Resource immobility refers to a resource which is difficult to obtain by competitors because the cost of developing, acquiring or using that resource is too high. An example would be the benefits of economies of scale, a theory identified in some detail some 40 years ago by Pratten (1971), and still used today in a number of industries ranging from public transport (Farsi *et al*, 2007) through to banking (Mautin, 2011) and timber haulage (Soirinsuo & Mäkinen, 2011). The RBV view of the firm suggests that an organisation's human capital can contribute significantly to sustaining competitive advantage by creating resource diversity via increasing knowledge and skills, especially that which is difficult to imitate (Meso & Smith, 2000; Halawi *et al*, 2005; Afiouni, 2007; Brown, 2007).

It is in the area of resource diversity which CI&IM plays its part as the output of such a programme will be unique to the firm and will enhance its intellectual capital generation. Barney (1991), Mata *et al* (1995), Swart (2006), Afiouni, (2007) and Brown,

(2007) also comment that in order to create human capital resource diversity and immobility, an organization must engage in the right managerial practices, use the right organisational processes and offer the right tools and educational opportunities for the practitioner to do their job right. This aspect of the creation of intelligence-based competitive advantage was addressed specifically in the work of Fleisher & Wright (2010) in which they presented a unique four-level hierarchical model of analysis failure and guiding principles for firms to follow in order to discharge their organisational level responsibility in this regard.

In one of very few empirical studies of its type, Newbert (2008) addressed the position of RBV that the exploitation of valuable, rare resources and capabilities contributes to a firm's competitive advantage, which in turn contributes to its performance. In testing these hypotheses, Newbert (2008) found that "value and rareness are related to competitive advantage, that competitive advantage is related to performance and that competitive advantage mediates the rareness-performance relationship" (p. 745).

CI&IM also aligns with the *sense making school of decision making* which rejects the notion of decision making as a point of inflection in managerial action (Weick, 1995; Weick, *et al*, 2005), rather it sees the process as much more tacit and emergent. Winch & Maytorena (2009), describe the sense making school as one where managers are continually seeking cues from their context. Information arrives as "news" which may, or may not, be surprising. They use this information to make sense of their context and then shape that context based on the sense made. It follows, therefore, that there are no independent criteria for the evaluation of the sense made, and that action is based more upon pragmatic interpretation of the context than optimisation of the data.

In an empirical study of high-tech firms, Liu and Liu (2008), drawing on the work of Bock *et al* (2005) showed the significance of individual knowledge acquisition and sharing behaviour within the firm. Through their results, they were able to conclude that this "needs to be emphasised since it will contribute to the critical foundation of organisational knowledge creation" (p. 424) and as a consequence, the reduction of risk in decision making (Renzl, 2008). Van den Hooff & Huysman (2009) also showed in their study that "knowledge sharing is not stimulated by imposing structures and tools, but by rich social interaction and its immersion in practice" (p. 1), a view voiced both previously and subsequently by Yang (2008; 2010).

The role which CI&IM can play in the development of *organisational learning* and the creation of *organisational memory* has only recently been realised. In a seminal article, Spender (1996) said "knowledge is too problematic a concept to make the task of building a dynamic knowledge based theory of the firm easy" (p. 45). He goes on to state "since the origin of all tangible resources lies outside the firm, it follows that competitive advantage is more likely to arise from the intangible firm-specific knowledge which enables it to add value to the incoming factors of production in a relatively unique manner. Thus it is the firm's knowledge and its ability to generate knowledge, that lies at the core of a more epistemologically sound theory of the firm" (p. 46).

The core of most definitions of organisational learning (OL) is one of a change which occurs as the organisation acquires experience, but researchers have debated whether OL should be defined as a change in cognition or behaviour (Crossan *et al* 1990; Easterby-Smith *et al*, 2000). However, there is agreement with defining OL as a change in the organisation's knowledge which occurs as a function of experience, which manifest itself in changes in cognitions or behaviour, including both explicit and tacit, or difficult to articulate, components (Garvin, 2000; Argote & Miron-Spektor, 2009).

Kandemir & Hult (2005) and Sánchez *et al,* (2009) claim that OL may be the only source of sustainable competitive advantage for a firm in today's complex and dynamic world. It is certainly the resource which is least able to be mimicked (Spender, 2008). Empirical studies have confirmed the benefits of OL on customer orientation (Hult *et al,* 2001), market orientation (Santos *et al,* 2005) and the strategic supply process (Hult *et al,* 2002).

In a refreshing diversion from academic theorising, Yakhlef (2010) prefers to support an embodied, corporeal approach to the evolving practice based work on learning and knowing. He suggests that learning and knowing are grounded in practical, bodily, emotional experiences. However, he notes that the "practice turn" in contemporary social theories has not escaped the attention of organisation theorists who have also placed practices front and centre in their studies of various organisational phenomena (Jarzabkowski *et al,* 2007, Johnson *et al,* 2007; Whittington, 2007).

Quoted by Rowlinson *et al,* (2010), Nissley & Casey (2002) regard organisational memory (OM) as potentially being "the static repository model where some objectified truth is stored". They use the metaphor of a corporate museum to illustrate the way in which organisations can choose to "selectively remember or forget", and that "what is remembered or what is forgotten shapes an organisation's identity and image" (p. 44). In attempting to persuade firms to take organisational knowledge and memory ser- iously, a decade and a half ago, Van Daal *et al,* (1998) proposed a knowledge matrix which would identify the location of current knowledge, capture this for future gen- erations and identify where rectification was needed. It would appear from the writings of Wood (2002), Martin de Holan & Phillips (2003; 2004), Harris & Wegg-Prosser (2007), Besanko *et al* (2010), Kosinen (2010) and Rowlinson *et al* (2010), that that message has yet to be heard.

At around the same time, Prescott, (1999) theorised on the future of CI from the perspective of that year. His prediction was that CCI would become a core capability in organisations, CI courses would be taught in business schools across the world, inte- gration would be formal and informal, orientation would be strategic, analysis would have a qualitative emphasis, top management interest would be high and the link to decision making would be direct. The principal location of CI personnel would be in CI units or in marketing or planning departments and that the key issues would be managing the parallel process, developing the CI function as a learning mechanism and designing an intelligence infrastructure for multi-national firms. This latter element was more recently highlighted by Kalkan (2008) who identified it as a problem still to be fully resolved.

The adoption of CI&IM as an organisation wide philosophy and a platform for *IBCA©* places it as an important concept within organisational learning and the crea- tion of organisational memory. The symbiosis between CI&IM and the RBV of the firm is also a tangible benefit, as indeed are the cross-functional areas of theory and practice. As a consequence, this provides significant risk reduction in the decision making process.

Capitalising on Existing Organisational Intelligence Systems

An organisation will typically benefit from a number of intelligence acquisition efforts, most likely, all operating to different objectives and to different time scales (Dishman &

Calof, 2008; Fleisher *et al*, 2008, Trim & Lee, 2008; Sharp, 2009). The role of *Competitive Intelligence* is to capitalise on these efforts, identify knowledge gaps, to supplement the output via a process of analysis and transformation to provide new knowledge for the firm. It is this latter process which is regarded as *Insight Management*.

The traditional intelligence systems from which a firm can capitalise are *Knowledge Management System, Management Information System, Marketing Information System* and *Competitor Monitoring System*. Buckman (2004) and Liebowitz (2006) imply that whilst it is clear that not all firms will have all of these systems set up in a formal manner, or that their information gathering programmes operate perfectly, the intelligence flows from these sources, would still be regarded as contributing to the intelligence capital of the organisation. As such, it is appropriate to identify the purpose of each system, the elements which comprise them and the primary applications to which the information is applied in the pursuit of *IBCA*©. Each of these systems has value in its own right but collectively, they form the Critical Intelligence Portals Approach to CI&IM, a concept first introduced by Wright (2005c). Subsequently developed (Wright, 2011) the resultant framework is provided in Figure 1.1. This approach embraces pre-existing systems and extends far beyond "environmental scanning", a term and activity often used, interchangeably, yet inaccurately, with CI. Environmental scanning is a passive activity which reports on a myriad of external events, typically regardless of relevance, after they have happened. In contrast, CI&IM is a focused, active and multi-level, organisational effort which encourages internal and external information sharing with the over-riding purpose being to acquire and/or maintain *IBCA*©.

This approach has been developed by Wright (2011) as a consequence of viewing companies as learning organisations and employees as willing learners as suggested by Miller *et al* (2006). A case study on this subject reported on by Scheeres *et al* (2010), centred on how learning still takes place through organisational practices even when there is no formalised learning agenda, whilst Geiger & Schreyögg (2009, p. 477) state "the need to select and distinguish useful from useless knowledge, outdated from valid knowledge, and accurate from misleading suggestions and so on is becoming increasingly challenging in today's societies and organizations. Contemporary organizations and knowledge societies are not so much troubled by a lack of knowledge, but rather by the selection of relevant, useful or right knowledge".

It is in this area that CI&IM plays its part, as a complementary, rather than confrontational element to existing systems of knowledge acquisition. Joseph Luft and Harry Ingham, in their work on how to understand inter-personal relationships, developed a framework, naming it, somewhat unimaginatively, as the Johari Window (Luft & Ingham, 1955). Applying their principles, with minor changes, this model can be applied equally to categorise the different types of knowledge which either exist, or are absent, in a firm's systems. This novel application of the 2x2 Johari window was first introduced by Wright & Pickton (1998) and developed by Weiss & Wright (2006). The original 2x2 Johari Window has also been loosely applied at a basic level by Shenton (2007) who claimed that "no previous paper has applied the Johari Window to

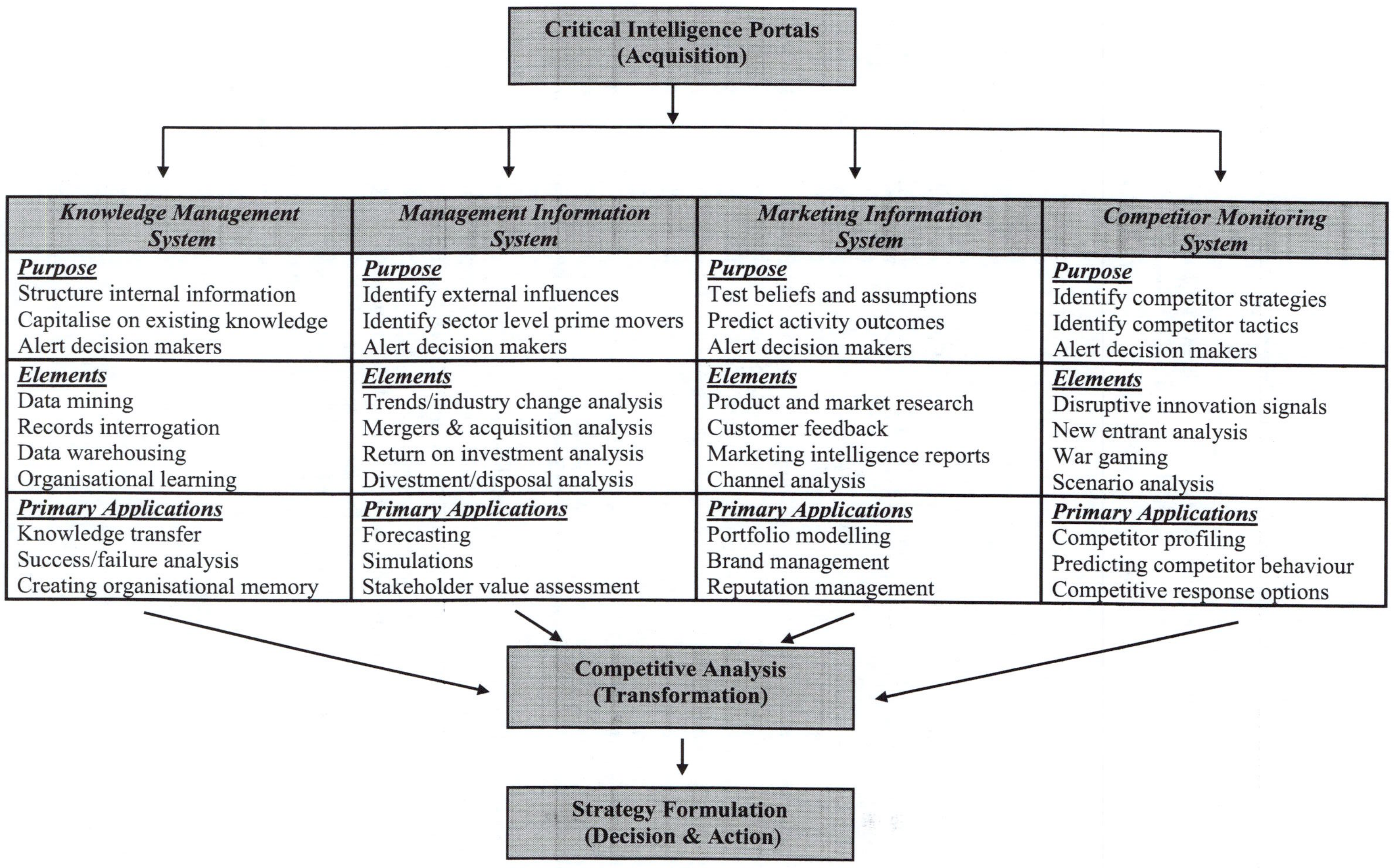
Critical Intelligence Portals (Acquisition)
Knowledge Management System
Purpose
Structure internal information
Capitalise on existing knowledge
Alert decision makers
Elements
Data mining
Records interrogation
Data warehousing
Organisational learning
Primary Applications
Knowledge transfer
Success/failure analysis
Creating organisational memory
Management Information System
Purpose
Identify external influences
Identify sector level prime movers
Alert decision makers
Elements
Trends/industry change analysis
Mergers & acquisition analysis
Return on investment analysis
Divestment/disposal analysis
Primary Applications
Forecasting
Simulations
Stakeholder value assessment
Marketing Information System
Purpose
Test beliefs and assumptions
Predict activity outcomes
Alert decision makers
Elements
Product and market research
Customer feedback
Marketing intelligence reports
Channel analysis
Primary Applications
Portfolio modelling
Brand management
Reputation management
Competitor Monitoring System
Purpose
Identify competitor strategies
Identify competitor tactics
Alert decision makers
Elements
Disruptive innovation signals
New entrant analysis
War gaming
Scenario analysis
Primary Applications
Competitor profiling
Predicting competitor behaviour
Competitive response options
Competitive Analysis (Transformation)
Strategy Formulation (Decision & Action)

Figure 1.1 Critical Intelligence Portals Approach to CI&IM

the investigation of information needs" (p. 487). Not only was this an inaccurate claim but it was inaccurate by, at worst, 11 years, at best, two years.

Understanding the Organisational Knowledge Matrix

Having identified the range of knowledge which can be held by a firm, it is now possible to map the four Critical Intelligence Portals shown in Figure 1.1 onto an Organisational Knowledge Matrix, illustrated in Figure 1.2. This is an extension of the previously cited matrices, which now embrace aspects which are not present in any other depiction.

Knowledge Management System

Dawson (2000) drew attention to the danger of regarding the phrase "Knowledge Management" as implying that knowledge already exists and simply needs to be managed to produce benefit. To emphasise his point, Dawson draws comparisons with "asset management" and "property management". Drawing on the work of Damodaran & Olphert (2000) and Haseman *et al* (2005), Lin & Huang (2008, p. 410) provide a succinct definition of idealised Knowledge Management Systems (KMSs). They suggest that "KMSs increase organisational learning by capturing internal knowledge and making it available to employees for reuse. KMSs maintain corporate history, experience and expertise of long-term employees. Employee knowledge is incorporated into the systems that help them and their successors run the business". The problem with KMSs is that they are typically IT driven, using historical, internal data as their primary source, typically with a past and present only perspective. Choi *et al* (2008) referring to Hansen *et al* (1999) notes that KMS "strategy attempts to increase organizational efficiencies by codifying and reusing knowledge mainly through advanced IT", and that by its very nature, a KMS is a delivery system rather than an interpretation mechanism. That is not to disregard the worth of a good KMS, but their potential to deliver more than a forecast based on historical records is limited.

Feng *et al* (2004) and Lee *et al* (2005) examined the direct relationship between KMS usage and organisational performance and reported only a few positive effects. Kalling (2003) argued that current research on KM fails to offer a detailed understanding of the role of knowledge in improving an organisation's performance. Khalifa *et al* (2000, p. 121) also states that "the mere usage of KMS does not necessarily lead to the anticipated benefits". A KMS system, whilst not in itself a panacea (Stapleton, 2003), would seem to provide a tangible and obvious contribution to understanding the "known-knowns" and as such, represents the *Known Box* in an organisation's knowledge matrix.

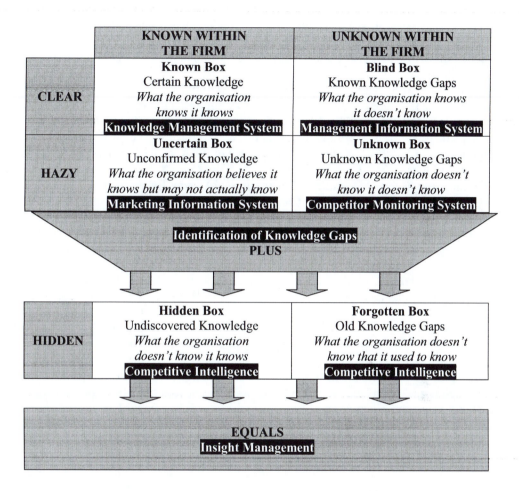

Figure 1.2 Organisational Knowledge Matrix

Management Information System

The focus of a Management Information System (MIS) should be one of under-standing the external environment and assessing elements which could detrimentally affect the firm's sustainability or positively enhance its future success. However, Mou-tinho & Southern (2010, p. 100) point out that trying to draw the distinction between internally and externally focused systems is "becoming increasingly blurred" as the two converge through technological advancement. They confirm that "the key output of a traditional MIS would be management reports", which would suggest a backward facing orientation.

A more forward looking organisation would be utilising its MIS as input to the decisions which it knows it needs to make, but it should also be seeking information on the elements that it knows it is not yet fully prepared for. Gilad (2004) and Fuld (2004) refer to these as Early Warning Signals and these are precisely the drivers which can lead to sector level shifts, mergers and/or acquisition activity, investment and/or divestment plans.

In an expansive text which draws attention to the many functions which can make up an MIS, Oz (2009, p. 18) states that:

> Different types of information systems serve different functions for particular types of organizations, functions within organizations, business needs, and management levels of an organization. Business enterprises differ in their objectives, structure, interests, and approaches. In recent years the capabilities of many applications have been combined and merged. It is less likely that you will find ... stand-alone sys-tems with a single capability. Managers and other professionals plan, control, and make decisions. As long as a system supports one or more of these activities, it may be referred to as a Management Information System (MIS).

The purpose of an MIS therefore should be to provide the impetus for asking ques-tions about the future and spending more time on speculating, through the use of simulation, on the potential effect which significant change could have on the firm's success. (Filip, 2008) supports this view, drawing attention to the left or right brained orientations which an MIS can take. In a left-brained system, the emphasis would be on quantitative, computational, sequential and a logical approach to cause and effect. A right-brained system would draw on unbounded pattern recognition where simila-rities and uncertain information would prevail. Whilst agreeing in principle with this stance, Hodgkinson *et al* (2009), through numerous examples, draw attention to the value of intuition in the decision making process and identifies a shift in today's MISs which are "giving way to more sophisticated conceptions (of) intuitive and analytical approaches to decision making" (p. 277).

This suggests that a modern MIS would address the "known-unknowns", would be focusing its attention on learning more about how the firm's commercial future could evolve and would be seeking answers to the dilemmas raised by the *Blind Box* of an organisation's knowledge matrix.

Marketing Information System

According to Stair & Reynolds (2010, p. 412), a Marketing Information System (MkIS) "supports managerial activities in product development, distribution, pricing decisions, promotional effectiveness and sales forecasting". An important sub-system is market research which is ideally placed to obtain answers to specific questions which would normally relate to product or service features as well as customer preferences and buying behaviour. Hooley *et al* (2004) and Wilson (2002) identified the basic functions of an MkIS:

- conducting market research which obtains data with the purpose of answering specific questions which would normally relate to product or service features as well as customer preferences and buying behaviour
- use of statistical analysis techniques to manipulate raw data and prepare it for dissemination to interested parties
- creation of internal market models on the effect of price/sales relationship or changes to product offering
- creation of new market models which integrate and then simulate the effect of changing forces in demand, overall company performance and changes to brand reputation

However, Ranchhod & Gurău (2007) note that while many firms have developed multi-functional and centralised databases but they draw attention to the problems experienced when the organisation and storage of that information is handled only at departmental level. The dissemination of such data to decision makers can sometimes be detrimentally affected. As the name suggests, the general focus of an MkIS is on the market and the firm's activities within that market, which leaves a significant gap regarding technical, manufacturing, R&D and process intelligence. Whilst there are elements of known-knowns in an MkIS as its output can be used to obtain confirmation of those known-knows, it can also be used to expose mis-understandings or mis-beliefs about current activity. For that reason, an MkIS would be regarded as primarily adressing the "may not know-knowns" and would place it in the *Uncertain Box* of an organisation's knowledge matrix.

Competitor Monitoring System

The value of a Competitor Monitoring System (CMS) which provides input into decisions on how to respond to the competitive environment has long been recognised as a significant aspect of a firm's activity (Buchele, 1962; Ansoff, 1965; Brock, 1984; Fahey, 1999; Fahey, 2002). Yet today, despite the decades-old warnings of Oxenfeldt & Moore (1978; 1981), Uttal, 1979), Wong *et al* (1989), Whittington & Whipp (1992), Slater & Narver, (1994, MacDonald (1995) and more recently, Zhou *et al* (2007), the analysis of competitors can still be subordinated as greater emphasis is placed on understanding customers and consumers. Clearly, important though customers and consumers are, it is debateable whether they should dominate a firm's thinking (Pickton & Wright, 2000).

Even less well understood is the process of how firms identify their competitors (Rothschild *et al*, 1991; Paley, 1994; Francis *et al*, 1995; Francis, 1997; Clark &

Montgomery, 1999), how they track them (Kydd, 1996), where they get their information from (Clark, 1983; Kendrick, 2001; Keep *et al*, 1994; Kahaner, 1995; Teitelbaum, 1992), how they assess competitive arenas (Day, 1997a; Park & Smith, 1990; Bennett, 2003), how they analyse their capabilities (Band, 1986; Press, 1990; Harari, 1994; Porter, 1998a; Porter, 1998b; Subramanian & IsHak, 1998; Wilkinson, 1998; Saxby *et al*, 2000; Rivette, 2001; Gordon, 2002; Marchi, 2005), how they maintain their competitive edge (Day, 1997b; Fuld, 1985) or how they devise their own response strategies to competitor action (Porter, 1983a; Piorier, 1993; Gatignon *et al*, 1997; Reibstein & Chussil, 1999; Robert, 1991). Of the work cited above, only that of Subramanian & IsHak (1998) reported on an empirical study.

An important element of the CMS is competitor profiling which provides the foundation for the formulation of action plans, either offensive or defensive (Linn, 1994; Clark *et al*, 1999; Heil *et al*, 1997; Vella & McGonagle, 2000) and assesses a competitor's predisposition to compete (Werther, 2000, Wells, 2001).

No empirical research has been published on competitor monitoring or profiling practices since 2001 although it remains a critical activity of a firm's decision making process. It is also regarded as a "must have" function, even if it is not formally recognised as such. It is hard to image any business, marketing or competitive strategy textbook being regarded as complete, without a significant proportion of its pages being devoted to the importance of competitor knowledge and competitive analysis as input to the competitive strategy design process (Hart, 1992; Nutt, 1993; Fuld, 1995; April 2002; Jaworski *et al*, 2002; Warren, 2002; Fleisher & Bensoussan, 2003; Hussey, 2003; Loshin, 2003; Metcalfe & Warde, 2003; Rifat, 2003; Robinson, 2003; Savioz, 2003; Allee, 2004; Badr & Wright, 2004a; 2004b; Boisot, 2004; Callingham 2004; Hurd & Nyberg, 2004; Rothberg & Erickson, 2004; Mostert, 2005; Woodside, 2005; Comai & Tena, 2006; Fuld, 2006; Goldmann & Nieuwenhuizen, 2006; Harding, 2006; Fahey, 2007; Zhou *et al*, 2007; Dishman & Calof, 2008; Sharp, 2009).

Due in part to the apparent confusion as to the importance of competitor monitoring, and perhaps the mistaken impression that "everybody does that, don't they", the evidence would suggest that in reality, if competitor monitoring and competitor profiling is conducted at all, it is conducted in reactive, rather than proactive, mode (Jayachandran & Varadarajan, 2006; Landrum *et al,* 2000) or r is confined to the tactical issues of price and product offering (Miller & Chen, 1996).

As such a CMS would be representative of the "unknown-unknowns". In other words, if nobody knows which questions to ask, and nobody is sufficiently concerned to consider what they might be, then the firm doesn't know what it doesn't know. Whilst *monitoring* competitors is a relatively easy task in this information rich age (Griffiths, 2011), the proliferation of automated competitor dashboard systems sold by software vendors, results in a lack of human interface which means the task of understanding, predicting and simulating their future moves is less so (Quinto *et al*, 2010). A CMS which did not embrace those features would be placed in the *Unknown Box* of an organisation's knowledge matrix.

Identification of Knowledge Gaps

It is upon the components identified above which CI&IM draws, not only for its intellectual input but the identification of areas which are not being satisfied. It stands alongside, yet apart from, existing systems in order to provide the overview which is essential to ensure adequate intelligence coverage for the firm. Taking this approach avoids duplication of effort, providing greater benefit and streamlined input for the firm's decision makers (Sharp, 2009). By adopting a process of knowledge conversion (Ammann, 2009), and the management of expert knowledge (Waring & Currie, 2009) a CI&IM framework also addresses both the *Hidden Box* and the *Forgotten Box* of an organisation's knowledge matrix.

In attempting to address the elements which might come into the *Hidden Box*, a formalised CI&IM structure ensures that there is a known location, and a process, through which employees can report information which on the face of it may not necessarily seem important, but, when combined with other elements of unstructured and structured information, may provide insight on, or confirm the existence of, a situation which requires immediate attention (Ringland, 2002; Allard, 2004; Tyson, 2005; Pai, 2006). In one of the few empirical studies conducted on undiscovered knowledge, Pai (2006, p. 117) argues that it is "necessary to elucidate the tacit knowledge that often remains undiscovered and is not shared in the organizational knowledge base and to make this personal knowledge explicit at the organizational level". Pai (2006) also points out the problems of securing such tacit knowledge as it is linked to the individual. It is argued here that this is best addressed via an active CI&IM function which can facilitate the extraction of this knowledge, either formally, through interviews, workshops and seminars or informally, from conversation, debate and encouragement.

Potentially, the more damaging box to ignore would be the *Forgotten Box*. Harris & Wegg-Prosser, 2007 and Besanko *et al* (2010) refer to a number of studies which suggest that organisations can forget the know-how which made them successful, stating that this is inevitably due to employee turnover and a failure to garner the tacit knowledge held by those individuals, to benefit the next generation. As noted by Fernandez & Sune, (2007, p. 620), "since the 1970s and 1980s, the subject of organizational forgetting has been studied by a small number of researchers working in the areas of operations and/organization theory".

Organisational forgetting has been defined as the intentional or unintentional loss of organisational knowledge at any level (Martin de Holan & Phillips, 2003; 2004), yet inattention to this area of old knowledge retention and new knowledge creation can be devastating. Wang *et al* (2009) also emphasised the role of firm-specific knowledge resources, as being an important element in the attainment of sustainable competitive advantage. Benkard (2000) and Martin de Holan & Phillips (2004) point out the dangers of organisational forgetting whilst Kosinen (2010) warns that as firms increasingly move towards a project-based structure from a silo-style functional structures, "knowledge, not labour, raw material or capital, is the most important resource" (p. 149). Argote & Ingram (2000) argue that by embedding knowledge in interactions involving people, organisations can both effect knowledge transfer internally and impede knowledge transfer externally. Thus, knowledge embedded in the firm, stays within the firm, and becomes the basis for *IBCA*©. A proactive CI&IM attitude, if properly embedded and implemented within a firm, is ideally placed to deliver the desired competitive advantage. It does this by posing, and seeking answers to, question that the firm does not even know it should be asking, speculating on those questions which could be asked, as well as ensuring that those questions are not addressing issues about which the firm already has the answer, if only it knew where to look (Schatzki 2005; 2006).

Whatever a firm might wish to call the activity of gathering, assessing, analysing and acting upon an intelligence acquisition process is almost irrelevant, but it has to be advantageous and add to a firm's intellectual capital. To suggest otherwise, surely, would have little basis in the world of common sense.

Cross-Boundary, Inter-Disciplinary Benefits

As a field of academic study, CI&IM is a strong candidate for being regarded as a truly inter-disciplinary subject. In order to fully capitalise on its benefits, practitioners, and academics, need to have an understanding of the roles which all other functions play in an organisation's commercial effort (Wright *et al,* 2002; Felin & Hesterly, 2007). Knowledge of the activities which each function undertakes, and some appreciation of their technical lexicon is essential, otherwise it is impossible to communicate. This is a concern voiced by those seeking to capitalise fully on project management techniques applied to multi-team working (Fong, 2003; Jugdev *et al,* 2007; Mathur *et al,* 2007).

As has been shown already in this section, the real-world work of CI&IM, as well as academic research, has touch points with strategic planning, organisational learning, decision making, organisational culture, management style, competitive behaviour, corporate taboos, myths and legends as well as the more traditional functional areas of Accounting, Treasury, Legal, HRM, IT, R&D, Marketing and Manufacturing.

Other inter-disciplinary areas of study which enjoy similar cross-boundary influence to CI&IM would be Total Quality Management, Corporate Reputation Management, Corporate Social Responsibility, Customer Relationship Management, Customer Service, Talent Management, Process Improvement and Innovation Management. All of these require an organisational mind-set, an operational structure and a management style which empowers each and every employee, regardless of position or rank, to deliver results. CI&IM also sits alongside other cross-functional, inter-disciplinary activities which generally remain the responsibility of senior staff, such as Strategic Planning, Mergers & Acquisitions, Capital Investment, Strategic Alliances, R&D Management and Technology Marriages.

There are some areas which have a natural fit with the component parts of CIAS and CI&IM, one being marketing which typically carries the responsibility for revenue critical activities such as product/service offering, pricing, promotion, distribution strategies, product portfolio management, competitor monitoring and profiling to name a few. It is not surprising therefore that a symbiotic relationship exists between CI&IM and marketing (Badr & Wright, 2004a; 2004b; Wright, 2005a; 2005b; Vorhies & Morgan, 2005; Weiss & Wright, 2006; Menguca *et al,* 2007; Fleisher *et al,* 2008; Wright *et al,* 2008; Wright *et al,* 2009a; 2009b). Linkages in product use for example, can indicate new segments or the need for modified products (Leenders & Wierenga, 2008) which can encourage better targeting (Chen *et al,* 2010). An example cited by Frates & Sharp (2005) referred to widespread use and acceptability of text messaging. Recognising this as a complementary service for the majority of its customers, mobile phone manufacturers realised that it was a primary service for a hitherto inaccessible segment – the deaf and hard of hearing. It is in these "serendipitous product functions" and actions such as: walking in the customer's shoes, redefining the competitive arena, converting problem customers into new market segments, examining the value chain access points and acting on customer feedback, that issues of drifting market share, reducing revenues and product obsolescence can be viewed (Kristensson *et al*, 2008; Zott & Amit, 2008). CI&IM can be nothing but a valuable ally in the search for marketing's Holy Grail, the hitherto unidentified, unexploited yet potentially highly profitable niche (Trinh *et al*, 2009; Toften & Hammervoll, 2010).

Changes in a firm's situation, whether that be of a positive or negative nature can provide opportunities upon which competitors can capitalise which brings into play all other functions in the firm. CI&IM embraces the serendipitous and one-off aspects of intelligence gathering which leads to better visioning and more exciting scenario development. It really does epitomise the 'no surprises' style of management which is embodied in a firm-wide management style (Gilbreath, 2010) implemented not only at the strategic level (Fahey, 2007) but at both the tactical and operational levels where, arguably, more immediate effects may be observed (Azvine *et al*, 2006; Desouza & Evaristo, 2006; Wright & Calof, 2006; Andreou & Bontis, 2007; Dishman & Calof, 2008; Ashton & Stacey, 2009). CI&IM output informs competitive opportunities and/ or threats which frequently require swift action. Empowering managers to make informed decisions and embrace the CI&IM mind-set fully, at all levels, encourages firms to look for the unusual, consider the implications, act upon this if necessary, but always attempt to anticipate shifts in the competitive landscape.

Erickson & Rothberg (2005) draw attention to the requirement for a firm, in this information rich age to be more aware of how it manages the critical information and knowledge which is passed around the many networks within a firm. The potential for greater exploitation of the increasingly large amounts of valuable information which reside in downstream networks is obvious, as is the number of interfaces which occur across functions (Bhatt *et al*, 2010; Mathur *et al*, (2007). This adds further evidence for the need for a firm-wide CI&IM attitude which encourages employee engagement with all aspects of their work, the identification of intelligence acquisition opportunities but equally as important, their care and diligence in ensuring that vital data and information does not fall into the wrong hands (Richelson, 2006; Gorge, 2008; Hahn *et al*, 2009). Clearly, managerial style and culture play an important part in securing a successful CI&IM operation. O'Gorman (2005) identified cultural tendencies, or memes, which act as an aid to understanding the complexity of strategic decisions and competitive behaviour. These issues have been addressed in the broader context by illustrious writers such as Day *et al* (1997), Fahey (1999), Heil & Robertson (1991), Porter (1983a; 1983b; 1985; 1998a; 1998b; 1998c) and Smith *et al* (1997).

During the past decade, writers such as Leeflang & Wittink (2001), Debruyne *et al* (2002), Gordon (2002), Warren, (2002), Pauwels (2004), Mostert (2005), Neilsen (2005), Steenkamp *et al* (2005), Pietersen (2006), Magin (2006), Michaluk (2007), Tully (2007), Wagner (2007), de Bruijn *et al* (2008), Warren, (2008), Moatti (2009), Pandza & Thorpe (2009), and Reibstein & Wittink (2009) have developed a more focused approach to questions such as why an organisation takes a particular stance in different competitive situations. Why is reaction activity predictable in one scenario but unpredictable in another? What is the meme-set of a competitor's top management team and how does this influence that firm's decision- making output? At the product level, how emotionally tied is the firm to a particular product line? How vigorously will the firm defend its territory, even in light of irrefutable evidence that this is not a wise move? In other words, is there a meme-set at work which is responsible for the way in which a firm conducts itself? Understanding why competitors, customers and individual influencers behave in the way they do has to be a core element of any CI&IM programme. Otherwise, the entire effort becomes one of data collection and mechanistic analysis with little or no regard for the psychology of competitive behaviour.

Creative Thinking for Intelligence-Based Competitive Advantage

IBCA© goes beyond the understanding of knowledge, typically past events, and strives to create fore-knowledge which is future orientated and addresses the "what if?" and the "what now?" questions. A firm which embraces this concept and takes steps to ensure it is fully operationalised with the added ingredient of employee empowerment, will be better placed than most to succeed.

The philosophical and intellectual approach of CI&IM in its quest to deliver *IBCA©* also embraces the theory of "thin-slicing" postulated in *Blink* by Gladwell (2005). He states: "Thin-slicing is not an exotic gift. It is a central part of what it means to be human. We thin-slice whenever we meet a new person or have to make sense of something quickly or encounter a novel situation. We thin-slice because we have to and we come to rely on that ability because there are a lot of hidden fists out there, lots of situations where careful attention to the details of a very thin slice, even for no more than a second or two, can tell us an awful lot" (p. 34–44).

This refreshing approach to data reduction is exactly how skilled CI practitioners deal with information overload and impossible deadlines. There is never enough time to completely dot the "I"s or cross the "T"s and sorting the "relevant" from the "functional" becomes the only thing which matters as time-sensitive decisions are being taken. Without *thin-slicing*, there is always the risk that any potential *IBCA©* will quickly disappear, simply because the action taken is too late to have any notable impact. Gladwell challenges the conventional, structured approaches to problem solving and in his earlier work, *Tipping Point* Gladwell (2002) and urges us to look again at the way in which we consider risk. These works sit alongside the wise words in other visionaries texts such as *Hypercompetition: Managing the Dynamics of Strategic Maneuvering* (D'Aventi, 1994), *Strategic Supremacy: How Industry Leaders Create Growth, Wealth and Power Through Spheres of Influence* (D'Aventi, 2001), *Seeing What's Next: Using the Theories of Innovation to Predict Industry Change* (Christenson *et al*, 2004), *Fooled by Randomness: The Hidden Role of Chance in Life and in the Markets* (Taleb, 2004), *The Black Swan: The Impact of the Highly Improbable* (Taleb, 2007), *The Wisdom of Crowds* (Surowiecki, 2005), *Blue Ocean Strategy: How to Create Uncontested Market Space and Make Competition Irrelevant* (Kim & Mauborgne, 2005), *Microtrends: The Small Forces Behind Tomorrow's Big Changes* (Penn & Zalesne, 2007) and *The Red Queen in Organizations: How Competitiveness Evolves* (Barnett, 2008).

The views of these authors and their books should be required reading for any aspiring CI&IM practitioner as well as any academic researcher seeking to understand the realities and problems of generating a firm's intellectual capital, its application to risk reduction in decision making and subsequent manifestation as Intelligence-Based Competitive Advantage ©.

Addressing the CIAS Connection: Symbiosis, Osmosis, or Segregation?

The individual chapters in this book address in some detail, the contribution which various components of CIAS practice can make to the achievement of *IBCA©* . They cover those issues which challenge decision makers and are grouped into three main themes.

Competitive Intelligence

Chapter 2 takes the unique perspective of examining the nature of support provided to the SME community by Chambers of Commerce and Industry in four regions of France (Smith *et al*, 2010). Led by Jamie Smith, the research team from De Montfort University, UK, applied the results of their findings to a typology of CI attitudes and assessed how the CI Programme Directors viewed their SME managers. They reported a noticeable change in the awareness and attitudes of SMEs towards CI since the programmes were initiated some ten years ago. Equally pleasing was the finding that the CI programmes themselves were innovative, decentralised, constantly evolving and original. Some unique methods are employed, such as the use of professional actors and play-writing to convey the importance of intelligence acquisition, analysis and subsequent integration into the decision making process. It would seem that state funded support for what is more commonly termed as "Intelligence Economique" in France is growing apace. Other countries, European and elsewhere, could learn a thing or two from the state supported CI programmes offered to SMEs in France. This contribution was awarded the Best Paper in Track Prize at the 2010 Academy of Marketing Conference, sponsored by the *Journal of Strategic Marketing*.

Chapter 3 by Sophie Larivet and François Brouard from ESCE, Paris, France and Carleton University, Ottawa, Canada respectively, delves into the world of customer complaint management (Larivet & Brouard, 2010). The authors propose an exploratory model, drawn from the literature, which attempts to profit from the strategic intelligence gathered from the customer complaints process. Far from viewing these incidents as a nuisance, or an irritation, the authors highlight the different elements of their model by identifying the various steps which attempt to understand why customers complain and also the measures which can be taken to improve the handling of complaints when they are received. Examples of the type of strategic intelligence which can be gathered from complaints are outlined and the authors have grouped these into four key categories: technological, competitive, commercial and societal.

Chapter 4 also looks at behaviour and attitudes in the SME sector, this time in Turkey (Wright *et al* 2012). Written by Sheila Wright, De Montfort University, Christophe Bisson, Kadir Has University and Alistair Duffy, also of De Montfort University, the article reports on an empirical study undertaken in Istanbul, using a constructivist/pragmatic approach with the aim of applying the findings to an evidence based typology of practice covering six strands: gathering, attitude, use, location, technology support and IT systems. Following initial contact through the Istanbul Chamber of Industry, 371 firms indicated a willingness to take part in the online survey, with 314 usable responses recorded, representing a response rate of 84.6 per cent. The findings revealed that the sector was not operating at optimum level on any of the six strands. The undeniable conclusions was that if Turkey were to exhibit the levels of growth it has enjoyed over the past ten years, into the next ten years, then serious attention would have to be paid to the SME sector to make it more competitive and competitor aware. The support programmes referred to in Chapter 1, as provided by the public organisations in France may well be a model for Turkey to consider for its SME sector.

Chapter 5, also by Larivet & Brouard (2012), presents an empirical study of the attitudes of SME senior managers towards intelligence programmes in the Walloon region of Belgium. They present the findings from 250 phone interviews analysed within an attitude framework of cognitive, affective and behavioural measures. As a consequence of a decline in their heavy industry base, the *Agence de Stimulation Économique* was created as a public institution in 2006 and was charged with the task of delivering services and training for the SME and entrepreneurial sector. One of their goals was to develop what they termed as *Strategic Intelligence* awareness among SMEs and as a consequence, their efforts represent the first large-scale SI development project in Belgium. Primarily a French-speaking southern region of Belgium, and geographically close to France, similarities with the longer established efforts of Chambers of Commerce and Industry in France, with their programme of SME training in *Intelligence Economique* was inevitable. The findings from the study were illuminating in that it appears that ASE's task is far from complete and there is much yet to do to fully engage their SME sector with the concept of intelligent intelligence.

Competitive Analysis

Chapter 6 by Lyndon Simkin, Oxford Brookes University and Sally Dibb, Open University identifies a new dawn of appreciation for market-led analytical tools among firms which, as a result of the current economic climate, are being forced to drastically re-assess their approaches to corporate planning and decision making (Simkin & Dibb 2012). One hundred firms were contacted and it was found that the senior decision making table, which had once been dominated by the "quant jocks" from accounting and treasury was now being inhabited by those skilled in the use of identifying and understanding the relevance of market environment drivers, competitor reviews, customer insights and capability audits. These allowed the firm to re-think strategies for turbulent times, a situation which a high percentage of firms stated, would not have occurred, without the credit crunch and current fragile economic environment. The authors report on the excitement among their interviewees at the discovery of market-led analytical approaches and an almost palpable image of freedom at addressing the questions which marketers have concerned themselves with for decades. The apparent promotion from the marketing floor to the executive floor of questions such as where is our revenue coming from? Where could it come from? How do we defend or improve our market position? What do we need to do to remain a going concern? Has to be applauded, if only to show that they should have been listening to us all along. This stimulating contribution is illustrated with real examples and evidence of the changes taking place in the firms the authors have dealt with. One can only hope that their efforts will be further disseminative with other firms which are not afraid to think again at the way in which they approach the analytical and strategy formulation task.

Chapter 7 by Anthony Patterson, Lee Quinn and Steve Baron, University of Liverpool, tackles what the authors expertly argue, is a devalued aspect of strategic marketing - the power of intuitive thinking (Patterson *et al*, 2012) . Their empirical study, based on in-depth interviews with the senior decision making managers of ten large firms, draws attention to the advantages and benefits of gut-feel and intuition in data deficient decision-making scenarios. Despite the received wisdom that crucial decisions should only be made when the data set is complete, has been analysed, considered with a view to the future landscape and the myriad options quantified, mapped, discussed and evaluated, the instances of this being the 'norm' are far from numerous. Interview evidence provided by the authors testify to the reality of decision making time horizons and data absence requiring much more than the numbers. Therefore, the skill of managers who are able to operate confidently with a less than perfect data set should not be underestimated and they should certainly not feel the need to work up a post-event rationalisation which might then attempt to suggest that they acted rationally. They know they didn't and so much the better for that. This work goes a long way towards questioning the notion that good decisions are only those made with perfect information and it also challenges the current trend towards metric based marketing decision making in a refreshingly honest way.

Chapter 8 by Craig S. Fleisher, Aurora DC, USA and Sheila Wright, De Montfort University, UK, looks at the problems of analysis failure (Fleisher & Wright, 2010). They highlight that there are several levels at which analysis failure can occur, but focus their work on the causes of failure at an individual level. They identify a number of danger areas ranging from differing levels of natural ability and motivation through cognitive biases, perceptual distortion, insufficient use of the right tools to use, through to poor preparedness by higher education. The authors go on to present ten key continua which they regard as essential for an effective CI analyst to master before they can consider themselves truly competent in their work. The authors also emphasise that a CI analyst needs tangible support from their firm and provide six insightful guiding principles which an enlightened firm should follow.

Chapter 9 by Dag Bennett and Charles Graham, both from the Ehrenberg Centre for Research in Marketing, at London South Bank University, UK, reports on findings from a study carried out on brand loyalty in the car market in Thailand (Bennett & Graham, 2010). This is a dynamic category of infrequent purchases where loyalty to an existing brand might be expected to dominate. However, through their research, the authors have been able to identify that brand share growth in Thailand, has come primarily from first time customers who have been attracted by the brand's size and brand exposure. Growth through penetration rather than retention may not sit comfortably with those who subscribe to the 'brand loyalty at all costs' philosophy of marketing, but this research has shown that in certain markets, it can be easier, and more cost effective, to attract new buyers to your brand than spend time and money trying to convince existing customers to stay with it.

Chapter 10 also looks at customer loyalty but this time by developing a computer assisted quantitative approach in which a clustering model and a classification model are employed for defining and predicting customer churn (Tamaddoni Jahromi, *et al*, 2010). Led by Ali Tamaddoni Jahromi, the research team from Tarbiat Modares University, Tehran, Iran employed a data mining approach to select, explore and model large amounts of data to discover meaningful patterns and construct a representation of activity in the non-contractual pre-paid mobile telephony sector. Of concern to most firms is the propensity of customers to discontinue doing business with them and the research presented here provides some guidance on how firms can use predictive models to determine the likelihood of customer churn. As the sector under investigation is arguably the most volatile and most difficult one in which to develop brand loyalty, the model presented here would seem to be a very welcome aid to those charged with identifying potential lost revenue and separating churners from non-churners.

Competitive Strategy

Chapter 11 comes from Trevor Hartland, University of Glamorgan and Nicola Williams-Burnett, University of Wales Institute Cardiff. Their research looked at a very timely conundrum - how to protect the branding of one of the most well recognised events in the world - the Olympic Games (Hartland & Williams-Burnett, 2012). Interestingly, the full effects of the obligatory Host City Contract required the UK to honour promises made in its bid document, to bring into force the London Olympic and Paralympic Games Act which gives powers to the organising committee to prevent any unauthorised representations or associations with the London Games. Hartland and Williams-Burnett pick through the details of this Act and it is quite amazing to see the way in which infringements and representation is interpreted, not only in the eyes of the law, but in the eyes of the public. The problem is that ambush marketing is highly successful, albeit not quite what the British would call 'cricket'. Legislation has not proved to be very effective as marketers and firms work diligently around the clock looking for ways in which they can get away with it, legally or illegally. The Chartered Institute of Marketing has argued that the Act prevents firms, especially SMEs from getting some benefit from the London Games but at the same time admit that few marketers are aware of the details of the Act. Even iconic buildings and event locations are protected under the terms of the Act. The authors ask if this a step too far? And through a series of descriptive research and content analysis exercises identified the frequency of infringements under the terms of the Act, which are taking place on a daily basis. They discovered over two and a quarter million infringements on one day alone and address some of the frustrations which the organisers and strategic marketers must face when trying to sell sponsorship, advertising and branding associations with event supporters. It is hard to see how one can survive without the other yet clearly there is no legal redress available which can prevent freeloaders engaging in ambush marketing and taking without giving.

Chapter 12, written by Thomas Mejtoft from Umeå University, Sweden looks at the effects of vertical integration in the Swedish commercial printing industry and comes up with some very interesting consequences for competitive strategy formulation (Mejtoft, 2010) . The study's results reveal that firms which are direct customers are perceived as more loyal and profitable than advertising agencies and/or print brokers, therefore, integration of content creation is common to increase relations with direct customers. This brings into conflict the relationship that printing firms have with advertising agencies which remain an important revenue stream, but are not as valuable as direct customers. Strategies to resolve this conundrum are presented and firms are invited to challenge their perception that obvious vertical integration will naturally produce more profit. The author suggests ways in which printing firms can retain the benefits of vertical integration without alienating a valued customer segment. This is a valuable example, and contra-view, of competitive advantage theory which may not always translate into practice.

Chapter 13 by Pratik Modi from the Institute of Rural Management Anand, India examined the theory of market orientation in relationship to a number of performance related variables in a non-profit context (Modi, 2012). The extensive empirical study of 579 non-profit organisations in India, all of which were engaged in service delivery, provides an interesting contrast to the market orientation thinking more commonly found in commercially driven firms. Structural equation modelling was used to test a series of hypotheses using measures for performance, effectiveness/social desirability, innovativeness, resource scarcity, size/age and market orientation. The results showed that market orientation in an non-profit organisation not only increases the satisfaction level of beneficiaries, but also enhances the organisation's reputation among its peer group. Despite being limited to organisations which rely on third-party funding, this large scale and thorough study was able to demonstrate that regardless of funding sources, a market orientation would result in better performance and this inevitably has a direct influence on the strategic thinking, and lexicon, of decision makers. For his work in this regard, Professor Modi, was awarded the Best Paper in Track Prize at the 2011 Academy of Marketing Conference, sponsored by the *Journal of Strategic Marketing*.

Chapter 14 comes from Daniel Bretonès of ESCEM Business School, France, with Bernard Quinio and Gilbert Réveillon from Université Paris Ouest, CEROS, France. This is a fascinating article on how firms can develop and test the effects of strategy through the use of virtual worlds and virtual social networks (Bretonès, *et al*, 2010). These include serious games, multiplayer role playing games and well known virtual worlds such as *Second Life*. The authors suggest that the investment cost required in developing the virtual world and training employees in its use is far outweighed by the resultant unhindered creativity which employees experience when taking part, and the very real benefits of being able to test-drive strategies and tactics in the virtual world before committing expenditure to the real world. This sea-change in management practices indicates that between the digital environment and reality, there is a mutual enrichment process. Should this type of work become more common than it is today, the resultant impact on how managers are trained for employment and the creative skills which would need to be mastered in order to operate in this fashion could be highly significant to educators and curricula?

Conclusion

Within the Chapters in this book, it is possible to identify a number of touch-points with the areas depicted in Figure 1.1. Each can be aligned to one, or more, of the critical intelligence portals, their purpose, elements and principal applications. In that regard, it could be argued that both individually, and collectively, this book provides a significant contribution to the body of knowledge in the discipline.

From a practitioner point of view, when considering the benefits of encouraging an overarching CI&IM philosophy, executives often ask *"what's in it for me"*? That one is easy to answer. It provides:

- an objective view of the market place
- a reduction in decision making time, minimising risk and avoiding surprises
- identification of opportunities before the competition does
- identification of early warning signals of competitor moves
- time to consider counter moves
- input to idea generation
- challenges to, and/or verification of, assumptions
- challenges to, and/or verification of, intuition
- a proactive decision making attitude
- support for prioritisation of decisions
- stimulation for perusing improvement rather than mediocrity
- a reduction in uncertainty
- the attainment of intelligence-based competitive advantage

That said, it falls onto the shoulders of those who successfully achieve *IBCA©* to share their methods so that others can learn and develop. Paradoxically, this is exactly what you would advise a successful firm *not* to do, otherwise they comprise the value of the advantage they have gained by being better organised and more astute at converting input to insight. There remains the ever increasing, difficult task of producing more real life case examples, developing models which can put values onto such intangible activities (because that is all the accountants will listen to) and demonstrating that it is not the cost of operating an active CI&IM programme which should be upper most in the minds of decision-makers, but the cost of *not* doing so. This book is both timely and relevant to the field. If these contributions encourage more people to examine the practices of firms in the areas of competitive intelligence, competitive analysis and competitive strategy in the broadest sense of all those terms, then so much the better. At the risk of preaching to the converted, my question is this. Has everybody fallen so much in love with consumer behaviour, country of origin, advertising, PR, fair-trade, social media, branding, eco-marketing, digi-everything and the like? Is it just easier to focus on the tactical and operational issues of the day such as the pre-disposition of youths to use social networking devices, the fizzy drinks buying habits of the under-18s, the profit potential of the over-50s and the sales tactics used in the mobile phones industry? In contrast, the attainment of *IBCA©* offers long-term benefits, meets the test of being sustainable, significantly reduces the risk in decision-making but more importantly, it is costly and incredibly difficult for competitors to imitate. How any firm could view this as an optional extra is simply unfathomable.

References

Adidam, P.T., Gajre, S. & Kejriwal, S. (2009), 'Cross-Cultural Competitive Intelligence Strategies', *Marketing Intelligence & Planning,* 27(5), 666-680

Adidam, P.T., Banerjee, M. & Shukla, P. (2012), 'Competitive Intelligence and Firm's Performance in Emerging Markets: An Exploratory Study in India'. *Journal of Business & Industrial Marketing,* 27(5), 242-254

Afiouni, F. (2007), 'Human Resource Management and Knowledge Management: A Road Map Toward Improving Organizational Performance', *Journal of American Academy of Business,* 11 (2), 124-131

Allard, C.K. (2004), *Business as War: Battling for Competitive Advantage,* Hoboken, NJ: John Wiley & Sons

Allee, V. (2004), *The Knowledge Evolution: Building Organizational Intelligence,* Boston, MA: Butterworth-Heinemann Ltd

Ammann, E.M. (2009), 'The Knowledge Cube and Knowledge Conversions', *Volume I, Proceedings of the World Congress on Engineering,* 1st-3rd July 2009, London, UK

Andreou, A.N. & Bontis, N. (2007), 'A Model for Resource Allocation Using Operational Knowledge Assets', *The Learning Organization,* 14(4), 345-374

Ansoff , I. (1965), 'Checklist for Competitive and Competence Profiles', pp 98-99 in Ansoff, I. *Corporate Strategy,* New York, NY, McGraw Hill

Appelbaum, S.H. & Gonzalo, F. (2007), 'Effectiveness and Dynamics of Cross-Functional Teams: A Case Study of Northerntranspo Ltd.', *Journal of American Academy of Business,* 10 (2), 36-44

APQC International Benchmarking Clearing House (1998), *Managing Competitive Intelligence Knowledge in a Global Economy,* Houston, TX: American Productivity & Quality Center

APQC International Benchmarking Clearing House (2000), *Developing a Successful Competitive Intelligence Program: Enabling Action, Realizing Results,* Houston, TX: American Productivity & Quality Center

APQC International Benchmarking Clearing House (2003), *User-Driven Competitive Intelligence: Crafting the Value Proposition,* Houston, TX: American Productivity & Quality Center

April, K. (2002), 'Guidelines for Developing a K-Strategy', *Journal of Knowledge Management,* 6 (5), 445-456

April K, & Bessa J. (2006), 'A Critique of the Strategic Competitive Intelligence Process within a Global Energy Multinational', *Problems and Perspectives in Management,* 4(2), 86-99

Argote, L, & Ingram, P. (2000), 'Knowledge Transfer: A Basis for Competitive Advantage in Firms', *Organizational Behavior and Human Decision Processes,* 82(1), 150-169

Argote, L. & Miron-Spektor, E. (2009), 'Organizational Learning: From Experience to Knowledge', *Proceedings: New Perspectives in Organization Science Conference, Carnegie Mellon University,* May 2009, USA

Ashton, W.B. & Stacey, G.S. (2009), 'Technical Intelligence in Business: Understanding Technology Threats and Opportunities', *International Journal of Technology Management,* 10(1), 79-104

Azvine, B., Cui, Z., Nauck, D.D. & Majeed, B. (2006), 'Real Time Business Intelligence for the Adaptive Enterprise', pp 29-39 in *Proceedngs: 8th IEEE International Conference on Enterprise Computing, E-Commerce, and E-Services,* 26th-29th June 2006, San Francisco, USA

Badr, A. & Wright, S. (2004a), 'Competitive Intelligence and Marketing Strategy Formulation', *Competitive Intelligence,* 7(3), 35-38

Badr, A. & Wright, S. (2004b), 'Integration of Competitive Intelligence into all stages of Marketing Strategy Formulation', in *CD-ROM Proceedings: 9th Annual European Conference, Society of Competitive Intelligence Professionals,* 27th-29th October 2004, Milan, Italy

Badr, A., Madden, E. & Wright. S. (2006), 'The Contribution of CI to the Strategic Decision Making Process: Empirical Study of the European Pharmaceutical Industry', *Journal of Competitive Intelligence and Management,* 3(4), 15-35

Band, W. (1986), 'How to Evaluate a Competitor's Marketing Strategy'. *Sales & Marketing Manager Canada,* 27(8), 19-21

Barnett, W.P. (2008), *The Red Queen in Organizations: How Competitiveness Evolves,* Princeton, NJ: Princeton University Press

Barney, J.B. (1991), 'Firm Resources and Sustained Competitive Advantage', *Journal of Management,* 17(1), 99-120

Benkard, C.L. (2000), 'Learning and Forgetting: The Dynamics of Aircraft Production', *American Economic Review,* 90(4), 1034-1054

Bennett, R. (2003), 'Competitor Analysis Practices of British Charities', *Marketing Intelligence & Planning,* 21(6), 335-345

Bennett, D. & Graham, C. (2010), 'Is Loyalty Driving Growth for the Brand in Front? A Two-Purchase Analysis of Car Category Dynamics in Thailand', *Journal of Strategic Marketing,* 18 (7), 573-585

Besanko, D., Doraszelski, U., Kryukov, Y. & Satterthwaite, M. (2010), 'Learning-by-Doing', Organizational Forgetting, and Industry Dynamics', *Econometrica,* 78(2), 453-508

Bhatt, G., Emdad, A., Roberts, N. & Grover, V. (2010), 'Building and Leveraging Information in Dynamic Environments: The Role of IT Infrastructure Flexibility as Enabler of Organizational Responsiveness and Competitive Advantage', *Information & Management,* 47(5/6), 341-349

Bock, G.W., Zmud, R.W., Kim, Y.G. & Lee, J.N. (2005), 'Behavioral Intention Formation in Knowledge Sharing: Examining the Role of Extrinsic Motivators, Social-Psychological Force and Organizational Climate', *MIS Quarterly,* 29(1), 87-112

Boisot, M. (2004), *Knowledge Assets: Securing Competitive Advantage in the Information Economy,* Oxford, UK: Oxford University Press

Bratianu, C., Jianu, I. & Vasilache, S. (2011), 'Integrators for Organizational Intellectual Capital', *International Journal of Learning and Intellectual Capital,* 8(1), 190-201

Bretonès, D.D., Quinio, B. & Réveillon, G. (2010), 'Bridging Virtual and Real Worlds: Enhancing Outlying Clustered Value Creations', *Journal of Strategic Marketing,* 18(7), 613-625

Brock, J.J. (1984), 'Competitor Analysis: Some Practical Approaches', *Industrial Marketing Management,* 13(4), 225-231

Brown, E.D. (2007), 'Information Technology Human Capital as Competitive Advantage'. Retrieved from: http://ericbrown.com/docs/Information%20Technology%20Human%20Capital %20as%20Competitive%20Advantage.pdf (accessed 3rd May 2011)

Buchele, R. (1962), 'How to Evaluate a Firm', *California Management Review,* 5(1), 5-16

Buckman, R. (2004), *Building a Knowledge-driven Organization,* London, UK: McGraw Hill Higher Education

Callingham, M. (2004), *Market Intelligence: How and Why Organizations Use Market Research,* London, UK: Kogan Page Ltd

Carr, A.S., Kaynak, H. & Muthusamy, S. (2008), 'The Cross-Functional Co-ordination between Operations, Marketing, Purchasing and Engineering and the Impact on Performance', *International Journal of Manufacturing Technology and Management,* 13(1), 55-77

Chen, E.L., Katila, R., McDonald, R. & Eisenhardt, K.M. (2010), 'Life in the Fast Lane: Origins of Competitive Interaction in New vs. Established Markets', *Strategic Management Journal,* 31(13), 1527-1547

Choi, B., Poon, S.K. & Davis, J.G. (2008), 'Effects of Knowledge Management Strategy on Organizational Performance: A Complementarity Theory-based Approach', *International Journal of Management Science,* 36(2), 235-251

Christensen, C.M., Anthony, S.D. & Roth, E.A. (2004), *Seeing What's Next: Using the Theories of Innovation to Predict Industry Change,* Boston, MA: Harvard Business School Press

Clark, B.H. & Montgomery, D.B. (1999), 'Managerial Identification of Competitors', *Journal of Marketing,* 63(33), 67-83

Clark, L.A., Cleveland, W.S., Denby, L. & Liu, C. (1999), 'Competitive Profiling Displays; Multivariate Graphs for Customer Satisfaction Data', *Marketing Research,* 11(1), 24-33

Comai, A. & Tena, J. (2006), *Mapping & Anticipating the Competitive Landscape,* Barcelona, Spain: Emecom

Crossan, M.M., Lane, H.W. & White, R.E. (1990), 'An Organizational Learning Framework: From Intuition to Institution', *Academy of Management Review,* 24(3), 522-537

D'Aventi, R. (1994), *Hypercompetition: Managing the Dynamics of Strategic Maneuvering,* New York, NY: Free Press

D'Aventi, R. (2001), *Strategic Supremacy: How Industry Leaders Create Growth, Wealth and Power Through Spheres of Influence,* New York, NY: Free Press

Damodaran, L. & Olphert, W. (2000), 'Barriers and Facilitators to the Use of Knowledge Management Systems', *Behaviour & Information Technology,* 19(6), 405–413

Dawson, R. (2000), 'Knowledge Capabilities as the Focus of Organisational Development and Strategy', *Journal of Knowledge Management,* 4(4), 320-327

Day, G.S. (1997a), 'Assessing Competitive Arenas: Who Are Your Competitors?', pp 23-47 in Day, G.S. & Reibstein, D.J. (Eds), *Wharton on Dynamic Competitive Strategy*, New York, NY: John Wiley & Sons

Day, G.S. (1997b), 'Maintaining the Competitive Edge: Creating and Sustaining Advantages in Dynamic Competitive Environments', pp 48-75 in Day, G.S. & Reibstein, D.J. (Eds), *Wharton on Dynamic Competitive Strategy*, New York, NY: John Wiley & Sons

Day, G.S. & Reibstein, D.J. w/Gunther, R. (1997), *Wharton on Competitive Strategy Dynamics,* Hoboken, NJ: John Wiley & Sons Inc

de Bruijn, E.R.A., Niedl, S.F. & Bekkering, H. (2008), 'Fast Responders Have Blinders On: ERP Correlates of Response Inhibition in Competition', *Cortex,* 44(5), 580-586

Debruyne, M., Moenaert, R., Griffin, A., Hart, S., Hultink, E.J. & Robben, H. (2002), 'The impact of New Product Launch Strategies on Competitive Reaction in Industrial Markets', *Journal of Product Innovation Management,* 19(2), 159-170

DeNisi, A.S. Hitt, M.A. & Jackson, S.E. (2009), 'The Knowledge-Based Approach to Sustainable Competitive Advantage', pp 3-36 in Jackson, S.E., Hitt, M.A. & DeNisi (Eds), *Managing Knowledge for Sustained Competitive Advantage*, San Francisco, CA: Jossey-Bass

Desouza, K.C. & Evaristo, J.R. (2006), 'Project Management Offices: A Case of Knowledge-Based Archetypes', *International Journal of Information Management,* 26(5), 414-423

Dishman, P.L. & Calof, J.L. (2008), 'Competitive Intelligence: A Multiphasic Precedent to Marketing Strategy', *European Journal of Marketing,* 42(7/8), 766-785

Easterby-Smith, M., Crossan, M. & Niccolini, D. (2000), 'Organizational Learning: Debates Past, Present and Future', *Journal of Management Studies,* 37(6), 783-796

Erickson, S.G. & H.N. Rothberg (2005), 'Expanding Intelligence Capabilities: Downstream Knowledge Targets', *Journal of Competitive Intelligence and Management,* 3(2), 8-15

Fahey, L. (1999), *Competitors: Outwitting, Outmaneuvering and Outperforming,* New York, NY: John Wiley & Sons Inc

Fahey, L. (2002), 'Invented Competitors: A New Competitor Analysis Methodology', *Strategy & Leadership,* 30(6), 5-12

Fahey, L. (2007), 'Connecting Strategy and Competitive Intelligence: Refocusing Intelligence to Produce Critical Strategy Inputs', *Strategy & Leadership,* 35(1), 4-12

Farsi, M., Fetz, A. & Filippini, M. (2007), 'Economies of Scale and Scope in Local Public Transport', *Journal of Transport Economics and Policy,* 41(3), 345-361

Felin, T. & Hesterly, W.S. (2007), 'The Knowledge-Based View, Nested Heterogeneity, and New Value Creation: Philosophical Considerations on the Locus Of Knowledge', *Academy of Management Review,* 32(1), 195–218

Feng, K., Chen, E.T. & Liou, W. (2004), 'Implementation of Knowledge Management Systems and Firm Performance: An Empirical Investigation', *Journal of Computer Information Systems*, 45(2), 92-104

Ferguson N, (1998), *The House of Rothschild*, 1998 cited in *Who's Who in British History*, Cico Books (2002), pp 698

Fernandez, V. & Sune, A. (2007), 'Organizational Forgetting and its Causes: An Empirical Research', *Journal of Organizational Change Management*, 22(6), 620-634

Filip, F.G. (2008), 'Decision Support and Control for Large-Scale Complex Systems', *Annual Reviews in Control*, 32(1), 61-70

Fiol, C.M. (2009), 'Organizing for Knowledge-Based Competitiveness: About Pipelines and Rivers', pp 37-63 in Jackson, S.E., Hitt, M.A. & DeNisi (Eds), *Managing Knowledge for Sustained Competitive Advantage*, San Francisco, CA: Jossey-Bass

Fleisher, C.S. & Bensoussan, B. (2003), *Strategic and Competitive Analysis: Methods and Techniques for Analyzing Business Competition*, Upper Saddle River, NJ: Prentice Hall

Fleisher, C.S. & Wright, S. (2010), 'Competitive Intelligence Analysis Failure: Diagnosing Individual Level Causes and Implementing Organisational Level Remedies', *Journal of Strategic Marketing*, 18(7), 553-572

Fleisher, C.S., Wright, S. & Allard, H.T. (2008), 'The Role of Insight Teams in Integrating Diverse Marketing Information Management Techniques', *European Journal of Marketing*, 42 (7/8), 836-851

Fong, P.S.W. (2003), 'Knowledge Creation in Multidisciplinary Project Teams: An Empirical Study of the Processes and their Dynamic Interrelationships', *International Journal of Project Management*, 21(7), 479-486

Francis, D.B. (1997), 'Your Competitors: Who Will They Be?', *Competitive Intelligence Review*, 8 (1), 16-23

Francis, D.B., Sawka, K.A. & Herring, J.P. (1995), 'Competitors: Who to Watch, What to Watch, Who to Ignore, and How to Tell the Difference', *Competitive Intelligence Review*, 6(3), 41-46

Franco, M., Magrinho, A. & Silva, J.R. (2011), Competitive Intelligence: A Research Model Tested on Portuguese Firms', *Business Process Management Journal*, 17(2), 332-356

Frates, J. & Sharp, S. (2005), 'Using Business Intelligence to Discover New Market Opportunities', *Journal of Competitive Intelligence and Management*, 3(2), 16-28

Fraumann, E. (1997), 'Economic Espionage, Security Missions Redefined', *Public Administration Review*, 57(4), 303-308

Fuld, L.M. (1985), 'Sizing up the Competition', *Canadian Business Review*, 12(2), 35-37

Fuld, L.M. (1995), *The New Competitor Intelligence: The Complete Resource for Finding, Analyzing, and Using Information About Your Competitors*, New York, NY: John Wiley & Sons

Fuld, L.M. (2004), 'Early Warnings', *Pharmaceutical Executive*, 24(4), 82-86

Fuld, L.M. (2006), *The Secret Language of Competitive Intelligence: How to See Through and Stay Ahead of Business Disruptions, Distortions, Rumors, and Smoke Screens*, New York, NY: Crown Business

Garvin, D.A., 2000, *Learning in Action: A Guide to Putting the Learning Organization to Work*, Harvard Business School Press, Boston, MA.

Gatignon, H. & Reibstein, D.J. (1997), 'Creative Strategies for Responding to Competitive Strategies', pp 237-255 in Day, G.S. & Rubenstein, D.J. (Eds), *Wharton on Dynamic Competitive Strategy*, New York, NY: John Wiley & Sons

Geiger, D. & Schreyögg, G. (2009), 'Coping with the Concept of Knowledge: Toward a Discursive Understanding of Knowledge', *Management Learning*, 40(4), 475-480

Gilad, B. (2004), *Early Warning: Using Competitive Intelligence to Anticipate Market Shifts, Control Risk and Create Powerful Strategies*, New York, NY: AMACOM

Gilbreath, R. (2010), *The Next Evolution of Marketing*, New York, NY: McGraw-Hill

Global Intelligence Alliance. (2006), *Competitive Intelligence in Large Companies -Global Study,* GIA White Paper 4/2005, Retrieved from: http://www.globalintelligence.com/insights-analysis/white-papers/ci-in-large-companies-global-study (accessed: 12th May 2007)

Gladwell, M. (2002), *The Tipping Point: How Little Things Can Make A Big Difference,* New York, NY: Black Bay Books

Gladwell, M. (2005), *Blink: The Power of Thinking Without Thinking,* New York, NY: Little Brown Company

Global Intelligence Alliance. (2006), *Competitive Intelligence in Large Companies -Global Study,* GIA White Paper 4/2005, Retrieved from: http://www.globalintelligence.com/insights-analysis/white-papers/ci-in-large-companies-global-study (accessed: 12th May 2007)

Goldmann, G. & Nieuwenhuizen, C. (2006), *Strategy: Sustaining Competitive Advantage in a Globalised Context,* Cape Town, SA, Juta & Co Ltd

Gordon, I.H. (2002), *Competitor Targeting: Winning the Battle for Market and Customer Share,* Etobicoke, Ontario: John Wiley & Sons Canada Ltd

Gorge, M. (2008), 'Data Protection: Why are Organisations Still Missing the Point?', *Computer Fraud & Security,* 2008(6), 5-8

Griffiths, P. (2011), 'Where Next for Information Audit?', *Business Information Review,* 27(4), 261-224

Hahn, E.D., Doh, J.P. & Bunyaratavej, K. (2009), 'The Evolution of Risk in Information Systems Offshoring: The Impact of Home Country Risk, Firm Learning and Competitive Dynamics', *MIS Quarterly,* 33(3), 597-616

Halawi L.A., Aronson J.E. & McCarthy, R.V. (2005), 'Resource-Based View of Knowledge Management for Competitive Advantage', *The Electronic Journal of Knowledge Management,* 3(2), 75-86. Retrieved from: www.ejkm.com (accessed: 17th April 2011)

Hansen M., Nohria, N. & Tierney, T. (1999), 'What's Your Strategy for Managing Knowledge?' *Harvard Business Review,* 77(2), 106-116

Harari, O. (1994), 'The Hypnotic Danger of Competitive Analysis', *Management Review,* 83(8), 36-38

Harding, R. (2006), *Corporate Intelligence Awareness: Securing the Competitive Edge,* Oshawa, ON: Multi-Media Publications Inc

Harris, M. & Wegg-Prosser, V. (2007), 'Post Bureaucracy and the Politics of Forgetting: The Management of Change at the BBC, 1991-2002', *Journal of Organizational Change Management,* 20(3), 290-303

Hart, S.L. (1992), 'An Integrative Framework for Strategy Making Processes', *Academy of Management Review,* 17(2), 327-3251

Hartland, T. & Williams-Burnett, N. (2012), 'Protecting the Olympic Band: Winners and Losers', *Journal of Strategic Marketing,* 20(1), 69-82

Haseman, W.D., Nazareth, D.L. & Souren, P. (2005), 'Implementation of a Group Decision Support System Utilizing Collective Memory', *Information & Management,* 42(4), 591-605

Heil, O., Day, G.S. & Reibstein, D.J. (1997), 'Signalling to Competitors', pp 277-292 in Day, G.S. & Reibstein, D.J. (Eds), *Wharton on Dynamic Competitive Strategy,* New York, NY, John Wiley & Sons

Heil, O. & Robertson, T.S. (1991), 'Toward a Theory of Competitive Market Signalling: A Research Agenda', *Strategic Management Journal,* 13(6), 403-418

Heppes, D.W. (2006), *An Assessment Of The Level Of Maturity Of The Competitive Intelligence Function Within A South African Retail Bank,* Magister Commercii in Business Management Dissertation, University of Johannesburg, South Africa

Hodgkinson, G.P., Sadler-Smith, E., Burke, L.A., Claxton, G. & Sparrow, P. (2009), 'Intuition in Organizations: Implication for Strategic Management', *Long Range Planning,* 42(3), 277-297

Hooley, G., Piercy, N.F. & Nicoulaud, N. (2008), *Marketing Strategy and Competitive Positioning 4/E,* Harlow, UK: Pearson Education Ltd

Hult, G.T.M., Ketchen, D.J. & Reus, T.H. (2001), 'Organizational Learning Capacity and Internal Customer Orientation within Strategic Sourcing Units', *Journal of Quality Management,* 6 (2), 173-192

Hult, G.T.M., Ketchen, D.J. & Slater, S.F. (2002), 'A Longitudinal Study of the Learning Climate and Cycle Time in Supply Chains', *Journal of Business & Industrial Marketing,* 17(4), 302-23

Hurd, M. & Nyberg, L. (2004), *The Value Factor: How Global Leaders Use Information for Growth and Competitive Advantage,* New York, NY: Bloomberg Press

Hussey, D. (2003), *CBI Series in Practical Strategy, Competitor Analysis: Turning Intelligence into Success,* Hoboken, NJ: John Wiley & Sons Inc

Jarzabkowski, P., Balogun, J. & Seidl, D. (2007), 'Strategizing: The Challenges of a Practice Perspective', *Human Relations,* 60(1), 5-27

Jaworski, B.J., Macinnes, D.J. & Kohli, A.K. (2002), 'Generating Competitive Intelligence in Organisations, *Journal of Market-Focused Management,* 5(4), 279-307

Jayachandran, S. & Varadarajan, R. (2006), 'Does Success Diminish Competitive Responsiveness?, Reconciling Conflicting Perspectives', *Journal of the Academy of Marketing Science,* 34 (3), 284-294

Johnson, G., Langley, A., Molin, L. & Whittington, R. (2007), *Strategy as Practice: Research Directions and Resources,* Cambridge, UK: Cambridge University Press

Jugdev, K., Mathur, G. & Fung, T.S. (2007), 'Project Management Assets and their Relationship with the Project Management Capability of the Firm', *International Journal of Project Management,* 25(6), 560-568

Juhari, A.S. & Stephens, D.P. (2006), 'Tracing the Origins of Competitive Intelligence Throughout History", *Journal of Competitive Intelligence and Management,* 3(4), 61-82

Kahaner, L. (1995), 'What You Can Learn From Your Competitors' Mission Statements', *Competitive Intelligence Review,* 6(4), 35-40

Kalkan, V.D. (2008), 'An Overall View of Knowledge Management Challenges for Global Business', *Business Process Management Journal,* 14(3), 390-400

Kalling, T. (2003), 'Knowledge Management and the Occasional Links with Performance', *Journal of Knowledge Management,* 7(3), 67-81

Kandemir, D. & Hult, G.T.M. (2005), 'A Conceptualization of an Organizational Learning Culture in International Joint Ventures', *Industrial Marketing Management,* 34(5), 430-439

Keep, W.W., Omura, G.S. & Calantone, R.J. (1994), 'What Managers Should Know About Their Competitors' Patented Technologies', *Industrial Marketing Management,* 23(3), 257-264

Kendrick, T. & Blackmore, J. (2001), 'Ten Things You Really Need to Know about Competitors', *Competitive Intelligence Magazine,* 4(5), 12-15

Khalifa, M., Yu, A.Y. & Shen, K.N. (2000), 'Knowledge Management Systems Success: A Contingency Perspective', *Journal of Knowledge Management,* 12(1), 119-132

Kim, W.C. & Mauborgne, R. (2005), *Blue Ocean Strategy: How to Create Uncontested Market Space and Make Competition Irrelevant,* Boston, MA; Harvard Business School Press

Kosinen, K.U. (2010), 'Organisational Memories in Project-based Companies: An Autopoietic View', *The Learning Organisation,* 17(2), 149-162

Kristensson, P., Matthing, J. & Johansson, N. (2008), 'Key Strategies For The Successful Involvement of Customers in the Co-Creation of New Technology-Based Services', *International Journal of Service Industry Management,* 19(4), 474-491

Kydd, P.H. (1996), 'Tracking Your Competitors', *Research Technology Management,* 59(1), 12-14

Landrum, N.E., Howell, J.P. & Paris, L. (2000), 'Leadership for Strategic Change', *Leadership & Organisation Development Journal,* 21(3), 150-156

Larivet, S. & Brouard, F. (2010), 'Complaints are a Firm's Best Friend', *Journal of Strategic Marketing,* 18(7), 537-551

Larivet, S. & Brouard, F. (2012), 'SMEs' Attitude towards SI Programmes: Evidence from Belgium', *Journal of Strategic Marketing,* 20(1), 5-18

Lee, K.C., Lee, S. & Kang, I.W. (2005), 'KMPI: Measuring Knowledge Management Performance', *Information & Management,* 42(3), 469-82

Leeflang, P.S.H. & Wittink, D.R. (2001), 'Explaining Competitive Reaction Effects', *International Journal of Research in Marketing,* 18(1/2), 119-137

Leenders, M.A.A.M. & Wierenga, B. (2008), 'The Effect of the Marketing-R&D Interface on New Product Performance: The Critical Role of Resources and Scope', *International Journal of Research in Marketing,* 25(1), 56-68

Liebowitz, J. (2006), *Strategic Intelligence: Business Intelligence, Competitive Intelligence, and Knowledge Management,* Boca Raton, FL: Auerbach Publications

Lin, T-C. & Huang, C-C. (2008), 'Understanding Knowledge Management System Usage Antecedents: An Integration of Social Cognitive Theory and Task Technology Fit', *Information & Management,* 45(6), 410-417

Linn, T.A. (1994), 'Learning From the Competition', *Journal of Accountancy,* 177(2), 43-46

Liu, M-S. & Liu, N-C, (2008), 'Sources of Knowledge Acquisition and Patterns of Knowledge-Sharing Behaviors: An Empirical Study of Taiwanese High-Tech Firms', *International Journal of Information Management,* 28(5), 423-432

Loshin, D. (2003), *Business Intelligence: The Savvy Manager's Guide,* Burlington, MA: Elsevier Science & Technology Books

Luft, J. & Ingham, H. (1955), The Johari Window: A graphic Model for Interpersonal Relations, *University of California Western Training Laboratory*

MacDonald, S. (1995), 'Too Close for Comfort?: The Strategic Implications of Getting Too Close to the Customer', *California Management Review,* 37(4), 8-27

Magin, V. (2006), *Competition in Marketing,* PhD Thesis, Johannes Gutenberg-Universität at Mainz, Germany

Marchi, S (2005), 'Using a Visual Tool to Analyse Competition', *Competitive Intelligence Magazine,* 8(4), 9-14 & 59

Martin de Holan, P. & Phillips, N. (2003), 'Organizational Forgetting', pp 393-409 in Easterby-Smith, M. & Lyles, M.A. (Eds), *Handbook of Organizational Learning and Knowledge Management,* Oxford, UK: Blackwell

Martin de Holan, P. & Phillips, N. (2004), 'Remembrance of Things Past: The Dynamics of Organizational Forgetting', *Management Science,* 50(11), 1603-1613

Mata, F. J., Fuerst, W.L., & Barney, J.B. (1995), 'Information Technology and Sustained Competitive Advantage: A Resource-Based Analysis', *MIS Quarterly,* 19(4), 487-505

Mathur, G., Jugdev, K. & Fung, T.S. (2007), 'Intangible Project Management Assets as Determinants of Competitive Advantage', *Management Research News,* 30(7), 460-475

Mautin, O.K.E.D. (2011), 'Bank Consolidation and Scale Economies: Trend of Banks in a Developing Country', *Journal of Economic Theory,* 5(1), 15-21

Mejtoft, T. (2010), 'Moving Closer to the Customers: Effects of Vertical Integration in the Swedish Commercial Printing Industry', *Journal of Strategic Marketing,* 18(7), 599-611

Menguca, B., Auhb, S. & Shiha, E. (2007), 'Transformational Leadership and Market Orientation: Implications for the Implementation of Competitive Strategies and Business Unit Performance', *Journal of Business Research,* 60(4), 314-321

Meso, P. & Smith, R. (2000), 'A Resource-Based View of Knowledge Management Systems', *Journal of Knowledge Management,* 4(3), 224-234

Metcalfe, S. & Warde, A. (2003), *Market Relations and the Competitive Process (New Dynamics of Innovation & Competition),* Manchester, UK: Manchester University Press

Michaluk, G. (2007), *The Marketing Director's Role in Business Planning and Corporate Governance,* Chichester, UK: John Wiley & Sons Ltd

Miller, D. & Chen, M-J. (1996), 'The Simplicity of Competitive Repertoires: An Empirical Analysis', *Strategic Management Journal,* 17(6), 419-439

Miller, G.J., Brautigam, D. & Gerlach, S.V. (2006), *Business Intelligence Competency Centers: A Team Approach to Maximizing Competitive Advantage,* Hoboken, NJ: John Wiley & Sons Inc

Moatti, V. (2009), 'Learning to Expand or Expanding to Learn? The Role of Imitation and Experience in the Choice Among Several Expansion Modes', *European Management Journal,* 27(1), 36-36

Modi, P. (2012), 'Market Orientation in Non-Profit Organizations: Innovativeness, Resource Scarcity, and Performance', *Journal of Strategic Marketing*, 20(1), 55-67

Mostert, D.G. (2005), *Competitive Analysis: A tool to Enhance the Process of Strategy Formulation,* MPhil Information & Knowledge Management Dissertation, University of Stellenbosch, South Africa

Moutinho, K. & Southern, G. (2010), *Strategic Marketing Management*, Andover, UK: South Western/Cengage Learning Course Technology

Neilsen, C. (2005), 'The Global Chess Game.. Or is It Go? Market Entry Strategies for Emerging Markets', *Thunderbird International Business Review,* 47(4), 397-427

Newbert, S.L. (2008), 'Value, Rareness, Competitive Advantage, and Performance: A Conceptual-Level Empirical Investigation of the Resource-Based View of the Firm', *Strategic Management Journal,* 9(7), 745-768

Nissley, N. & Casey, A. (2002), 'The Politics of the Exhibition: Viewing Corporate Museums Through the Paradigmatic Lens of Organizational Memory', *British Journal of Management,* 13(SI), 35-46

Nutt, P.C. (1993), 'The Formulation Processes and Tactics Used in Organizational Decision Making', *Organization Science*, 4(2), 226-251

O'Gorman, D. (2005), 'Memes, CI and Marketing: A Preliminary Framework', *Journal of Competitive Intelligence and Management*, 3(2), 29-43

Oxenfeldt, A.R. & Moore, W.L. (1978), 'Customer or Competitor: Which Guideline for Marketing?', *Management Review,* 67(August), 43-48

Oxenfeldt, A.R. & Moore, W.L. (1981), 'Competitor Analysis: A Prize-centered Approach', *Management Review,* 70(5), 23-28

Oz, E. (2009), *Management Information Systems, 6/E*, Boston, MA: Thomson Course Technology

Pai, J-C. (2006), 'An Empirical Study of the Relationship between Knowledge Sharing and IS/IT Strategic Planning (ISSP)', *Management Decision*, 44(1), 105-122

Paley, N. (1994), 'Choose Competitors Carefully', *Sales and Marketing Management,* 146(6), 57-58

Pandza, K. & Thorpe, R. (2009), 'Creative Search and Strategic Sense-making: Missing Dimensions in the Concept of Dynamic Capabilities', *British Journal of Management*, 20(1), S118-S131

Park, C.W. & Smith, D.C. (1990), 'Product Class Competitors as Sources of Innovative Marketing Strategies', *Journal of Consumer Marketing,* 7(2), 27-38

Patterson, A., Quinn, L. & Baron, S. (2012), 'The Power of Intuitive Thinking: A Devalued Heuristic of Strategic Marketing, *Journal of Strategic Marketing*, 20(1), 35-44

Pauwels, K. (2004), 'How Dynamic Consumer Response, Competitor Response, Company Support and Company Inertia Shape Long-Term Marketing Effectiveness', *Marketing Science,* 23 (4), 596-610

Penn, M.J. & Zalesne, E.K. (2007), *Microtrends: The Small Forces Behind Tomorrow's Big Changes,* New York, NY: Twelve-Hatchett Book Group

Peteraf, M.A. (1993), 'The Cornerstones of Competitive Advantage: A Resource-Based View', *Strategic Management Journal,* 14(3), 179-191

Pickton, D.W. & Wright, S. (2000), 'Poor Understanding of Marketing Principles Has Led to Poor Marketing Management performance: Consideration of Four Marketing Myths', *Comportamento Organizacional e Gestao (Organisational Behaviour and Management), Instituto Superior de Psicologia Aplicada*, Lisbon, Portugal, 6(1), 109-118

Pietersen, M.A. (2006), *Competitive Intelligence at the Medical Research Council,* MPhil Information and Knowledge Management Dissertation, University of Stellenbosch, South Africa

Piorier, C.A. (1993), 'Personality Intelligence: Anticipating Your Competitor's Next Decision', *Manage*, 44(4), 22-25

Porter M.E. (1983a), 'Analyzing Competitors: Predicting Competitor Behavior and Formulating Offensive and Defensive Strategy', pp 192-209 in Leontiades, M. (Ed), *Policy, Strategy and Implementation,* New York, NY: Random House

Porter, M.E. (1983b), *Cases in Competitive Strategy,* New York, NY: The Free Press

Porter, M.E. (1985), *Competitive Advantage: Creating and Sustaining Superior Performance,* New York, NY: The Free Press

Porter, M.E. (1998a), *Competitive Strategy: Techniques for Analysing Industries and Competitors,* New York, NY: The Free Press

Porter, M.E. (1998b), *On Competition,* Boston, MA; Harvard Business School Publishing

Porter, M.E. (1998c), *The Competitive Advantage of Nations,* New York, NY: The Free Press

Pratten, C.F. (1971), *Economies of Scale in Manufacturing Industry,* Cambridge, UK: University Press

Prescott, J.E., (1999), 'The Evolution of Competitive Intelligence', *Proposal Management,* Spring, pp 37-52

Press, G. (1990), 'Assessing Competitors' Business Philosophies', *Long Range Planning,* 23(5), 71-75

Qiu, T. (2008), 'Scanning for Competitive Intelligence: A Managerial Perspective', *European Journal of Marketing,* 42(7/8), 814 - 835

Qingjiu T. & Prescott, J.E. (2000), 'China: Competitive Intelligence Practices in an Emerging Market Environment", *Competitive Intelligence Review,* 11(4), 65-78

Quinto, I., Buckingham Shum, S., DeLiddo, A. & Iandoli, L. (2010), 'A Debate Dashboard to Enhance On-Line Knowledge Sharing', *Proceedings of the IFKAD Conference: Intellectual Capital in a Complex Business Landscape,* 24-26 June 2010, Matera, Italy

Ranchhod, A. & Gurău, C. (2007), *Marketing Strategies: A Contemporary Approach,* Harlow, UK: Pearson Education Ltd/Prentice Hall

Reibstein D.J. & Chussil, M.J. (1999), 'Putting the Lesson before the Test: Using Simulations to Analyse and Develop Competitive Strategies'. *Competitive Intelligence Review,* 10(1), 34-48

Reibstein, D.J. & Wittink. D.R. (2009), 'Competitive Responsiveness', *Marketing Science,* 24(1), 8-11

Renzl, B. (2008), 'Trust in Management and Knowledge Sharing: The Mediating Effects of Fear and Knowledge Documentation', *International Journal of Management Science,* 36(2), 206-220

Rhee, K.S. & Honeycutt Sigler, T. (2010), 'Developing Enlightened Leaders for Industry and Community: Executive Education and Service-Learning, *Journal of Management Education,* 34(1), 163-181

Richelson, J.T. (2006), 'The Whole World is Watching', *Bulletin of the Atomic Scientists,* 62(1), 26-35

Riege, A.M. (2003), 'Validity and Reliability Tests in Case Study Research: A Literature Review with "Hands-on" Applications for Each Research Phase', *Qualitative Market Research: An International Journal,* 6(2), 75-86

Rifat, T. (2003), *Remote Viewing and Sensing for Managers: How to Use Military Psiops for a Competitive Edge,* London, UK: VISION Paperbacks

Ringland, G. (2002), *Scenarios in Business,* Chichester, UK: John Wiley & Sons

Rivette, K. (2001), 'Beware: Competitors Leveraging 'Hidden Assets', *Competitive Intelligence Magazine,* 4(5), 16-18

Robert, M.M. (1991), 'Attack Competitors by Changing the Game Rules', *Journal of Business Strategy,* 12(5), 53-56

Robinson, M.L. (2003), *Beyond Competitive Intelligence: The Business of Counterintelligence and Trade Secrets Protection,* Bloomington, IN: AuthorHouse

Rothberg, H.R. & Erickson, G.S. (2004), *From Knowledge to Intelligence: Creating Competitive Advantage in the Next Economy,* Burlington, MA: Elsevier Science & Technology Books

Rothschild, R., Swann, P. & Taghavi, M. (1991), 'Identifying Competitors from Market Share Data: A Technique and an Application', *Applied Economics,* 23(3), 525-529

Rowlinson, M., Booth, C., Clark, P., Delahaye, A. & Procter, S. (2010), 'Social Remembering and Organizational Memory', *Organization Studies*, 31(1), 69-87

Sánchez, J.A.L., Vijande, M.L.S. & Gutiérrez, J.A.T. (2009), 'Organisational Learning and Value Creation in Business Markets', *European Journal of Marketing*, 14(11/12), 1612-1641

Santos, M.L., Sanzo, M.J., Alvarez, L.I. & Vazquez, R. (2005), 'Organizational Learning and Market Orientation: Interface and Effects on Performance', *Industrial Marketing Management*, 34(3), 187-202

Savioz, P. (2003), *Technology Intelligence: Concept Design and Implementation in Technology Based SMEs*, Basingstoke, UK: Palgrave Macmillan

Saxby, C.L., Nitse, P.S. & Dishman, P.L. (2000), 'Managers' Mental Categorization of Competitors', *Competitive Intelligence Review*, 11(2), 31-38

Schatzki, T.R. (2005), 'Peripheral Vision: The Sites of Organizations, *Organization Studies*, 26(3), 465-484

Schatzki, T.R. (2006), 'On Organizations as they Happen', *Organization Studies*, 27(12), 1863-1873

Scheeres, H., Solomon, N., Boud, D. & Rooney, D. (2010), 'When is it OK to Learn at Work? The Learning Work of Organisational Practices', *Journal of Workplace Learning*, 22(1/2), 13-26

Sharp, S, (2009), *Competitive Intelligence Advantage*, Hoboken, NJ: John Wiley & Sons

Shenton, A.K. (2007), 'Viewing Information Needs Through a Johari Window', *Reference Services Review*, 35(3), 487-496

Simkin, L. & Dibb, S. (2012), 'Leadership Teams Rediscover Market Analysis in Seeking Competitive Advantage and Growth During Economic Uncertainty', *Journal of Strategic Marketing*, 20(1), 45-54

Slater, S.F. & Narver, J.C. (1994), 'Does Competitive Environment Moderate the Market Orientation-Performance Relationship?', *The Journal of Marketing*, 58(1), 46-55

Smith, J.R. (2009), 'Competitive Intelligence in Small Companies: A Synthesis of Studies and Research Agenda', in *CD-ROM Proceedings: Academy of Marketing Conference, Competitive Intelligence, Analysis & Strategy Track*, 7th-9th July 2009, Leeds Metropolitan University, Leeds, UK

Smith, K.G., Grimm, C.M., Young, G. & Wally, S. (1997), 'Strategic Groups and Rivalrous Firm Behavior: Towards a Reconciliation', *Strategic Management Journal*, 18(2), 149-157

Smith, J.R., Wright, S. & Pickton, D.W. (2010), 'Competitive Intelligence Programmes for SMEs in France: Evidence of Changing Attitudes', *Journal of Strategic Marketing*, 18(7), 523-536

Soirinsuo, J. & Mäkinen, P. (2011), ' Growth and Economies of Scale Among Timber Haulage Companies', *Journal of Small Business and Enterprise Development*, 18(1), 170-184

Spender, J-C. (1996), 'Making Knowledge the Basis of a Dynamic theory of the Firm', *Strategic Management Journal*, 17(SI Winter), 45-62

Spender, J-C. (2008), 'Organizational Learning and Knowledge Management: Whence and Whither?', *Management Learning*, 39(2), 159-176

Stair, R. & Reynolds, G. (2010), *Principles of Information Systems*, , Boston, MA: Cengage Learning Course Technology

Stapleton, J.J. (2003), *Executive's Guide to Knowledge Management: the Last Competitive Advantage*, New York, NY: John Wiley & Sons

Steenkamp, J.E.M., Nijs, V.R., Hanssens, D.M. & Dekimpe, M.G. (2005), 'Competitive Reactions to Advertising and Promotion Attacks', *Marketing Science*, 24(1), 35-54

Subramanian, R. & IsHak, S.T. (1998), 'Competitor Analysis Practices of US Companies: An Empirical Investigation', *Management International Review*, 38(1), pp 7-23

Surowiecki, J, (2005), *The Wisdom of Crowds*, New York, NY: Anchor House

Swart, J. (2006), 'Intellectual Capital: Disentangling an Enigmatic Concept', *Journal of Intellectual Capital*, 7(2), 136-159

Taleb, N.N. (2004), *Fooled by Randomness: The Hidden Role of Chance in Life and in the Markets,* London, UK: Penguin Books

Taleb, N.N. (2007), *The Black Swan: The Impact of the Highly Improbable,* London, UK: Penguin Books

Tamaddoni Jahromi, A., Sepehri, M.M., Teimourpour, B. & Choobdar, S. (2010), 'Modeling Customer Churn in a Non-Contractual Setting: The Case of Telecommunications Service Providers'. *Journal of Strategic Marketing,* 18(7), 587-598

Teitelbaum, R. (1992), 'The New Race for Intelligence: Your Competitors May Well be Mounting Sophisticated Information-Gathering Operations', *Fortune,* 126(10), 104-107

Toften, K. & Hammervoll, T. (2010), 'Niche Marketing and Strategic Capabilities: An Exploratory Study of Specialised Firms', *Marketing Intelligence & Planning,* 28(6), 736-753

Trim, P.R.J. & Lee, Y-I. (2008), 'A Strategic Marketing Intelligence and Multi-Organisational Resilience Framework', *European Journal of Marketing,* 42(7/8), 731-745

Trinh, G., Dawes, J. & Lockshin, L. (2009), 'Do Product Variants Appeal to Different Segments of Buyers Within a Category?', *Journal of Product & Brand Management,* 18(2), 95-105

Tully, K.A. (2007), *Déjà Vu: Why Firms Respond More Than Once to a Competitor Action,* PhD Thesis, University of Pittsburgh, PA, ISA

Tyson, K.W.M. (2005), *The Complete Guide to Competitive Intelligence: Gathering, Analysing and Using Intelligence,* Englewood Cliffs, NJ: Prentice Hall

Tzu, S. (1988), *The Art of War.* Oxford, UK: Oxford University Press

Uttal, B. (1979), 'The Gentleman and the Upstarts Meet in a Great Mini Battle', *Fortune,* 23rd April 23, pp 98-108

Van Daal, B., de Haas, M. & Weggeman, M. (1998), ' The Knowledge Matrix: A Participatory Method for Individual Knowledge Gap Determination', *Knowledge and Process Management,* 5(4), 255-263

Van den Hooff B. & Huysman, M. (2009), 'Managing Knowledge Sharing: Emergent and Engineering Approaches', *Information & Management,* 46(1), 1-8

Vella, C.M. & McGonagle, J.J. (2000), 'Profiling in Competitive Analysis', *Competitive Intelligence Review,* 11(2), 20-30

Vorhies, D.W. & Morgan, N.A. (2005), 'Benchmarking Marketing Capabilities for Sustainable Competitive Advantage', *Journal of Marketing,* 69(1), 80-94

Wagner, R. (2007), *Creative Search and Strategic Sense-making: Missing Dimensions in the Concept of Dynamic Capabilities,* MPhil Information & Knowledge Management Dissertation, University of Stellenbosch, South Africa

Wang, H.C., Jinyu, H.E. & Mahoney, J.T. (2009), 'Firm-Specific Knowledge Resources and Competitive Advantage: The Roles of Economic-and Relationship-Based Employee Governance Mechanisms', *Strategic Management Journal,* 30(12), 1265-1285

Waring, J. & Currie, G. (2009), 'Managing Expert Knowledge: Organizational Challenges and Managerial Futures for the UK Medical Profession', *Organization Studies,* 30(7), 755-778

Warren, K. (2002), *Competitive Strategy Dynamics,* Chichester, UK: John Wiley & Sons Ltd

Warren, K. (2008), *Strategic Management Dynamics,* Chichester, UK: John Wiley & Sons Ltd

Weick, K.E. (1995), *Sense Making in Organizations,* Thousand Oaks, CA: Sage

Weick, K.E., Sutcliffe, K.M. & Obstfeld, D. (2005), 'Organizing and the Process of Sense Making', *Organization Science,* 16(4), 409-421

Weiss, A. & Wright, S. (2006), 'Dealing with the Unknown - A Holistic Approach to Marketing and Competitive Intelligence', *Competitive Intelligence Magazine,* 9(5), 15-20

Wells, C.A. (2001), 'Analysing Corporate Personalities', *Competitive Intelligence Magazine,* 4(4), 17-20

Wernerfelt, B. (1984), 'A Resource Based View of the Firm', *Strategic Management Journal,* 5(2), 171-180

Werther, G.F.A. (2000), 'Profiling Change as a Strategic Analysis Tool', *Competitive Intelligence Magazine,* 3(1), 19-22

Whittington, R. (2007), 'Strategy Practice and Strategy Process: Family Differences and the Sociological Eye', *Organization Studies,* 28(10), 1575-1586

Whittington, R. & Whipp, R. (1992), 'Professional Ideology and Marketing Implementation', *European Journal of Marketing,* 26(1), 52-63

Wilkinson, S. (1998). 'Competitors Reveal Own Strengths, Weaknesses', *Chemical & Engineering News,* 76(15), 27-30

Williams, R. (2006), 'Narratives of Knowledge and Intelligence: Beyond the Tacit and Explicit', *Journal of Knowledge Management,* 10(4), 81-99

Wilson, A. (2002), *The Marketing Audit Handbook*, London, UK: Kogan Page Ltd

Winch, G.M. & Maytorena, E. (2009), 'Making Good Sense: Assessing the Quality of Risky Decision-Making', *Organization Studies,* 30(2/3), 181-203

Wong, V, Saunders, J. & Doyle, P. (1989), 'The Barriers to Achieving Stronger Marketing Orientation in British Companies: An Exploratory Study', pp 34-64 in *Proceedings: Marketing Education Group Conference,* Glasgow Business School, Glasgow, UK

Wong, A., Tjosvold, D. & Liu, C. (2009), 'Cross-Functional Team Organizational Citizenship Behavior in China: Shared Vision and Goal Interdependence among Departments', *Journal of Applied Social Psychology,* 39(12), 2879-2909

Wood, M. (2002), 'Mind the Gap? A Processual Reconsideration of Organizational Knowledge', *Organization,* 9(1), 161-171

Woodside, A.G. (2005), *Market-Driven Thinking: Achieving Contextual Intelligence,* Oxford, UK: Butterworth-Heinemann Ltd

Wright, S. (2005a), 'Seven European Nations, A Profile of Current CI Practice', *Competitive Intelligence,* 8(4), 20-27

Wright, S. (2005b), 'The CI:Marketing Interface', *Journal of Competitive Intelligence & Management,* 3(2), 3-7

Wright, S. (2005c), 'Competitive Intelligence for Competitive Advantage: What it is, Why it Matters', *Royal United Services Institute for Defence and Security Studies Annual Conference,* Whitehall, London, UK

Wright, S. (2011), *A Critical Evaluation of Competitive Intelligence and Insight Management Practice,* Doctor of Philosophy (PhD) thesis, De Montfort University, Leicester, United Kingdom

Wright, S., Badr, A, Weiss, A. & Pickton, D.W. (2004), 'Competitive Intelligence Through UK Eyes', *Journal of Competitive Intelligence and Management,* 2(2), 68-87

Wright, S., Bisson, C. & Duffy, A.P. (2012), 'Applying a Behavioural and Operational Diagnostic Typology of Competitive Intelligence Practice: Empirical Evidence from the SME Sector in Turkey, *Journal of Strategic Marketing,* 20(1), 19-33

Wright, S. & Calof, J.L. (2006), 'The Quest for Competitive, Business and Marketing Intelligence: A Country Comparison of Current Practice', *European Journal of Marketing,* 40(5/6), 453-465

Wright, S., Eid, E.R. & Fleisher, C.S. (2009a), 'Empirical Study of Competitive Intelligence Practice: Evidence from UK Retail Banking', in *CD-ROM Proceedings: Academy of Marketing Conference, Competitive Intelligence, Analysis & Strategy Track,* 7th-9th July 2009, Leeds Metropolitan University, Leeds, UK

Wright, S., Eid, E.R. & Fleisher, C.S. (2009b), 'Competitive Intelligence in Practice: Empirical Evidence from the UK Retail Banking Sector', *Journal of Marketing Management,* 25(9/10), 941-964

Wright, S. & Pickton, D.W. (1998), 'Improved Competitive Strategy through Value Added Competitive Intelligence', pp 73-83 in *Proceedings: Third Annual European Conference, Society of Competitive Intelligence Professional,* Berlin, Germany

Wright, S, Pickton, D.W. & Callow, J. (2002), 'Competitive Intelligence in UK firms: A Typology', *Marketing Intelligence & Planning,* 20(6), 349-360

Yakhlef, A. (2010), 'The Corporeality of Practice-Based Learning', *Organization Studies*, 131(4), 409-430

Yang, J-T. (2008), 'Individual Attitudes and Organisational Knowledge Sharing', *Tourism Management*, 29(2), 345-353

Yang, J-T. (2010), 'Antecedents and Consequences of Knowledge Sharing in International Tourist Hotels', *International Journal of Hospitality Management*, 29(1), 42-52

Zangoueinezhad, A. & Moshabaki, A. (2009), 'The Role of Structural Capital on Competitive Intelligence', *Industrial Management & Data Systems*, 109(2), 262-280

Zhou, K.Z., Brown, J.R., Dev, C.S. & Agarwal, S. (2007), 'The Effects of Customer and Competitor Orientations on Performance in Global Markets: A Contingency Analysis', *Journal of International Business Studies*, 38(2), 303-319

Zott, C. & Amit, R. (2008), 'The Fit between Product Market Strategy and Business Model: Implications for Firm Performance', *Strategic Management Journal*, 29(1), 1-26

Part I: Competitive Intelligence

Competitive Intelligence programmes for SMEs in France: evidence of changing attitudes

Jamie R. Smith, Sheila Wright and David Pickton

Department of Marketing, De Montfort University, Leicester, UK

This paper reports on an empirical study of the French Chambers of Commerce and Industry Competitive Intelligence (CI) programmes. Semi-structured interviews were undertaken with the directors of 15 CI programmes from four regions of France. The research questions focused on definitional issues, CI programme content, Small and Medium-sized Enterprise (SME) CI practices and innovative methods used to change attitudes towards CI. The interview transcriptions were sorted, analysed and classified in NVivo software. The findings show that tangible results have been achieved despite resistance from small businesses in regard to their Competitive Intelligence practices. The paper also identifies the public and private sector entities which were named as sources of advice for small businesses for their Competitive Intelligence needs. The SMEs were also classified by the application of a CI attitude typology. The insights elicited can help future initiatives by public/private partnerships in both CI programme design and implementation.

Introduction

Over the last 10 years France has implemented regional programmes to increase the awareness of, and change attitudes towards, the Competitive Intelligence (CI) practices of enterprises. Dedijer (1994) identified France as the first country in the world to look closely at the relationships between government, intelligence and society. Uniquely in France, and in contrast to other European and North American countries, CI support is considered to be a state role (Carayon, 2003; Dou, 2004; Martre, 1994; Smith & Kossou, 2008) and to be implemented throughout French regions (Goriat, 2006; Moinet, 2008). The emphasis has primarily been on Small and Medium-sized Enterprises (SMEs) with the Chambers of Commerce and Industry (CCI) playing a central role (Clerc, 2009). The overall objective of this study is to investigate the emerging French paradigm of CI as a public policy. Specifically, this paper addresses the roles and perspectives of the CI programme directors who interact with SMEs in the field. Table 1 summarises the research design.

Methodology

Gilmore, Carson, and Grant (2001) argued for a phenomenological approach to SME research with an emphasis on explanation and not prediction. A qualitative approach provides insight into the issue being explored (Creswell, 2007) illuminating the rich data

39

Table 1.   Research design.

Sample frame	Chambers of Commerce and Industry in France
Sampling method	Purposive/snowballing
Sample size	15 interviews
Research approach	Qualitative, Exploratory, Descriptive
Data collection methods	Semi-structured interviews and document analysis, face to face and telephone
Data analysis	NVivo software to code, sort, classify and identify common themes
Research questions	What is the content of your CI programme?
	What types of firms are targeted in terms of size and sector?
	Which organisations from both the private and public sectors do you collaborate with in your CI programmes?
	Which organisations have the most credibility for advising on CI practices?
	What terminology is used in the intelligence gathering process?
	Who is responsible for CI in the SMEs?
	What are the attitudes of the SME decision makers towards CI practices?
	What actions do you take to change the SME decision makers' attitudes?
	How motivated are the SME managers to follow your advice?
	How do SMEs evaluate the effectiveness of their CI practices?

found in local contexts (Johnson & Onwuegbuzie, 2004). CI itself has been defined as both art and science (Calof & Skinner, 1998) and, essentially, being qualitative in nature (McGonagle & Vella, 2002). Interviewing can be focused on meanings and frameworks as well as events and processes (Rubin & Rubin, 2005), all of which were captured in this evaluation research. The transcripts were uploaded into NVivo for coding and analysis. A case node was created for each CI director to form a constellation of sources around a person (Bazely, 2007). Coding the transcripts identified topics and brought together data where they occurred (Bazely, 2007). The construction of ranked tables identified emerging themes, frequencies and patterns (Neuman, 1997).

The sample frame

All but one CCI stipulated that their actions could be considered programmes. The sample frame included only CCI CI programmes that had been running for at least one year. The sampling methods used were purposive and snowballing. Purposive sampling enables the researcher to build a sample frame around a specific subject matter (Denscombe, 2007). Riley, Wood, Clark, Wilkie, and Szivas (2003) considered that sample units which provide information about themselves and about other units (snowball sampling) an effective social science method to identify suitable respondents. The programmes have evolved over time often solidifying related services and activities which started before the noted years. Rennes has two ongoing programmes; one interview was undertaken with each programme manager. Estimates were stated by the CI programme directors as to the numbers of SMEs which have participated in the CI programmes. The directors have considerable exposure to SMEs in terms of CI needs, SME attitudes towards CI and the effectiveness of the CCI activities. Most have interacted with over a hundred SMEs in some form of their programme implementation. There is an accumulated experience of 59

Table 2.   Participating CCI.

Chamber of Commerce	Year CI programme started	Estimated number of SMEs involved in programmes
Bourgogne	2000	Over 100 in 2008
Chalons en Champagne	'activities' since 1989	Currently around 200
Chambery	2007	Around 12 companies
Colmar	2000	Around 250 in 2008
Dordogne	2008	50
Franche-Comté (regional)	2006	Around 150
Le Mans	1998	80 a year face to face
Lille	2006	Around 140
Paris	2004	Around 120
Rennes (regional) Dufour	2005	Around 100
Rennes (regional) Rodrigez	2007	Around 400
Rhone-Alpes (regional)	2006	Many hundreds
Rouen 2007	2007	115
Tours	2007	Around 100
Versailles Val-d'Oise	2006	Between 300 and 400

years for the interviewees in terms of directing CI programmes. Table 2 lists the participating CCI alphabetically.

Competitive Intelligence for small businesses

The case for SME research has been well established by management scholars (McGregor, 2005; Nkongolo-Bakenda, Anderson, Ito, & Garven, 2006; Ruzzier, Hisrich, & Antoncic, 2006). The investigation of CI in SMEs has not been as well documented as in larger companies (Burke & Jarratt, 2004; Tarraf & Molz, 2006). Early work by Groom & David (2001) suggested that SMEs were not very concerned with CI. A recent study in France by Oubrich (2007) suggested that SMEs were limited to conducting surveillance of markets and competition whereas large companies were integrating CI programmes into strategy development. Nevertheless, a few quite major studies have focused on SMEs. In Canada, Brouard (2006) looked at environmental scanning practices in SMEs. Salles (2006) examined the information needs of SMEs in France in order to conduct Competitive Intelligence. In Switzerland, a research-action approach showed the necessity of a strategic assessment to determine CI needs in SMEs (Bégin, Deschamps, & Madinier, 2008). A comparative study of Belgium and South Africa by Saayman et al. (2008) found that there were few differences between small and large companies in terms of intelligence practices. However, French CI research has highlighted the different practices between large and small companies (Bégin et al., 2008; Bulinge, 2001; Salles, 2006). In France, the situation is quite different in that Competitive Intelligence as a business discipline, especially for SMEs, is supported by government-sponsored programmes that are being implemented country wide (Moinet, 2008; Smith & Kossou, 2008).

The variables which influence CI activity are not well defined (Tarraf & Molz, 2006). There is a calling for more insightful ways to assess SMEs (Spickett-Jones & Eng, 2006). Qiu (2008) investigated how entrepreneurial attitude and normative beliefs influence managerial scanning for CI in large companies. The antecedent investigation of CI awareness and attitudes in SMEs however, remains a gap in the literature. This exploratory study can be considered an incremental step towards addressing the roles of attitudes and awareness in a CI programme context.

CCI Competitive Intelligence programmes

The CCI in France represent networking organisations that bridge the public and private sectors with an intimate knowledge of the entrepreneurial community (Clerc, 2009). The CI programmes are decentralised and do not take on a common format. However, as can be seen from Table 3, all the CCI disseminate CI concepts through conferences and virtually all engage in training and workshops. Many provide a diagnosis of the SME CI practices to determine which training and assistance is appropriate. Many also speak of accompanying the SME with their CI needs and this may go as far as setting up a CI system for them. Table 3 illustrates the CCI programme content.

Innovative approaches towards changing attitudes and practices

Approaches towards changing attitudes and behaviours surfaced during the interviews. As can be seen, the CCI were using both conventional and non-conventional means.

Theatre

One CCI used professional actors and a play to convey the importance of strategic information and other CI concepts to SMEs. The head of the programme was convinced it worked but more senior officials were reluctant to continue such an alternative method.

SME managers sharing experiences

Many CCI invite SME managers who have implemented CI programmes to forums to share their experiences with other SME managers. SME counterparts are considered by the CCI as the most credible source.

Table 3.   Summary of CCI Competitive Intelligence programmes.

Interviewee code	Conferences	Training/ workshops	Sharing of best practices amongst SMEs	Diagnosis of SME CI practices	Assistance in implementing a CI system
C1	✔	✔	✔	✔	
C2	✔	✔	✔		
C3	✔	✔			✔
C4	✔	✔		✔	
C5	✔	✔		✔	
C6	✔	✔			
C7	✔	✔			
C8	✔	✔	✔		✔
C9	✔	✔			
C10	✔	✔	✔	✔	
C11	✔		✔		
C12	✔	✔		✔	
C13	✔	✔			
C14	✔	✔			
C15	✔	✔		✔	

A CI animator split between four SMEs each in a different industry

An interesting approach was used by another CCI which created an original employment contract for a qualified CI specialist to work in four different SMEs. The consultant, who has a degree in *Intelligence Economique*, spent one day a week with each enterprise to set up tools and systems and train employees on CI techniques. As the four SMEs were from different industries there were no confidentiality issues. The four SMEs jointly paid 50% of the consultant's salary, the other 50% paid by the CCI. The result was very successful. It was considered that a person who came every week becomes familiar with people and practices and therefore can be more sensitive to needs than a consultant who comes for three days and then leaves. In this case, the exceptional nature of the consultant trained and certified in CI, trilingual with eight years' overseas experience, clearly contributed to the success. In fact, the arrangement only came to an end, after one year, because the consultant moved on to other opportunities. The SMEs wanted to continue and were willing to pay 100% of the salary.

Conferences

Seminars, speeches, 'breakfasts', are all approaches to creating awareness for the SMEs. The CCI believe that over the recent years these have contributed to a change of attitude. However, this type of activity is limited to creating awareness or changing attitudes. More structured and customised actions such as training, needs analysis and setting up systems, are required to change behaviours.

Financial assistance

The more advanced programmes of the CCI such as setting up a CI unit, following up after a needs analysis, or training, are financed by the State (funds are distributed through the regional government). The subsidy can be implemented in different ways and typically represents 50% to 80% of total cost but sometimes it is 100%. One programme stated that the first year the SME paid almost nothing, much more in the second year and 100% in the third year. They will not participate if there is no financial assistance. Many CCI fear however that they are giving the SME managers the false impression that information is free.

Education/training

Many CCI fund and work closely with business schools. There are instances where SME managers follow a CI module. More targeted training for using CI tools is often part of a CI programme.

Collaborating entities

Table 4 presents organisations and entities from both the private and public sectors. These were identified by the CCI CI programme directors as sources of advice for Competitive Intelligence for SMEs in France.

Alain Juillet, the former Inter-ministerial Representative for *Intelligence Economique*, stepped down in 2009 and has been replaced (La Tribune, 2009). The top three named entities were CCI, consultants and gendarmerie.

Table 4. Collaborating entities.

French entity	Who they are	Number of times entity was named	Percentage of CCIs naming entity ($n = 15$)
State organisations			
DRIRE	Regional government for industry, research, and the environment	12	20
DCRI	The intelligence department of the Ministry of the Interior (still referred to as DST by some)	12	53
INPI	Intellectual property registry	2	13
Gendarmerie	A military body with police responsibilities	24	60
Alain Juillet	(Former)Inter-ministerial Representative for *Intelligence Economique*	13	53
Quasi-state organisations			
CCI/ARIST	Chambers of Commerce and Industry/Agency for Strategic and Technology Research (part of CCI)	137	100
ADIT	Agency for the Diffusion of Technology Information	2	13
MEDEF	A French employers 'union' with 750,000 members	32	40
CGPME	A French 'union' for SMEs	5	27
Private organisations			
Consultants – consultancies	Individuals or companies which sell CI related services	152	87
Chartered accountants	Known in France as *experts comptables* (State Certified Accountants)	15	47
Media	Internet, blogs and the press	22	87

Definitional issues

Defining CI has created significant debate for both practitioners and academics in France (Bulinge, 2002; Jakobiak, 2006; Larivet, 2001) and in the English speaking world (Brody, 2008; Fleisher & Bensoussan, 2007; Wright & Calof, 2006). How respondents refer to CI is a good indicator of how they position the concept in their minds (Wright, Eid, & Fleisher, 2009). The commonly accepted translation of CI into French or indeed vice versa is *Intelligence Economique* but this does not resolve equivalence issues (Jakobiak, 2006). *Intelligence Economique* is arguably a larger concept than CI because it is a public policy (Carayon, 2003) and it has a defensive orientation (Larivet, 2009). These equivalence issues should be born in mind when interpreting the term CI in this paper.

In this study CI facilitators unanimously stated that in their view, the SME managers would not be able to give a precise CI definition, even if they appeared to understand the concept. Associations with espionage and other pejorative behaviours were widely noted even if a clearer, more credible appreciation of CI concepts was emerging. Some CCI went so far as to refuse to use the term CI, fearing SME managers' potentially negative reactions. Other CCI were implementing CI services and actions while using other names

Table 5. The terminology of Competitive Intelligence.

Interviewee code	Selected responses to the question: *'Can the SMEs give a definition of CI?'*
C14	'Not all, environmental scanning is used as a synonym'
C14	'The vocabulary is evolving, we don't speak of CI but of Strategic Monitoring'
C5	'They are very defensive, for many it is associated with espionage and hacking which is often how the media have presented it'
C1	'Some have never heard of IE, they can all relate to environmental scanning, but IE, no'
C9	'No, one must explain it, in any case, I don't believe in the definition myself'
C3	'Yes, but incompletely, they associate it with environmental scanning. Those who are aware of CI do relate it to anticipation and adaptation, that is, a strategic application'
C10	'You can associate everything to the word *economique*, it depends on the characteristics of the manager, protection is the priority'
C11	'No, we speak of environmental scanning, we do not use the term CI'
C12	'A complete definition no but I believe they are beginning to get a grasp as to what it's all about'
C15	'If we ask they often say espionage or trickery'

such as environmental scanning or strategic information. Still others used the term CI with confidence and conviction. Overall, definitional and scope issues related to CI programmes were considered a problem. The merging of CI programmes with Innovation or Sustainable Development programmes was seen as one way of circumventing, or alleviating, the issue. Even if there is an acknowledgement that information, intelligence and innovation share relations the area is not well researched (Julien & Ramangalahy, 2003; Savioz, 2004), suggesting this could be a risky path to follow. The findings presented here corroborate Brody (2008) who proposed that CI is a constantly evolving concept. Table 5 presents a selection of responses from the CI programme directors concerning SME interpretations of CI.

Attitudes towards CI

Attitudes, even if they are latent hypothetical constructs, are observable in a wide variety of ways (Ajzen, 2005). Previous research has explored the influencing drivers of awareness, attitude, process and structure (Wright & Calof, 2006) in CI processes. More recently, Dishman & Calof (2008) examined the role of CI as a multiphasic precedent to marketing strategy where 'organisational awareness and culture' was identified as an influence driver.

In the face-to-face interviews, the Rouach and Santi (2001) CI attitude typology was presented to the CI programme directors. This framework was chosen as it allowed for differing levels of CI development and was itself born out of a sample frame including French SMEs. This typology has been used to position British charities on their competitor analysis attitudes (Bennett, 2003) and to position CI attitudes for multinational divisions (April & Bessa, 2006). The CI typology by Wright, Pickton, and Callow (2002) which also addressed CI attitude was developed from larger firms in the UK. In this typology attitude type is intrinsically linked to three other facets of CI practice (Hudson & Smith, 2008) which are not necessarily relevant in a small business context. The similarity of the attitude types between the two typologies nevertheless lends credibility to the chosen framework.

Table 6. Identifying SME attitude typologies.

Company typology	CI directors' commentary
Type 1: Sleepers/Immune/Passive • No fear of competition • No interest in Competitive Intelligence • Not invented here syndrome • Minimal or no support from management	'I'm not sure if type 1 exists, they are all afraid of the competition' 'I don't know of any for the first type' 'I would phrase this type differently, I think there are a lot of enterprises who don't express their needs effectively' 'We call these ostriches and we have a lot of them' 'I'm sure at least half of our enterprises are either type 1 or 2'
Type 2: Reactive/Task Driven • Only responds when competitors are hostile • Opportunists • Very limited budget for Competitive Intelligence • Task driven attitude • Ad hoc basis Top management doesn't believe in the benefits of Competitive Intelligence	'It's important but not a priority' 'They expect CI to be free' 'They decide quickly without a lot of reflection' 'I've never had an SME come to me ask – I need help with Competitive Intelligence' 'SME managers have a very nebulous concept of CI, not least of all because it remains nebulous at the state level' 'If there is no immediate need the message passes slowly – if there is an urgent need the message passes quickly' 'We have the majority in type 2'
Type 3: Active/Operational • Actively observing the competition • Limited resources • Beginning of an operational network • Trying to understand, analyse and interpret markets • Unwilling or unable to have a long term vision on Competitive Intelligence • Management can see that Competitive Intelligence could increase profit	'There are a lot that have passed from type 2 to type 3' 'I have some type 3 enterprises I work with for CI, they are going towards type 4' 'I think type 3 is the most common type we have'
Type 4: Strategic/Assault/Pro-active • Hunt for strategic information • Professional, ethical approach • Significant resources • Human intelligence valued • Monitoring competitors' moves • Top management support • An integrated procedure • Scenario planning	'Type 4 exists but it is the SME that belongs to a bigger group, they are well structured' 'I had one SME that I would position between type 4 and 5, the only hesitation is they had limited resources' 'We have types 1, 2 & 3, rarely type 4, never type 5'
Type 5: Highly Proactive/Value Creation • An offensive stance/war mentality • Very pro-active in managing the Competitive Intelligence process • Sophisticated tools/experts	'An SME with a war mentality, no, we don't have that' 'I've seen this mentality but never this level of pro-activity' 'They exist as SMEs but they are the subcontractors in defence'

(continued)

Table 6. *Continued*

Company typology	CI directors' commentary
• Unlimited resources • Team approach/Competitive Intelligence integrated into decision making	'Type 5 exists but not in SME, it's the big companies' 'I had a type 5, he managed a company with 1500 employees' 'We had a type 5 in an SME, he had gone to "l'École de Guerre", a real case, but I'm not sure if he is still in business, it was absolutely exceptional'

Source: Rouach and Santi (2001).

The CCI programme directors were asked to identify which typologies existed in the SMEs they served. Overall, every type was referenced but not by every CCI. Table 6 shows the characteristics of each type and a summary of comments received from the CCI directors. These would appear to reflect the diversity of the economic fabric represented regionally. *Type 4: Strategic/Assault/Pro-active* and *Type 5: Highly Proactive/Value Creation* were very rare but cases could be identified. *Type 3: Active/Operational* was the most common response. A significant insight was the sense of transition from *Type 1: Sleepers/Immune/Passive* and *Type 2: Reactive/Task Driven* types to arguably a more progressive state often supported by the CCI programme.

Another approach for evaluating SME managers' attitudes towards CI was undertaken by a direct question to the CI programme directors. The principal responses are presented in Table 7.

While the perceived attitudes of SMEs towards CI are heterogeneous, certain themes can nonetheless be identified. First, attitudes can be, and have been, changed by the collective efforts of the CCI and the collaborating entities. Mainly this has been achieved through creating greater awareness of the stakes in managing strategic information. Second, evidence of benefits and the provision of support are necessary in both the short and the long term. Third, two recurring perceived handicaps are the lack of resources of SMEs, including time, and lastly, the lack of conceptual clarity surrounding CI processes from an SME perspective.

Evaluating CI effectiveness

One CI programme director argued that CI is never, or very rarely internalised in an SME, therefore evaluation is meaningless. However, even if an external entity provides the CI processes for an SME there is still the need for evaluation. Two CI directors stated that they did not believe that SMEs evaluated their CI effectiveness, at least not factually. Table 8 classifies CI director responses on how they see SMEs evaluating CI effectiveness. They are shown both quantitatively and qualitatively. The answers were largely unstructured. In other words, the CI programme directors were aware that SMEs are mostly interested in CI effectiveness, but they did not witness many systematic processes.

These findings at least provide the potential for SMEs to combine multiple dimensions, a prerequisite for CI evaluation (Blenkhorn & Fleisher, 2007). Buchda (2007) argued for the inclusion of qualitative factors for any attempts to measure CI return on investment.

Table 7.   SME attitudes towards Competitive Intelligence.

CCI Code	Principal responses of CI programme directors
C13	'It's important but not the priority, they are over-stretched by daily operations'
C13	'In France, they expect information to be free'
C14	'It's always the personality of the SME owner that plays the biggest role'
C13	'They think it is necessary but they haven't got the time'
C5	'There is scanning, protection and networks. They are always strong on one but never at all three, they are either technical, managerial or sales oriented'
C5	'For now they don't see a return on investment for information'
C4	'They are not disappointed, it is rather a question of non-comprehension at the beginning'
C1	'It depends more on the personality of the manager than the sector'
C6	'There are two attitudes, those that are really enthusiastic and think it will solve all their problems, and those who might be curious but lack conviction'
C6	'For those SME we accompany who ask for help, we have never had one dissatisfied'
C6	'Now, for them, they understand that information is important, in fact, they want information on everything, which is not possible'
C8	'They are sceptical before starting, but once we get going they really get on board'
C7	'It's always the same problem, everyone has their own interpretation of Competitive Intelligence'
C9	'Often the SMEs are run by engineers who have no notion as to what is a market'
C9	'They are a lot more open than they used to be'
C9	'I don't think they are structured in their attitudes'
C9	'They don't know their needs, that's why we do the needs analysis'
C2	'Now they are much more involved because of the economic crises'
C2	'They state that they cannot have these competences internally'
C2	'When it is put in place correctly they see right away the benefits'
C3	'For them it remains conceptual, it is for large companies'
C15	'For many SMEs it takes an event, a lost client, a burglary, poor performance, they are very reactive'
C15	'They are interested, the more examples I give the more convinced they are but when they leave they drop right back into their world'
C10	'They only commit if there is financial assistance'
C12	'What is missing is a global approach, everyone in the company is in their corner, and that is not how CI works'
C12	'It depends a lot on who helps them with their CI, if it was someone questionable, well, CI is to blame'

Table 8.   Evaluating Competitive Intelligence effectiveness.

Qualitative evaluation	Quantitative evaluation
Customer satisfaction	Win more bids
Concrete decisions	Integrate with quality system generating quantitative criteria
Improve their overall situation	Register patents
Anticipate new markets before competitors	Launch new products
Business development	Win market share/sales
Security test	Bigger markets
	Higher margins
	Apply consultant's evaluation tool

Conclusion

Ganesh, Miree, and Prescott (2003) spoke of the importance of identifying 'key informants' for CI field research. Indeed, the CI programme directors of the CCI have proved to be a rich source for qualitative research into SME CI practices. A summary of the findings are given in Table 9.

The programmes themselves are innovative, decentralised, constantly evolving and original. This undoubtedly allows them to adapt to their various environments. A weakness of earlier CI regional programmes in Canada had been the assumption that CI concepts were well known and thus needed no introduction (Bergeron, 2000). Activities to create awareness together with the innovative nature of the programmes have resulted in a balanced approach. The awareness and attitudes of SMEs towards CI have indeed changed since these programmes were initiated a decade ago. The snowball effect of multiple players should however be acknowledged. The CCI is but one of numerous public and private entities that influence SME CI practices. Collectively, they have changed attitudes towards CI practices. A theme that permeates the CI directors' responses is that despite resistance SME attitudes towards CI have evolved in a positive manner. The resistance from SMEs is due to limited resources, limited time, and an inability to know their CI needs. It can also be claimed that resistance may be born from the terminology used. The assertion that the decision makers' personality and style is central to defining the strategic process (Burke & Jarratt, 2004) would also seem to be justified by these findings. It should be kept in mind however that attitudes are evaluative in nature towards a person, object or target. Personality traits are not necessarily evaluative and they focus on the individual him or herself (Ajzen, 2005). Despite all of these observations, the provision of financial assistance is necessary to win commitment from SMEs.

The findings of this research are consistent with previous research in France on CI for SMEs in the sense that the SME manager is central to the processes (Larivet, 2009), and that CI needs are related to company nature, company strategy and company environment

Table 9.   Summary of findings.

Research question	Most common response
What is the content of your CI programme?	Conferences, training always, perhaps a needs analysis, rarely setting up a CI system
What types of firms are targeted in terms of size and sector?	Below 250 employees (the EU definition). Sectors depend on region and government strategy
Which organisations from both the private and public sectors do you collaborate with in your CI programmes?	Consultants were named first, CCI second, the gendarmerie third
Which organisations have the most credibility for advising on CI practices?	CCI first (modestly disclosed)
What terminology is used in the intelligence gathering process?	Competitive Intelligence (i.e. *Intelligence economique*) is *not* the language of SMEs. No common substitute has emerged but environmental scanning is the easiest to relate to SMEs
Who is responsible for CI in the SMEs?	The SME manager, could be someone else for SMEs with more than 20 employees
What are the attitudes of the SME decision makers towards CI practices?	Mixed attitudes, mostly interested but don't have the time or resources, attitudes are moving in a positive direction

(Salles, 2006). However, whereas Larivet (2009) found company size to have little bearing on CI practices this research identified 20 employees as a pivotal size in terms of SME manager involvement. While the debate on CI definitions and scope is far from over the data here suggest that a management science CI concept is evolving in a positive manner, albeit slowly and incompletely. The Rouach and Santi (2001) typology is effective for positioning SMEs on attitude and practices. To a degree this satisfies the need for a CI typology for SMEs as identified by Bergeron (2000). Finally, a French paradigm for CI in SMEs cannot exclude the multitude of private and public players hereby identified.

Limitations

One potential limitation of this study lies in its exploratory and descriptive nature. A larger sample and quantitative analysis could elicit cause and effect relationships and increase the potential for extrapolation and generalisations (Johnson & Onwuegbuzie, 2004). The interviews were carried out with willing subjects from CCIs which were known to be providing active CI programmes for the SMEs in their region. There was clearly a benefit to the programme directors in engaging with this study but significant steps were taken in the interview process to secure unbiased answers and challenge over-optimistic views. It would be very interesting to carry out a comparative study in a different region of France to assess just how well SMEs are being served in the provision of CI programmes by their CCI throughout the country.

Implications for future research

Future research could investigate these research questions quantitatively and directly address the SME decision makers themselves. Focusing on the SMEs would permit an analysis of company performance by those participating in CI programmes compared to those which do not. Longitudinal studies, such as panels, could investigate how SMEs progress through the typology stages and how they emerge in practice. Whereas this research has focused on SME attitudes towards CI concepts and processes, future research could examine the role of personality in SME owner/managers in determining a predisposition, willingness or otherwise, towards engaging in Competitive Intelligence activities. It would also be very interesting to replicate this study in other Western European countries as well as selected states in the USA.

References

Ajzen, I. (2005). *Attitudes, personality and behaviour* (2nd ed.). Maidenhead: McGraw-Hill.

April, K., & Bessa, J. (2006). A critique of the strategic Competitive Intelligence process within a global energy multinational. *Problems and Perspectives in Management, 4,* 86–99.

Bazely, P. (2007). *Qualitative data analysis with NVivo.* London: Sage.

Bégin, L., Deschamps, J., & Madinier, H. (2008). *Une approche interdisciplinaire de l'intelligence economique* (Les Cahiers de Recherche No. 07/4/1). Retrieved September 21, 2010 from http://papers.ssrn.com/sol3/papers.cfm?abstract_id=1083943

Bennett, R. (2003). Competitor analysis practices of British charities. *Marketing Intelligence and Planning, 21,* 335–345.

Bergeron, P. (2000). Regional business intelligence: The view from Canada. *Journal of Information Science, 26,* 153–160.

Blenkhorn, D., & Fleisher, C.S. (2007). Performance assessment in Competitive Intelligence: An exploration, synthesis, and research agenda. *Journal of Competitive Intelligence and Management, 4*(2), 5–22.

Brody, R. (2008). Issues in defining Competitive Intelligence: An exploration. *Journal of Competitive Intelligence and Management, 4*(3), 3–16.

Brouard, F. (2006). Development of an expert system on environmental scanning practices in SME: Tools as a resouce program. *Journal of Competitive Intelligence and Management, 3*(4), 37–55.

Buchda, S. (2007). Rulers for business intelligence and Competitive Intelligence: An overview and evaluation of measurement approaches. *Journal of Competitive Intelligence and Management, 4*(2), 23–54.

Bulinge, F. (2001, October). *PME-PMI et intelligence economique: Les difficultés d'un marriage de raison.* Paper presented at the Colloque VSST, Barcelona, Spain.

Bulinge, F. (2002). *Pour une culture de l'Information dans les petites et moyennes organisations: Un modèle incrémentale d'intelligence économique* (Doctoral dissertation). Retrieved September 21, 2010, from http://bulinge.univ-tln.fr/Franck_Bulinge/These/These.pdf

Burke, G.I., & Jarratt, D.G. (2004). The influence of information and advice on competitive strategy definition in small-and medium-sized enterprises. *Qualitative Market Research: An International Journal, 7,* 126–138.

Calof, J.L., & Skinner, B. (1998). Competitive Intelligence for government officers: A brave new world. *Optimum, 28*(2), 38–42.

Carayon, B. (2003). *Intelligence économique, compétitivité et cohésion social.* Retrieved September 21, 2010, from http://www.ie-news.com/fr/pdf/carayon.pdf

Clerc, P. (2009, February). *The role of the CCI in the French Competitive Intelligence system.* Paper presented at the 1st Portuguese-French Meeting on Competitive Intelligence, Fernando Pessoa University, Porto, Portugal.

Creswell, J. (2007). *Qualitative inquiry and research design.* London: Sage.

Dedijer, S. (1994). Opinion: Governments, business intelligence – a pioneering report from France. *Competitive Intelligence Review, 5*(3), 45–47.

Denscombe, M. (2007). *The good research guide: For small-scale social research projects.* Maidenhead: McGraw-Hill.

Dishman, P.L., & Calof, J.L. (2008). Competitive Intelligence: A multiphasic precedent to marketing strategy. *European Journal of Marketing, 42,* 766–785.

Dou, H. (2004). Quelle intelligence economique pour les PME? *Journal of Business Research, 50,* 235–244.

Fleisher, C.S., & Bensoussan, B.E. (2007). *Business and competitive analysis: Effective application of new and classic methods.* Upper Saddle River, NJ: FT Press.

Ganesh, U., Miree, C., & Prescott, J. (2003). Competitive Intelligence field research: Moving the field forward by setting a research agenda. *Journal of Competitive Intelligence and Management, 1*(1), 1–12.

Gilmore, C., Carson, D., & Grant, K. (2001). SME marketing in practice. *Marketing Intelligence and Planning, 19*(1), 6–11.

Goriat, S. (2006). *L'Expression du problème dans la recherche d'informations: Application à un contexte d'intermédiation territoriale* (Doctoral dissertation). Retrieved September 21, 2010, from http://tel.archives-ouvertes.fr/tel-00011918/

Groom, J., & David, F. (2001). Competitive activity among small firms. *SAM Advanced Management Journal, 66*(1), 12–20.

Hudson, S., & Smith, J.R. (2008, March). *Assessing Competitive Intelligence practices in a non-profit organization.* Paper presented at Proceedings of 2nd European Competitive Intelligence Symposium, Lisbon, Portugal.

Jakobiak, F. (2006). *L'intelligence economique, la comprendre, l'implanter, l'utiliser.* Paris: Editions d'Organisation.

Johnson, R., & Onwuegbuzie, A. (2004). Mixed methods research: A research paradigm whose time has come. *Educational Researcher, 33*(7), 14–26.

Julien, P.A., & Ramangalahy, C. (2003). Competitive strategy and performance of exporting SMEs: An empirical investigation of the impact of their export information search and competencies. *Entrepreneurial Theory and Science, 27,* 227–245.

Larivet, S. (2001, June). *Intelligence économique: Acceptation française et multidimensionnalité.* Paper presented at the 10th Conference de L'Assoication Intenationale de Management Strategique, Université Laval, Quebec.

Larivet, S. (2009). *Intelligence economique enquête dans 100 PME.* Paris: L'Harmattan.

La Tribune. (2009, September 30). *Olivier Buquen nouveau délégué interministériel à l'intelligence économique.* Retrieved September 21, 2010, from http://www.latribune.fr/actualites/

economie/france/20090930trib000428218/olivier-buquen-nouveau-delegue-interministeriel-a-l-intelligence-economique.html

Martre, H. (1994). *Intelligence économique et stratégie des entreprises*. Retrieved September 21, 2010, from La Documentation Française website: http://www.ladocumentationfrancaise.fr/rapportspublics/074000410/index.shtml

McGonagle, J., & Vella, C. (2002). *Bottom line Competitive Intelligence*. Westport, CT: Quorum Books.

McGregor, S. (2005). Consumer transactions with SMEs: Implications for consumer scholars. *International Journal of Consumer Studies*, 29(1), 2–16.

Moinet, N. (2008, March). *L'Intelligence economique territoriale de la théorie à la pratique: Reflexions autour du dispositif régional Poitou-Charentes*. Paper presented at Proceedings of 2nd European Competitive Intelligence Symposium, Lisbon, Portugal.

Neuman, W.N. (1997). *Social research methods: Qualitative and quantitative approaches*. Boston, MA: Allyn & Bacon.

Nkongolo-Bakenda, J.-M., Anderson, R., Ito, J., & Garven, G. (2006). Globally oriented small and medium-sized enterprises: In search of an integrative framework and competitive determinants. *International Journal of Globalisation and Small Business*, 1, 374–392.

Oubrich, M. (2007). L'Intelligence economique, un outil de management statégique orienté vers le développement de neuvelles connaissances. *La Revue de Science de Gestion*, Direction et Gestion, (226–227), 77–88.

Qiu, T. (2008). Scanning for Competitive Intelligence: A managerial perspective. *European Journal of Marketing*, 42, 814–835.

Riley, M., Wood, R.C., Clark, M.A., Wilkie, E., & Szivas, E. (2003). *Researching and writing dissertations in business and management*. London: Thomson.

Rouach, D., & Santi, P. (2001). Competitive Intelligence adds value: 5 intelligence attitudes. *European Management Journal*, 19, 552–559.

Rubin, H.J., & Rubin, I.S. (2005). *Qualitative interviewing: The art of hearing data*. London: Sage.

Ruzzier, M., Hisrich, R.D., & Antoncic, B. (2006). SME internationalisation research: Past present, and future. *Journal of Small Business and Enterprise Development*, 13, 476–497.

Saayman, A., Pienaar, J., de Pelsmacker, P.J., Viviers, W., Cuyvers, L., Muller, M.-L., & Jegers, M. (2008). Competitive Intelligence: Construct exploration, validation and equivalence. *Aslib Proceedings: New Information Perspectives*, 60, 383–411.

Salles, M. (2006). Decision making in SMEs and information requirements for Competitive Intelligence. *Production Planning and Control*, 17, 229–237.

Savioz, P. (2004). *Technology intelligence, concept design and implementation in technology-based SMEs*. Basingstoke: Palgrave Macmillan.

Smith, J.R., & Kossou, L. (2008). The emergence and uniqueness of Competitive Intelligence in France. *Journal of Competitive Intelligence and Management*, 4(3), 63–85.

Spickett-Jones, J., & Eng, T.-Y. (2006). SMEs and the strategic context for communication. *Journal of Marketing Communications*, 12, 225–243.

Tarraf, P., & Molz, R. (2006). Competitive Intelligence at small enterprises. *SAM Advanced Management Journal*, 71(4), 24–34.

Wright, S., & Calof, J.L. (2006). The quest for competitive, business and marketing intelligence: A country comparison of current practice. *European Journal of Marketing*, 40, 453–465.

Wright, S., Eid, E.R., & Fleisher, C.S. (2009). Competitive Intelligence in practice: Empirical evidence from the UK retail banking sector. *Journal of Marketing Management*, 25, 941–964.

Wright, S., Pickton, D.W., & Callow, J. (2002). Competitive Intelligence in UK firms: A typology. *Marketing Intelligence and Planning*, 20, 349–360.

Complaints are a firm's best friend

Sophie Larivet[a] and François Brouard[b]

[a]Department of Marketing, Ecole Superieure du Commerce Exterieur (ESCE), Pôle Universitaire Léonard de Vinci, Paris La Défense cedex, 92916, France; [b]Sprott School of Business, Carleton University, 1125 Colonel By Drive, 824 Dunton Tower, Ottawa, Ontario, K1S 5B6, Canada

The strategic intelligence literature includes many studies on the use of sales forces and exhibitions; however, customer complaints are generally sidestepped in the strategic intelligence context. This article takes a theoretical approach to the interaction between strategic intelligence and complaint management. From our literature review, we draw an exploratory model of the link between the two processes and emphasize the most important complaint handling initiatives for strategic intelligence, both for its gathering and protection aspects. An analytical presentation of the intelligence that can be collected from complaints is proposed. The research should be helpful to managers who want to understand better or design a complaint management system that is 'strategic intelligence oriented'.

Introduction

Managers can be deterred from implementing a strategic intelligence (SI) system because they fear its cost and presumed complexity. While strategic intelligence can in fact have a sophisticated organizational shape (an Intelligence Head Office, for instance), companies can also use existing informational practices to contribute to an intelligence system. Thus much of the literature stresses that a great deal of information already exists within companies and is simply not circulated. For example, salespersons are continually collecting marketing intelligence as a by-product of their work, but many of them fail to pass on the intelligence. Their managers need to motivate them and develop a positive attitude towards strategic intelligence in order to make them play the game (Le Bon, 2006). Yet strategic intelligence development can rely on what is already available in the firm (Brouard, 2007) and simply requires the integration of independent marketing information techniques (Fleisher, Wright, & Allard, 2008).

In order to introduce or expand strategic intelligence culture into existing organizational systems, it is important to give managers some food for thought. After all, most firms do not have to build a strategic intelligence system from scratch. The strategic intelligence literature includes studies about the use of sales forces (Le Bon, 2006) or exhibitions (Calof & Fox, 2003) for strategic intelligence purposes, but customers' complaints are generally ignored. This article tries to fill in this gap by studying interactions between complaint management and strategic intelligence. In addition to this central and theoretical objective, this research encourages the use of marketing information processes to develop or improve strategic intelligence systems.

The outline of the article is as follows. First, fundamental concepts are defined. The next section explains the contributions of complaint management to strategic intelligence and presents the interactions of both concepts in a conceptual model. The key elements of complaint handling for strategic intelligence are then detailed. A section discussing some findings and presenting managerial implications follows. Future research is suggested in the conclusion.

Definitions of fundamental concepts

The fundamental concepts of the article are strategic intelligence and complaint management.

Strategic intelligence

Strategic intelligence is both a process and an output. It is the output of the informational process by which an organization stays attuned to its environment in order to make strategic decisions. Strategic intelligence can be divided into four more specific types of intelligence (Brouard, 2000; Daft & Weick, 1984; Jennings & Lumpkin, 1992).

- Competitive Intelligence is related to actual and potential competitors.
- Technological intelligence involves the technological dimension of an organization's products, services or processes.
- Commercial intelligence is about customers or prospects (marketing intelligence) and suppliers.
- Societal intelligence is concerned with all other elements, including demographic, economic, socio-cultural and political factors.

Strategic intelligence is also another name for the global informational process, which can be divided into two sub-cycles: the gathering cycle and the protection cycle (see Figure 1).

The gathering cycle has four phases: planning; collection; analysis; and dissemination (Ghoshal & Westney, 1991; Miller, 2000; Peyrot, Childs, van Doren, & Allen, 2002). In the planning phase, the organization identifies the intelligence needs of its management team.

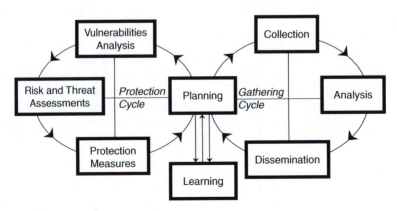

Figure 1.   Intelligence cycle.

Collection refers to the acquisition of relevant data. Analysis creates information by linking data together and identifying patterns and trends, while the dissemination phase consists of transmitting results to the decision makers.

More and more authors now also include protection activities in SI practices (Francq, 2001; Larivet, 2006; Nolan & Quinn, 2000). During the planning phase of this cycle, organizations identify critical assets and determine their protection requirements, since they realize that it is impossible and costly to protect everything. Vulnerability analysis assesses the weaknesses that may exist in relation to protection needs, while risk and threat assessments estimate the potential effects of vulnerabilities on organizational activities and serve as a basis for designing safety and security measures. Protection measures are designed to safeguard information and intangible assets (knowledge, databases, reputation, image …) from others (competitors, hackers, etc.) or from accidents (fire, etc.). Both the gathering and the protection cycle include a learning phase (Figure 1) to evaluate past actions and react accordingly for the future.

While some academic research in SI focuses on various marketing information sources, no article in this field concentrates on complaints even though marketing specialists recognize that complaints are a source of intelligence.

Complaints and complaint management

Complaint management is a widely studied subject in the marketing literature (Harris & Ogbonna, 2010; Orsingher, Valentini, & de Angelis, 2010). The objective of this section is not to present an exhaustive literature review but to review some essential characteristics of complaint management in order to present our model and explain how complaint management can be useful in strategic intelligence.

Complaints

A customer complaint can be defined as a customer's protest to a firm with the goal of obtaining an exchange, refund or apology (Singh & Widing, 1991). It is a form of negative feedback from the customer (Bell, Mengüç, & Stefani, 2004), and can be considered reasonable or unreasonable (McCole, 2004). Different customers will have different objectives in their complaints. Some may look for a redress or recovery action; some may only want to comment on a situation.

Customer reaction can be divided into two phases. The initial customer reaction follows a business transaction for a product/service. The subsequent actions or customer reaction follows the business' reaction.

The first (initial) reaction can be analysed using Hirschman's (1970) typology. Initial dissatisfaction can be divided into two main categories: exit and voice (Andreassen, 1999; Maute & Forrester, 1993). The exit response is probably the worst for the organization because customers will stop buying the product/service and change their patronage. They could also switch brands or reduce their consumption. This article focuses more on voice response, of which complaint is the main form. This response can be directed to the organization, but also to friends and consumer organizations. These third-party complaints could bring the dispute into the legal system or to a public forum by organizing a boycott or setting up a protest website (Ward & Ostrom, 2006). By complaining, however, the customer offers another chance to the organization. In addition to exit and voice, Hirschman's typology also includes the loyalty response, seen as a passive response (Maute & Forrester, 1993). This could be viewed as a wait-and-see approach. The customer 'does nothing', making this kind of reaction less important for this study.

The second customer reaction depends on the customer's satisfaction with the recovery reaction. It can increase the level of complaint and provide additional information for strategic intelligence purposes (Voorhees & Brady, 2005).

Complaint management

According to Fornell and Wernerfelt (1988) and Fornell and Westbrook (1979), complaint management is much more than complaint handling. The process by which a company will give (or not) compensation to unsatisfied customers. Complaint management is also about facilitating complaint expression and its dissemination within the firm (Fornell & Wernerfelt, 1988).

Resistance to complaint management comes in many forms (Détrie, 2007): customers are viewed as whiners, complaints are seen as denunciations, suppliers are incriminated and so on. Negative reactions are not what a firm prefers to hear. However, many studies show that there can be a positive impact from complaint management. For example, complaint management can:

- increase consumer satisfaction, product evaluation and purchase likelihood by allowing customers to vent their dissatisfaction (Kowalski, 1996; Nyer, 2000);
- heighten the customer retention rate (Ang & Buttle, 2006; Tax, Brown, & Chandrashekaran, 1998);
- limit the spread of potentially damaging negative word-of-mouth information (Blodgett & Anderson, 2000; Blodgett, Granbois, & Walters, 1993);
- enhance the likelihood of repurchase (Gilly, 1987);
- have a positive impact on customer loyalty (Andreassen, 1999).

Thus complaint management's contribution to a company's results can follow different paths. Most of the time, authors highlight this one: complaint management can increase satisfaction, thus can have a positive impact on loyalty, and thus can improve profitability, in a Customer Relationship Management (CRM) perspective. But another path has to be explored: complaint management can contribute to strategic intelligence, and thus to competitive advantage. This article focuses on the first step of this route (complaint management contributions to strategic intelligence).

Contributions of complaints and complaint handling to strategic intelligence

Collecting intelligence from complaints

Intelligence from complaints is a source of strategic opportunity (Harari, 1992). Fornell (2007) suggests that complaints should be encouraged in order to extract more information from customers. Most articles only take into account the contribution of complaints to the clientele dimension of commercial intelligence, also known as customer or marketing intelligence (Xu & Kaye, 1995). However, data from customers do not only contain customer intelligence, in the strict sense of the word. For example, a business might collect information about suppliers' technology and rates, about competitors' rates and about new regulation using complaints (Larivet & Brouard, 2007). Albrecht (2000) and Gordon (2002) give several examples of potential intelligence that could be gathered from complaints. Table 1 summarizes the different kinds of information that can be found in complaints: not only marketing intelligence, but also competitive, technological or societal intelligence.

Table 1.   Examples of strategic intelligence gathered from complaints.

Technological	New technology on the market, default in technology, new technology or production process by a competitor, new technology or material of a supplier, etc.
Competitive	Product/service by competitors, comparison with competitors' product/service; customers' perception of the organization, customers' perception of competitors, change in competitors' rates, etc.
Commercial	Reasons for customers' satisfaction/dissatisfaction, failure examples, customers' expectations, customers' needs, customers' requirements, customers' service evaluation, other suppliers of the customer, level of customer loyalty, customers' experience, quality of relationship, reasons for brand preferences, possible solutions to a problem, complaint rate and frequency, level of return, history of some transactions, types of information sought, preferred mode of entry for complaints, pricing sensibility, preferred pricing structure, billing problems, satisfaction with resolution and business reaction, future purchase timing, explanations on account receivables, problem with a salesperson/distributor, retention rate, etc.
Societal	Customers' needs by age group or location, new trends, protest websites, protest organizations, new regulation, etc.

Protecting the reputation of the company

As already mentioned, strategic intelligence includes protection measures. In a governmental or military context, intelligence services not only collect, analyse and disseminate information, but they also try to protect the knowledge of the country (strategic technologies for instance). In a competitive perspective, it is logical for a firm to gather intelligence about its competitors or its environment, but it is also logical to try to prevent competitors from doing so: competitive advantage stems from informational asymmetry.

The protection scope varies depending on authors. The traditional approach concentrates on information assets that could be stolen or discovered by the competitors. A broader view includes perception management (Francq, 2001; Harbulot, Moinet, & Lucas, 2002). Applied to private firms, perception management can be considered as legal actions designed to affect perceptions of the image, identity or reputation of an organization (Elsbach, 2006). Reputation is an intangible asset that needs to be protected, not only from competitors, but also from dissatisfied customers. It belongs in the scope of the strategic intelligence protection process.

Quite recently, the French cable operator Noos was unable to respond to the very numerous complaints of its customers. It chose to change its name following such a precipitous fall in reputation that returning to the status quo was unthinkable (Aguila, 2007). This example recalls the importance of the quality of complaint handling in protecting reputation: dissatisfied complainants have higher levels of brand loyalty than non-complainants, but only if the complaint management system ends up giving them satisfaction (Fornell & Wernerfelt, 1988).

When a negative rumour spreads (whether or not it is based on truth), the complaint handling system will be in the firing line and will have to answer questions or reassure worried customers. Procter & Gamble has been receiving mail related to its relationship with Satan for years after the birth of the rumour (Kimmel, 2004). The complaint handling process provides the opportunity to prevent or fight rumours and to respond to false (or true) accusations and helps limit the spread of negative word of mouth (Blodgett & Anderson, 2000; Blodgett et al., 1993).

Patents are traditional tools of strategic intelligence that help to protect the knowledge of a company. Efficient complaint handling and management can help protect a brand or a reputation. Fornell and Wernerfelt (1988) call complaint management defensive marketing. Thus it is also a contribution to the defensive cycle of strategic intelligence.

Process interaction

As explained above, complaint management interacts with both the gathering and protection cycles of strategic intelligence. In Figure 2, a conceptual and exploratory model sketches the link between the complaint process and strategic intelligence. We define the complaint process as the cycle of a complaint from the customer's initial reaction to his or her secondary reaction. More details about this process are given in the next section, but preliminary explanations of Figure 2 are needed now.

As shown in Figure 2, a transaction (product or service) occurs between the customer and the business that generates a customer reaction. Some of the factors that affect customer behaviour (customer characteristics, context and customer attitudes) will not be developed here because they are not directly related to the interaction between the complaint process and strategic intelligence.

The customer reaction itself can be classified into three main categories: positive (compliments, positive word of mouth, commitment), neutral (do nothing, request information) or negative. When his reaction is negative, the customer may voice a complaint. The voicing of the complaint is the first step of a cyclical complaint process, about which further explanations will be provided in the next section and in Figure 3. The complaint should generate a business reaction, which is the reaction of both the organization itself and the employee(s) in contact with the customer. Organization reaction and employee reaction are impacted by various factors such as characteristics, context and attitudes. Only the most important factors are presented in the following paragraphs.

Employees' perceptions have an impact on customer behaviour and perception of justice (Homburg & Stock, 2004; Maxham & Netemeyer, 2003). The literature has classified employees' attitude towards the customer into avoidance, collaboration, accommodation and

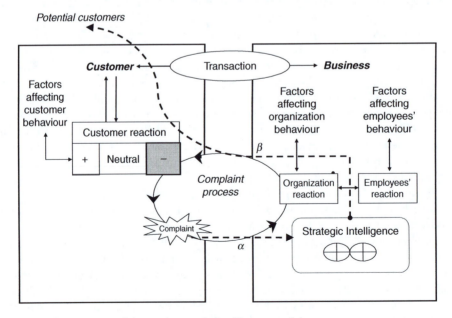

Figure 2. Customer complaints and strategic intelligence model.

competition (Bell & Luddington, 2006; Bell et al., 2004; Bitner, Booms, & Mohr, 1994). Of course, some employee attitudes are useful for efficient complaint management – reliability, promptness, experience with complaints and seeking behaviour.

Business characteristics, attitude and context are also very important for complaint management. In particular, professional standards, consumer associations, the level of competition, human resources training, managerial style, reputation sensibility and costs of compensation will make the business more or less attentive to its complaint management.

Those elements are the standard components cited in complaints literature. The model also depicts the strategic intelligence process with its two sub-cycles, both of which interact with the complaint management system.

Gathering cycle and complaint process

In Figure 2, a dotted arrow (named α) moves from the complaint process to the strategic intelligence process. It is the symbol for the information flow that, coming from complaint handling, feeds the gathering cycle. The complaint handling system will determine how intelligence enters the firm. The complaint management policy will establish the way a complaint is analysed and circulated, which makes it very important to be aware that complaints intelligence is useful for other purposes than increasing customer satisfaction. All dissemination solutions are possible, from very informal systems in small businesses (Larivet, 2009) to interrelated databases and search engines in large corporations.

Protection cycle and complaint process

A second dotted arrow (named β) goes from strategic intelligence to the customer, through the complaint process. The arrow depicts the protective effects of a good complaint management on the firm's image and reputation. The information and/or compensation given to an unsatisfied customer will help prevent or limit any negative impacts of the customer's dissatisfaction (secondary reaction). If there is no complaint management system, or if the customer sees the company's reaction as inappropriate, there is a potential danger of negative word of mouth or of public action (through a consumer association, for instance). Both can damage the firm's reputation and brand image.

Because complaint management is a process that connects a firm with its environment (like sales do, for example), it is an area where information flows inside and outside the company. It appears that both components of strategic intelligence can rely on complaint management. Complaint management is already known for its customer knowledge function, but it is obvious that it can also have a larger strategic intelligence function. In order to describe better the variables that are important for its implementation or improvement (in a strategic intelligence perspective), we now present a more comprehensive model of the complaint process.

Key elements of the complaint process for strategic intelligence

Complaining behaviour is a dynamic and complex process (Blodgett et al., 1993). Since many factors affect stakeholders' reactions, Figure 3 identifies the features of our complaint process model. The model consists of a description of the customer complaint route and of some handling initiatives. Its design incorporates ideas from many authors (Andreassen, 2000; Bell & Luddington, 2006; Blodgett & Anderson, 2000; Blodgett, Wakefield, & Barnes, 1995; Estelami, 2000; Fornell & Wernerfelt, 1987, 1988; Maxham

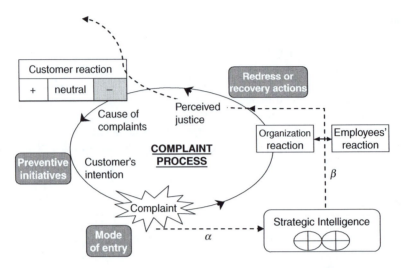

Figure 3.   Complaint process.

& Netemeyer, 2002; McCole, 2004; Palmatier, Dant, Grewal, & Evans, 2006; Santos & Boote, 2003; Singh, 1988; Singh & Widing, 1991, Singh & Wilkes, 1996; Stephens & Gwinner, 1998; Szymanski & Henard, 2001; Tax et al., 1998; Zeithaml, Berry, & Parasuraman, 1993).

Our complaint process distinguishes two sets of concepts. The first series (inside the circle) depicts some steps of customer complaining behaviour. The second series (outside the circle) depicts some handling initiatives that could be of importance in a strategic intelligence perspective.

The first series includes concepts ranging from the cause of complaints to perceived justice.

Cause of complaints

The major reasons for complaints are core product or service failure, billing, scheduling, slow service, pricing, inappropriate employee behaviour, consumer did not like product anymore, product did not fit, product not compatible, delivery problem, poor repair work, product damaged in repair or poor product design (Estelami, 2000). Having a reason to complain is not sufficient to set a customer in motion. He or she might not have the intention to complain.

Customer's intention to complain

Customer complaint intention is a major variable in complaining behaviour and depends on factors such as perceived value, prior experience of complaining, attitude towards complaining or culture (Kim, Kim, Im, & Shin, 2003; Liu & McClure, 2001; Maute & Forrester, 1993; Sharma, Marshall, Reday, & Na, 2010; Singh, 1988; Voorhees & Brady, 2005). If a customer indeed complains, he or she will have a secondary reaction to the way his or her complaint was handled. At this stage, the perceived justice related to the business and employees' reaction is decisive (Prim-Allaz & Sabadie, 2005; Smith, Bolton, & Wagner, 1999).

Perceived justice

The perceived justice concept can be divided into three dimensions: distributive justice, procedural justice and interactional justice (Blodgett & Anderson, 2000; Maxham & Netemeyer, 2002; McCole, 2004; Tax et al., 1998). All refer to fairness. Distributive justice refers to the fairness of the remedy in the exchange (outcomes). Procedural justice refers to the fairness of the procedures and policies used (decision-making procedures). Interactional justice refers to how fairly a customer is treated during the complaint process (interpersonal behaviour).

The second group of variables (inside the circle) in Figure 3 is related to handling measures taken by the organization.

Preventive initiatives

Preventive initiatives help preventing failures or set in place the basis to handle complaints. Examples are quality control, customer service policies, codes of conduct, refunds, return and exchange policies, guarantees, training activities, benchmarking, internal audit and product trial.

Mode of entry

The mode of entry for complaints varies greatly in terms of points of entry and formats. Some complaints are solicited and others are voluntary. Some are written and others are oral. Modes of entry include front-line employees, intermediaries, managers, third-party recipients of complaints, complaint cards, suggestion cards, satisfaction cards, website questionnaires, surveys, personal letters, email, oral comments requested and informal oral comments (Mattila, 2004; Robertson & Shaw, 2006; Voss & Gruber, 2005). Depending on the mode of entry, strategic intelligence collection might be easier or harder. For example, written satisfaction cards are easier to process systematically, compared to informal oral comments. Different industries have standard practices to solicit and handle complaints, like the praise and assessment cards in the hospitality industry (Jones, McCleary, & Lepisto, 2002; Voss & Gruber, 2005).

Redress/recovery actions

Following a complaint, businesses will react and will or will not offer something to the complainant. Kelley, Hoffman and Davis (1993) identify 12 redress/recovery strategies: discount for problems or inconvenience, correction (e.g. repair, adequate information), manager/employee intervention, correction plus (compensation added to correction), replacement, apology (oral/written), refund, customer initiated correction, business credit, unsatisfactory correction, failure escalation and 'nothing'. The last three strategies are considered unacceptable recovery strategies and should not be used when designing a complaint handling process.

Those actions are important because effective service recovery can have a positive impact on consumer trust and commitment (Blodgett & Anderson, 2000; Tax et al., 1998). Defensive marketing with compensation could be seen as more cost effective than advertising (Fornell & Wernerfelt, 1988), which is of importance in a perception management perspective. Without a proper response, organizations may create additional customer dissatisfaction (Goodwin & Ross, 1993). In cases of conflict and the absence of resolution, the public court system could be used by the customer. Dissatisfaction can be voiced by other means (consumer associations, blogs, reviews and other new media techniques).

For strategic intelligence, the mode of entry and recovery actions are very important. First, in order to have an efficient gathering cycle, the complaint process has to be able to incorporate all complaints, no matter which form they take (mode of entry). Second, the type of recovery action chosen by the company influences the perceived justice (by the customer) and thus his or her future talk about the brand or the firm, which could reach other customers or prospects. In a perception management perspective, the message delivered to the customer at this moment of the complaint handling process is crucial. A strategic intelligence culture could help complaint managers to be more aware of their role in influencing customers' opinion and word of mouth.

Discussion and managerial implications

Complaints are 'weak signals'

Two interesting questions about complaints as a source for actionable intelligence are: are complaints typical enough of what happens to consumers to be considered? Are they 'important' enough to be processed in a strategic intelligence system? Indeed, in the field of mass consumption products, only 4% of dissatisfied customers who have bought packaged goods or other small ticket items complain to the producer. For large ticket items, the percentage varies from 5 to 10% (Goodman, 1999). As stated by Sharma et al. (2010), complainers and non-complainers have different characteristics, which make the second ones not fully representative of customers in general. Some rare customers, sometimes called jaycustomers, deliberately act in an abusive manner (Harris & Reynolds, 2004). As mentioned by Moyer (1984), complaint handling systems must be complemented by other intelligence gathering instruments to avoid the bias of complainers (exaggerations, for instance).

However, according to Ansoff's (1975) theory of weak signals, whether complainers or complaints are representative or not is not that important. Something new or unusual in a complaint might be a sign of a strategic surprise, an unfamiliar, sudden and urgent event (Ansoff, 1975). In a strategic intelligence perspective, such a signal in a complaint should ring a bell and cause further investigation (Lesca & Blanco, 2002). The idea is not to rely only on complaints intelligence, but to use it like any other source, check it and analyse the correlation with other data.

Internal vs. external handling initiatives

An organization often implements internal handling initiatives to handle complaints itself. Examples are in-house customer service representatives or organization ombudsmen. Some industries and organizations implement external handling initiatives using a third party as an intermediary. Examples include dispute resolution mechanisms using third-party mediation and arbitration, private tribunals, outsourced call centres and industry association ombudsmen. These outsourcing solutions may be cost effective, but they raise the issue (among others) of what intelligence will be collected and how it will be processed. Moreover, can perception management be efficiently conducted in case of a sudden negative rumour, if a call centre is outsourced (not to mention that the outsourced call centre is often the focus of the complaint)? Nothing is less certain. At the very least, this issue should be considered carefully by complaint managers.

Dissemination of intelligence

Beyond the commercial relevance of complaint management, the research emphasizes its usefulness in gathering strategic intelligence. Considering the importance of complaints from an information perspective, marketing professionals should consider complaints as a strategic source that is likely to provide better understanding of both customer issues and a larger marketing environment. They also should be aware that such intelligence could be of great importance for non-marketing managers. Resources (human, financial, material) should be allocated to capture complaint data systematically, and those responsible for strategic intelligence should make sure that data held by customer services are correctly handled and disseminated. Table 1 can be helpful for the design of a collection grid that might be used to gather customer complaints. The responsibility of strategic intelligence managers is to help marketers to design the grid and then to analyse and disseminate the analytical output to interested parties in the firm. They should also benefit from collaboration with marketing managers and employees by using the complaint handling system as an interface with the firm's environment, where information can move in and out.

However, this research cannot provide a ready-made integration programme. A cross-functional team might be an interesting organizational answer. Fleisher et al. (2008) give an example of a successful insight team that managed to integrate market research, customer relationship information and Competitive Intelligence. The authors are clear that such a process is not readily replicable in other organizations, even though they put forward minimum conditions for success: a planned integration strategy, a structure, appropriate resources and executives supporting the project (Fleisher et al., 2008).

Conclusion and research implications

This paper has explored the complexity of complaint management from a strategic intelligence perspective. It is a new contribution to the body of research showing how the strategic intelligence gathering cycle can rely on existing practices. Moreover, it highlights the link between the strategic intelligence protection cycle and complaint management process using the perception management concept.

The most important finding of this research is an exploratory and theoretical model of the interactions between the complaint process and strategic intelligence. It offers a synthesis of past research but also raises questions. In particular, although the study shows the theoretical overlap of complaint management and strategic intelligence, the issue of the implementation of such an idea, that is, the allocation of the roles between complaint managers and any strategic intelligence managers, remains to be addressed. Future research should focus on identifying formal and informal processes of collaboration between the people who collect and process complaints (whether there is a formal complaint management system or not) and those who are in charge of strategic intelligence (whether this function is official or sparingly allocated).

Future research could also investigate the efficiency of the various complaint handling initiatives in collecting intelligence that is not only 'satisfaction' oriented, or in influencing perception improvement. An interesting question would be to look at the effect of perceived justice on the collection of more valuable insights.

Marketing practices can have an impact on strategic intelligence just as strategic intelligence can impact marketing practices. Complaints can not only open a dialogue between the customer and the business, but can be a vital initiator of high quality communication between marketing researchers and strategic intelligence specialists.

Acknowledgements

The authors want to thank Sheila Wright for her trust and support, as well as all the reviewers who have provided such useful comments and ideas at the different stages of this article. Thank you also to Maria Crawford for her helpful editorial assistance.

References

Aguila, N. (2007, July 12). Noos Numéricâble change de nom [Noos Numericable changes name]. *Infos du net*. Retrieved from http://www.infos-du-net.com/actualite/11161-noos-numericable.html

Albrecht, K. (2000). *Corporate radar: Tracking the forces that are shaping your business*. New York: Amacom.

Andreassen, T.W. (1999). What drives customer loyalty with complaint resolution? *Journal of Service Research, 1*, 324–332.

Andreassen, T.W. (2000). Antecedents to satisfaction with service recovery. *European Journal of Marketing, 34*, 156–175.

Ang, L., & Buttle, F. (2006). Customer retention management processes: A quantitative study. *European Journal of Marketing, 40*, 83–99.

Ansoff, H.I. (1975). Managing strategic surprise by response to weak signals. *California Management Review, 18*(2), 21–33.

Bell, S.J., & Luddington, J.A. (2006). Coping with customer complaints. *Journal of Service Research, 8*, 221–233.

Bell, S.J., Mengüç, B., & Stefani, S.L. (2004). When customers disappoint: A model of relational internal marketing and customer complaints. *Journal of the Academy of Marketing Science, 32*, 112–126.

Bitner, M.J., Booms, B.H., & Mohr, L.A. (1994). Critical service encounters: The employees' viewpoint. *Journal of Marketing, 58*(4), 95–106.

Blodgett, J.G., & Anderson, R.D. (2000). A Bayesian network model of the consumer complaint process. *Journal of Service Research, 2*, 321–338.

Blodgett, J.G., Granbois, D.H., & Walters, R.G. (1993). The effects of perceived justice on complainants' negative word-of-mouth behavior and repatronage intentions. *Journal of Retailing, 69*, 399–428.

Blodgett, J.G., Wakefield, K.L., & Barnes, J.H. (1995). The effects of customer service on consumer complaining behavior. *Journal of Services Marketing, 9*(4), 31–42.

Brouard, F. (2000). Que la veille stratégique se lève: Faisons le point sur la terminologie et le concept [Let strategic intelligence rise: An assessment of the terminology and the concept]. *Administrative Sciences Association of Canada & International Federation of Scholarly Associations of Management Joint Conference (ASAC-IFSAM), 21*(6), Strategy [CD-ROM], 22–33.

Brouard, F. (2007). Awareness and assessment of strategic intelligence: A diagnostic tool. In M. Xu (Ed.), *Managing strategic intelligence: Techniques and technologies* (pp. 122–140). Hershey, NY: Information Science Reference.

Calof, J., & Fox, B. (2003). Trade show intelligence: Intensive, exhaustive and fun. *Competitive Intelligence Magazine, 6*(6), 6–10.

Daft, R.L., & Weick, K.E. (1984). Toward a model of organizations as interpretation systems. *Academy of Management Review, 9*, 284–295.

Détrie, P. (2007). *Les réclamations clients* [Customer complaints]. Paris: Éditions d'Organisation.

Elsbach, K.D. (2006). *Organizational perception management*. Mahwah, NJ: Lawrence Erlbaum Associates.

Estelami, H. (2000). Competitive and procedural determinants of delight and disappointment in consumer complaint outcomes. *Journal of Service Research, 2*, 285–300.

Fleisher, C.S., Wright, S., & Allard, H.T. (2008). The role of insight teams in integrating diverse marketing information management techniques. *European Journal of Marketing, 42*, 836–851.

Fornell, C. (2007). *The satisfied customer: Winners and losers in the battle for buyer preference*. New York: Palgrave-McMillan.

Fornell, C., & Wernerfelt, B. (1987). Defensive marketing strategy by customer complaint management: A theoretical analysis. *Journal of Marketing Research, 24*, 337–346.

Fornell, C., & Wernerfelt, B. (1988). A model for customer complaint management. *Marketing Science, 7*, 287–298.

Fornell, C., & Westbrook, R.A. (1979). The relationship between consumer complaint magnitude and organizational status of complaint processing in large corporations. In R.L. Day & H.K. Hunt (Eds.), *New dimensions of consumer satisfaction and complaining behavior* (pp. 95–98). Bloomington, IN: Bureau of Business Research.

Francq, A. (2001). The use of counterintelligence, security, and countermeasures. In C.S. Fleisher & D.L. Blenkhorn (Eds.), *Managing frontiers in competitive intelligence* (pp. 40–50). Westport, CT: Quorum Books.

Ghoshal, S., & Westney, D.E. (1991). Organizing competitor analysis systems. *Strategic Management Journal, 12*(1), 17–31.

Gilly, M.C. (1987). Postcomplaint processes: From organizational response to repurchase behaviour. *Journal of Consumer Affairs, 21*, 293–313.

Goodman, J. (1999). Basic facts on customer complaint behavior and the impact of service on the bottom line. *Competitive Advantage, 9*(1), 1–5.

Goodwin, C., & Ross, I. (1993). Consumer evaluations of responses to complaints: What's fair and why. *Journal of Consumer Marketing, 7*(2), 39–47.

Gordon, I.H. (2002). *Competitor targeting: Winning the battle for market and customer share.* Etobicoke, Ontario: John Wiley & Sons.

Harari, O. (1992). Thank heaven for complainers. *Management Review, 81*(1), 59–60.

Harbulot, C., Moinet, N., & Lucas, D. (2002, September). *La guerre cognitive: A la recherche de la suprématie stratégique* [Cognitive war: Looking for strategic supremacy]. Paper presented at the 6th Competitive Intelligence Forum of the French Aeronautical and Astronautical Association [VIème Forum Intelligence Économique de *l'Association Aéronautique et Astronautique Française*], Menton, France. Retrieved from http://www.infoguerre.fr/fichiers/3AF25092002.pdf

Harris, L.C., & Ogbonna, E. (2010). Hiding customer complaints: Studying the motivations and forms of service employees' complaint concealment behaviours. *British Journal of Management, 21*, 262–279.

Harris, L.C., & Reynolds, K.L. (2004). Jaycustomer behavior: An exploration of types and motives in the hospitality industry. *Journal of Services Marketing, 18*, 339–357.

Hirschman, A.O. (1970). *Exit, voice, and loyalty: Responses to decline in firms, organizations and states.* Cambridge, MA: Harvard University Press.

Homburg, C., & Stock, R.M. (2004). The link between salespeople's job satisfaction and customer satisfaction in a business-to-business context: A dyadic analysis. *Journal of the Academy of Marketing Science, 32*, 144–158.

Jennings, D.E., & Lumpkin, J.R. (1992). Insights between environmental scanning activities and Porter's generic strategies: An empirical analysis. *Journal of Management, 18*, 791–803.

Jones, D.L., McCleary, K.W., & Lepisto, L.R. (2002). Consumer complaint behavior manifestations for table service restaurants: Identifying sociodemographic characteristics, personality, and behavioral factors. *Journal of Hospitality & Tourism Research, 26*, 105–123.

Kelley, S.W., Hoffman, K.D., & Davis, M.A. (1993). A typology of retail failures and recoveries. *Journal of Retailing, 69*, 429–452.

Kim, C., Kim, S., Im, S., & Shin, C. (2003). The effect of attitude and perception on consumer complaint intentions. *Journal of Consumer Marketing, 20*, 352–371.

Kimmel, A.J. (2004). *Rumors and rumor control: A manager's guide to understanding and combating rumors.* Mahwah, NJ: Lawrence Erlbaum Publishers.

Kowalski, R.M. (1996). Complaints and complaining: Functions, antecedents, and consequences. *Psychological Bulletin, 119*, 179–196.

Larivet, S. (2006). L'intelligence économique: Un concept managérial [Economic intelligence: A business concept]. *Market Management, 6*(3), 22–35.

Larivet, S. (2009). *L'intelligence économique: Enquête dans 100 PME* [Economic intelligence: A survey in 100 SMEs]. Paris: L'Harmattan.

Larivet, S., & Brouard, F. (2007). Faire de l'intelligence économique au quotidien: Application à la gestion des réclamations [Practising economic intelligence daily: The exemple of complaint management]. *Market Management, 7*(4), 5–25.

Le Bon, J. (2006). La force de vente et les activités d'intelligence économique [Sales force and economic intelligence activities]. *Revue Française de Gestion, 32*(163), 15–30.

Lesca, H., & Blanco, S. (2002, October). *Contribution à la capacité d'anticipation des entreprises par la sensibilisation aux signaux faibles* [Contribution to companies' anticipation capability by raising awareness of weak signals]. Paper presented at the 6th International Conference on Small and Medium Businesses [6ème Conférence Internationale sur les Petites et Moyennes Entreprises, CIFEPME], Montreal, Canada. Retrieved from http://web.hec.ca/airepme/images/File/2002/108FA%20-%20Sylvie%20Blanco.pdf

Liu, R.R., & McClure, P. (2001). Recognizing cross-cultural differences in consumer complaint behavior and intentions: An empirical examination. *Journal of Consumer Marketing, 18*(1), 54–75.

Mattila, A.S. (2004). Consumer complaining to firms: The determinants of channel choice. *Journal of Services Marketing, 18*, 147–155.

Maute, M., & Forrester, W.R. (1993). The structure and determinants of consumer complaint intentions and behaviour. *Journal of Economic Psychology, 14*, 219–247.

Maxham, J.G., & Netemeyer, R.G. (2002). Modeling customer perceptions of complaint handling over time: The effects of perceived justice on satisfaction and intent. *Journal of Retailing, 78*, 239–252.

Maxham, J.G., & Netemeyer, R.G. (2003). Firms reap what they sow: The effects of shared values and perceived organizational justice on customers' evaluations of complaint handling. *Journal of Marketing, 67*(1), 46–62.

McCole, P. (2004). Dealing with complaints in services. *International Journal of Contemporary Hospitality Management, 16*, 345–354.

Miller, J. (Ed.). (2000). *Millenium intelligence: Understanding and conducting competitive intelligence in the digital age.* Medford, NJ: CyberAge Books.

Moyer, M.S. (1984). Characteristics of consumer complainants: Implications for marketing and public policy. *Journal of Public Policy and Marketing, 3*(1), 67–84.

Nolan, J.A., & Quinn, J.F. (2000). Intelligence and security. In J. Miller (Ed.), *Millennium Intelligence* (pp. 203–224). Medford, NJ: CyberAge Books.

Nyer, P.U. (2000). An investigation into whether complaining can cause increased consumer satisfaction. *Journal of Consumer Marketing, 17*(1), 9–19.

Orsingher, C., Valentini, S., & de Angelis, M. (2010). A meta-analysis of satisfaction with complaint handling in services. *Journal of the Academy of Marketing Science, 38*, 169–186.

Palmatier, R.W., Dant, R.P., Grewal, D., & Evans, K.R. (2006). Factors influencing the effectiveness of relationship marketing: A meta-analysis. *Journal of Marketing, 70*(4), 136–153.

Peyrot, M., Childs, N., van Doren, D., & Allen, K. (2002). An empirically based model of competitor intelligence use. *Journal of Business Research, 55*, 747–758.

Prim-Allaz, I., & Sabadie, W. (2005). Les apports de la théorie de la justice à la gestion des réclamations [Justice theory contribution to complaint management]. *Décisions Marketing, 38*, 7–19.

Robertson, N., & Shaw, R. (2006, December). *Consumer complaint channel choice in self-service technology encounters.* Paper presented at the Australian and New Zealand Marketing Academy (ANZMAC) Conference, Brisbane, Queensland. Retrieved from http://smib.vuw.ac.nz:8081/WWW/ANZMAC2006/documents/Robertson_Nichola.pdf

Santos, J., & Boote, J. (2003). A theoretical exploration and model of consumer expectations, post-purchase affective states and affective behaviour. *Journal of Consumer Behaviour, 3*, 142–156.

Sharma, P., Marshall, R., Reday, P.A., & Na, W. (2010). Complainers versus non-complainers: A multi-national investigation of individual and situational influences on customer complaint behaviour. *Journal of Marketing Management, 26*, 163–180.

Singh, J. (1988). Consumer complaint intentions and behavior: Definitional and taxonomical issues. *Journal of Marketing, 52*(1), 93–107.

Singh, J., & Widing, R.E. (1991). What occurs once consumers complain? A theoretical model for understanding satisfaction/dissatisfaction outcomes of complaint responses. *European Journal of Marketing, 25*(5), 30–46.

Singh, J., & Wilkes, R.E. (1996). When consumers complain: A path analysis of the key antecedents of consumer complaint response estimates. *Journal of the Academy of Marketing Science, 24*, 350–365.

Smith, A.K., Bolton, R.N., & Wagner, J. (1999). A model of customer satisfaction with service encounters involving failure and recovery. *Journal of Marketing Research, 36*, 356–372.

Stephens, N., & Gwinner, K.P. (1998). Why don't some people complain? A cognitive-emotive process model of consumer complaint behaviour. *Journal of the Academy of Marketing Science, 26*, 172–189.

Szymanski, D.M., & Henard, D.H. (2001). Customer satisfaction: A meta-analysis of the empirical evidence. *Journal of the Academy of Marketing Science, 29*(1), 16–35.

Tax, S.S., Brown, S.W., & Chandrashekaran, M. (1998). Customer evaluation of service complaint experiences: Implication for relationship marketing. *Journal of Marketing, 62*(2), 60–76.

Voorhees, C.M., & Brady, M.K. (2005). A service perspective on the drivers of complaint intentions. *Journal of Service Research, 8*, 192–204.

Voss, R., & Gruber, T. (2005). Complaint handling at the Schinlerhof Hotel with praise and assessment cards. *Management Services, 49*(3), 16–19.

Ward, J.C., & Ostrom, A.L. (2006). Complaining to the masses: The role of protest framing in customer-created complaint web sites. *Journal of Consumer Research, 33*, 220–230.

Xu, X., & Kaye, G.R. (1995). Building market intelligence systems for environment scanning. *Logistics Information Management, 8*(2), 22–29.

Zeithaml, V.A., Berry, L.L., & Parasuraman, A. (1993). The nature and determinants of customer expectations of service. *Journal of the Academy of Marketing Science, 21*(1), 1–12.

Applying a behavioural and operational diagnostic typology of competitive intelligence practice: empirical evidence from the SME sector in Turkey

Sheila Wright[a], Christophe Bisson[b] and Alistair P. Duffy[c]

[a]Strategic Management & Marketing, Faculty of Business and Law, De Montfort University, Hugh Aston Building, The Gateway, Leicester, LE1 9BH, UK; [b]Kadir Has University, Kadir Has Caddesi, 34083, Cibali, Istanbul, Turkey; [c]Department of Engineering, De Montfort University, The Gateway, Leicester, LE1 9BH, UK

This paper reports on an empirical study conducted within the SME sector in the city of Istanbul, Turkey. The findings from this study enabled the creation of a behavioural and operational typology of competitive intelligence practice, one developed from the work of S. Wright, D.W. Pickton and J. Callow (2002. Competitive intelligence in UK firms: A typology. *Marketing Intelligence & Planning, 20*, 349–360). Using responses to questions which indicated a type of behaviour or operational stance towards the various strands of CI practice under review it has been possible to identify areas where improvements could be made to reach an ideal situation which could garner significant competitive advantage for the SMEs surveyed.

Introduction

While most EU countries are still trying to recover from the last financial crisis (Chen, 2011), Turkey is today a fast rising economic power with a 7.3% economic growth in 2010 (Central Intelligence Agency, 2011). Small and medium enterprises (SMEs) play an important role, yet Kavcioglu (2009) reported that Turkish SMEs have marketing problems and a lack of information and technology expertise. It is suggested here that one solution would be for Turkish SMEs to become adept at, and fully embrace the practice of competitive intelligence (CI).

CI has received different definitions over the years (Brody, 2008) and has often been assimilated with competitor intelligence, business intelligence or environmental scanning. The study reported in this paper adopts a much less restrictive definition of CI, one provided by Rouach and Santi (2001, p. 553) which is the

> art of collecting, processing and storing information to be made available to people at all levels of the firm to help shape its future and protect it against current competitive threat: it should be legal and respect codes of ethics; it involves a transfer of knowledge from the environment to the organization within established rules.

The scope of this study deals with market intelligence, competitor intelligence and technological intelligence (Deschamps & Nayak, 1995) as well as strategic and social intelligence (Rouach & Santi, 2001). Thus, this research addresses an important scientific gap by studying the CI practices of SMEs in Turkey.

The importance of SMEs in the Turkish economy

Turkish SMEs play a vital role as they comprise 98–99% of all firms in Turkey (Kavcioglu, 2009). They represent 81% of all employment and contribute 36% of the total GDP of Turkey (Kavcioglu, 2009). SMEs are responsible for 60% of Turkey's overall exports (typical sectors being textiles, clothing, automotive, iron, steel, white goods, chemicals, pharmaceuticals and shipping) and 40% of Turkey's overall imports (typical sectors being machinery, chemicals, semi-finished goods, fuels and transport equipment) (*Hurriyet Daily News*, 2011). Turkey's main trading partners are the European Union (57% exports, 40% imports), Russia and the USA (State Institute of Statistics, 2011). None of these are showing financial buoyancy yet according to Blanke and Mia (2006), Turkey is expected to be in the top 10 economies in 2020. The UK Trade and Investment Report (2009) also states that whilst Turkey has started to face global competition, this has typically come from emerging markets such as China and India.

Competitive intelligence in SMEs and emerging countries

Priporas, Gatsoris and Zacharis (2005, p. 665) noted that 'CI seems to be the key ingredient for success in today's uncertain business environment', regardless of size. Indeed, CI has proved to be an important source of competitive advantage for companies and is a key investment area in the EU (Priporas et al., 2005). Studies in France (Larivet, 2009; Smith, Wright, & Pickton, 2010) note the high level of government intervention and support which provides practical and intellectual assistance to their SME sector. This leads to a heightened awareness of the commercial benefit of such practice and the desire to acquire essential skills to help develop their CI practice. CI practices in SMEs is a growing topic of interest and the sector has been studied in Canada (Brouard, 2006; Tannev & Bailetti, 2008; Tarraf & Molz, 2006), in France (Afolabi, 2007; Bisson, 2003; Knauf, 2007; Salles, 2006; Smith et al., 2010) and in Switzerland (Begin, Deschamps, & Madinier, 2007). Bisson (2010) demonstrated that to compete successfully, SMEs must acquire CI tools and methodologies. A year earlier, Mazzarol, Reboud and Soutar (2009, p. 338) reported that 'owner-managers from small firms need to be alerted to environmental changes, committed to innovation and willing to change or take action if required'. Some five years earlier, Lesca, Caron-Fasan, Janissek-Muniz, and Freitas (2005, p. 1) said that 'in order to become more and more competitive, SMEs and above all SMEs of emergent countries, need to capture international and transnational markets'. Thus, the use of CI methods and tools by SMEs is especially vital in an ambitious nation such as Turkey. There is also compliance with the findings of Bisson (2010, p. 24) who noted that 'in most countries, SMEs constitute the main source of employment and are increasingly active participants in the globalized economy'. Only one study into this area has been carried out in Turkey. Taşkin, Adali, and Ersin (2004) investigated the technological intelligence in Turkish companies, using a sample of 300 firms but no identification of firm size was evident. The evidence above suggests that the use of CI methods and tools by SMEs is critical, not only for all countries, but especially for a nation such as Turkey which relies so heavily on that sector of its commercial constitution, for fiscal, trade and employment success.

Research design

A constructivist/transformative approach was adopted as the aim was to explore the views of a community working in a variety of industry sectors. Elements of pragmatism were present as there was an acceptance that any data collected could only be a reflection of 'provisional knowledge' as opposed to the discovery of indisputable 'facts'. From empirical evidence, the aim was to identify and classify CI behaviour and attitudes of SMEs in Turkey, against an extended typology of practice, based on that first produced by Wright et al. (2002).

A self-completion questionnaire using a mixture of closed and open style questions was used to initiate the data set. The questions were determined according to the model developed from a study of CI active firms in the UK by Wright et al. (2002) and based on four strands: Attitude, Gathering, Use and Location. This model has been a platform or inspiration for further work and/or replication studies by authors such as Adidam, Gajre, and Kejriwal (2009), April and Bessa (2006), Badr (2003), Bouthillier and Jin (2005), Dishman and Calof (2008), Hudson and Smith (2008), Larivet (2009), Liu and Wang (2008), Madden (2004), Oerlemans, Rooks, and Pretorius (2005), Priporas et al. (2005), Santos and Correia (2010), Smith (2005), Suntharamoorthy (2009), Tryfonas and Thomas (2006), Whitehurst (2008), Wright, Eid, and Fleisher (2009a, 2009b) and Wright, Fleisher, and Madden (2008). This provides evidence of validation of the measures developed and as such it was deemed to be one which was entirely appropriate to use as the foundation for this study.

The research reported on here, sought to extend that model by adding two new strands, Technological Support, identified as the degree of investment made to assist with gathering competitive information and IT Support, identified as the type of systems used to manage the flow of competitive information. To ensure compatibility of analysis, the questionnaire used by Wright et al. (2002) was adapted and each of the strands were defined into questions which could then be translated into a typology verdict for that individual firm. Set apart from the main category questions, a self-declared position statement was offered which was used to either confirm or contradict answers given within each category. This served as a clarification mechanism which revealed any inconsistency in a typology verdict based on the allocations of answers to individual questions and the self-declared position statement.

Questions relating to general information such as turnover, sector, employee numbers, main markets and export activity were also asked and placed at the end of the questionnaire which was translated from English to Turkish, back-translated from Turkish to English, tested via a pilot study and subsequently launched in its final on-line format in September 2010. The target group was SMEs located in Istanbul, a city which represents 55% of Turkey's trade, 45% of the country's wholesale trade and generates 21.2% of Turkey's gross national product (Istanbul Metropolitan Municipality, 2009).

The Istanbul Sanayi Odasi (Istanbul Chamber of Industry) provided a membership list which was then cleaned for the purposes of this research. Duplicate data were deleted, as were companies which were deemed to be outside the EU definition (EU Commission Recommendation, 2003) of an SME in terms of turnover ($<$ €50 million) and/or number of employees ($<$ 250). A self-selecting sample of 371 firms indicated a willingness to take part in the survey and the link to the on-line questionnaire was sent to those firms. Only 28 recipients of the invitation, subsequently declined to respond. A total of 22 responses were deleted as their answers to the firm classification questions revealed that they too fell outside the scope of the EU's definition of an SME. A further seven responses were identified as being from firms which had identified themselves as the local branch of a global company. These firms, although small in number, were considered to be less independent than a typical SME, would not behave in a comparable fashion and would potentially be acting under the direction of a much larger, potentially more resourceful entity. For these reasons, their responses were removed from the data set which resulted in a total of 314 returns being recorded, representing a response rate of 84.6%.

Of the 343 firms which started the survey, 94 dropped out after they had answered the first section on their firm's *gathering* strategies. A further 66 dropped out after they had completed both the gathering and *attitude* sections. The questionnaire proved to be sufficiently interesting to the remaining 154 respondents who answered all the following sections on the final four strands: *technological support, IT support systems, use* and *location*, with the exception of two respondents who failed to complete the final section on location. The percentage response rates for each stage of the survey are shown in Table 1 and it is argued that these are sufficiently high so as to produce meaningful analysis.

Sample profile

Of the 144 firms which declared their industry sector, 59.7% came from the manufacturing sector. The next highest representative was from the IT section with 13.2%. Other sectors were represented, but in less than double digits. These were: construction; food and consumer goods; energy; healthcare; services; retail; textiles; packaging; and veterinary pharmacy. It could be argued that it was very refreshing to see so many manufacturing firms taking an interest in the subject, sufficient so as to complete the survey and offer their contact details in order to receive a copy of the summary report. Manufacturing firms, by their very nature, epitomise the transformational process from input (raw materials) to output (finished goods) and this, more than perhaps any other sector, would appreciate the process which transforms raw data via competitive analysis, into competitive intelligence which delivers insight.

The same number of respondents (144) identified their revenue band with 65 firms (45.13%) reporting <€2 million (micro), 60 firms (41.67%) reporting <€10 million (small) and 19 firms (13.20%) reporting <€50 million (medium). The same number of respondents provided details of their employee numbers with 23 firms (15.97%) having less than 10 employees (micro), 72 firms (50%) having less than 50 employees (small) and 49 firms (34.03%) having less than 250 employees (medium). A majority of 80 firms (55.55%) declared their main markets as both local and global with 49 firms (34.03%) concentrating on their local market and the remaining 15 firms (10.42%) focusing on global markets. Given that this research was aimed at the SME sector, operating in a mix of local and global markets, these returns confirmed that the right contact database had been selected for this task.

Table 1. Response rates for each stage of the survey.

Typology strand	Section heading	Number	%
Gathering	Intelligence Gathering strategies	314	100
Attitude	Attitude toward CI	220	70.06
Technology support	Technology support used for CI	154	49.04
IT systems	IT systems used by manage CI	154	49.04
Use	Use of CI in the decision making process	154	49.04
Location	Location for intelligence gathering in the firm	152	48.40

Applying the results to a behavioural and operational typology of CI practice

As previously cited, building on previous research efforts, pilot study results and subsequent development, a set of descriptors was agreed. These are provided in Appendix 1 and the findings from the survey were applied to this framework. The italic categories are deemed to be those to which a firm could aspire, if it wished to perform competitive intelligence at an optimal level.

Gathering

This was perhaps the easiest section for the respondents to tackle. It asked about the type of information they gathered, the sources they used, how much competitive information they gleaned from their own employees, how they prepared their employees for contact with competitors, what types of financial return they expected from their CI effort and how much financial support was provided for CI activities. Over 2200 responses were recorded to the question on what type of information was collected, with customers, competitors, products in own market, suppliers and laws taking the top five places, closely followed by taxation, economy and finance. Somewhat worryingly, the items which were revealed as being of less interest were ISO standards, politics, scientific articles/publications, industrial processes and patents. Given the sector profile of this sample and the emphasis on manufacturing and IT, this reveals a concerning lack of awareness, or even disinterest, in key elements of their sector which could significantly affect their competitiveness, either positively or negatively.

The most popular source of information was stated to be own knowledge, followed by websites and then trade fairs. This is indicative of reliance on a relatively easily available and not especially well informed set of sources and concurs with the findings that 60% of respondents who said they obtained either a moderate or high amount of competitive information from their own employees. In contrast, the remaining 40% received either none, or only a low amount, which would suggest that they are under-using, or ignoring, a potential reservoir of competitive information. The more sophisticated, and arguably more valuable, sources such as written/verbal evidence from verified sources, forecasting models and management consultants were the least used.

Only 57.8% of respondents stated that they trained and prepared their employees before they went to trade shows, exhibitions, conventions and other public events to make them aware of the type of information they should look for. For the remaining 42.2% which did this only 'occasionally' or 'never', it begs the question as to why not and what are they attending for if obtaining competitive information is not part of their brief? More interestingly, 69.5% of respondents said that they briefed their employees on what they should *not* talk about to competing firms which is a pleasing result, demonstrating a proactive attitude towards protecting the firm's sensitive information. Unfortunately, this leaves 30.5% which pay little attention to this area, a situation which can only be regarded as either naive or reckless.

Whilst 74.4% of respondents stated that they evaluated the reliability of their sources of information, given the dominance of personal knowledge, websites and trade fairs reported above, it is difficult to understand how this is achieved. It is possible that the respondents' understanding of 'checking' is not quite as robust as would be expected.

In terms of financial support given by the organisation to support the task of monitoring the competitive environment, the most common reply was 'minimal to cover the basic task and simple gathering'. A staggering 86.3% of respondents stated that no funds were available as the tasks were done by interested people rather than intelligence experts, or that funds were available provided that an immediate financial benefit could be produced. Anybody working in CI knows that this is an almost impossible objective to achieve, especially in advance of an investigation, so by default, funds in these firms would be unlikely to be released. In others, funds were considered to be either just about adequate, or not enough, to do a reasonable job.

Taking the findings from these questions and related answers, the overall verdict was very slightly tipped towards a Hunter Gathering level yet the self-declared position for an overall gathering approach was significantly biased, to a factor of nearly 2:1 towards an *Easy Gathering* stance. This suggests that whilst the firms may think they are operating in a sophisticated manner, this represents their desire, rather than reality, a view further supported by the responses which indicated that 64.9% of the firms used *only* public domain sources for their competitive information.

Attitude

When asked how often the firm collected information about competitors, technologies and customers, three vital ingredients which make up the competitive landscape, the most frequently selected choice was the same for all three: 'irregularly, when it becomes available'. This reinforces the conclusion shown above, that firms claiming to have Hunter Gathering traits in the previous section, gave conflicting responses in this section, which suggests that in practice, they do not. Only 14.9% reported that their firm had a written process and a system dedicated to CI with nearly 7.7% saying they did not know, which would suggest that none exists. This leaves a staggering 77.4% which has no formalised process or dedicated system which handles gathered information.

Having said that, 25.5% stated that their firm provided 'full commitment for understanding competitors', and advocated the benefits which that brought, with 23.8% claiming there was 'active support for current activities'. One wonders how on earth that is achieved given their earlier responses. Contrast this further with the self-declared control statement where 47.9% agreed that 'we are too busy thinking about today to worry about tomorrow' and 'CI is a waste of valuable time'. Even those who were in support of CI could only record short-term interest (15.1%) and one-off projects (37%) where CI had been taken seriously. Nobody selected the option which indicated that they had an integrated competitive information process where competitors were monitored, their moves anticipated or reaction plans were formulated. This is strongly indicative of a *Task-Driven Attitude*.

Use

The use of CI by decision makers is, of course, the principal objective of such a programme. The most frequently selected choice, which received nearly twice that of the nearest other option was 'there is no organised process for feeding CI output into the decision-making process'. This was followed some way behind, in almost equal numbers respectively by 'we use CI for short-term decisions' (14.5%) and 'day-to-day operations, as soon as we receive information, we act' (13.6%). The choice of 'long-term decisions' was also reported by 12.9% which suggests a real dichotomy of purpose and use of CI by the sample. By some distance, the highest percentage of responses to this question (37.3%), fell into the *Joneses User* category.

In considering the impact which various elements have on their firm's decision making, 'customer demands' was the most frequent choice, followed by 'technological/technology standard changes' and 'competitor(s) short-term behaviour'. Given the findings in earlier sections which identified shortcomings in both gathering activities and attitudinal styles, the findings here suggest that a significant change of approach is needed if these firms are to use CI to address those areas which they say have a direct impact on their decision making and as a consequence, their performance. This agrees with the self-declared statement where the largest number of respondents (43.2%) selected 'we use competitive information to help us make decisions about price changes and promotional efforts'. Clearly, looking at websites, relying on public domain information and thinking that CI is a waste of time does not improve their potential to use competitive information in a timely or expert manner. It might even be possible to question whether they do indeed recognise valuable information when it comes their way. The findings from this section, coupled with that of the previous paragraph would suggest not and are indicative of a *Knee-Jerk User*.

Location

It was important to establish if the respondents felt that a dedicated location for the CI effort was beneficial. It was pleasing, if a little surprising that 83.8% of respondents said that their employees 'always' knew who to pass information to, with only 16.2% stating this was rarely the case. The top five departments which took responsibility for collecting CI were first Sales (20.0%) and then Marketing (19.8%). The next two most frequently selected choices were Procurement/Purchasing (10.3%), followed closely by R&D (8.9%). Dissecting the last two in terms of popularity was agreement by 9.4% of respondents who stated that 'all departments take responsibility'. It was possible for multiple choices to be made in answer to this question, garnering a total of 404 individual responses from just 155 firms. This would suggest that despite the data above, few firms have any idea as to who takes overall responsibility and the process operates in a very loose manner.

Contrastingly, a significantly high 33.5% of respondents agreed that a dedicated intelligence unit was 'always' essential to accomplish successfully the monitoring task with 21.9% agreeing that this was 'sometimes' essential but not always. A similar number of respondents (23.2%) thought that a dedicated CI unit was 'a good idea but not always essential' with the remainder indicating that they did not think it was needed at all.

As a consequence, it came as no surprise that 94.2% of respondents stated that they did *not* have a dedicated intelligence unit with 80% of respondents stating that they did not have a person in their firm whose job it was gather, analyse, disseminate and store competitive information. This stands in contradiction of the findings above which indicated that 83.8% of firms said their staff 'always' knew who to pass competitive information to. Of the remaining firms, 31 (20%) said that they did have an employee dedicated to CI with a high figure of 24 indicating that this individual participated in senior management meetings but the remaining seven did not. One can only wonder what they do with the information they receive and what on earth they do with their time. This is not to take any credit away from the 24 firms which could claim to have a reasonably mature and professional approach to CI but it has to be noted that this is an incredibly small number and a disappointing revelation. In total, 89.6% of respondents indicated an *Ad-Hoc Location* approach.

Technology support

This section addressed the type of tools used to assist in the gathering task. From a total of 384 selections across 10 choices the most frequently used tools were websites (36.1%) and

Google (35.7%). Very small numbers were recorded against free search alert tools (0.08%), software allowing statistical analysis and dissemination (0.06%) and specialist websites such as Espacenet for patents (0.06%). This was confirmed in the self-declared position statement section where an astonishing 87% of respondents agreed that they used 'common, freely available tools for web searching such as Google' as their tool of choice. Only eight respondents indicated 'we use full versions of meta-search engines and are familiar with specialist databases for patents and financial information', which further concurs with the Easy Gathering verdict reached earlier. For the technology support section however, the responses indicated an overwhelming 94.9% verdict of a *Simple Technology Support* stance.

IT systems

The level of IT support used by the respondent firms to manage their competitive information was the subject of this section. Of the 173 responses received, 56.1% stated that they did not use any systems at all to manage their competitive information, agreeing with the statement that it was in their minds and they relied on their memory. The next largest category which received agreement was representative of a large gap, as only 12.7% of respondents said they used IT systems to manage competitive information *but* they preferred paper records and did not really like relying on computers, or somebody else for the safety of their information.

The next largest category in answer to whether the firm used any IT systems for CI purposes, was 'I don't know', representing 9.8% of respondents and an unimpressive confirmation of a degree of ignorance regarding their firm's procedures and processes. This agreed with the self-declaration statement with 63.9% of respondents saying they relied on the good will of staff to share what they knew. There can be no question that this was indicative of a *Dismissive IT Systems* stance.

Implications for practice

The findings from this study provide a valuable template to inspire not only SMEs in Turkey, but elsewhere, to achieve competitive advantage. As can be seen from our behavioural and operational typology of competitive intelligence practice in Figure 1, the firms represented in this study have some ground to make up if they wish to reach an optimal state.

It is recognised that not all SMEs have either the desire, or the financial resources to do this, but it is important that this is a considered decision, made with the full knowledge of just how far the firm is from an optimal state. Identifying the firm's position on the typology reveals where improvements need to be made in order to bring them closer to the ideal situation which can only be of benefit to their competitive performance. SMEs especially, need to take full advantage of what competitive information and intelligence can deliver if they are to compete efficiently with large firms which already reap the benefits of CI practice. Firms which ignore this, have no excuse when they are overtaken by more agile rivals who have invested heavily with the aim of achieving an optimal CI effort. In order to remain and increase their performance, there really is no choice but to commit wholeheartedly to CI. 'Do nothing' never was a wise option and it is especially so in today's increasingly complex and dynamic competitive environment.

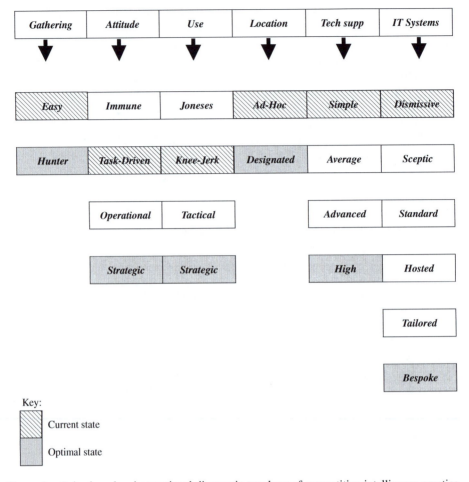

Figure 1.   Behavioural and operational diagnostic typology of competitive intelligence practice.

Recommendations for corrective measures

Gathering

> Sector verdict: Easy Gathering
> Ideal/optimum state: Hunter Gathering

There are only two categories in this strand and it is not that difficult to operate at an ideal level. Currently, the evidence suggests that there is far too much effort being spent on easy gathering from public sources. This typically produces volume not value. More attention to decision-maker requirements with greater focus on 'need to know' rather than 'like to know' would produce more intelligent intelligence. The verdict for this category is a key indicator, and potentially a root cause of failings in others. It is symptomatic of an overall failure to engage with CI practice in a professional and diligent manner.

Attitude

> Sector verdict: Task-Driven Attitude
> Ideal/optimum state: Strategic Attitude

A proactive attitude which can address all issues facing the firm is essential when trying to develop a CI philosophy within the firm. A task-driven attitude, where questions are asked, and answered, with little value added is very comfortable for those involved and is the natural habitat of the un-inquisitive, the disengaged and those who are too ready to say 'it's not my job to think'. A supportive attitude needs to embrace all strategic issues and be seen as essential for future success, otherwise the CI effort will never mature beyond a 'stick-fetching' activity.

User

Sector verdict: Knee-Jerk User
Ideal/optimum state: Strategic User

It is not surprising that with Easy Gathering and a Task-Driven Attitude that confusion exists about what intelligence should be used for. The predominant use of CI in this sample was for price changes and promotional effort. Whilst CI can indeed help with tactical decisions, this should be the base-level expectation, not the overall ambition. If the sector wants to embrace CI at the strategic level, it has to shift from applying CI output purely to day-to-day decisions and start to use it for predictive purposes such as scenarios and 'what if' analysis.

Location

Sector verdict: Ad-Hoc Location
Ideal/optimum state: Dedicated Location

For a CI programme to be successfully implemented, firms need to define roles, responsibilities and establish a defined location for all CI elements. Only then can duplication of effort be eliminated and the technical and cognitive skills of full-time staff developed. This also ensures that employees are always aware of where to send valuable competitive information when they obtain it.

Technology support

Sector verdict: Simple Technology Support
Ideal/optimum state: High Technology Support

The dominance of web-based, public domain sources accessed by this sample is insufficient to secure any competitive advantage. It is the use to which that information is put, rather than simply identifying it, which is important. Websites are notoriously fickle and can be subject to bias or PR treatment such that they offer little advantage in terms of unique intelligence. The very fact that any information is on a website means it is old news. Everybody who is interested has already seen it, most likely your competitors as well, and as such, the information has very limited value. Firms need to invest in cross-functional integrated systems which can evolve as needs change. Advanced tools such as semantic-based algorithms should be used, which can interrogate and manipulate the competitive information collected.

IT systems support

Sector verdict: Dismissive IT Systems Support

Ideal/optimum state: Bespoke IT Systems SupportNot using any IT system to support CI is highly risky and short-sighted. Five stages of development exist before the optimum bespoke state is reached. Any one of those stages would represent significant improvement on current practice. A standardised or hosted system is entirely achievable by most firms, however small, with a tailored system being the immediate, minimal state with bespoke being set as the firm's ambition.

Implications for SME support networks

Clearly a lot of development and support is needed within the sector if SMEs in Turkey are to reach even a moderately professional approach to competitive intelligence. One or two firms stand out as being somewhat skilled and having the right attitude and support systems but these are very definitely in the minority. It is quite normal for firms to become totally committed to CI once they have observed the benefits and can understand how it applies to their activities.

The French government has readily grasped this and through its Chambers of Commerce & Industry (CCI) network, offers a range of workshops and training courses, delivered by respected University Business Schools. As identified by Smith et al. (2010), SME managers are encouraged to take a CI module and improve their CI analysis skills as part of an overall provision of intelligence awareness. Subject to some not too onerous conditions, some CCIs are able to provide support for setting up a CI unit, typically 50–80% of the total cost, but sometimes this can be 100%. This is the type of skill level and state-funded CI programmes which Turkey's SMEs could find themselves in competition with.

Better awareness of the role which investment in technology can play in enhancing the gathering, analysis and dissemination tasks is essentials as this reduces the perceived and actual cost of a CI programme. Technological assistance also enables the operators to spend less time on data handling and more time on interpretation and developing insight which the firm can use to its advantage.

With the current GDP figures and a 'feel-good' factor in Turkey, is there a danger of complacency setting in? Is Turkey witnessing a 'false dawn'? Do they recognise the need to be more competitive and to what degree would their answer influence their future behaviour? Has anybody thought to consider how vulnerable the sector might be to attack, and if so, from where and whom? It is recommended that a well-funded programme of CI awareness and skills training would be the best method to address these issues.

Implications for future research

In considering the next steps for this work, it is intended to conduct a parallel study in the SME sectors of other, similarly placed countries. It would be intriguing to devise a number of success measures for SMEs and then to apply those to firms at different stages in the typology, and by implication, CI maturity. A comparative study in France for example, would be a fascinating indicator of the value and/or effectiveness of the CI programmes funded by their government. If this turned out to be positive, and given the high expectations for revenue and job creation placed on the SME sector in Turkey, there would clearly be an impetus for the Turkish government to consider how it could provide professional CI training and support for this critically important sector of their economy. This could result in an avalanche of interest as firms strive to remain competitive and seek to address the deficiencies which exist in comparison to their neighbours.

It would also be interesting to establish through empirical evidence, whether skilled CI practitioners are able to demonstrate that their work secures and defends the competitive advantage it promises. One could speculate on precisely which type of scenario(s) could be identified quicker, or be analysed more productively, with CI work as opposed to the passive, somewhat pedestrian approach, preferred by the majority of firms which took part in this study.

References

Adidam, P.T., Gajre, S., & Kejriwal, S. (2009). Cross-cultural competitive intelligence strategies. *Marketing Intelligence & Planning, 27*, 666–680.

Afolabi, B.S. (2007). *La conception et l'adaptation de la structure d'un système d'intelligence economique par l'observation des comportements de l'utilisateur* (Unpublished doctoral dissertation). Université Nancy 2, France.

April, K., & Bessa, J. (2006). A critique of the strategic competitive intelligence process within a global energy multinational. *Problems and Perspectives in Management, 4*(2), 86–99.

Badr, A. (2003). *The role of competitive intelligence in the formulation of marketing strategy* (Unpublished doctoral dissertation). De Montfort University, UK.

Begin, L., Deschamps, J., & Madinier, H. (2007). Une approche interdisciplinaire de l'intelligence economique. *Les Cahiers de Recherche,* 07/4/1. Retrieved August 29, 2008, from http://papers.ssrn.com/sol3/papers.cfm?abstract_id=1083943

Bisson, C. (2003). *Application de méthodes et mise en place d'outils d'intelligence compétitive au sein d'une PME de haute technologie* (Unpublished doctoral dissertation). Université Aix-Marseille, France.

Bisson, C. (2010). Development of competitive intelligence tools and methodology in a French high-tech SME. *Competitive Intelligence Magazine, 13*, 18–24.

Blanke, J., & Mia, I. (2006). *Turkey's competitiveness in a European context.* Geneva: World Economic Forum.

Bouthillier, F., & Jin, T. (2005). Competitive intelligence and webometrics. *Journal of Competitive Intelligence and Management, 3*(3), 19–39.

Brody, R. (2008). Issues in defining competitive intelligence: An exploration. *Journal of Competitive Intelligence and Management, 4*(3), 3–16.

Brouard, F. (2006). Development of an expert system on environmental scanning practices in SME: Tools as a research program. *Journal of Competitive Intelligence and Management, 3*(4), 37–55.

Central Intelligence Agency. (2011). *The world fact book: Turkey.* Retrieved January 24, 2011, from https://www.cia.gov/library/publications/the-world-factbook/geos/tu.html

Chen, K. (2011). *Debt crisis and the economic outlook in Europe.* Retrieved January 24, 2011, from http://ezinearticles.com/?2011-Debt-Crisis-and-the-Economic-Outlook-in-Europe&id=5702809

Deschamps, J.-P., & Nayak, P.R. (1995). *Product juggernauts: How companies mobilize to generate a stream of market winners.* Boston, MA: Harvard Business School Press.

Dishman, P.L., & Calof, J.L. (2008). Competitive intelligence: A multiphasic precedent to marketing strategy. *European Journal of Marketing, 42*, 766–785.

EU Commission Recommendation. (2003). *2003/361/EC,* Official Journal of the European Union 2003/361/EC, 124, p. 36.

Hudson, S., & Smith, J.R. (2008, March). *Assessing competitive intelligence practices in a non-profit organisation.* Proceedings: 2nd European Competitive Intelligence Symposium, Lisbon, Portugal, pp. 1–20.

Hurriyet Daily News. (2011). *SMEs lead Turkish exports.* Retrieved January 24, 2011, from http://www.hurriyetdailynews.com/n.php?n=smes-lead-turkish-export-2011-01-13

Istanbul Metropolitan Municipality. (2009). *Characteristics of the study area* (Special report). Istanbul, Turkey: Istanbul Metropolitan Municipality.

Kavcioglu, S. (2009, April). *The Turkish experience in SME finance and non-financial services streamlining.* Paper presented at the SMEs in the Globalized World Conference, Istanbul.

Knauf, A. (2007). *Caracterisation des roles du coordinateur-animateur: Emergence d'un acteur necessaire à la mise en pratique d'un dispositif regional d'intelligence economique* (Unpublished doctoral dissertation). Université Nancy 2, France.

Larivet, S. (2009, June). *Economic intelligence in small and medium business in France: A survey,* Proceedings: 3rd European Competitive Intelligence Symposium, Mälardalen University, Stockholm, Sweden, pp. 128–144.

Lesca, H., Caron-Fasan, M.-L., Janissek-Muniz, R., & Freitas, H. (2005). *La veille stratégique: Un facteur clé de success pour les PME/PMI brésiliennes voulant devenir fourniseeur de grandes companies transnationales*. Sao Paulo: Revista FACEF Pesquisa.

Liu, C.-H., & Wang, C.-C. (2008). Forecast competitor service strategy with service taxonomy and CI data. *European Journal of Marketing, 42*, 746–765.

Madden, E. (2004). *Competitive intelligence in the UK pharmaceutical industry* (Unpublished MBA dissertation). De Montfort University, UK.

Mazzarol, T.W., Reboud, S., & Soutar, G.N. (2009). Strategic planning in growth oriented small firms. *International Journal of Entrepreneurial Behaviour & Research, 15*, 320–345.

Oerlemans, L., Rooks, G., & Pretorius, T. (2005). Does technology and innovation management improve market position? Empirical evidence from innovating firms in South Africa. *Knowledge, Technology & Policy, 18*(3), 38–55.

Priporas, C.-V., Gatsoris, L., & Zacharis, V. (2005). Competitive intelligence activity: Evidence from Greece. *Marketing Intelligence & Planning, 23*, 659–669.

Rouach, D., & Santi, P. (2001). Competitive intelligence adds value: Five intelligence attitudes. *European Management Journal, 19*, 552–559.

Salles, M. (2006). Decision making in SMEs and information requirements for competitive intelligence. *Production Planning and Control, 17*, 229–237.

Santos, M., & Correia, A. (2010, September). *Competitive intelligence as a source of competitive advantage: An exploratory study of the Portuguese biotechnology industry*. Proceedings: 11th European Conference of Knowledge Management, Universidade Lusiada de Vila Nova de Famalacão, Famalacão, Portugal, pp. 867–873.

Smith, J.R. (2005, January). *The effectiveness of competitive intelligence: An Anglo-French comparative study*, CD-ROM Proceedings: 1st European Competitive Intelligence Symposium, Poitiers, France.

Smith, J.R., Wright, S., & Pickton, D.W. (2010). Competitive intelligence programmes for SMEs in France: Evidence of changing attitudes. *Journal of Strategic Marketing, 18*, 523–536.

State Institute of Statistics. (2011). *Turkey balance of trade*. Retrieved January 24, 2011, from http://www.tradingeconomics.com/Economics/Balance-of-Trade.aspx?Symbol=TRY

Suntharamoorthy, P. (2009). *Competitor profiling in the UK manufacturing sector* (Unpublished MSc Strategic Marketing dissertation). De Montfort University, UK.

Tanev, S., & Bailetti, T. (2008). Competitive intelligence information and innovation in small Canadian firms. *European Journal of Marketing, 42*, 786–803.

Tarraf, P., & Molz, R. (2006). Competitive intelligence at small enterprises. *SAM Advanced Management Journal, 71*(4), 24–34.

Taşkin, H., Adali, M.R., & Ersin, E. (2004). Technological intelligence and competitive strategies: An application study with fuzzy logic. *Journal of Intelligent Manufacturing, 15*, 417–429.

Tryfonas, T., & Thomas, P. (2006, June). *Intelligence on competitors and ethical challenges of business information operations*. Proceedings: 5th European Conference on Information Warfare and Security, National Defence College, Helsinki, Finland, pp. 237–244.

UK Trade & Investment Report. (2009). *FCO country updates for business, Turkey: Global competitiveness: Making the grade*. Ankara: British Embassy.

Whitehurst, G.R. (2008). *How today's top companies evaluate and use intelligence on their competitors* (Unpublished MBA dissertation). University of Warwick, UK.

Wright, S., Eid, E.R., & Fleisher, C.S. (2009a, July). *Empirical study of competitive intelligence practice: Evidence from UK retail banking*. CD-ROM Proceedings: Academy of Marketing Conference, Competitive Intelligence, Analysis & Strategy Track, Leeds Metropolitan University, Leeds, UK.

Wright, S., Eid, E.R., & Fleisher, C.S. (2009b). Competitive intelligence in practice: Empirical evidence from the UK retail banking sector. *Journal of Marketing Management, 25*, 941–964.

Wright, S., Fleisher, C.S., & Madden, E. (2008, September). *Characteristics of competitive intelligence practice in R&D driven firms: Evidence from the UK pharmaceutical industry*. CD-ROM Proceedings: EBRF Conference: Understanding Business in the Knowledge Society, Viking Line, Helsinki, Finland and Stockholm, Sweden.

Wright, S., Pickton, D.W., & Callow, J. (2002). Competitive intelligence in UK firms: A typology. *Marketing Intelligence & Planning, 20*, 349–360.

Appendix 1. A behavioural and operational typology of competitive intelligence practice.

Gathering	
Easy Gathering	Firms which use general publications and/or specific industry periodicals and think these constitute exhaustive information. Unlikely to commit resources to obtain information which may be difficult or costly to obtain. Always looking for an immediate return on investment
Hunter Gathering	*Firms knowing that easy gathering information is available to all who care to look. Realise that if CI is to have a strategic impact then additional, sustained effort is required. Resources are available which allow researchers to access sources within reasonable cost parameters, back their instinct, follow apparently irrelevant leads, spend time talking, brainstorming and thinking about CI problems without always being pressured for 'the answer'. Firms which appreciate and support intellectual effort*
Attitude	
Immune Attitude	Too busy thinking about today to worry about tomorrow. Thinks that the firm is either so small, so big or so special that it enjoys immunity from competitors and thus CI is a waste of time. Minimal or no support from either top management or other departments
Task-Driven Attitude	Finding answers to specific questions and extending what the firm knows about its competitors, usually on an ad-hoc basis. Departments more excited about CI than top management who do not see the benefits
Operational Attitude	A process, with the company at its centre, trying to understand, analyse and interpret markets. Top management usually trying to develop a positive attitude towards CI because they can see it might increase profit, and therefore personal bonuses. Unwilling or unable to think about the application of CI for the long term
Strategic Attitude	*An integrated procedure, in which competitors are determined as those who are satisfying our customers' needs, current and/or future. Monitoring their moves, anticipating what they will do next and working out response strategies. Receives both top management support, co-operation from other departments and is recognised by all as essential for future success*
Use	
Joneses User	Firms trying to obtain answers to disparate questions with no organisational learning taking place. Has commissioned a CI report from a consultant because that is what everybody else has done
Knee-Jerk User	Firms which obtain some CI data, fail to assess its quality or impact, yet act immediately. Can often lead to wasted and inappropriate effort, sometimes with damaging results. Such firms are most vulnerable to planted mis-information by competitors who are more CI aware
Tactical User	CI used mostly to inform tactical measures such as price changes, promotional effort. Some firms can successfully argue that CI loses its impact and timeliness if it gets stuck at the strategic level but are, nevertheless, acutely aware of its potential value to the business

(continued)

Appendix 1. (*Continued*).

Strategic User	*CI is used to identify opportunities/threats in the industry and to aid effective strategic decision making. All levels of staff, management and operational, are aware of Critical Success Factor (CSFs) and their attendant CI requirements. Continuous, legal measures used to track competitors, simulate their strengths and weaknesses, build scenarios and plan effective counter attacks. CI data are applied to 'what-if?' discussions. Contingency planning and counter intelligence is a part of normal strategic thinking. Action plans are implemented and mistakes are seized upon as learning, rather than blaming, opportunities. Open and facilitative management culture which displays trust and encourages involvement*
Location	
Ad-Hoc Location	No dedicated CI unit. Intelligence activities, where undertaken are on an ad-hoc basis, subsumed into other departments, with intermittent or non-existent sharing policies
Designated Location	*Firms with a specific intelligence unit, full-time staff, dedicated roles, addressing agreed strategic issues. Staff have easy access to decision makers, status is not a barrier to effective communication*
Technology support	
Simple Tech Support	The company is just using the free web such as a search engine or looking at some websites which require no specific knowledge. Also use general office software such as spreadsheet
Average Tech Support	Using off-the-shelf products such as meta-search engines which simply reorganise publicly available information for own use. Company might use websites requiring specific knowledge (e.g. Espacenet) and pay to use specialised websites and databases (e.g. patent and finance)
Advanced Tech Support	This information system holds vital and high level information as well as operational and tactical material. Is fully integrated across the business and continually evolves to meet the firm's requirements. Content analysis (e.g. statistical analysis) provided
High Tech Support	*In addition to advanced tools, firms use 'clever' algorithms aimed at understanding automatically the competitive information collected. These algorithms are based on semantics*
IT systems	
Dismissive IT Systems	Does not use any IT system to manage competitive information
Sceptic IT Systems	Has a system to manage competitive information but prefers to use paper based records. Does not trust IT systems sufficiently and is wary of their reliability
Standardised IT Systems	A standard existing system is purchased from a software vendor and installed on computers located within an organisation
Hosted IT Systems	A standard system is used, but it is not managed by the company itself (e.g. pay per view system)
Tailored IT Systems	In a tailored development, an off-the-shelf system or hosted solution is tailored according to an organisation's needs regarding its competitive information
Bespoke IT Systems	*Unique to the firm system which has been designed in-house and aiming at collecting, analysing and disseminating competitive information*

SMEs' attitude towards SI programmes: evidence from Belgium

Sophie Larivet[a] and François Brouard[b]

[a]ESCE, Pôle Universitaire Léonard de Vinci, Paris La Défense cedex, 92916, France; [b]Sprott School of Business, Carleton University, 1125 Colonel By Drive, 824 Dunton Tower, Ottawa, Ontario, K1S 5B6, Canada

This paper presents the findings of an empirical study of Strategic Intelligence (SI) in Belgian (Walloon) small and medium enterprises (SMEs). The main objective of the research was to take stock of the attitude towards SI initiatives directed at small businesses. More precisely, the research aimed to establish whether or not some threats to such programmes, identified by previous studies, needed to be taken into account in the Walloon approach. These threats mainly lay in the cognitive, affective and behavioural dimensions of SMEs' attitudes, used as a framework for analysis. A total of 250 phone interviews were carried out with the head or a top manager of each SME. The research reveals a lack of awareness of SI and SI programmes and a gap between the SMEs' self-confidence in their information level and their intelligence practices. In short, findings show that Wallonia is a virgin territory for SI and does not suffer from all the handicaps that have been identified in studies of other countries' programmes.

Introduction

Public policy supporting Competitive Intelligence (CI) is scarce. The involvement of the French government and public institutions in implementing a national CI programme, mainly directed towards SMEs, could even be considered unique (Smith, Wright, & Pickton, 2010). In her seminal research, Bergeron (2000) found that most countries do not focus on CI, but rather implement more general plans involving scientific and technological information, foresight, or knowledge management. In countries such as Sweden or the USA, private-based initiatives are more common. Therefore, the recent Belgian initiative of developing Strategic Intelligence (SI) in SMEs through a public institution, about 10 years after France implemented its policy, deserves attention. Previous research (Bergeron, 2000; Salles, 2001) has shown that SMEs' attitude might be a threat to CI programme implementation. In this particular setting, and based on a tri-component view of attitude, this paper addresses the issue of SME decision-makers' attitude towards SI programmes.

The outline of the article is as follows: the first section of the article describes the research context and the concept of SI. Research positioning and relevance are then explained, followed by the research question and framework. The next section delineates the methodology, followed by results and a discussion. Future research is suggested in the conclusion.

Research context: ASE's SI conception and programme

The *Agence de Stimulation Économique* (ASE; Economic Stimulation Agency) is a public institution created in 2006 as part of what is known as the Marshall Plan for Wallonia. Wallonia is the mainly French-speaking southern region of Belgium; over the past decades, it has suffered from a sharp decline in heavy industry. It has its own regional government, which launched this recovery plan in 2004. The Walloon government has charged the ASE with organising and co-ordinating a group of services and tools dedicated to entrepreneurs. One of these programmes consists of developing SI among SMEs and is the first large-scale SI development project in Belgium.

The expression SI was chosen by the ASE in order to differentiate from the French and Anglo-Saxon concepts of Economic Intelligence and CI (ASE, no date a). Nevertheless, the ASE definition of SI is very close to the French concept of Economic Intelligence. The Walloon organisation considers it a 'multidisciplinary approach based on three fundamental pillars: intelligence, protection, and influence' (ASE, no date b, authors' translation). This definition, similar to those of many French experts (Clerc, 1995; Harbulot, 1995; Larivet, 2004; Levet & Paturel, 1996), is broader than the Anglo-Saxon definition of CI. SI includes CI, defined by Wright and Pickton (1998, p. 76) as 'the strategic process of identifying, understanding and using Critical Success Factors', but also encompasses safety or security measures (designed to safeguard information and intangible assets such as knowledge, databases or reputation) and influence or lobbying practices.

The ASE programme is a public initiative directed towards SMEs that is more or less comparable to the French chambers of commerce programmes as depicted by Smith et al. (2010). The main difference is that the ASE SI network is made up of 'operators' that are far from being exclusively regional chambers of commerce but are still local economic development actors. Unlike in France, in Belgium SI is not considered to be a responsibility for the State although state institutions might play a role (for instance, a draft agreement concerning the protection aspects was signed with the Belgian State Security Service). Besides, even though its geographic and language proximity made France the main benchmark over other countries, the ASE wanted to avoid one of the French pitfalls in using the concept of Economic Intelligence: the confusion with economic espionage. This confusion is so frequent in France that some chambers of commerce no longer use the expression Economic Intelligence, fearing negative reactions from entrepreneurs (Smith et al., 2010). Consequently, when the ASE started its own programme in 2007, it decided to adopt the use of an expression that French speakers would not be as likely to associate with illegal practices.

As in French chambers of commerce, the ASE programme includes awareness actions (such as conferences), training (several theoretical and practical training sessions about different aspects of SI) and coaching (SI audits and personalised advising). By the end of 2010, awareness programmes had reached 680 SMEs, training sessions were delivered to 140 SMEs and 99 SMEs had been individually coached (ASE, personal communication, 19 November 2010). These SMEs had been subjectively selected by Walloon economic development operators. At this stage of the programme, the ASE felt a need for further investigation in order to design future programmes. They thus decided to survey two samples: first, SMEs that had been trained in SI, and second, a random sample of SMEs. This second part of the research is presented in this article.

Research positioning and relevance

Engaged research

This research, as it was initiated by the ASE, is in line with what Van de Ven (2007) calls 'engaged scholarship', that is, a participative form of research involving academics and practitioners working together to solve a problem. According to Van de Ven (2007), this co-production of knowledge is better grounded and more insightful and useful than research conducted by researchers alone.

In pursuance of engaged scholarship principles, each step of the research was co-constructed by the various stakeholders. Among them, the ASE started and funded the project. Several people from the ASE, mainly the Director, the Head of SI and Innovation and an SI coach, were involved in the research process. A marketing agency named Expansion was also part of the project, mainly through two senior consultants. Their competencies lay in designing and conducting a quantitative survey and in making recommendations about how to promote the SI programme. One of the authors of this paper was engaged in each step of the research process and frequently interacted with the other actors, developing a closer relationship to the setting, whereas the other one was positioned as a 'detached, impartial onlooker' (Van de Ven, 2007, p. 269) with a less context-specific point of view. Both researchers were already familiar with SI in SMEs. Other stakeholders, mainly professors, other SI experts and local economic actors, took a small part in the data interpretation step.

Thus, each research activity, notably problem formulation, research design and recommendations, was negotiated and shared or discussed by some or all participants, depending on their competencies. The objective was to try to meet the goal of both scholarly quality and practical relevance (Pettigrew, 2001), with researchers and practitioners acting as equals in the process (Van de Ven, 2007).

This research positioning made it compulsory for the ASE and researchers to share an interest in SI in Walloon SMEs. The ASE's concern with the subject and setting of the research is obvious, but the academic relevance should be further detailed.

Academic relevance

One reason for our interest in this research was that no study of CI or SI had ever been done in Wallonia. A quantitative survey of CI in Belgium (and South Africa) was published by De Pelsmacker et al., in 2005 (see also Saayman et al., 2008), but the Belgian sample was made up of Flemish companies only, and is thus nearly impossible to consider as a study of the same country. In practical terms, Flanders and Wallonia can be regarded as two separate countries, even if they officially make up one state. Indeed, 'business and social conditions in Flanders, Brussels-Capital, and Wallonia have always been significantly different and will probably become more so' (Economist Intelligence Unit, 2010, p. 8).

The context of the Walloon and Belgian economy also created a good case for studying this region. Belgium is the 20th largest economy in terms of gross domestic product (International Monetary Fund, 2010), and Wallonia's contribution to the Gross Domestic Product (GDP) is greater than that of Flanders (Institut Wallon de l'Evaluation, de la Prospective et de la Statistique, 2011). Moreover, Belgium is ranked just before Sweden, known as a CI benchmark (Bergeron, 2000; Commissariat Général du Plan, 1994).

In addition, for a number of reasons, we do not fully agree with Wright and Calof (2006) when they suggest that country-level studies are now of little use because they remain at the macro level. First, this kind of applied research is useful for practitioners, which is one of the objectives of engaged research. The ASE initiative is directly inspired by similar French initiatives, but awareness, culture and attitude towards SI might be different in Belgium and thus have consequences for the programme design. According to Bergeron (2000), some national cultural traits might favour CI programme implementation. Second, as stated by Wright and Calof (2006) themselves, some of the numerous CI country-level studies they have examined present measurement problems. Before them, Bergeron (2000) had been more severe, writing that some nations' reputations for CI, such as those of Sweden or Japan, might be based on misunderstandings, exaggerations, scarce examples frequently repeated or, at the least, lack of sufficient documentation. There is thus room for improvement. A third reason why repeated country-level surveys remain interesting is that awareness, attitudes, and behaviour might change over the years. Smith, Wright and Pickton (2011) suggest that this is the case in France after over 10 years of public initiatives.

Lastly, CI research focusing on small businesses is not a saturated field. As far as we can tell, SME-focused research has been conducted in a rather small number of countries: Canada; France; Switzerland; Turkey; and the USA (Bergeron, 2000; Brouard, 2006; Bulinge, 2002; Groom & David, 2001; Koseoglu, Karayormuk, Parnell, & Menefee 2011; Larivet, 2004; Madinier, 2007; Phanuel & Levy, 2002; Salles 2001; Smith et al., 2010; Tarraf & Molz 2006; Wright, Bisson, & Duffy 2011). Burt's (2005, p. 245) invitation still seems relevant in this particular field: 'When you have an opportunity to learn how someone in another group does what you do differently – go.'

Research question and framework

As explained above, the ASE SI programme was built following the French example. From 2007 to 2010, the ASE and its network of 'operators' experimented with awareness, training and coaching sessions. The latter were often offered to SMEs whose dynamism or innovativeness gave the ASE a reason to believe that their owners would have a positive attitude toward SI and the SI programme. Before enlarging its offer to the general Walloon SME population, the ASE needed to take stock of the attitudes of Walloon SME decision-makers towards SI programmes and of their intention to participate in such programmes. Considering the centrality of the decision-maker in SMEs, 'SMEs' will be used as shorthand for 'SME decision-makers' in the paragraphs below.

Even if recent theory shows a far more complex process, attitude is still considered an antecedent to intention, which is an antecedent to behaviour (Ajzen, 2005). Here the research objective was not to draw a predictive model of the demand for ASE programmes, but to explore Walloon SMEs' attitude and intention towards such programmes, in order to detect any potential threats that could prevent SMEs from participating in SI programmes. As a matter of fact, previous work had identified threats to the development of CI initiatives; these threats can be categorised into attitudinal (cognitive, affective, behavioural) dimensions using Rosenberg and Hovland's (1960) tri-component model.

Threats related to the cognitive dimension

In her seminal work, Bergeron (2000) describes the lack of an informational and strategic culture. As many authors have found (Bergeron, 2000; Larivet, 2004; Smith et al., 2010), the majority of SMEs lack a clear understanding of SI (or the similar term used in different countries), seeing the concept as vague or abstract (Brouard, 2006; Smith et al., 2010). SMEs are not always conscious of their needs, or their needs can be unclear. Salles (2001) thus notes aberrations in the expression of information needs in SMEs. For instance, SMEs engaged in cost and delay reduction plans do not feel the need to collect information about production. Bergeron (2000) concludes that the importance of CI is simply not recognised, and that SMEs are thus unfamiliar with CI programmes.

Threats related to the affective dimension

In France, which is very close to Wallonia in terms of language and geography, CI is often associated with economic espionage (Smith et al., 2010). The confusion is even considered to be responsible for a negative emotional response (fear or mistrust) to the promotion of CI programmes. The research group therefore decided to make the following hypothesis: SMEs might feel reluctant or hesitant about SI programmes, with the idea that 'SI is for big companies only'. Many authors (cf. Bulinge, 2001; Phanuel & Levy, 2002; Salles, 2001) have indeed noticed a size effect on firms' practices. SMEs might thus not feel concerned by SI questions.

Threats related to the behavioural dimension

According to Bergeron (2000), there is no real demand for CI programmes from SMEs, due to a lack of awareness. One of the French CI directors quoted by Smith et al. (2010, p. 530) says, 'I've never had an SME come to me ask – I need help with CI.' Other behaviours also have to be taken into account: for instance, exporting is considered to be related to CI practices (Phanuel & Levy 2002; Salles, 2001). Bergeron (2000) sees globalisation as a contributing factor to the development of CI programmes. Not having an international presence, or not wishing to have one, could have a negative (behavioural) impact on the demand for SI programmes. Finally, how actively Walloon SMEs are practising SI could be a threat for the development of SI programmes (if they are already very proactive), or would require a level adaptation. Previous research (Bergeron, 2000; Brouard, 2006; Bulinge, 2002; Groom & David, 2001; Koseoglu et al., 2011; Larivet 2004; Madinier 2007; Phanuel & Levy 2002; Salles 2001; Smith et al., 2010; Tarraf & Molz 2006; Wright et al., 2011) generally agrees that in each country studied, some SMEs do practise CI or SI, even if very proactive small businesses are rare.

Methodology

Questionnaire

The previous theoretical framework served as a guide to analysing potential threats to the ASE programme. Assessing these threats required building a new tool. Previous studies, such as those of Rouach and Santi (2001) or Wright, Pickton, and Callow (2002) were not replicable because they were designed for companies already aware of the concept. As 79% of Walloon SMEs employ between five and 20 employees (COFACE/EuroDB, 2007, quoted by Agence Wallonne des Télécommunications, 2007), it seemed highly probable, given previous research, that most of them would not know what SI is.

Consequently, a new questionnaire was built that involved 33 questions divided into eight topics (see Table 1). Yes/no questions, scaled questions and open-ended questions were used as described in Table 1. The questionnaire was written and administered in French (the translation in Table 1 was done for academic purposes only).

Sampling method

The survey was administered from 20 August to 8 September 2010. SMEs' names and phone numbers were extracted from the Ketels database, developed by the Spectron

Table 1.   Questionnaire structure.

Topic 1: Firm's satisfaction about its information level	Q1: Do you know your current clients' needs? *[semantic scale]*
	Q2: Do you know your prospects' needs? *[semantic scale]*
	Q4: Tell me if you keep yourself informed about developments in the following elements in your environment:
	   - Q4a: your Belgian competitors *[semantic scale]*
	   - Q4b: your foreign competitors *[semantic scale]*
	   - Q4c: your current or potential suppliers *[semantic scale]*
	   - Q4d: technologies and production methods useful to your company *[semantic scale]*
	   - Q4e: changes in regulations *[semantic scale]*

Topic 2: Strategic practices	Q3: Most of the time, when you approach a new market, it is *[a) to respond to a client's needs / b) to retaliate to a competitor's move / c) to seek out a new opportunity / d) through chance meeting or reading]* Q5: How often do you make strategic plans? *[semantic scale]* Q6: When was the last time you launched a new service/product in Belgium? *[semantic scale]* Q7: When was the last time you launched a new service/product outside Belgium? *[semantic scale]*
Topic 3: Spontaneous perception of SI	Q8: Could you tell me in a few words what the concept of 'Strategic Intelligence' means to you? *[open-ended question]* Q9: [only if they didn't answer 'I don't know' to Q8]: How did you become aware of what SI is? *[open-ended question]*

Before they proceeded to the following questions, telemarketers briefly explained SI:

'From now, we will call SI a business approach that consists of Strategic Information literacy and protection, including three practices: environmental scanning; information protection; and influence.'

Topic 4: Opinion about SI	Q10: Assess your level of concern about each of the following topics:
	   - Q10a: environmental scanning *[semantic scale]*
	   - Q10b: information protection *[semantic scale]*
	   - Q10c: influence and lobbying *[semantic scale]*
	Q11: Assess your level of command of each of the following topics:
	   - Q11a: environmental scanning *[semantic scale]*
	   - Q11b: information protection *[semantic scale]*
	   - Q11c: influence and lobbying *[semantic scale]*
	
	Q12: Do you agree with the following statements?
	   - Q12a: SI is only for big companies. *[Likert scale]*
	   - Q12b: SI can help in defining strategic medium- and long-term goals. *[Likert scale]*
	   - Q12c: SI is useful for the growth of your company. *[Likert scale]*
	   - Q12d: SI might help to position your company against the competition. *[Likert scale]*
	   - Q12e: SI is useful for international development. *[Likert scale]*
	Q20: Do you think that SI should be taught to future managers? *[yes / no / no opinion]*

Topic 5: SI practices	Q13: Which types of intelligence does your company do? *[Cite items, several answers accepted: Competitor intelligence / Client intelligence / Supplier intelligence / Technological intelligence, generally speaking / Patent intelligence / Brand intelligence / Political intelligence / Regulation intelligence / Public market intelligence / Others (which?) / None]*

(continued)

Table 1. (*Continued*).

	Q14: We are now going to talk about information search methods (for instance, the use of search engines, databases, specific software, libraries). Generally speaking, do you think that the use of these methods in your company, is *[very insufficient / insufficient / quite adequate / satisfying / very satisfying]*?
	Q15: How do you get information about your competitors? *[Cite items, several answers accepted: Internet / Clients / Suppliers / Sales force / External consultants / Others (which?) / Not applicable]*
	Q16a: Has your company faced a malicious attack? *[Yes / no / I don't know]*
	Q16b: If yes, of what nature? *[Cite items, several answers accepted: Data theft / Equipment / Material theft / Employee / Deception operation / Hacking / Other (which?)]*
	Q17: Have you ever called in external consultants in that field? *[yes / no]*
	Q18: I am now going to read you different statements about your company's influence. Tell me if you agree with them or not.
	Q18a: My company knows how to influence public opinion. *[Likert scale]*
	Q18b: My company contributes to the development of norms and regulations in our sector. *[Likert scale]*
	Q18c: My company uses the Internet to improve its reputation. *[Likert scale]*
	Q18d: My company is capable of reaching public decision-makers if needed. *[Likert scale]*
Topic 6: SI actors	Q19: As far as you know, who are the SI specialists in Wallonia? *[Open-ended question]*
Topic 7: Company and respondent identity	Q21: What is your position in your company? *[Open-ended question]*
	Q22: When was your company established? *[Open-ended question]*
	Q23: Which stage of the life cycle is your company in? *[Being set up or just set up / Development or growth / Handing over]*
	Q24: Sector? *[Open-ended question]*
	Q25: Is your company part of a corporate group?
	Q26: Turnover in 2009?
	Q27: In comparison with 2008, your 2009 turnover was *[More than 10% lower / Less than 10% lower / Stable / Less than 10% higher /More than 10% higher]*
	Q28: Your current clients' origin is mostly *[Regional / National / European / Worldwide]*
	Q29: In the medium term, your clients' origin will be *[Regional / National / European / Worldwide]*
	Q30: Percentage of export sales in your turnover?
	Q31: Are you a member of *[A professional federation / A Walloon cluster / A competitiveness cluster / A chamber of commerce / Union des Classes Moyennes / Union Wallonne des Entreprises / A social economy federation]*?
Topic 8: Interest in/intention for SI training	Q32: The ASE organises SI training sessions in your region. Would you like to receive more information about them? *[yes / no]*
	Q33: Would you be interested in pursuing more intensive and diploma SI training ? *[yes / no / don't know]*

Company, which is known as one of the most complete and up-to-date databases in Belgium. The target population consisted of Walloon SMEs employing between three and 250 employees, with the exception of companies belonging to sectors that are not eligible for the European Regional Development Fund (ERDF). Only eligible companies can receive ASE support, precisely because the ASE's mission is to co-ordinate economic stimulation projects that are co-funded by ERDF and other European funds. In short, the surveyed companies belonged to the following sectors: manufacturing; wholesale trade; building and civil engineering; freight transport; B-to-B services; agriculture; forestry; and mining (for an exhaustive non-eligible sectors list, see Service Public de Wallonie, 2010). The targeted population represented a total of about 13,000 companies. Random sampling was used to select a sample of 1000 SMEs.

Phone survey software was used to select randomly the order of the phone calls. Telemarketers made the calls until 250 questionnaires were completed and usable (this number was chosen considering time, budget and representativeness issues). Only heads of SMEs or top managers were interviewed. The final error of margin was $\pm 6.1\%$ for a 95% confidence interval.

Sample profile

Of the respondents, 85% were very small companies (under 20 full-time equivalent employees). This is quite similar to the Walloon average of 79%. Due to the sampling choice, it is difficult to compare the sample structure in terms of sectors to the overall Walloon SME population. The construction sector made up 38% of respondents; this sector is indeed the largest among Walloon SMEs (Agence Wallonne des Télécommunications, 2007). The remaining sectors broke down as follows: 23% of respondents belonged to the manufacturing sector, 17% to the service industry (mainly business to business (B-to-B) services), 12% wholesalers, 5% transport-related companies and 5% agriculture, forestry or mining firms.

A full 81% of respondents said that their clients are mainly national or regional; 71% thought that their clientele would not change in the future. A chi-square test clearly indicates that this result is not simply a sector effect due to the high proportion of construction companies.

Results

SI awareness

The concept of SI was unfamiliar to 66% of respondents, independent of their size. In our sample, medium firms (under 20 employees) were not more aware of SI than were very small ones. Only 20% spontaneously associated SI with the word 'strategy', while 6% thought of 'environmental scanning', 4% of 'anticipation' and 2.8% of 'information seeking'. Only one firm associated SI with protection, and none with influence or lobbying, the two other SI pillars. In short, Walloon SMEs did not understand the concept of SI, and a full 93% of them were unable to name a single SI Walloon specialist.

Importance of SI

After having heard a short explanation of SI (the 'three pillars' definition), SMEs had a globally positive understanding of the concept. A majority of 70.3% (fully or mostly) agreed that SI is useful for the growth of a company (14.1% disagreed), 66% thought that

SI can help in defining strategic medium- and long-term goals (10.9% disagreed), and 63.7% assumed that it helps to position the company against competition (14.5% did not). However, most respondents were not convinced that it is useful for international development (only 47.4% agreed with the statement).

Belief about own practices

A large proportion, 86%, of Walloon SMEs think they understand their clients' needs well or very well, and 67% are confident in their knowledge of their prospects' needs. SMEs' self-confidence is somewhat lower, but still significant, concerning other parts of their environment: 71.5% think they manage to stay informed about their current or potential suppliers quite or very easily (for 6% it is quite or very difficult); 68.5% think they manage to stay informed about technologies and production methods useful to the company quite or very easily (for 10.3% it is quite or very difficult).

However, SMEs recognise that it can be difficult to stay informed about regulations (48% said quite or very easily vs. 30.6% quite or very difficult) and competitors: 44.3% thought they managed to stay informed about their Belgian competitors quite or very easily (vs. 21% who said quite or very difficult), whereas only 24.5% thought they got information about their foreign competitors quite or very easily (vs. 51.1% quite or very difficult).

A substantial majority of 83% are satisfied or very satisfied with their information-seeking methods. But when asked to self-evaluate their SI skills, only 39.3% thought they had a (very or quite) good level of command of environmental scanning (21.5% a bad or very bad level). This is a first sign of the gap between the self-confidence shown in their previous declarations and their practices.

Practices

Looking more closely at the behaviour of SMEs, results show that only 48% watch their clients, 37% their competitors and 26% their suppliers. Only 25% do general technological intelligence, while 22% do legal intelligence. Brand and patent intelligence is practised by less than 7% of SMEs. No sector effect was detected (industrial firms might have been more attentive to patents, for instance, but that was not the case). In short, they practise little or no environmental scanning. The same types of results are found concerning the other SI pillars (protection and influence). Less than half the firms said they have an influence on public opinion, public decision-makers or norms. Only 17% had already obtained external help to protect information.

Walloon SMEs scarcely use the usual intelligence sources: in decreasing order, 36% use the Internet, 28% their clients, 22% their suppliers, 17% word-of-mouth and 11% their sales force and so on, while only 5% search in legal publications and 2% use trade shows. None of them mentioned spying.

Another interesting finding is that only 32% of SMEs approach new markets by seeking out a new opportunity, and 8% in reaction to a competitor's move. Most of them simply respond to their clients' needs (66%).

SMEs and SI programmes

Respondents showed interest in SI: 64.4% thought that SI should be taught to future managers, and 60.4% asked for more information about ASE training sessions. As many as 20.8% would be interested in pursuing intensive training to qualify in SI.

Feelings about SI

SMEs are moderately concerned by SI: 41.16% feel (very or rather) concerned about environmental scanning (29.7% don't); 44.6% feel (very or rather) worried about information protection (34.9% don't); and 35% only feel (very or rather) concerned about influence and lobbying (39.5% don't). However, they do not consider SI to be a practice for 'big companies only' (53.1% disagree with this idea vs. 32.9% who agree).

Quite surprisingly, not a single Walloon SME associated SI with espionage, economic patriotism or any other practice that could frighten a small business away from SI.

Discussion, research and managerial implications

A synthesis of results using the tri-component framework is presented in Table 2. One can hardly say that Walloon SMEs have a negative attitude towards SI or SI programmes, but some issues might be challenging for the ASE.

Wallonia, a virgin territory for SI

The Walloon SMEs' ignorance of the SI concept is remarkably high, compared to the 53% calculated by Larivet (2004) in France 10 years ago, when SI public programmes were beginning there. The spontaneous association with strategy by (only) 20% of respondents might be tautological reasoning. However, this lack of knowledge of the concept might be considered a threat to the ASE programme. To avoid the Canadian pitfall in regional programmes identified by Bergeron (2000) in a lack of awareness campaigns, the ASE

Table 2.   Walloon SMEs' attitude and intention to follow a SI programme.

Attitude	Threats to SI programme	Opportunities for SI programme
Cognitive	- 66% of SMEs don't know what SI is - 93% of SMEs don't know a single SI actor - SI importance for international development is not recognised - SMEs think they are well informed about clients, suppliers, technologies and production methods - SMES are satisfied with their information-seeking methods - SMEs are not conscious of their needs	- SI importance is recognised for growth, facing the competition & defining goals - SMEs don't think it is easy to stay informed about competitors and regulation evolutions - SMEs think they have an average level of SI - SMEs think SI should be taught to future managers
Affective		- SI is not associated with economic espionage (no fear) - SI is not associated with big companies (no reluctance)
	- SME moderately worried by SI questions (self-confidence)	
Behavioural	- SMEs have primarily Belgian clients and don't foresee (want?) any change - SMEs are mostly passive	- SMEs don't practise SI or even environmental scanning - SMEs don't use many of the usual intelligence sources - SMEs asked to receive more information about SI training sessions
Intention	About 1/5 interested in pursuing a training session leading to a diploma	

should consider a campaign of mass communication of the concept to make it more familiar to SMEs.

More worrying is the abysmal ignorance of the existence of local SI operators, which confirms previous statements about the lack of knowledge of SI programmes (Bergeron, 2000). There should be local communication campaigns by each actor to explain its SI role. Unlike in France, all of the Walloon SI operators have different names (BEP, SPI +, CCI, IDELUX, IDETA) and various legal statuses, which make them more difficult to identify. In this case, the ASE might try to appear as a one-stop SI service and communicate in its own name. A kind of SI brand or label could also be useful to unify the SI actors' publicity.

However, the poor SI awareness is not entirely negative. On the contrary, the fact that SMEs have no prejudice against SI might help the ASE to develop a more positive initial SI perception than, for example, this perception had been in France. Wallonia is a virgin territory for SI.

An overall positive attitude

It is tempting to use a review of Table 2 to make a final assessment of Walloon attitude and intention to participate in an ASE programme. An overview would indicate that the global attitude is quite good and that the ASE can easily reduce many of the threats. Communication, education initiatives and testimonies of previously trained (and satisfied) SMEs would help other SMEs to become more conscious of the room for progress and could have an effect on threatening cognitive items.

Affective threats are not salient, even if the size of the company was also found to be related to SI worries (chi-square test). Even if they were no more aware of the SI concept than were smaller firms, companies over 20 employees reported worrying more about it. This result is a step in the direction of previous qualitative findings about 20 employees being a 'pivotal size in terms of SME manager involvement' (Smith et al., 2010, p. 534). The ASE could take this pivotal size into account and target companies over 20 employees.

Concerning the behavioural dimension, the fact that SMEs do not currently practise SI is the justification for the ASE programmes. In fact, the intention to participate is not as low as expected, considering the results of Bergeron (2000). The demand for more information is encouraging: a full one-fifth of respondents have the intention to participate in a qualifying programme. Even if the links between attitude, intention and behaviour are not that simple, these positive signs are encouraging.

Of more concern are the two behavioural threats that have been identified. One is that Walloon SMEs are not willing to grow outside their borders, which could be a problem, considering the very small size of the internal Walloon or even Belgian market and the economic situation the country is facing. The other one is the passivity of some Walloon SMEs: they choose just to follow their clients and rarely react to the competition. These SMEs belong to the 'immune/passive' categories identified by Rouach and Santi (2001) and Wright et al. (2002). Far beyond the issue of SI, this problem raises strategic questions as well as questions of strategy (strategic autonomy, strategic culture, etc.).

Unconscious needs, practice and measurement problems

A final examination of Table 2 shows that, generally speaking, SMEs have environmental scanning or SI practices that lack consistency with their self-confidence about their level of information. The intuition of Salles (2001) about 'aberrations' in terms of SMEs' SI needs is confirmed. It seems almost as if these firms are unconscious of their needs. Given their ignorance about SI, it becomes very difficult to question them directly about their expectations, needs or even attitude towards SI.

SI attitude or behaviour measurement problems are not new (Brouard, 2006; Larivet, 2004; Wright & Callof, 2006), but they are particularly crucial in a small business context. SMEs' ignorance of SI terminology and informal practices are two of the main reasons why such substantial size effects are found when examining SI practices (Larivet, 2009). This bias is too often ignored. In most countries, it is almost impossible to use direct measures with SMEs; if at all, they must be done very carefully. Some attempts to confront these difficulties have been made by using indirect measures and scales (Larivet, 2004; Wright & Calof, 2006), or by using 'informed informants', to paraphrase Ganesh, Miree, and Prescott (2003, quoted by Smith et al., 2010). The solution definitely does not lie in rejecting from the samples the decision-makers who are unable to answer survey questions (Koseoglu et al., 2011), but in working harder on building good measurement instruments specifically dedicated to SMEs.

Wright and Calof (2006) are right to suggest the use of other fields' tools and to ask for more studies about 'how' CI is practised. However, their claim should not be understood as putting a stop to 'whether' (SI is practised) studies, but rather encouraging researchers to design them better. In the case of small businesses at least, the measurement of 'whether' is deeply linked to the measurement of 'how' something is concretely done (Brouard, 2006). For instance, looking for a formalised CI organisation in a small business would probably lead to the conclusion that the firm is not CI oriented, which might in fact be false. 'Whether' and 'how' are not opposing concepts but in fact complete each other.

Conclusion

This research has limitations, mainly typical of 'engaged research' constraints: it is descriptive, it is exploratory regarding its theoretical framework, the sample only takes into account sectors eligible for ASE support and the margin of error could be improved by interviewing more companies.

However, even taking these limitations into account, this survey answers a certain number of questions about Walloon SMEs' attitudes. It shows their lack of awareness concerning SI and SI programmes but reveals that the concept has not been contaminated by the French prejudice about espionage and has (when explained) a quite positive image. It also reveals a gap between the quite high level of confidence that SMEs have in their information level and their concrete intelligence practices. It would seem that SMEs are unsure of their needs or the opportunities that SI practice could open for them. At the same time, there seems to be some demand for information and training sessions. Furthermore, making SMEs aware of the usefulness of SI does not necessarily mean they will engage in SI if they lack the resources for it.

Finally, the exploratory use of the tri-component view of attitude reveals that it is a promising concept for future research. As already suggested by Smith et al. (2010), a deeper investigation into the theories and constructs surrounding attitude should help researchers to develop solid theoretical foundations for CI research.

Acknowledgements

The authors want to thank all the participants in this work of 'engaged scholarship', more specifically: Vincent Bory, director of ASE, Claude Lepère, former Head of SI and Innovation at

ASE, Olivia Santus, SI coach at ASE and Hadrienne Flahaux and her colleagues at Expansion. Thank you to all the Walloon SI actors, experts and also absolute beginners for their useful contributions and feedback. We are indebted to Maria Crawford for her manuscript editing. Many thanks to Sheila Wright and Jamie Smith for their always inspirational research and useful comments.

References

Agence de Stimulation Économique. (no date a). *Origine de l'Intelligence Stratégique* [Origin of Strategic Intelligence]. Retrieved from http://www.intelligencestrategique.be/site/ase_is-fr/ intelligence-strategique/origine-de-l-intelligence-strategique.html

Agence de Stimulation Économique. (no date b). *Les piliers de l'Intelligence Stratégique* [Strategic Intelligence pillars]. Retrieved from http://www.intelligencestrategique.be/site/ase_is-fr/ intelligence-strategique/les-piliers-de-l-intelligence-strategique/index.html

Agence Wallonne des Télécommunications. (2007). *PME wallonnes: Usages TIC 2006* [Walloon SMEs: ICT uses 2006]. Retrieved from http://www.awt.be/web/dem/index.aspx?page= dem,fr,pme,010,002

Ajzen, I. (2005). *Attitudes, personality, and behavior* (2nd ed.). Milton-Keynes: Open University Press/McGraw-Hill.

Bergeron, P (2000). *Veille stratégique et PME: Comparaison des politiques gouvernementales de soutien* [Competitive Intelligence and SMEs: A comparison between governmental support policies]. Sainte-Foy: Presses Universitaires du Québec.

Brouard, F. (2006). Development of an expert system on environmental scanning practices in SME: Tools as a research program. *Journal of Competitive Intelligence and Management, 3*(4), 37–58.

Bulinge, F. (2001, October 2). *PME-PMI et intelligence compétitive: les difficultiés d'un mariage de raison* [SMEs and competitive intelligence: Difficulties of a marriage in name only]. Proceedings of Veille Stratégique Scientifique & Technologique Conference, Barcelona, pp. 245–256.

Bulinge, F. (2002). *Pour une culture de l'information dans les petites et moyennes organisations: Un modèle incrémental d'intelligence économique* [In favour of an information culture in small and medium businesses: An incremental model of Economic Intelligence] (Doctoral dissertation). Retrieved from http://www.veille.com/ie/publications/these_franck_bulinge.pdf

Burt, R.S. (2005). *Brokerage and closure: An introduction to social capital.* Oxford, NY: Oxford University Press.

Clerc, P. (1995). Intelligence économique et stratégie [Economic Intelligence and strategy]. In *Encyclopedia Universalis* (pp. 194–197). Paris: Universalia.

Commissariat Général du Plan. (1994). *Intelligence économique et stratégie des entreprises* [Economic Intelligence and firms' strategies]. Paris: La Documentation Française.

De Pelsmacker, P.J., Muller, M.-L., Viviers, W., Saayman, A., Cuyvers, L., & Jegers, M. (2005). Competitive intelligence practices of South African and Belgian exporters. *Marketing Intelligence & Planning, 23*, 606–620.

Economist Intelligence Unit. (2010, February). *Financial services industry report: Belgium.* Retrieved from the Business Source Complete database, http://www.eiu.com/

Groom, J., & David, F. (2001). Competitive activity among small firms. *SAM Advanced Management Journal, 66*, 12–20.

Harbulot, C. (1995). *La machine de guerre économique: Etats-Unis, Japon, Europe* [The economic warfare machine: United States, Japan, Europe]. Paris: Economica.

Institut Wallon de l'Evaluation, de la Prospective et de la Statistique. (2011). *PIB volume* [GDP volume]. Retrieved from http://themes.iweps.be/content/Indicator_2094/

International Monetary Fund. (2010). *World economic outlook database.* Retrieved from http:// www.imf.org/external/pubs/ft/weo/2011/01/weodata/index.aspx

Koseoglu, M.A., Karayormuk, K., Parnell, J.A., & Menefee, M.L. (2011). Competitive Intelligence: Evidence from Turkish SMEs. *International Journal of Entrepreneurship and Small Business, 13*, 333–349.

Larivet, S. (2004). Les manifestations de l'intelligence économique en PME [Economic Intelligence manifestations in SMEs]. In A. Guilhon (Ed.), *L'intelligence économique dans la PME* [Economic Intelligence in SMEs] (pp. 129–148). Paris: L'Harmattan.

Larivet, S. (2009). *L'intelligence économique: Enquête dans 100 PME* [Economic Intelligence: A survey in 100 SMEs]. Paris: L'Harmattan.

Levet, J.-L., & Paturel, R. (1996, May). *L'intégration de la démarche d'intelligence économique dans le management stratégique* [The integration of the Economic Intelligence process into strategic management]. Proceedings of the Fifth International Conference of Strategic Management, Lille [CD-Rom].

Madinier, H. (2007). Quelle veille stratégique pour les PME de Suisse romande? [Which Competitive Intelligence for French-speaking Switzerland?]. *Documentaliste – Sciences de l'Information, 44*, 300–310.

Pettigrew, A.M. (2001). Management research after modernism. *British Journal of Management, 12*, S61–S70.

Phanuel, D., & Levy, D. (2002, June). *Intelligence économique ou économie d'intelligence dans les PME-PMI? L'exemple d'un département français* [Economic Intelligence or economy of intelligence? The example of a French department]. Proceedings of the Eleventh International Conference of Strategic Management, Paris [CD-Rom].

Rosenberg, M.J., & Hovland, C.I. (1960). Cognitive, affective, and behavioural components of attitudes. In C.I. Hovland & M.J. Rosenberg (Eds.), *Attitude organisation and change: An analysis of consistency among attitude components* (pp. 1–14). New Haven, CT: Yale University Press.

Rouach, D., & Santi, P. (2001). Competitive Intelligence adds value: Five intelligence attitudes. *European Management Journal, 19*, 552–559.

Saayman, A., Pienaar, J., de Pelsmacker, P.J., Viviers, W., Cuyvers, L., Muller, M.-L., & Jegers, M. (2008). Competitive Intelligence: Construct exploration, validation and equivalence. *Aslib Proceedings: New Information Perspectives, 60*, 383–411.

Salles, M. (2001, October). *Les besoins des PME en information d'Intelligence Economique: Présentation des résultats d'une enquête en Midi-Pyrénées* [SMEs' needs for information from Economic Intelligence: Presentation of the results of a survey in Midi-Pyrénées]. Proceedings of the Third Veille Stratégique Scientifique & Technologique Conference, Barcelona. Retrieved from http://ieut1.irit.fr/publications/Les_besoins_des_PME_en_information.pdf

Service Public de Wallonie. (2010, October). *Aide à l'investissement: Brochure d'information & notice explicative des formulaires de demande d'intervention* [Investment support: Information booklet and explanatory notice about intervention demand form]. Retrieved from http://formulaires.wallonie.be/Formulaires/NoticeAideInvestissement.pdf

Smith, J.R., Wright, S., & Pickton, D. (2010). Competitive Intelligence programmes for SMEs in France: Evidence of changing attitudes. *Journal of Strategic Marketing, 18*, 523–536.

Smith, J.R., Wright, S., & Pickton, D. (2011, July). *Competitive Intelligence effectiveness, terminology, and attitudes: Does size matter?* Proceedings of the Academy of Marketing Conference, Liverpool. Retrieved from https://marketing.conference-services.net/resources/327/2342/pdf/AM2011_0263.pdf

Tarraf, P., & Molz, R. (2006). Competitive Intelligence at small enterprises. *SAM Advanced Management Journal, 71*(4), 24–34.

Van de Ven, A.H. (2007). *Engaged scholarship: A guide to organizational and social research*. Oxford, NY: Oxford University Press.

Wright, S., Bisson, C., & Duffy, A. (2011, July). *A behavioural and operational typology of Competitive Intelligence practices in Turkish SMEs*. Proceedings of the Academy of Marketing Conference, Liverpool. Retrieved from https://marketing.conference-services.net/resources/327/2342/pdf/AM2011_0308.pdf

Wright, S., & Calof, J.L. (2006). The quest for competitive, business and marketing intelligence: A country comparison of current practices. *European Journal of Marketing, 40*, 453–465.

Wright, S., & Pickton, D. (1998, November). *Improved competitive strategy through value added Competitive Intelligence*. Proceedings of the Third Annual Society of Competitive Intelligence Professionals European Conference, Berlin, pp. 73–83.

Wright, S., Pickton, D.W., & Callow, J. (2002). Competitive Intelligence in UK firms: A typology. *Marketing Intelligence and Planning, 20*, 349–360.

Part II: Competitive Analysis

Leadership teams rediscover market analysis in seeking competitive advantage and growth during economic uncertainty

Lyndon Simkin[a] and Sally Dibb[b]

[a]Oxford Brookes University, Oxford, UK; [b]Open University, Milton Keynes, UK

Many of marketing's long-standing frameworks are finding an uprated role in the current economic turmoil. As companies' leadership teams strive to understand changing market dynamics, recognise that revenue streams are threatened, seek to provide customers with new propositions relevant to their evolving values and combat embattled rivals, core marketing analyses and strategic marketing tools are coming to the fore. In many organisations, it is the non-marketers amongst the leadership team that are turning to these marketing frameworks and incorporating market-led risk assessment of revenue streams to shape new business strategies. While this strategising does not necessarily involve marketers at this most senior level of decision making, it has put marketing's analytical and strategic components at the forefront of corporate decision making. This paper explains how, providing an insight into the strategising process emerging for undertaking such market-led risk assessment, opportunity identification, creation of bases for competing, strategic trade-offs and programme planning.

Many of marketing's long-standing frameworks are finding an uprated role in the current economic turmoil. As leadership teams strive to understand changing market dynamics and their implications, recognise that revenue streams are threatened and must be replaced, and seek to provide customers with new propositions relevant to their evolving values and purchasing needs, core marketing analyses and strategic marketing tools are coming to the fore. But not necessarily by marketers. In many organisations, it is the non-marketers amongst the leadership team that are turning to these marketing frameworks and incorporating market-led risk assessment of revenue streams in order to shape new-look business strategies.

While this strategising does not necessarily involve marketers at this most senior level of decision making, it certainly has put marketing's analytical and strategic components at the forefront of corporate decision making. This paper explains how and provides an insight into the strategising process emerging necessary for undertaking such market-led risk assessment, opportunity identification, strategic trade-offs and programme planning. We offer an insight into how chief executive officers (CEOs), chief financial officers (CFOs) and chief operating officers (COOs) are finding value in the marketing toolkit, as they seek to address economic meltdown and still achieve an edge over competitors. These insights stem partly from a survey of senior marketers, but also from working alongside a diverse set of corporations as they combat economic turmoil and rapidly altering market dynamics. The work builds on an earlier study of senior marketers and brand managers, in which the role of non-marketers adopting the strategic marketing toolkit was noted by many of the respondents. The paper overviews the approaches adopted by several large corporates, in order to illustrate how marketing's toolkit is benefiting organisations and their leadership teams.

Marketing in recession

The marketing mix is a long-established concept and is at the heart of brand management (cf. Elliott & Percy, 2007; Keller, 2007). Intuitively, it is to be expected that the current economic turmoil is altering corporate priorities and is impacting on the practices of brand management and the use of the marketing mix (e.g. Bush, 2009; Goodson & Walker, 2008; Mason & Staude, 2009; Spence, 2009; Veronikis, 2009). A study by us (cf. Simkin, 2010) indeed found that priorities for marketers were altering. This study also observed a growing expectation amongst directors on companies' leadership teams that their marketing colleagues would re-engineer their customer-facing propositions and brand strategies to show awareness of targeted consumers' changing priorities and new-found values.

There has been much published about how brands must demonstrate relevance and commitment to their consumers and trade customers, in order to ride out the current economic downturn (e.g. Bush, 2008; Keller, 2011; Marketing Society Forum, 2009; Passikoff, 2009; Ritson, 2009; Wong, 2009). It is not too surprising to find that these challenges are acknowledged by senior marketers and brand managers. The study by Simkin found that marketers' priorities, when faced with recession, were: (a) pricing manipulation; (b) the necessary repositioning of the brand's tone of voice; and (c) more cautious use of associated marketing communications, in order to be aligned to consumers' concerns for more judicious spending. Table 1 reveals the relative importance

Table 1. Marketing and brand managers' priorities.

The marketing mix elements now most important	% citing this aspect
Pricing strategy	92
Promos (P-O-S deals)	90
Branding	82
Tone of voice	82
MarComms	80
Digital	74
On-line activation	74
Product re-engineering/re-sizing	74
Portfolio clean-up/reduction	72
In-store activation	70
Packaging	68
Product development	62
Supply chain	60
Trade customer service	38
Channel selection/initiatives	34
Channel presence/penetration	30
Consumer service/support	18

Source: Simkin (2010).

to these marketers, of the executions of their brand strategies, to reflect the macro-drivers impacting on them and their consumers. Although the altered pecking order of marketers' tactics during recession is not the focus of this paper, the summary in Table 1 reveals the importance of market insight in order to make such decisions. The study also identified how the analytics of marketing were exciting senior decision-makers, who themselves were embracing such tools.

An unexpected finding from our poll of senior marketers' activities was that while they were tasked to re-engineer customer-facing propositions and modify brand strategy/ execution accordingly, non-marketing colleagues were themselves turning to the analytical toolkit of marketers in order to re-assess overall priorities for their businesses in terms of the opportunities to pursue, target market selection and the development of re-aligned business plans. Marketers were expected to re-think today's value propositions and ensure customers perceived relevancy in the company's brand, while the marketing toolkit was deemed highly pertinent to the leadership's re-thinking of the business plan and overall corporate strategy. Arguably, this poses a threat and an opportunity to marketers in these organisations.

The traditional strategic marketing process (cf. Dibb & Simkin, 2008; or McDonald & Wilson, 2011) that progresses from a process of market analysis, opportunity selection, target market choice and proposition development into execution of associated marketing programmes (cf. Piercy, 2008; or Hooley, Saunders, Piercy, & Nicoulaud, 2007), has become more routinised in many of these surveyed businesses, as they strive to maintain growth trajectories or simply retain market share. Perhaps this is not surprising, as marketing should be acting routinely as an organisation's radar or 'eyes and ears', sensing out changes in the market, opportunities and threats, and steering the business to re-align around changing customer expectations and competitive challenges (Keller, 2011; Srinivasan, Lilien, & Rangaswamy, 2005). However, in the vast majority of the businesses examined, the stimulus for such market-led strategising and planning was not the senior marketing team but the companies' leadership team and senior directors.

Follow-up interviews with those contacted in Simkin's original survey revealed that often CEOs and financial directors (FDs) are now turning to examinations of marketing environment drivers, competitor reviews, customer insights and capability audits in order to re-think strategies for turbulent times. Of the 100 companies contacted, 78% stated that without the Credit Crunch, this would not have occurred and there would have been no new market-led assessment of their business plans. The study revealed how many companies, including business to business (B2B) and business to consumer (B2C), goods and services had created revised strategic planning processes which harnessed the 'traditional' toolkit of marketing analysis and target market strategy development. This paper now focuses on several of these companies' processes in order to illustrate the types of strategising emerging and to reveal the role of marketing's toolkit in companies' business planning.

Corporate drivers

Our interviews and observations reveal that marketing is playing an increasing part in corporate re-shaping of strategies in the current economic uncertainty and turbulence, caused by global financial pressures and corporates faced with associated changing customer behaviours. However, it is not necessarily a firm's marketers who are instigating this or even involved, but their analytical toolkit – the long-standing strategic marketing armoury – is driving these businesses' strategic planning.

As the COO for a multi-billion defence and electronics corporation explains:

> We needed to sense-check our order projections to be certain about likely bookings and plug any shortfalls. A combination of (a) risk assessment based on customers' predicaments, *their* market drivers and financial constraints, (b) understanding where trading conditions are forcing competitors to seek revenue, sometimes at our expense, and (c) assessing emerging and potential opportunities, enabled us to maintain our growth trajectory and avoid unwelcome shortfalls in bookings and revenue. But we had to be better informed by market conditions and customers' requirements in these challenging times.

The process adopted by this company was designed to answer some fundamental questions in these changing circumstances, at a time when customers were re-appraising their priorities, some suppliers were struggling for viability, and US/UK governments were re-directing their budgets often away from certain defence projects. The leadership team had to answer these queries:

(1) Where has the money been coming from? Will it continue in this way? What do the market drivers/trends imply? What are the implications for us?

(2) Where is the money to come from? Both current and new sources/opportunities? How will we compensate at-risk orders?

(3) What are the resulting key objectives and implications for our strategy?

(4) What are the current unique selling points (USPs) and differentiators, plus current successes on which to build? Are they enough/adequate in the light of these analyses of market developments? Will we be credible in pursuing this revised strategy?

(5) What are the areas of weakness to sort out and the necessary actions? What must be changed in order to execute the emerging vision?

Risk assessing key accounts and order books is not new, nor is seeking growth opportunities. Combining them in a single strategising process, however, until now rarely has been the norm. The various tasks might have been undertaken, but not in a joined-up manner, simultaneously seeking to replace at-risk business with new opportunities or re-thought programmes. Often separate executives handled these tasks for very different reasons. Such a hybrid strategising process (Figure 1) – which also includes re-thinking target market strategy, the basis for competing, customer engagement and retention tactics, and which also appraises required capabilities, performance metrics and organisational alignment – has not been standard practice, and certainly not in these businesses.

In the leisure sector, the leading European player for gaming/gambling was similarly facing dramatically changing market conditions as recession forced consumers to re-think their spending priorities, major investment programmes in new super-casinos had to be re-thought because of changing political agendas, and the e-gaming revolution threatened traditional club, casino and betting shop operations. Decisions for how best to re-focus corporate priorities and ride the economic downturn impacting on consumers in core markets led the CEO and CFO to examine the drivers in the firm's core markets and to validate income projections. In order to maintain the corporation's growth projections and financial returns, additional opportunities had to be sought in order to rectify the dips in established operations revealed in their analyses, as explained by the company's CEO:

> We had a strong marketing team, good at supporting our separate businesses and engaging effectively with targeted consumers in those operations. Now we needed to harness such analytical prowess at a corporate level in order to fully inform major strategic trade-offs and steer our investment planning. Market analysis and market-informed risk planning fully

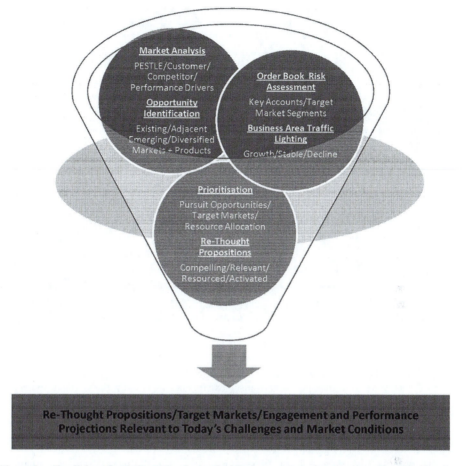

Figure 1.   Parallel market-informed order book risk assessment and new opportunity identification.

under-pinned the executive board's work. Without these market analyses, our strategy would not be as currently planned or our ability to combat emerging rivals.

In the cases of both businesses, a renewed interest in assessing market conditions, drivers and challenges re-directed the leaderships' strategic thinking and their planning. Understanding market trends, fast-changing customer priorities, competitor moves and financial performance – all standard analyses in the marketing toolkit – became front of mind for their leadership teams. A core component of such strategic planning was a risk assessment of expected incomes, but one informed by customers' pressures and altering priorities, competitor moves and the forces of the broader external trading environment. Economic and political uncertainty has led CFOs, COOs and CEOs to be highly motivated by learning about evolving conditions in core target markets.

The type of process emerging

A Vice President (VP) of a tier 1 US defence contractor expands:

For us, we had significant external turmoil and pressures on defence procurement. This coincided with constructing a new five-year plan. We decided to adopt a new-look approach, based on three core foundations: (1) an evaluation of market trends, threats and emerging

Phase I: Market analyses & risk assessment of revenues	Phase II: Strategic trade-offs & prioritisation	Phase III: Engagement & internal re-alignment
Analysis first – basis for decisions	Strategic decisions – informed by analyses	Engagement programmes – to deliver the emerging strategy
• Performance • Market sizes and trends • Market forces – PEST • Customer drivers • Competitors' developments • Traffic lighting of revenue streams – risk assessment • SWOT • Implications	• Likely revenues • Emerging opportunities • Attractiveness trade-offs • Capability shortfalls • Agreed priorities • Target market strategy • Basis for competing and positioning	• Sales & marketing programmes • Resourcing • Timelines • Responsibilities • Metrics & reporting • Reviews & remedial activities • Immediate and medium-term
➤ Risk assessment of existing orders/accounts. ➤ Acceptance of the urgency to generate additional revenues. ➤ Market-led opportunity analysis to address revenue shortfalls and generate growth.	➤ Trade-off choices to scope a viable and growth-led mix of pursuits. ➤ Understanding of the capability and organisational deficiencies for embracing the new vision. ➤ Target market strategy decisions and planning.	➤ Customer engagement activities and resourcing. ➤ Organisational re-structuring, skilling and capability development. ➤ Re-alignment of metrics and corporate performance expectations.

Figure 2.   Key activities and phase-by-phase outcomes.

opportunities, in existing markets but also new areas; (2) our technology roadmapping and projections; and (3) the anticipated shortfalls in existing contracts and with current customers – DoD and MoD mainly. We needed a process which included all of these elements, could be fulfilled in three to four months, would engender buy-in from our business areas, and which would add new options for growth.

The adopted process and principal activities were as in Figure 2.

The process that emerged for these corporates linked market analysis, financial forecasts and performance evaluation with opportunity selection, target market strategy and proposition development, before constructing go to market plans and full customer engagement programmes. These three phases are familiar to many marketers and strategists, and fit with suggested best practice (e.g. McDonald & Wilson, 2011; Slater, Hult, & Olson, 2010), but here the leadership teams – often without senior marketers present – were driving this market analysis-led process, one designed to stay ahead of fast-moving market changes, risk assess income streams and revenue forecasts, while opening up the field of vision for possible opportunities to help remedy glaring shortfalls in sales, and even achieving previously stated corporate growth expectations. In this way, these leadership teams aimed to stay abreast of market changes and ahead of the curve in terms of their competitors' ability to reflect changing customer priorities, which again reflected accepted best practice for strategy creation (cf. Casadesus-Masanell & Ricart, 2010; Day, 2006).

The primary drivers for these leadership teams were to:

(1) sense-check previous forecasts in the context of current market circumstances;
(2) rectify shortfalls by identifying additional opportunities;
(3) generate a platform for growth;
(4) seek to improve their organisations' capabilities and ability to deliver the agreed strategy;

(5) re-assess competitors;

(6) re-focus resource allocation around the most viable opportunities; and

(7) foster executive commitment to the new-look plan of action.

The leaders responsible for instigating such strategising wanted to 'get real' in the face of external market pressures and persuade colleagues to re-appraise their priorities. In all cases, there was a desire to ensure market dynamics and developments informed and directed the emerging strategy – a desire led by CEOs, FDs, COOs and not just marketing directors.

To these ends, the overall process often utilised was typically sequenced as in Figure 3, with clear milestones conveyed to core stakeholders and those selected to be part of the process. Step one was the market assessment, examining macro trends, opportunities and threats; performance; customer and competitor drivers; and the implications for existing revenues and planned bookings. This phase was intended to provide the insights necessary for developing a strategy and making the inevitable trade-offs faced when considering which new opportunities to pursue alongside certain retained current worthwhile activities. The strategy phase made the necessary trade-off choices between possible opportunities and target markets, and considered the overall revenue mix, alongside target market strategy, positioning and creation of a compelling and competitive proposition. The final phase (see also Figure 2) produced the engagement plan, aligned resourcing and determined changes necessary to combat the identified operational, resource, communication and behavioural blockers inside the organisations. In organisations with a strategic marketing director or VP, such a process and behaviour might not be unusual. However, in these cases, activities – informed by the market analysis toolkit – were being led by CFOs, COOs and CEOs struggling to come to terms with economic conditions and rapidly changing customer expectations.

Under-pinning this strategy process was a market intelligence-led analytical assessment of existing revenues or prospects, whether market, segment, product group or key account level. Such risk assessment of current income streams focused on red and amber 'traffic lighting', where red revenues were deemed highly vulnerable or certain to cease, and amber revenues were decidedly circumspect. Such decisions were based on insights into how

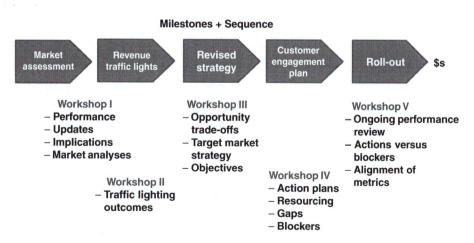

Figure 3.   Typical phasing of corporates' processes.

customers are altering their spending priorities, on competitors' enforced evolving strategies and on the ramifications from updated marketing environment (PESTLE) drivers on these businesses and their customers. In order to compensate for the inevitable shortfalls identified in such market-led risk assessment of bookings and forecasts, their processes also sought probable and possible market-led opportunities:

(1) consideration of PESTLE drivers and associated opportunities and threats;
(2) customer-led opportunities; and
(3) lessons to emulate from competitors.

In all cases, their assessment of opportunities borrowed from Ansoff's framework, thereby becoming an assessment of all emerging opportunities:

- Existing customers – existing products/programmes.
- Existing customers – new products/programmes.
- New customers – existing or new products/programmes.
- Adjacent markets – existing or new products/programmes.

However, their approach clearly included a reality check: whether suggested opportunities meshed with capabilities and a viable basis for competing. This would have impacted on likely success in achieving these desires, so strengths, USPs and differentiators for each identified income stream to pursue had to be considered.

Typical outcomes

For each of the businesses seen to be adopting this process, the so-called 'traffic lighting' risk assessment of current revenue streams and apparently secure bookings revealed only some to be 'green' and secure. This proportion in fact ranged from 40% to 60% across the businesses examined. All had a significant proportion flagged as 'amber' and thereby at risk of being terminated or reduced. Interestingly, several of these vulnerable accounts or orders had slipped somewhat under the radar of executives who had not recognised the extent to which macro external market trends or a customer's changing circumstances had placed an order or business area on the 'at risk' register. 'We were facing significant proportions of red and amber-flagged bookings. We had to seek sales to compensate for such dips', explained one COO. Perhaps more surprisingly, some firms identified 'red' orders/accounts which were being terminated, but where the significance of these lost pieces of business had not been appreciated; in many cases these activities under-pinned work for other customers, product development programmes or the firm's credibility and ability to compete in a particular market, so the implications were more far ranging than only the vulnerability of the specific order or account.

These businesses were not unaccustomed to seeking new opportunities, emerging technologies, adjacent markets, exploitation of key accounts and so forth. Far from it: their strategising and marketing planning, business development and key account management routinely sought growth. However, the integrated nature of their new processes meant that shortfalls identified from the market-informed traffic lighting of at-risk orders were immediately addressed through a rigorous and far-ranging exploration of emerging possibilities for new business and growth in current and additional areas. This was deemed by the CEOs, CFOs and COOs as the added value: rapid and provocative examination of anticipated revenue streams coupled with a pursuit plan for rectifying the identified shortfalls in likely revenue streams, properly shaped by the market's altered characteristics and drivers.

Nevertheless, this led to a further complication. In most cases, the additional and new revenue possibilities lay in adjacent markets, emerging technologies or in accounts barely impacted on previously. Such 'unchartered territory' inevitably carried development costs, issues of skills, competencies and incomplete market and competitor knowledge, and the need to manage re-orientation of priorities amongst the firms' personnel, systems, metrics and structures.

The overall strategising process had to include the operationalisation of the emerging new vision. This centred on trade-off analysis of the emerging view of likely revenue opportunities, along with detailed customer engagement and operational planning to execute the new plan. These activities are indicated in Figures 2 and 3. The Managing Director of a major fast-moving consumer goods (fmcg) player also adopting this market-led assessment approach explained:

> The current downturn, political direction and customer uncertainty have forced us to re-align our investment plans and strategy, and re-engineer our products, so we have needed to also re-direct our energies and capabilities. This has been very demanding. Our strategy re-think had to flow into our consumer engagement, trade relationships and then to our internal behaviours.

Conclusions

The over-arching outcome from these companies' experiences is that marketing is assisting in re-pitching products and services appropriate to today's climate and fast-changing customer drivers. Propositions relevant to customers' new pressures are required, which more effectively address competitors' moves. There is much reliance on marketing executives by CEOs/leadership teams, to provide:

- smarter target marketing and understanding of market conditions;
- re-engineering of go to market propositions;
- demonstrating relevance to consumers;
- staying abreast of evolving market dynamics.

However, CEOs, CFOs and COOs are themselves harnessing the analytical toolkit of marketing to reshape their strategies and to orientate their colleagues to fast-changing market challenges.

One CEO summed up thus:

> Adopt a new-look approach based on an evaluation of markets, roadmapping and anticipated shortfalls in existing contracts. Face up to the significant proportions of red and amber-flagged bookings. Look to compensate for such dips. Reflect new priorities in the propositions taken to market, consumer engagement, trade relationships and internal behaviours. Force the leadership team to change their activities to deliver to these re-shaped priorities. Be led by market insights and honesty about at-risk business. Or fail.

This rather stark 'call to arms' was reflected amongst the leadership teams of all the businesses harnessing such a market-led strategising or go to market planning approach.

As a result, market analysis certainly is contributing significantly to re-thinking business strategies in terms of: (1) traffic lighting of income stream risk; (2) opportunity identification to address identified gaps; and (3) re-engineering of take-to-market propositions likely to be attractive to target customer groups and of concern to competitors. The contribution of market analysis has become more fundamental and directional to many leadership teams, even if marketers do not necessarily become involved in the subsequent creation of a firm's strategy. The market-informed strategising process depicted here is typical of how many leadership teams are combining market-led risk assessment of apparent orders and income streams with market-led identification of replacement opportunities, linked to re-orientated target market priorities and re-thought customer engagement approaches. The irony for marketers is, perhaps, that in many firms it is the current economic meltdown and concerns about performance which have given marketing's toolkit more topicality and visibility in strategic decision making. Marketers' budgets are being pruned and they are turning to more prudent tactics in order to execute their marketing programmes, at a time when their market insights and analytical capabilities rarely have been more sought after by senior colleagues within corporate leadership teams. The evidence is that the marketing toolkit is under-pinning senior strategic planning like never before, but often in the hands of other directors, not marketing. But at least leaderships are seeking market insight.

References

Bush, M. (2008). Navigating recession with CRM, direct, online. *B2B, 93*(18), 3–28.

Bush, M. (2009). Recession lesson: Throw out your old algorithms. *Advertising Age, 80*(22), 5.

Casadesus-Masanell, R., & Ricart, J.E. (2010). From strategy to business models and onto tactics. *Long Range Planning, 43*, 195–215.

Day, G. (2006). Aligning the organization with the market. *MIT Sloan Management Review, 48*, 41–49.

Dibb, S., & Simkin, L. (2008). *Marketing planning*. London: Cengage South Western.

Elliott, R., & Percy, L. (2007). *Strategic brand management*. Oxford: Oxford University Press.

Goodson, S., & Walker, C. (2008). Beating the recession. *Adweek, 49*(33), p. 16.

Hooley, G., Saunders, J., Piercy, N., & Nicoulaud, B. (2007). *Marketing strategy and competitive positioning*. Harlow: FT/Prentice-Hall.

Keller, K.L. (2007). *Strategic brand management*. Harlow: Prentice-Hall.

Keller, K. (2011). Marketing in a recession. *Ideas*. Retrieved from www.tuck.dartmouth/today/ideas/marketing-in-a-recession

Marketing Society Forum. (2009, August 5). Should more FMCG companies launch their own value ranges? *Marketing*, p. 22.

Mason, R.B., & Staude, G. (2009). An exploration of marketing tactics for turbulent environments. *Industrial Management and Data Systems, 109*, 173–190.

McDonald, M., & Wilson, H. (2011). *Marketing plans: How to prepare them, how to use them*. Chichester: Wiley.

Passikoff, R. (2009). 10 branding trends for 2010: Value is the new black. *Functional Ingredients, 92*, 32–33.

Piercy, N. (2008). *Market-led strategic change: Transforming the process of going to market*. Oxford: Butterworth-Heinemann.

Ritson, M. (2009, October). Should you launch a fighter brand? *Harvard Business Review, 87*(10), 86–94.

Simkin, L. (2010, July). '9 out of 10 brand managers prefer...': The hierarchy of priorities for brand managers during recession. Academy of Marketing Conference Proceedings, Coventry.

Slater, S., Hult, G., & Olson, E. (2010). Factors influencing the relative importance of marketing strategy creativity and marketing strategy implementation effectiveness. *Industrial Marketing Management, 39*, 551–559.

Spence, R. (2009). Last brands left standing. *Media Week, 19*(6), p. 2.

Srinivasan, R., Lilien, G., & Rangaswamy, A. (2005). Turning adversity into advantage: Does proactive marketing during a recession pay-off? *International Journal of Research in Marketing, 22*, 109–125.

Veronikis, E. (2009). Behind the list with Mark Richwine. *Central Penn Business Journal, 25*(42), 35–40.

Wong, E. (2009). Value: It's what's for dinner. *Adweek, 50*(23), 7.

The power of intuitive thinking: a devalued heuristic of strategic marketing

Anthony Patterson, Lee Quinn and Steve Baron

The Management School, University of Liverpool, Liverpool, UK

Historically, the value of intuition in strategic marketing has been devalued. Consequently, the aim of this paper is to investigate empirically and articulate the ways in which the heuristic of intuition can prove, and is proving, helpful to marketing managers involved in making strategic-level decisions. Drawing upon extensive interviews conducted with marketing managers, we explore the extent to which intuitive insights are privileged over systematic, rational, logical evaluations. Our data evidence how intuition-led decision making becomes a powerful tool in instances where there is a paucity of data, when options are manifold, when the future is uncertain and when the logic of strategic choice needs to be confirmed. Ultimately, the paper seeks to place a new and affirmative subjectivity within the realm of marketing strategy that respects and legitimises the power of intuitive insight.

Introduction

To the detriment of the value placed on the intuition, judgement and subjective insight of marketing managers, the strategic marketing literature has long been guilty of giving undue prominence to analytical processes and approaches that rely heavily on market research data to drive strategy creation. So guilty, in fact, that many textbooks in this area seem to be prefaced with get-off-the-hook clauses that attempt to account, and even apologise, for this all too obvious omission in their work. By way of illustration, consider this quotation from Meldrum and McDonald (2007, p. 251) who state, 'no matter how important intuition, feel and experience are as contributory factors in this process of rationality...'. In other words, to be so bold as to articulate what they really mean, 'no matter how important these things may be, please, dear readers, just abide by the predetermined models and frameworks in our book'. Such privileging of pure rationality and reason is, of course, a mainstay of contemporary marketing theory and thought. In spite of the espousal of alternative modes of intuitive decision making, which gained prominence in the late 1990s (Day, 1997; Dolnick, 1998; Weintraub, 1998), continuing to gather pace in more recent times (Dane & Pratt, 2007; Duggan, 2007), the rational perspective has managed to remain very firmly rooted. Indeed, Boyett and Boyett (2003, p. 158), with tongue firmly in cheek, perfectly summarise the general attitude in strategic marketing thinking: 'intuition-based testosterone-driven marketing decision making is always bad and logic, analysis, and rationality is always the way to go'. Even Kotler and

Keller (2006, p. 724) long for the day that marks 'the demise of marketing intuition and the rise of marketing science'.

Despite receiving significant scholarly attention, both theoretically and conceptually, few studies have examined the prevalence and nature of intuition in practice (Henden, 2004). This is particularly noticeable in the marketing strategy literature despite the increasing attention that has been drawn to the reality of marketing managerial activity, with researchers frequently raising the issue of subjectively influenced managerial decision-making practices within their empirical inquiries (e.g. Alvesson, 1998; Ardley, 2008; Hackley, 2000; Quinn, 2009; Quinn, Hines, & Bennison, 2007). The notion and nature of intuitive decision making, in particular, has drawn significant attention within the organisational psychology literature and has been variously articulated as a managerial means of moving beyond the reliance on rational, numerical and complex flows of data to make quicker, or post-hoc rationalised, judgements based on what research participants have explained as 'gut feelings' recognisable within the business environment (Lank & Lank, 1995). However, whilst the theoretical antecedents underpinning what intuition is and thus how it can be explained have fragmented (cf. Dane & Pratt, 2007, p. 35) following a long history of attention in the organisational sciences, the area has become increasingly prominent as a legitimate realm of scientific inquiry, drawing particularly from debates within the fields of psychology and neuroscience (Dane & Pratt, 2007; Hodgkinson, Langan-Fox, & Sadler-Smith, 2008; Sadler-Smith, 2008). Consequently, therefore, it is surprising to note that calls to examine and articulate the adoption of a more critical and humanistic method of social-scientific inquiry within the superordinate management domain of marketing (Ardley, 2011; Brown, 2001; Hackley, 2001) have repeatedly been overlooked and, as Ardley (2011, p. 4) observes, there remains little acknowledgement of 'tacit knowledge and the "gut feelings" of humans which are often influential in decision-making' (Baumard, 1999; Hackley, 1999). Recent accounts noting occurrences of intuitive managerial behaviours in marketing managerial practices are few, although Quinn's (2009, p. 263) empirical account begins to frame the phenomenon of intuition in managerial practice as a non-linear, socially situated process of decision making, explained as 'the managerial ability to simplify evaluations of complexity for the purpose of decision-making'. Essentially, such conceptions have tended to rely on Weick's (1995, p. 88) definition of 'intuition as compressed expertise . . . [a process by] which people arrive at an answer without understanding all the steps that led up to it'. However, as Sadler-Smith (2008, p. 9) notes, managers across all professions are 'constantly being exhorted to be more creative, innovative, entrepreneurial and ethical – areas where intuition has an important if not invaluable role to play' without specifically articulating precisely how being intuitive will help them become better managers.

Consequently, the aim of this paper will attempt to investigate empirically and articulate the ways in which the devalued heuristic of intuition can prove, and is proving, helpful to marketing managers involved in making strategic-level decisions. We will demonstrate the power of intuitive thinking as practised by marketing managers on the frontline of strategy creation. We will attempt to delve deeply into what Faulkner (1998, p. 3), author of *The essence of intuition*, eloquently describes as, 'the nigglings, the gatherings, the foggy thoughts at the edge of consciousness' that encapsulate its essence. Specifically, we will draw upon extensive interviews conducted with marketing managers who make critical, strategic marketing decisions on a regular basis. We will explore the extent to which they privilege their intuitive insights over systematic, rational, logical evaluations. By doing so, we will hopefully glean some guidelines from the frontline about how best to incorporate

Table 1.   Organisation and key informant details.

Organisation descriptors	Company size (to end of 2006 financial year)	Key informant(s) role
Specialist clothing retailer A	£3.1bn turnover; £470m operating profit	Head of Marketing and Research
Specialist clothing retailer B	£101m turnover; £8.38m operating profit	Marketing and Research Executive
Specialist clothing retailer C	£762m turnover; £109m operating profit	Marketing Director
Grocery retailer	£1.6bn turnover; £61m operating profit	Marketing Manager
Independent brand A	Privately owned company – financial data not disclosed	Company Owner/CEO
Independent brand B	£56.5m turnover; £6m operating profit	Company Owner
Independent brand C	£62.7m turnover; £11.1m operating profit (UK/Eire)	Sales and Operations Director (UK/Eire)
Brand management company	£933m turnover; £19m operating profit	Group Market Researcher and Planner
Data consultant/supplier	£157m turnover; −£3.4m operating profit	(1) Director of Client Services (2) Senior Marketing Executive
Data consultant/supplier	Global sales of £1.9bn; 15,500 employees	(1) Business Consultant and/or (2) Director of Business Strategy

Source: Company files.

intuitive insights into the formation of marketing strategy. Ultimately, we seek to place within the realm of marketing strategy a new and affirmative subjectivity that respects and legitimises the power of intuitive insight.

Methodology

The requirement to examine a breadth of these tacit/subjective/intuitive/gut feel-driven practices in the strategic marketing domain guides the research focus of this paper towards an in-depth exploration of the prevalence and potential significance of practitioners' approaches to strategic, decision-led marketing activities. The study was carried out within a qualitative research framework which takes into consideration the contextuality of managerial action, allowing for an exploratory analysis of interpretations and constructions of intuitively derived managerial actions identifiable within the practices encountered. Drawing excerpts from an empirical study which examined the strategic activities of marketing personnel working within the UK's apparel retail sector, across all organisational levels, the study aims to explore the extent to which intuitive insights enabled marketing decision making in a strategic marketing context. The research inquiry adopted a qualitative design, consisting of individual depth-interviews with 12 key industry informants within 10 apparel retail sector-based organisations (Table 1).

Key informants were interviewed on the basis that their roles within each of their respective organisations provided them with day-to-day experiences of acting and directing strategic intentions within their respective businesses. Informants fulfilled a number of roles and participants were employed within positions across the organisational spectrum, ranging from company owners and chief executives to marketing executives. Three of the 12 informants were female. A depth-interviewing technique was used to guide key areas of each interview discussion in order to focus upon particular issues of interest that would inform our goal of understanding the extent of intuitive decision-making processes practised by our interviewees. The interviews were tape-recorded and transcribed immediately following each interview.

Many informants taking part in the study requested that their identities, brand examples provided, and any client data, remained sufficiently concealed within any subsequent publication. In order to respect those requests, and to maintain consistency throughout our presentation of the data, where illustrative quotations are used as narrative evidence, only the managerial role of the informant, their gender and their respective organisational format will be declared. Given the paucity of previous relevant studies of this nature, a non-probability sampling design offered the most appropriate opportunity for inviting the views of practitioners working in a strategic marketing capacity. The aim of the research was to emphasise the subjective nature of generated insights in order to provide an empirically evidenced narrative to expand upon this previously under-explored area of interest. The data were subjected to a thematic analysis (Boyatzis, 1998) and transparency in the analytical process was achieved by adopting a widely recognised process for analysing qualitative data. This process was conducted as follows: (1) familiarisation with the data; (2) generation of codes; (3) searching for themes; (4) reviewing meaningful themes generated; (5) defining the core themes; and (6) producing the final report (Braun & Clarke, 2006, pp. 86–93).

In the following findings section of our paper, the excerpts taken from our data capture an essence of meaning relevant to each of the key themes we present. Furthermore, we embed our narrative in a manner which clearly illustrates the story we are telling about our data. This narrative presents an argument which is meaningful in relation to the overall focus of our research attention. Specifically it discusses the important role which intuition plays when it comes to making data deficient decisions, selecting from a multitude of options, future gazing and confirming the logic of a metrics rich analysis.

Data-deficient decisions

Contrary to the rationalistic prescription to gather all salient information and make assessments on the basis of this full knowledge, our interview data reveal that marketing managers often do not have the 'full picture' prior to making important decisions. While it is absolutely true that some information gathering does take place in terms of analysing the possibilities of action, there is nearly always uncertainty and ambiguity as to what the best course of action actually is. Nonetheless, such irresolvable ambiguity in their view cannot stand in the way of making progress, of taking action and of moving forward. Taking difficult decisions that can have far-reaching consequences comes with the territory of being a marketing professional. As one manager commented:

> There are many times in the course of my working week that I have to make a decision, like for instance whether or not to run a promotion, or subtly change the packaging, or any number of things. And sure we could commission a market research project in an attempt to understand the effect this will have on our brand. We could trawl through the reports we already have on the sales associated with previous promotions. We could him and ha all day long, but ultimately it comes back to me and the team. It's our responsibility to make the call, to make the decision. And if I'm totally honest, I just tend to rely on myself, my experience, my God-given talent. And you know what, usually I'm right! (Marketing Manager, Grocery Retailer, Female)

This intuitive heuristic is described in the literature as 'satisficing', which Mumford and Norris (1999, p. 809) describe as, 'simply seizing on the first available approximation of a solution'. In an ideal world, of course, it might be preferable to embark upon a full elaboration and exploration of all alternatives, but the reality of a marketing practitioner's everyday life makes such a scenario virtually impossible. Despite this, marketing managers can often be reluctant to admit that they privilege intuitive insights. Many of them were, after all, schooled in the ways of strategic thinking. Most of them, having graduated from university with business studies degrees in their pockets, have been heavily steeped in the Kotlerite standard of analysis and implementation. They know that while their innate way of doing things might get results, it should not be publicly acknowledged as a method. They know that their bosses were also schooled in these same marketing decision-making marketing models and that they have an expectation that their employees will utilise them. Everyone it seems is pretending to abide by rationalistic modes of thought. As one interviewee made plain:

> I think most people are so engaged in the hand-to-hand combat that goes on that they're very reluctant to actually come forward about how they actually arrive at their decisions. I suspect that's why there's not a great deal of work being done in the area because people as respondents are not terribly forthcoming about how they do this, because being so candid might portray them in the way that they don't want to be portrayed. They want to be seen as rational, hard-working servants of their organisation. So, I think there's a kind of gap between the way that people want themselves to be portrayed and the way that they actually behave. (Company Owner, Independent Brand B, Male)

Overwhelmed by options

Intuitive thought processes really seem to come to the fore when marketing managers are confronted with a multitude of options from which to choose. Such a scenario can be bewildering at the best of times, but is especially so in today's unpredictable climate where 'black swan' events can unexpectedly cause chaos in the marketplace, and render best laid plans redundant. As Etzioni (2001, p. 46) writes, 'The flow of information has swollen to such a flood that managers are in danger of drowning; extracting relevant data from the torrent is increasingly a daunting task.' Moreover, when the data on these choices are conflicting, complicated and interconnected, selecting the 'best' option becomes even more difficult (Schön, 1983). Against this backdrop, faced with the prospect of wading through reams of data, knowing full well that a clear strategic choice is unlikely to emerge, marketers are most inclined to ditch the explicit analytical approach to marketing decision making and rely instead on intuition. One marketing manager we interviewed, reflected on the evolution of how research data within her organisation is used – or not as the case may be – to inform the decision-making process:

> When I first joined they hadn't got a formal research function at all but were buying into an awful lot of data that was just sitting there. I cancelled most of it because there is no point in doing research if you're not going to use it or if it's going to be misused. I think you've got to find ways of making a difference where you can and be prepared not to bother with those things that just cloud the picture … and it sounds defeatist, but I think gradually, over time, you follow the lines of least resistance – and research now is very broadly used within the company – but I'm realistic enough to know, or to acknowledge, that in the pecking order of data that get used for decisions, it's certainly well below the sales data and our own idea of what will and what won't work. (Head of Marketing and Research, Specialist Clothing Retailer A, Female)

Straying from the path of rationality can also be engrained in the culture of certain industries in which marketers operate. Many CEOs subscribe to the trite but true axiom that 'over-analysis leads to paralysis'. They can even be openly hostile to the frameworks of analysis that consultants produce and academics recommend. These experienced leaders see themselves as people of action, living in the moment. They take pride in their ability to reflect instantaneously and evaluate. In this sense, one of the business consultants interviewed provided the following observation:

> Research spend in fashion is not particularly high, erm, when I started in fashion retailing, you'd got Debenhams who had a big research department, Arcadia had a big research department, M&S had a big one. And now M&S have got one and that's kind of it, you know. Philip Green doesn't do research and he's binned all of theirs, Debenhams seemed to get thinned down – they still do some with us – but they thinned down quite a lot. It's kind of, perhaps, an underinvestment although many people in the retail sector say, 'you know, it's about the product'. Philip Green [apparently] says that 'if you don't get the product right it doesn't matter. (Business Consultant, Data Consultant/Supplier, Male)

Future gazing

While much of marketing thought and theory is predicated on being able to foresee the future, the truth is that doing so is extraordinarily difficult. Consider the role of marketing planning, an industry at the forefront of rational marketing. Its primary function is to predict the future. Yet as Brown's (2001) devastating critique of this industry highlights, despite reports to the contrary, future gazing of any kind from the predictions of Nostradamus to those of trend analysts like Faith Popcorn are extremely suspect. Moreover, marketing managers are more likely to ignore or conveniently forget their marketing plans, rather than slavishly attempt to realise the objectives and recommendations laid down therein. They frequently regard them as being out of date before the ink dries. The reason why marketers pay them so little regard is perhaps because they know that their contents are based primarily on extrapolating straight-line numerical trends from the past to the present. Dealing with the future, or even the here and now, with all its uncertainty and incomplete information, knowing what new product concepts to launch, what trends to predict and the direction and intensity of these trends, is therefore often left to the individual judgement of a few farsighted marketers, rather than a clinical and complete analysis of macro-marketing influences. The sidelining of data analysis in favour of running with intuitive solutions was commonly reported by several informants that we interviewed:

> There will be lots of this nice to know information which a lot of retailers buy into. It's a way of them going back to their buying teams and marketing teams and understanding how the market is changing. What can we forecast going forward and what is the size of the jeans market or the footwear market? So, a lot of retailers will buy this data. It's a nice to know really and probably sits on the in-tray of some marketing director for months ... It's quite interesting and it's useful when the managing director's making an announcement to the City, but the truth is we don't do much with it ourselves. (Director of Client Services, Data Consultant/Supplier, Male)

> Because we have to move quickly and grasp these opportunities and move forward with confidence then very often the way we deal with the risk of making wrong decisions is the sort of suck it and see approach and I know that our own CEO and people have talked about the risk in exposing ourselves in taking space in our out of town stores. And then someone said well, actually we do it in one store and our risk is limited to a million pound cost, which in a business this size is not a huge exposure. We're not saying, we don't make announcements that we're going to have 50 out of town stores by the end of the year unless there are certain plans, but what I mean is we're always prepared to say okay let's do it in a small way and if it looks like it's working, increase, or roll it out further. (Managing Director, Specialist Clothing Retailer C, Male)

There is also a widespread recognition among the experienced marketing professionals we interviewed that the metrics of strategic marketing leave a lot to be desired. Many understand that the sense of control marketing planning purports to offer simply does not manifest itself in reality. Future outcomes, they are only too well aware, are as reliant on uncontrollable factors such as accidental discoveries, serendipitous happenings and dumb luck rather than meticulous planning:

> Strategic planning is a bit of a pretence, really. It makes managers think or feel that they're in control. I think there's a tendency that when there are times of crisis they actually chuck out the strategy and go back to what made them successful as managers. There are many managers, in retailing particularly, who, when the pressure's on, will actually go back to what made them their success in the 1980s and that's usually about discounting and the appeal of the value proposition. So you would find it very rare for any manager to say: 'I think we should put the prices up and move ourselves up market.' They're much more prepared to go back to what's been successful [in the past]. The eclectic part of strategy is the vision of where you're going and somebody having a clear idea of that vision. A lot of strategy creation is bedevilled by elaborate mission statements that are all about being passionate, and yet the fact of the matter is that in some years we increased the bottom line simply because we got lucky. (Company Owner, Independent Brand A, Male)

Confirming logic

Intuition seems also to function particularly well when marketers want to establish if the logic of a rational marketing analysis equates with the reality of the marketplace. Regardless of how flawless an argument may seem, a rational analysis that has as its starting point a faulty premise can never be realised. For example, after considering the statistical evidence, one might have logically concluded, just as Acer Inc. unfortunately did, that the consumer market for netbooks would grow exponentially over the next few years, and that investing in and producing more of these devices would be a tactically astute move. With the unexpected rise of the tablet market, this would, of course, have been an absurd conclusion, and a potentially costly mistake for any computer manufacturer to have followed. Incidentally, since making this tactical blunder, Acer's chief executive has been fired, its share price has plunged 30%, jobs have been cut and sales forecasts have slumped (Halliday, 2011). A marketer's intuition, with his ear close to the ground, with his years of experience in the swiftly changing technological sector might have sensed that change was afoot, not perhaps that the revolutionary iPad era was imminent, just that placing one's faith in the continued vitality of the netbook market would be a terrible strategic move. It is for these reasons that marketers are very wary of the marketing metrics that regularly land on their desk. When asked about the inherent role of intuition used to support their decisions, one of the data consultancy-based informants argued:

> Yeah, yeah, I think intuition really does come into it a lot, definitely. I was at *Company X* the other day and I was telling them: 'you wanna watch out because the kidswear market is going out of town, basically'. I mean if you're Next you're moving out of town – not completely – but as there's Tesco, Asda, Matalan ... those people are massive in the kidswear market and, of course, it's all out of town. The trend in kidswear is mostly for convenience and parking, so we were saying to *Company X* you'd better watch that. And they said, yeah, we've been thinking that as well and can you provide this data to kind of support our argument that we need to look at our out of town stores. So, sometimes, it's kind of like, we might take the lead or they might take the lead or we'll say it and they'll use it to support their argument. And then, say *Company Y*, I think they've got too trendy and for a while we were showing them that all their sales were to the under 25s, so getting a bit narrow, their customer base was becoming too small, they needed to expand it, so you know, in that sense it's up to them how they use it. (Business Consultant, Data Consultant/Supplier, Male)

Moreover, when asked to justify their own strategic decisions there is definitely a sense that marketers consciously select evidence which will support their intuitive argument, while at the same time ditching data that do not support it as another one of our informants made clear:

There's kind of a big gap between the theory of decision models and how decisions are made in that kind of context. I think what goes on in real life is a lot messier really. I would think that in business, modelling decisions and how decisions are made would be extremely difficult because I don't think decisions are made on the basis of totally rational, logical, thought; that would be my experience. There's still a lot of autocratic behaviour in organisations where people promulgate decisions and these decisions are made by individuals and the process by which they come to those decisions isn't always logical. I think sometimes it's very intuitive … sometimes they get a bee in their bonnet about certain situations. And then I think people want to justify those decisions, probably being quite selective about how they select the research, the evidence that they want to support on that basis. (Group Market Researcher and Planner, Brand Management Company, Male)

A number of the managers in our study even rail against the excessive use of logical marketing speak which, they claim, has a way of asserting facts with unflinching certainty, as though they contained an inherent rightness, when really the information, the impressive discourse adopted, can be a smokescreen that hides an ill-informed analysis. Thankfully, many of our key informants were wise to those that promulgated marketing 'mumbo-jumbo', as one of our key-informants stated:

I suppose what really irritates me the most [is that] a lot of people say 'everyone is our customer', which I find really quite irritating. I'll say who are your customers? And they'll say oh, it's ABC1, female, 18–50. Brilliant, that's really superb! No, that just really irritates me. It shows maybe a lack of knowledge. And then taking a step back from that I'm talking to say commercial directors who say: 'don't you talk to me about retail location and retail marketing, I've been doing this for 50 years and I've built this business from 2 units to 50 stores, £10 million turnover', or whatever, and there's a lot to be said for that as well. There's a lot to be said for intuition. (Business Consultant, Data Consultant/Supplier, Male)

Conclusion

Our empirical findings dispute the commonly held contention that intuition should be strenuously avoided if 'good' strategic marketing decisions are to be taken. On the contrary, this research shows how intuition is widely practised by marketing managers striving to make better decisions. As the qualitative themes of analysis illustrate, intuition becomes a particularly powerful tool in instances where there is a paucity of data, when options are manifold, when the future is uncertain, and when the logic of strategic choice needs to be confirmed. Moreover, since people in business are generally rewarded for displaying logic and supporting strategic choices with facts, we would estimate that the use of intuitive processes actually runs much deeper than this empirical study suggests. Since the practice, in certain industries at least, is frowned upon, we posit that some of the marketing professionals interviewed, when asked to explain their actions, inexplicable though they may truthfully be (and we say this with full knowledge of the inherent irony), intuitively use a post-hoc rationalisation process that utilises the dominant discourse and language of marketing analysis and planning to justify decisions that were in fact of an intuitive nature. In effect, as Wagner (2002, p. 51) astutely asserts, they 'make up an explanation that may be fictitious, perhaps not intentionally, but only in the spirit of trying to satisfy the questioner'.

Though let us be clear, the abiding recommendation of this paper is not that marketing managers should forget frameworks, reject rationality and abandon analysis, or that their work philosophy should be a banal motto of the 'just do it' variety. This is not what we are suggesting at all. For one thing, if one were to rely entirely on gut instinct, tacit knowledge and innate skill, the obvious conclusion would be that formulating marketing strategy amounts to little more than common sense and as Furnam (2006, p. 11) suggests, 'experience, intuition and modern technology is essentially all you need to get on in business'. To be sure, relying purely on intuition is problematic. Intuitive hunches can be plain wrong, especially when people allow their idiosyncratic prejudices, and self-interests to dominate their decision making. O'Hara-Devereaux (2004), for instance, explicitly warns against the use of 'old intuition', essentially intuition developed in the past, which can sometimes be disastrous because of the tumultuous changes that might have occurred in the micro economic environment since this intuition was derived. What is more, relying on intuitive leaders can be challenging since while they might be inspiring, often they do not pay sufficient attention to the finer details of implementing strategy (Michaluk, 2007).

Nonetheless, what we do maintain is that mainstream marketing intelligentsia is an excessively metrics-driven culture that undervalues the heuristic of intuition as commonly practised by marketing professionals. The logic of our paper feeds into a rich vein of popular management literature, such as Gladwell's (2005) *Blink* which illustrates how 'thinking without thinking' instantly assesses a situation or person and is as accurate as forming a judgement over a protracted period of time. While logic clearly remains important, intuitive marketers are in touch with their feelings, even when the origins of those same feelings cannot be accurately pinpointed. It is little wonder then that Brown (2001, p. 116) so fervently believes that, 'Intuition, inspiration and imagination are just as important as analysis, planning and control, possibly more so.' We would suggest, too, that companies should not be so intent on measuring and accounting for the minutia of all marketing activity. Scary though it may be, when it comes to dealing with managers who make strategic marketing choices, they should be more tolerant of ambiguity and inconsistency. They should learn to tolerate marketers who do not conform to type, whose offbeat strategic thinking, which might seem like guesswork, may just save a floundering company (Peat, 2002). And here is a truly radical suggestion. Maybe they should employ more of those people underrepresented in this study whose hotly contested inclination for intuition, empathy and all round emotional intelligence is certainly ripe for further debate (Agor, 1986; Hayes, Allinson, & Armstrong, 2004), namely – women. Unsurprisingly, the undervalued nature of intuition runs in tandem with the widely acknowledged underestimation of women as key contributors to every company's activities, marketing or otherwise. It is high time both wrongs were righted.

References

Agor, W.H. (1986). *The logic of intuitive decision making: A research-based approach for top management*. New York: Quorum Books.

Alvesson, M. (1998). Gender relations and identity at work: A case study of masculinities and femininities in an advertising agency. *Human Relations, 51*, 969–1005.

Ardley, B. (2008). A case of mistaken identity: Theory, practice and the marketing textbook. *European Business Review, 20*, 533–546.

Ardley, B. (2011, forthcoming). Marketing theory and critical phenomenology: Exploring the human side of management practice. *Marketing Intelligence and Planning, 29*.

Baumard, P. (1999). *Tacit knowledge in organizations*. Thousand Oaks, CA: Sage.

Boyatzis, R. (1998). *Transforming qualitative information: Thematic analysis and code development*. London: Sage.

Boyett, J.H., & Boyett, J.T. (2003). *The guru guide to marketing: A concise guide to the best ideas from today's top marketers*. Hoboken, NJ: John Wiley & Sons.

Braun, V., & Clarke, V. (2006). Using thematic analysis in psychology. *Qualitative Research in Psychology, 3*(2), 77–101.

Brown, S. (2001). *Marketing: The retro revolution*. London: Sage.

Dane, E., & Pratt, M.G. (2007). Exploring intuition and its role in managerial decision making. *Academy of Management Review, 32*, 33–54.

Day, L. (1997). *Practical intuition for success: A step-by-step program to increase wealth today*. New York: HarperCollins Publishers.

Dolnick, B. (1998). *The executive mystic: Psychic power tools for success*. New York: Harper Business.

Duggan, W. (2007). *Strategic intuition: The creative spark in human achievement*. New York: Columbia University Press.

Etzioni, A. (2001). Humble decision making. In *Harvard Business Review on decision making* (pp. 45–57). Boston, MA: Harvard Business School Press.

Faulkner, C. (1998). *The essence of intuition*. New York: PL Comprehensive [Audio cassette].

Furnam, A. (2006). *Management mumbo-jumbo: A skeptic's dictionary*. New York: Palgrave MacMillan.

Gladwell, M. (2005). *Blink: The power of thinking without thinking*. Boston, MA: Little Brown.

Hackley, C. (1999). Tacit knowledge and the epistemology of expertise in strategic marketing management. *European Journal of Marketing, 33*(7–8), 1–13.

Hackley, C. (2000). Silent running: Tacit, discursive and psychological aspects of management in a top UK advertising agency. *British Journal of Management, 1*, 239–254.

Hackley, C. (2001). *Marketing and social construction: Exploring the rhetorics of managed consumption*. London: Routledge.

Halliday, J. (2011, April 12). Apple told of iPad boom and warned about android threat. *Guardian*, p. 24.

Hayes, J., Allinson, C., & Armstrong, S. (2004). Intuition, women managers and gendered stereotypes. *Personnel Review, 33*, 430–417.

Henden, G. (2004). *Intuition and its role in strategic thinking*. Sandvika: Nordberg Hurtigtrykk.

Hodgkinson, G., Langan-Fox, J., & Sadler-Smith, E. (2008). Intuition: A fundamental bridging construct in the behavioural sciences. *British Journal of Psychology, 99*, 1–27.

Kotler, P., & Keller, K. (2006). *Marketing management* (12th ed.). Upper Saddle River, NJ: Pearson Education.

Lank, A.G., & Lank, E.A. (1995). Legitimizing the gut feel: The role of intuition in business. *Journal of Managerial Psychology, 10*(4), 18–23.

Meldrum, M., & McDonald, M. (2007). *Marketing in a nutshell: Key concepts for non-specialists*. London: Butterworth-Heinemann.

Michaluk, G. (2007). *The marketing director's role in business planning and corporate governance*. Chichester: John Wiley & Sons.

Mumford, M.D., & Norris, D.G. (1999). Heuristics. In M.A. Runco & S.R. Pritzer (Eds.), *Encyclopedia of creativity* (Vol. 1, pp. 807–813). London: Academic Press.

O'Hara-Devereaux, M. (2004). *Navigating the badlands: Thriving in the decade of radical transformation*. London: Wiley.

Peat, D.F. (2002). *From certainty to uncertainty: The story of science and ideas in the twentieth century*. Washington, DC: Joseph Henry Press.

Quinn, L. (2009). Market segmentation in managerial practice: A qualitative examination. *Journal of Marketing Management, 25*, 253–272.

Quinn, L., Hines, T., & Bennison, D. (2007). Making sense of market segmentation: A fashion retailing case. *European Journal of Marketing, 41*, 439–465.

Sadler-Smith, E. (2008). *Inside intuition*. Abingdon: Routledge.

Schön, D.A. (1983). *The reflective practitioner: How professionals think in action*. London: Temple Smith.

Wagner, R. (2002). Smart people doing dumb things: The case of managerial incompetence. In R.J. Sternberg (Ed.), *Why smart people can be so stupid* (pp. 42–63). London: Yale University Press.

Weick, K. (1995). *Sensemaking in organizations*. Thousand Oaks, CA: Sage.

Weintraub, S. (1998). *The hidden intelligence: Innovation through intuition*. London: Butterworth-Heinemann.

Competitive Intelligence analysis failure: diagnosing individual level causes and implementing organisational level remedies

Craig S. Fleisher[a] and Sheila Wright[b]

[a] *Chief Learning Officer, Aurora WDC, PO Box 32, Madison, WI 53701, USA;*
[b]*Department of Marketing, Faculty of Business and Law, De Montfort University, Hugh Aston Building, The Gateway, Leicester, LE1 9BH, UK*

It is anticipated that any Competitive Intelligence (CI) professional would want to perform the analysis task and execute their responsibilities successfully over time. Such competencies would normally come with added experience on the job, as should the ability to reduce the risk of failure by diagnosing potential pitfalls. This paper presents: (a) a unique four-level hierarchical model of analysis failure; (b) identification of common causes of failure at the individual level; (c) 10 key continua of CI analysis skills which we believe an analyst has to master to become competent in their work; and (d) guiding principles for an enlightened firm to follow if they wish to discharge their organisational level responsibility of reducing the potential for analysis failure. We believe that the issues raised in this paper are of significance and should ultimately contribute towards creating a more successful analysis function. This can only be of benefit to educators, practitioners and others who rely on skilful CI output to inform their decision making.

Introduction

It hardly needs to be said that organisations and managers can learn from failures (Brown, 2007). However this requires individuals to talk thoughtfully about them and examine their causes, something which is rarely done except in cases of catastrophic, publicly visible failures (Edmonson & Cannon, 2005). Although analysis of failure is an accepted part of contemporary manufacturing industry practice, its application to an enterprise's intelligence, planning and decision making functions is less common (Heuer, 2005; Underwood, 2006). In identifying the possibility and causes of CI analytical failure, we believe that much can be learned by managers and practitioners, with the first task being awareness of the location of failure.

Failure location

The highest level of commercial failure is, arguably, that of business failure, whereby a business is no longer able to continue as a viable entity. If failure is defined as 'discontinuance of business', then it is likely that approximately two-thirds of all start-ups will fail within their first 10 years (Hogarth & Karelaia, 2008; Koopman & Lucas, 2005), and at even higher rates in some particularly difficult sectors such as retailing and restaurants (Stanton & Tweed, 2009). The findings of an in-depth longitudinal study of small business managers' in Sweden by Delmar and Wiklund (2008) found that manager motivation has a unique influence on a firm's success when measured as growth in the number of employees but less so when measured as growth in sales. This is especially prevalent in family owned business where the goal of the enterprise may not be growth per se, but the provision of income and employment to the family (Fairlie & Robb, 2007; Tokarczyk, Hansen, Green, & Down, 2007). Most of these business failures are anecdotally attributed to the conflict caused by balancing the emotional cost against the emotional return in small firms, as illustrated by Astrachan and Jaskiewicz (2008), or a general lack of effective planning and management skills which affects firms of all size equally, regardless of location (Belbin, 2010; Bloom & van Reenen, 2007; Fuller-Love, 2006; Palmer, Simmons, & deKervenoael, 2010; Pansiri & Temtime, 2008). In an influential article, exposing the problem of poor managerial talent management, Capelli (2008, p. 74) reminds us that:

> Failures in talent management are an ongoing source of pain for executives in modern organizations. Over the past generation, talent management practices, especially in the United States, have by and large been dysfunctional, leading corporations to lurch from surpluses of talent, to shortfalls, to surpluses and back again.

Beneath the level of the firm, we encounter planning, decision making and implementation failures (Westney et al., 2009). These are partly composed of intelligence failures and can be further disaggregated into failures along the traditional intelligence cycle functions of planning, data collection, analysis, dissemination and communication (Chao & Ishii, 2003; McMullen, Shepherd, & Patzelt, 2009).

Intelligence failures are distinguishable from more task-oriented intelligence errors, which are viewed as factual inaccuracies in analysis, resulting from poor and/or missing data. Intelligence failure is defined by Johnston (2005, p. 6) as 'systemic organizational surprise resulting from incorrect, missing, discarded, or inadequate hypotheses'. These failures may be due, in part, to failed analysis, but they can also be caused by other factors that interact with the CI analysis process. Attempting to disentangle or disaggregate the analysis portion of the process from other related processes is never an easy or straight-forward task. At a minimum, it is important that analysts and their decision makers routinely carry out a post-mortem on projects to try and determine any areas for improvement.

Having suggested the need for post-task assessment of the analysis process, it is recognised that there are a variety of problems associated with the evaluation of CI analysis and reporting that makes this task more challenging. The range of cognitive biases impacting on the process is outlined in depth by Heuer (1999). Briefly summarised, he notes that:

- analysts normally overestimate the accuracy of their past judgements;
- CI clients or consumers normally underestimate how much they learned from analysis products such as reports or briefs;
- overseers of CI production who conduct post-mortem analyses of an intelligence failure normally judge that events were more readily foreseeable than was in fact the case.

When analysis is ineffective, it is often the case that neither the analyst nor the decision maker are aware of this, in sufficient enough time, and frequently cannot identify the root cause(s) of the errors, problems or failure (Marr, 2006). It is essential therefore that the following questions are addressed to identify the potential for underlying errors.

Analysis problem definition

- How well was the analysis problem, the Key Intelligence Topic (KIT)/Key Intelligence Question (KIQ) specified at the outset?
- Did the analysis process allow for, or encourage, subsequent redefinitions of the problem?

Analysis project planning

- Was a project management plan or statement of work produced to perform the analysis process?
- How well did the analyst implement the process according to the plan?
- Were iterative steps built into the plan to enable a re-assessment of the task?

Data gathering error

- How accessible was the appropriate data to the analyst?
- Were the data acquired efficiently?
- Did the analyst properly account for data or information gaps?
- Was the analysis failure caused primarily by poor data collection?

Tool and technique-related error

- Was the analyst fully familiar with the range of analytical tools to conduct the analysis?
- Was the analyst fully capable of using the range of analytical tools to conduct the analysis task?
- Were the right tools used, and in the right sequence?

Synthesis error

- Did the analyst arrive at the optimal conclusion or insight?
- Did the analyst 'connect the dots' in a defensible manner?
- Would other experienced and successful analysts have conducted the task differently?

Communication transmission or channel error

- Did the analyst communicate their insights to their decision maker effectively?
- Was the analysis failure really a communication failure or a channel blockage?

Communication reception error

- How familiar was the decision maker with the analytical tools selected for the task?
- Did the decision maker understand the limitations of differing analytical tools and allow for these in the decision making process?
- Was the decision maker fully able to comprehend all aspects of the analysis output?

Unsystematic development error

- Did events arise during the course of the process that derailed the analysis or analyst?

- What impact did unexplained variance or random factors have on the outcome of the analysis task?

Errors of analysis can occur in one, or combination of several, of these categories. Having located the source, or sources, of error, only then is corrective action effective.

Four-level hierarchical model of analysis failure

Whatever the reasons experienced for CI analysis failures, it is valuable to identify why it happens and this is represented in a four-level model for identifying the barriers to generating effective CI analysis. These four levels, and the primary factors associated with each, are illustrated in Table 1.

While each of these sections warrants a full discussion on its own, for the purposes of this paper, the concentration will be on the aspects which, it is proposed, can be most effectively influenced by the individual analyst. Some of these factors may be present in other categories and it is recognised that there may be secondary or tertiary impact at other levels.

Causes of failure at individual analyst level

The CI analysis task is fundamentally performed by individuals, although they will also co-operate and collaborate with others to get their tasks accomplished. From consulting and educational assignments, as well as research, it has been possible to observe the following hindrance factors as being primarily present at the level of the individual analyst.

Different natural analytical abilities

People rely on a limited set of mental models, have preconceptions on issues and exhibit a wide range of cognitive bias when reviewing information (Clayton & Kimbrell, 2007). People also think differently. Some, in a left-brained, analytical, logical and verbal fashion, whereas right-brained people tend to be creative, holistic and spatial (Hines, 1987). Innovation is a right-brain activity, not a left-brain activity yet both educational institutions and business organisations reward left-brain *work*, while discouraging right-brain *thinking* (Pink, 2005). This is important when viewed in light of analysis being a mixture of both scientific and non-scientific techniques. In other words, analysis benefits from the adoption of a whole-brain approach to thinking (Spreng & Grady, 2010).

Naturally limited mental capacities

The content and context facing most CI analysts have become more complicated, complex and fast moving in recent years. Having said that, the brain's natural abilities to effectively process additional information has not evolved to match this. The popular view is that we only use 10% of our brain's ability and while one could argue with the figure, it is clear that human beings still only use a limited percentage of their brain capacity (Sousa, 2009). Scientific record though, still does not have a sense of what that percentage might be (Klingberg, 2009). In his influential article, Miller (1956) suggested that the magical number describing our natural information processing capabilities is seven things at one time, plus or minus, two. This could be a major problem for CI analysts who often have a far higher number of issues to keep in their mental calculus at any one time. Although information technology systems have developed to assist in the analysis task, we still have to use our brains in the same way as we have always done (Shacham, Cutlip, & Brauner, 2008).

Table 1.   Four-level hierarchical model of analysis failures.

Level	Nature of problem
Individual analyst-level failures	• Different natural analytical abilities • Naturally limited mental capacities • Natural motivation • Cognitive biases and perceptual distortion • Insufficient understanding and application of analysis tools and techniques • Poor preparedness by higher education
Analysis task-level failures	• Part of larger task • Task discontinuity • Unsatisfactory data inputs • Disconnects from decision making • Imbalance among key task facets
Internal organisational-level failures	• Some decision makers don't understand and appreciate analysis • Clients cannot articulate/specify their critical intelligence needs • Clients cannot articulate/specify their intelligence questions • Under-resourcing the analysis function • Lack of analysis-specific IT support • Lack of thinking time • Organisational culture and politics • Time and trust • Invisibility and mystery • Misconception that everyone can do analysis
External environment-level failures	• Growing range of competitive factors • Complexity and turbulence • Data overload • Globalisation • Educational deficiencies

Natural motivation

Given a choice between a more difficult, and a less difficult task, with identical outcomes, the majority of people would opt for the easier task. As may be coming patently obvious by now, analysis is not an easy task and as suggested by Rhee and Honeycutt Sigler (2010), can require the use, or expenditure of, significant levels of cognitive, intellectual, organisational and social resources to achieve optimum performance. One reason it is so difficult is because we have far fewer published heuristics or 'rules of thumb' to use in performing CI analysis than we do in many other fields of organisational endeavour such as engineering (Burvill et al., 2009), science (van Raan, 2004) accounting (Manassea & Roubini, 2009) or process management (Benhabib & Bisin, 2008). Some CI analysts think that volume of delivered outputs is the answer, not value. This form of sufficing behaviour is unlikely to meet the needs of today's demanding decision making clients.

Cognitive biases and perceptual distortion

In spite of the presence of the broad range of analytical techniques, some organisations still adopt poor strategies and their decision making processes are vulnerable to individual cognitive biases or 'groupthink'. Researchers have identified a variety of common cognitive biases that can enter into an individual's or group's process of analysis

(Bazerman, 2002; Keil, Depledge, & Rai, 2007; Sawyer, 1999; Tversky & Kahneman, 1986). These are identified in Table 2.

The existence of cognitive biases and groupthink raises issues of how to bring critical intelligence to bear on organisational decision making mechanisms so that the decisions made are realistic (Fahey, 2007). Thom, Reichert, Chiao, Iochpe, and Hess (2008) point out that people in organisations often tend to collect more information than strictly necessary for decision making, partly to influence others and partly to be viewed as thorough in their work. In other words, analysis is often used not just for objective decision making but also for political or symbolic organisational purposes.

Insufficient understanding and application of analytical tools and techniques

Studies on the use of CI analysis tools and techniques have consistently demonstrated that the individuals responsible will use only a very limited set of tools and techniques, usually those they know the best and have previously applied with some perceived success (Gib & Gooding, 1998; Rigby, 2001, 2003, 2009; Thom et al., 2008). This has also been identified as 'tool rut' by Fleisher and Bensoussan (2007). Even when an analyst is willing to use an enlarged tool box and attempt techniques outside their usual scope, they often lack the knowledge, understanding and experience to do it well. It is no surprise therefore, that they will stick to the safe, but well worn path of technique familiarity (Marteniuk, 2003; Morecroft, 2006; Self, 2003; Swanson, 2007).

Poor preparedness by higher education

There is a common misconception that almost anyone can do CI analysis. Ask a business graduate whether they developed good CI analytical skills in their university programme and you will almost always get an affirmative answer, yet few recognise the differences between the process of analysis and the ability to think (Kavanagh & Drennan, 2008; Tynjälä, Slotte, Nieminen, Lonka, & Olkinuora, 2006). In the higher and executive education system there is little evidence that teaching the skill of pragmatism and realism is

Table 2. Cognitive bias elements.

Elements	Nature of problem
Estimation bias	Over or under estimation of the magnitude of the effect of future events
Escalating commitment	Continual commitment of time, effort and finance to support a failing project, even when there is evidence that it is a fruitless task
Group-think	Lack of pertinent questioning of underlying assumptions and an unwillingness to challenge entrenched leadership, engrained cultures and senior executives
Illusion of control	An individual's mis-placed confidence in their ability to control and immunity to error. Illusion and group-think are common bed-fellows
Prior hypothesis bias	Individuals prone to this bias use data only when they confirm their beliefs, even when presented with contradictory analytical evidence
Reasoning by analogy	Individuals use simple analogies to make sense of challenging problems. Oversimplifying complex problems can lead to detrimental judgement
Representativeness	The error of extrapolating data from small samples to explain larger phenomena. Inexperienced analysts find it hard to distinguish between apparent and real facts

taken seriously, albeit such a skill set is lauded as a distinct competitive advantage for an individual in their career (Andrews & Higson, 2008; Dacko, 2006; Dacre Pool & Sewell, 2007; Fleisher, 2004; Nabi, 2003). In their review of marketing curricula, Evans, Nancarrow, Tapp, and Stone (2002, p. 579) concluded that 'many marketing graduates are not being well equipped for the "new marketing"'. Andrews and Higson (2008) and Lynch (2007) also observed that unless graduates are able to master the broader range of 'soft' skills (of which we would claim critical analysis is one), then their ability to apply their subject knowledge will be severely limited. Lynch (2007) also reported on research with employers which revealed that their requirements from graduates went well beyond the application of subject knowledge, and into the realms of intuition, creativity and common sense. In their research on employer emphasis when recruiting graduates Raybould and Sheedy (2005, p. 263) reported that 'competence based questions have become increasingly prevalent over the past 10 years. There is focus upon the all-round skills such as team-working, leadership, problem solving as well as technical abilities.'

There is also the issue over whether analysis, per se, is actually a craft, a discipline, a field, or a profession (Davis, 2002; Fleisher, 2003; Johnston, 2005; Marr, 2006; Marrin & Clemente, 2005). Much of this debate centres on how a CI analyst has to balance the need to be creative with the need to employ documented methods in their effort to produce good output (Fleisher & Bensoussan, 2007; Pawelski, 2006). Although these two 'art' and 'science' elements are not necessarily diametrically opposed, they are generally perceived as two ends of a single continuum (Johnston, 2005). It is a rare kind of instructor who can accomplish this level of flexibility in the context of a discipline driven curriculum. In reporting on an innovative approach to leadership teaching by Foster and Carboni (2009), Schmidt-Wilk (2009, p. 657) writes:

> As management educators we aim to help students learn content about leadership, power, justice and social responsibility. We also aim to help them grow and develop for their future professional responsibilities. Developmental theory suggests that teaching to only the surface levels of the mind will not develop students' greatest potentials.

It is now over 10 years since Atkins (1999) challenged the assumptions held at that time regarding the employability of students who had successfully passed through higher education. Her position then was that 'over the last decade there has been a steady stream of reports and papers urging the higher education sector to take key, core, transferable and employability skills into the heart of students' learning experience' (p. 267). She also argued that (pp. 268–269):

> general intellectual skills span both the work required to obtain a degree and many of the attributes deemed desirable in employment in the next century, particularly in the knowledge-based production sector with its concepts of knowledge management and intellectual capital. They include:
>
> - critical engagement with evidence and its interpretation;
> - error-free reasoning;
> - the ability to analyse and synthesise information;
> - thinking flexibly;
> - attacking problems quantitatively;
> - creating valid new knowledge.

In a recent wide-ranging survey of senior executives from 694 companies, the Confederation of British Industry ([CBI] 2010) reported on their findings on the state of Education and Skills in those firms. Between them, they employ more than 2.4 million people, 1 in 12 of the workforce. The CBI (2010, p. 24) reported that 24% of respondent firms expressed dissatisfaction with graduates' problem-solving skills, stating that they had expected that the ability to use creative thinking to develop appropriate solutions to problems 'should be a prime outcome of higher education'. Add to this, the finding that 26% of respondents were unimpressed by the self-management skills of graduates and the inevitable conclusion has to be that little, if anything, has changed to address the problems identified in the 1990s. Analysts may indeed be left short-changed by many higher education providers.

Developing intelligence insight

CI analysis requires a unique and differentiated form of pragmatic thinking. Most individuals have neither been formally trained, nor have the natural ability, to perform this type of activity. Although there has been a natural and healthy evolution of offerings available to those wishing to receive formal analysis instruction (Fleisher & Bensoussan, 2003, 2007), few educational developments in this area have been positive, due in part, to the lack of experienced faculty staff and ambiguity of scope.

The potential for the teaching of critical and intuitive analysis has been debated in the arena of business ethics (Burton, Dunn, & Goldsby, 2006; Griseri, 2002; Locke, 2006), multiculturalism (El-Hani & Mortimer, 2007; Kim, 2006), technology/science (Davies, 2003) and popular culture (Snævarr, 2007). A conceptual paper by Clark, Gray, and Mearman (2006) identified scope within the marketing curriculum and Herrmann (2005, p. 111) spoke of the need for scholars and practitioners to conceive 'new dominant paradigms in strategic management that revolve around the concepts of knowledge, learning and innovation'. Miller and Ireland (2005) agreed and stated that in their view, the benefits of intuition had not received sufficient attention. More recently, Stepanovich (2009, p. 725), through the vehicle of a six-part unfolding tale, illustrated how students can be, and argues that they should be, encouraged not to 'accept blindly what they are told. . . . to challenge assumptions, conduct research, and form their own opinions'.

A somewhat unconventional approach to analysis was also advocated by Wright and Pickton (1995) in their paper titled *What marketers can learn from photography*. Not to be confused with satellite imagery or photo interpretation, they suggested the employment of visual arts graduates as intelligence analysts by firms, with the expectation that they might be able to look more creatively at situations and think in a less formulaic or structured manner.

Ten key continua of Competitive Intelligence analysis

In an effort to address this, Figure 1 outlines 10 continua which identify those skills that we believe a CI analyst has to master before they can consider themselves to be truly competent in their work.

These continua have been developed not only from research and experience of teaching competitive analysis, but also from discussions with a variety of practitioners of differing experience around the globe. A few elements of the 10 continua will inevitably overlap, but the intention has been to establish those with lower degrees of redundancy and repetition. In order to carry out their work effectively, competitive analysts must be willing, able and competent at moving across the continuum to suit the situation to hand.

Creative ↔ Scientific

CI analysts need to be skilled in the application of both creative and scientific techniques. Good analysts will seek to combine differing intellectual patterns, which are reflected in the wider, often unique processes in any firm's decision making process (Clark, 2004).

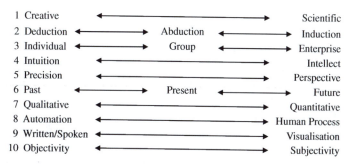

Figure 1.   The 10 key continua of Competitive Intelligence analysis.

Experienced CI analysts develop the ability over time to know how to achieve the appropriate balance between the various elements and differing approaches to the analytical task (Davis, 2002). Although recent efforts have sought to document and replicate the approaches, methods and skills needed to perform this analysis properly (Davis, 2002), most experienced CI analysts recognise that the creativity which comes from first-time or one-time connections or techniques can also be a source of valuable insight (Smith, Flowers, & Larkin, 2009). If all CI analysis is done scientifically, then the development of artificial intelligence, computational algorithms, and solutions-generating software would already have become the norm, a situation that at least a few experts suggest would be debilitating for analysis and decision making in most organisations (Fahey, 2007; Fuld, 2003; Gilad, 1994, 2004; Wright & Calof, 2006).

Deduction ↔ Abduction ↔ Induction

This continuum examines the sequence of analysis arising between assumptions, facts and conclusions. It is important because many CI analysts begin their tasks with a plethora of data, facts and rumour, while others start with nothing. It is just as important in cases where analogies or benchmarks are readily available, as it is in situations where they are lacking (French et al., 2009).

Deduction is the process of reasoning employed by CI analysts, whereby their conclusions follow from the stated premises (Clark, 2004; Loviscky, Treviño, & Jacobs, 2007). In other words, analysts deduce inferences by reasoning from the general to the specific. Deductive reasoning works best in so-called closed systems, which rarely exist in the competitive business arena. Nevertheless, as a critical mode of inquiry, it can be very useful in refuting specific hypotheses and helping the analyst arrive at more definitive estimates of the likelihood of prospective outcomes (Morse & Mitcham, 2002).

Induction typically happens when a CI analyst is able to postulate causality among related phenomena. It can also involve drawing out or analysing assumptions or premises used in forming conclusions (Clark, 2004; Morse & Mitcham, 2002).

Abduction is the process of generating an original hypothesis to explain evidence that does not easily or readily offer a common explanation (Spens & Kovács, 2006). Compared to inductive reasoning, abduction expands the number and set of hypotheses available for scrutiny to the analyst (Lundberg, 2007; Schum, 1987). Some experts have referred to this as the 'a-ha' type of reasoning whereby the analyst generates responses in a spontaneous fashion and probably cannot consciously articulate the steps they used to arrive at their outcome (Schmidlin, 1993).

Individual ←→ Group ←→ Enterprise

CI analysts work on tasks across three generic levels of their organisations – individual, group and enterprise. As in many problem solving and decision making endeavours, achieving success at all three levels involves more than just the added burden of having to integrate more people into one's task. Much of the analysts' work is done at the individual level whereby they alone are responsible for the outputs (Buchanan & O'Connell, 2006).

When working at the group level, CI analysts will commonly work in collaboration with others, with the final product being the result of a joint effort (Baker, 2010). In these cases, the individual effort is difficult to identify as it becomes entwined and develops as a result of the group process (Goncaloa & Duguid, 2008).

At the enterprise level, a CI analyst's own group, and other groups within the enterprise will generate insights that are utilised by decision makers. This is the most complex process in an organisation and a large part of the CI analyst's role is to consider and integrate both the firm and the market context into their analytical process (Short, Ketchen, Palmer, & Hult, 2007). There is a paramount need for them to be cognisant of, and factor in, the social, political, historical and cultural lenses through which their colleagues view the world (Fleisher & Bensoussan, 2007). At the same time, it is important that they do not over-play the role of such corporate norms, otherwise they can become paralysed and ineffective (Chira, Adams, & Thornton, 2008; Langley, 1995).

Intuition ←→ Intellect

Similar, but not the same as the creative–scientific continuum, this one suggests that CI analysts must employ their intuition, sometimes referred to as 'immediate cognition' or the 'Eureka effect' (Cutting & Kouzmin, 2004). Intuition is inevitably influenced by past experience, coupled with a natural proclivity to come to a judgement, often recognised as instinctive ways of knowing (Davis, 2002; Eriksen, 2009). Analysts will have a 'hunch' or sense of something which they cannot readily express in writing. What makes intuition so important in a CI analytical context is that not only will the analyst use this to some degree in processing data, but the decision maker will almost always use a similar skill in assessing the recommendations of the analyst. Intuition is a prevailing power within that process (Sinclair & Ashkanasy, 2005).

The use of intellect is where the CI analyst is operating in a well thought out, calculated and rational manner. Intellect is driven by a data gathering plan and a strategy which is subject to time, social and other performance pressures which can impair it.

Intellect and intuition may converge eventually, in an analyst's recommendation, but the intellectual portion of their recommendation can be more easily communicated to recipients in the form of rules, concepts and/or techniques. Intuition is less tangible, less easy to prove and rationally, less easy to account for (Sadler-Smith & Sparrow, 2007).

Precision ←→ Perspective

It is suggested that the majority of CI analysts will work in the broader context of the firm, rather than the more narrow and specific facets of precision (Saaty & Shih, 2009). This is often analogised as the trade-off between seeing the 'wood for the trees' (Bebbington, Gray, & Owen, 1999). A decision maker will not usually need to know the fact that a competitor earned precisely 34.5632% of their total revenues from a product called 'Shiny Hair to Go', rather, the perspective view that they generated approximately a third of their revenues from one product line. In other words, ensuring that the CI analyst does not leave themselves open to the damning response of, 'thank you for the figures, but what do they mean?' (Sutcliffe, 2010).

While the perspective view can sometimes be valuable, this does not mean that there is no room for precision in coming to that view. It is all a matter of what is reported and how it is done. CI analysts should always seek to attain a reasonable level of precision without spending any more time than is necessary to produce a recommendation with an agreed level of confidence. This will change by project, by situation, by decision maker and by decision urgency (Mintzberg & Westley, 2001/2010).

Past ↔ Present ↔ Future

CI analysts make trades-off between the use of their time and the direction, in which both their data, and their recommendations, are pointing. Accounting data, competitor sales figures, information from financial statements and balance sheets, market share figures and the like, are the result of actions which have taken place in the past. This information is of value when operating in static and simple market conditions, where forecasting, trends analysis and chain ratios, based on past events, are common place (Hooley, Piercy, & Nicouloud, 2008, pp. 177–190). In dynamic and complex markets, concept testing, scenarios, strategic planning, cross-impact analysis and expert opinion are required (Hooley, Piercy, & Nicouloud, 2008, pp. 191–198). The simple collection and assimilation of past data is insufficient to assess the future.

CI analysts also need to use leading indicators of present/future activity and factor these into their understanding of the evolving competitive environment. They need to tap into their organisational memory (Rowlinson, Booth, Clark, Delahaye, & Procter, 2010) but recognise that this will only summarise what is already known, it will not necessarily predict the future. Practising the art of reflection is critical to producing good analytical output. Reflection, as identified by Jordan, Messner, and Becker (2009, p. 466) 'denotes a practice of inquiry that is concerned with past, current or future phenomena, such as decisions, actions, processes and events. Reflection means engaging in comparison, considering alternatives, seeing things from various perspectives, and drawing inferences.' Judgements, propositions and recommendations about the future are where CI analysts earn their money and reputation, providing value added analytical output for use by the firm's decision makers.

Qualitative ↔ Quantitative

Qualitative analysis methods are those which are typically associated with interpretative approaches, rather than measuring discrete, observable events. Qualitative methods are most helpful in those areas that have been identified as potential weaknesses within the quantitative approach. The use of interviews and observations provide deeper, rather than broader, data about a particular phenomenon. These methods can be particularly valuable in helping to describe and explain the longitudinal evolution of competition and competitive behaviour (Johnston, 2005).

Quantitative methods are more commonly used to examine a context at a single point in time. The weaknesses of quantitative analytical process lie mainly in their failure to ascertain deeper underlying meanings and explanations of marketplace competition, even when they produce results that are significant, reliable and valid (Gilad, 2004).

Recent surveys of tools used in assisting decision making show that the majority of managers and companies tend to favour the use of quantitative methods (Rigby & Bilodeau, 2007), principally because they tend to produce results which can be replicated and are more easily disseminated. Quantitative analysis and results tend to be viewed as being more rigorous and free from interpretational bias (Davis, 2002), but it is also well understood that statistics are not always as 'squeaky clean' as purported (Best, 2001, 2004).

Effective CI analysts need to be able to apply and use both qualitative and quantitative methods as well as be able to communicate both the results and the processes underlying their analyses. They need to operate pragmatically, in order to ensure that they select the best methods to suit the task rather than be hide-bound by just one dominant approach (Wallenius et al., 2008). Without understanding from where, and how, their results were derived, as well as the trade-offs made in achieving them, they leave themselves open to criticism.

Automation ↔ Human Process

One aspect that every CI analyst must assess is the desire to automate their processes. Many business processes have benefited greatly from the 'systems' approach and it certainly has its place (Bose, 2008). Even a number of data gathering tasks that form the larger process of CI, such as setting up targeted Really Simple Syndication (RSS) feeds, monitoring of competitor website changes or media about competitor activity, have been productively automated (Vibert, 2001). Unfortunately, software developed to support the CI analytical process has, to date, not been impressive in performing or promoting effective analysis (Fuld, 2003).

No 'magic bullet' or 'plug-in' solution exists which can replace the ability of the human brain to understand, assimilate and assess the type of data that CI analysts regularly deal with, or make sense of (Ball, Edwards, & Ross, 2007). While some automation may benefit the process, what automation cannot yet carry out, and may never be able to, is to replicate the unique processes of strategic thinking that human beings can achieve (Nielsen & Michailova, 2007; Zangoueinezhad & Moshabaki, 2009). This is especially true when this thinking includes the application of creativity and intuition previously described.

Written/Spoken ↔ Visualisation

The issue of clearly communicating analytical processes and outcomes is ever-present. In volume terms, the written/spoken word is, arguably, the most frequent form of delivery used. Unfortunately, not all spoken or written words are meaningful because of poor delivery, poor language skills and/or overuse of codes or acronyms which do not translate or travel across divisions or strategic business units (SBUs) (Grewal & Slotegraaf, 2007).

Visualisation on the other hand, allows analysts to share their ideas in graphic, illustrative, pictorial formats (Bose, 2009; Chung, 2009). Being able to 'draw a picture' of a situation, visually describe competitors or their likely behaviours and use metaphors to aid understanding is far more powerful, and memorable, to busy decision makers than a 35 page report of closely typed text and figures (Magnusson, 2010). The onus is on the analyst to make the story 'live', interpret their findings and provide a recommendation, rather than simply present the bare facts. Astute CI analysts also need to be aware of the preferences of their differing audiences and be able to develop the skills required to deliver to those needs (Fox, 2009). Research by Militello, Bowers, Boehnlein, Olding, and Ambrose (2009, p. 255) into decision communication methods reported that the challenge for analysts is to resist creating 'visualizations for communicating complex multivariate relationships. Simple, familiar visualizations may be the most effective.'

Objectivity ⟷ Subjectivity

Nearly all tenets of analysis suggest that CI analysts must be objective, detached, dispassionate and unbiased in their work (Buchanan & O'Connell, 2006). This does not mean that individuals can, or should, surrender their personal views but the analysis process is often more akin to the social sciences than to pure science (Saaty, 2008). Consequently, there will always be some degree of error present. Individuality by a CI analyst is highly desirable in the appropriate circumstances but they need to recognise when they are being objective and when they are not (Clark & Montgomery, 1996). This balance is not always easy to achieve.

Subjectivity in CI analysis requires the same justification as any other form of objective measure. It must be properly clarified so that decision makers can make their own judgement on the quality of the analysis and recommendations presented. The analyst should always enter an assignment with an open mind, try to see things through the perspective of their data gatherers and decision makers as well as market competitors in order to be empathetic to better understanding their own preconceived notions.

Responding to analysis failure: guiding principles for the firm

Clearly, effective CI analysts must know how to position properly their efforts and focus across the continuum over time. That is not to say that it is always necessary to find the middle ground on each continuum. In fact, the middle ground may be exactly the wrong place to be. Rather, the analyst needs to determine where they should be on a project along each of the continua, and be able to adapt along each, as the project and its evolution demands. There is however, a responsibility on the part of the firm to provide a suitable environment within which the CI analyst can carry out their work, one in which they can learn their craft, experiment, develop and hone their skills. It is the CI analyst who provides the intellectual input but it is the analysis process which determines success or otherwise. No matter how skilled the analyst or the decision making process into which analytical output is inevitably fed, performance will be significantly enhanced if the firm takes it responsibility seriously and pays heed to the following guiding principles. Only then will they reap the full benefits of an effective and efficient CI analysis function.

Provide empowerment

Without intelligence, decision makers cannot take responsibility. With it, they cannot avoid taking responsibility. Clearly, the more that decision makers are equipped with insight, the better they will perform. This is why the importance of CI analysis needs to be recognised in its own right. Both analysts and executives should promote the reality that CI analysis is critical to an organisation's competitive success. Analysts and their internal customers ought to be comfortable with, and publicise to others, the real benefit which emanates from their work. Competitive Intelligence is a fast growing discipline in its own right and CI analysts are skilled professionals, operating no differently than other professionals in the firm.

Realise the value of analysis

Even if the benefits and value of the process cannot be easily quantified by existing performance measurement systems, executives need to realise that effective CI analysis cannot be achieved through 'quick fixes' or by the introduction of new software or hardware applications. The value of CI analysis comes from human perception and interception, the identification of apparently unrelated items of information, and the evaluation of such to produce competitive insight. This adds value to the decision making process and ultimately benefits the enterprise. Sharing examples of good and bad analytical outputs is a powerful way of demonstrating the relationship between CI analysis quality and decision making effectiveness. It will show how using analysis insights can significantly lower the number of uncontrollable or perceived risks associated with decisions.

Ask the right questions

Consumers of CI analysis products should know what to ask for from analysts and be realistic in what they expect to receive. Executives and departmental managers, like many other employees within the organisation, often misunderstand the true functions and proper operations of CI specialists. Decision makers will ask for the wrong information and will then have difficulty in making sense of the analytical products they receive. For the CI analyst, it is important that executives communicate just what it is that will make a difference to their agenda. Only then will the analyst be able to provide products that are tailored not only to decision makers' specific information requirements, but also presented in a usable format.

Position the analyst correctly

It is vital that a CI analyst is positioned where they can make a difference. They need to be actively involved in the networks of information collectors and their clients, but also be given sufficient time to do their work. The more time that an analyst has to focus their efforts on particular specialties needed by decision makers, the quicker they will move up the learning curve in terms of producing quality outputs. As CI analysis is primarily a human process, there is always the potential for human error. It is essential that the firm engages in post-mortem exercises of *all* significant decisions, regardless of whether these were regarded as successful or not, to encourage learning from such errors. This will help to develop shared trust between a CI analyst and their decision makers. CI analysts are at their most creative and most effective when they can rely on the trust and confidence of their clients.

Provide the right tools

As with any other skilled worker, the CI analyst needs to have access to all the proper tools of their craft. Analytic applications, reliable data inputs, access to sources, time to think, advanced information and communication infrastructure and so on. Analysts cannot be expected to provide insight without having access to rich sources of data, enabling technology, the open door of their organisational colleagues and clearly articulated KITs/KIQs. The outputs will then be focused to capture the client's imagination and provide assistance on complex issues both quickly and comprehensively. The CI analyst's job is not to intimidate clients with information, but to entice them with it.

Differentiate the task

Last, but certainly not least, CI analysts must differentiate the nature of the analysis they perform from other forms of analysis concurrently being done within their enterprises. CI analysts and their decision makers should be careful not to overrate, overemphasise or try and duplicate the analysis of organisations, industries and macro-level issues, which are typically provided by economists, financial analysts and/or sector analysts. These individuals are primarily concerned with short-term financial gains, not competitiveness and strategic development. Executives who understand the reasons these functions vary, and the respective benefits each generates, will be far better served by their CI analyst and their potential contribution to decision making.

Conclusion and practical implications

Competitive Intelligence produces insight about externally motivated change, future developments and their implications to the organisation. Done well, data analysis and the CI developed from it, helps the organisation to reduce its risk level in strategically dealing with both threats and opportunities in its competitive environment. Paradoxically, the CI analysis function tends to suffer during recessionary periods, when organisations reduce their commitment to what they deem as less essential functions. Those working in CI analysis know that this is precisely the time when investment in such activity should increase, in order to prepare the firm better for the challenges ahead.

Causes of failure at the individual level have been identified and we would draw special attention to the issue of cognitive bias, a factor of which both CI analysts and educators should be acutely aware. It is noted that the teaching of CI analysis receives superficial attention among educators and at best, is haphazard. Analysis is a critical component in aiding executives in their decision making. As such, effective analysts must know how to position properly their efforts and focus, over time, across the 10 key continua presented in this paper. Unfortunately, teaching the art of pragmatism, intuition and 'gut feel' is less evident in practice and is an element of learning which continues to evade educators.

This may be due to a their lack of experience of actually doing this sort of work in a commercial environment, a lack of experience at having to defend the findings of analysis when critical decisions will be taken on the basis of their work or their almost inevitable lack of understanding of what is needed by employers. It may even be a heady mixture of all three. Buchanan and O'Connell (2006, p. 38) noted that 'we don't admire gut decision makers so much as for their courage in making them. Gut decisions testify to the confidence of the decision maker, an invaluable trait in a leader.' Perhaps it is a simple matter of courage.

The problems inherent in CI analysis failure can be corrected and we have presented a set of guiding principles for implementation at the organisational level. This can only improve the potential for the delivery of high quality analysis output. When the full realisation of the impact that skilled CI analysts can have on a firm's success is understood, it makes sense that this would be one way of promoting better practice. The ultimate ambition would be the development of a validated education path which leads to a recognised qualification with standards of practice and a dedicated Chartered Competitive Intelligence Analyst status. Such a development would certainly be good news for employers seeking to recruit such talent to support the decision making challenges they face in the dynamic, globalised markets within which they compete.

References

Andrews, J., & Higson, H. (2008). Graduate employability, 'soft skills' versus 'hard' business knowledge: A European study. *Higher Education in Europe, 33*, 411–422.

Astrachan, J.H., & Jaskiewicz, P. (2008). Emotional returns and emotional costs in privately held family businesses: Advancing traditional business valuation. *Family Business Review, 21*, 139–149.

Atkins, M.J. (1999). Oven-ready and self-basting: Taking stock of employability skills. *Teaching in Higher Education, 4*, 267–280.

Baker, D.F. (2010). Enhancing group decision making: An exercise to reduce shared information bias. *Journal of Management Education, 34*, 249–279.

Ball, K., Edwards, J.D., & Ross, L.A. (2007). The impact of speed of processing training on cognitive and everyday functions. *Journal of Gerontology, Series B, 62*(1), 19–31.

Bazerman, M.H. (2002). *Judgment in managerial decision making* (5th ed.). New Jersey: Wiley & Sons.

Bebbington, J., Gray, R., & Owen, D. (1999). Seeing the wood for the trees: Taking the pulse of social and environmental accounting. *Accounting, Auditing and Accountability Journal, 12*(1), 47–51.

Belbin, R.M. (2010). *Management teams: Why they succeed or fail* (3rd ed.). Oxford: Butterworth-Heinemann.

Benhabib, J., & Bisin, A. (2008). Choice and process: Theory ahead of measurement. In A. Caplinand & A. Schotter (Eds.), *Handbook of economic methodology* (pp. 320–335). New York: Oxford University Press.

Best, J. (2001). *Damned lies and statistics: Untangling the numbers from the media, politicians, and activists.* Berkeley: University of California Press.

Best, J. (2004). *More damned lies and statistics: How numbers confuse public issues.* Berkeley: University of California Press.

Bloom, N., & van Reenen, J. (2007). Measuring and explaining management practices across firms and countries. *Quarterly Journal of Economics, 122*, 1351–1408.

Bose, R. (2008). Competitive Intelligence process and tools for intelligence analysis. *Industrial Management & Data Systems, 108*, 510–528.

Bose, R. (2009). Advanced analytics: Opportunities and challenges. *Industrial Management & Data Systems, 109*, 155–172.

Brown, S. (2007). *Fail better: Stumbling to success in sales & marketing.* London: Cyan.

Buchanan, L., & O'Connell, D. (2006). A brief history of decision making. *Harvard Business Review, 84*(1), 32–41.

Burton, B.K., Dunn, C.P., & Goldsby, M. (2006). Moral pluralism in business ethics education: It's about time. *Journal of Management Education, 30*(1), 90–105.

Burvill, C., Mead, G., Weir, J., McGowan, P., Reuter, M., Schiavone, F., & Leary, M. (2009). Evaluation of operational environmental performance: An engineering-based approach. *International Journal of Sustainable Design, 1*, 180–198.

Capelli, P. (2008). Talent management for the twenty-first century. *Harvard Business Review, 86*(3), 74–81.

Chao, L.P., & Ishii, K. (2003, September). *Design process error-proofing: Failure modes and effects analysis of the design process.* Paper presented at the Design Engineering Technical Conference, Chicago, IL.

Chira, I., Adams, M., & Thornton, B. (2008). Behavioral bias within the decision making process. *Journal of Business & Economics Research, 6*(8), 11–20.

Chung, W. (2009). Enhancing business intelligence quality with visualization: An experiment on stakeholder network analysis. *Pacific Asia Journal of the Association for Information Systems, 1*(1), Article 9. Retrieved from http://aisel.aisnet.org/pajais/vol1/iss1/9

Clark, B.H., & Montgomery, D.B. (1996). Perceiving competitive reactions: The value of accuracy (and paranoia). *Marketing Letters, 7*, 115–129.

Clark, P., Gray, D., & Mearman, A. (2006). The marketing curriculum and educational aims: Towards a professional education. *Marketing Intelligence and Planning, 24*, 189–201.

Clark, R.M. (2004). *Intelligence analysis: A target-centric approach.* Washington, DC: CQ Press.

Clayton, P., & Kimbrell, J. (2007). Thinking preferences as diagnostic and learning tools for managerial styles and predictors of auditor success. *Managerial Finance, 33*, 921–934.

Confederation of British Industry (CBI). (2010, May). *Ready to grow: Business priorities for education and skills: Education and skills survey.* London: CBI.

Cutting, B., & Kouzmin, A. (2004). A synthesis of knowing and governance: Making sense of organizational and governance polemics. *Corporate Governance, 4*(1), 76–114.

Dacko, S.G. (2006). Narrowing the skills gap for marketers of the future. *Marketing Intelligence & Planning, 24*, 283–295.

Dacre Pool, L., & Sewell, P. (2007). The key to employability: Developing a practical model of graduate employability. *Education+Training, 49*, 277–289.

Davies, D. (2003). Pragmatism, pedagogy and philosophy: A model of thought and action in primary technology and science teacher education. *International Journal of Technology and Design Education, 13*, 207–221.

Davis, J. (2002). Sherman Kent and the profession of intelligence analysis. *Occasional Papers, The Sherman Kent Center for Intelligence Analysis, 1*(5), 1–16.

Delmar, F., & Wiklund, J. (2008). The effect of small business managers' growth motivation on firm growth: A longitudinal study. *Entrepreneurship Theory and Practice, 32*, 437–457.

Edmonson, A., & Cannon, M. (2005). Failing to learn and learning to fail (intelligently): How great organizations put failure to work to improve and innovate. *Long Range Planning, 38*, 299–319.

El-Hani, C.N., & Mortimer, E.F. (2007). Multicultural education, pragmatism and the goals of science teaching. *Cultural Studies of Science Education, 2*, 657–701.

Eriksen, M. (2009). Authentic leadership: Practical reflexivity, self-awareness, and self-authorship. *Journal of Management Education, 33*, 747–771.

Evans, M., Nancarrow, C., Tapp, A., & Stone, M. (2002). Future marketers: Future curriculum: Future shock. *Journal of Marketing Management, 18*, 579–596.

Fahey, L. (2007). Connecting strategy and Competitive Intelligence: Refocusing intelligence to produce critical strategy inputs. *Strategy & Leadership, 35*(1), 4–12.

Fairlie, R.W., & Robb, A. (2007). Families, human capital, and small business: Evidence from the characteristics of business owners survey. *Industrial and Labor Relations Review, 60*, 225–245.

Fleisher, C.S. (2003). Are Competitive Intelligence practitioners professionals? In C.S. Fleisher & D.L. Blenkhorn (Eds.), *Controversies in Competitive Intelligence: The enduring issues* (pp. 29–44). Greenwich, CT: Praeger.

Fleisher, C.S. (2004). Competitive Intelligence education: Competencies, sources and trends. *Information Management Journal, 38*(2), 56–63.

Fleisher, C.S., & Bensoussan, B. (2003). *Strategic and competitive analysis: Methods and techniques for analysing business competition.* Upper Saddle River, NJ: Prentice Hall.

Fleisher, C.S., & Bensoussan, B. (2007). *Business and competitive analysis: Effective application of new and classic methods.* Upper Saddle River, NJ: Financial Times/Pearson.

Foster, P., & Carboni, I. (2009). Using student-centered cases in the classroom: An action inquiry approach to leadership development. *Journal of Management Education, 33*, 676–698.

Fox, T. (2009). *An empirical investigation of the effects of pre-decision agreement, group development and communication style on group decision making performance* (PhD thesis, Pacific University). Retrieved from http://commons.pacificu.edu/cgi/viewcontent.cgi?article=1184&context=spp

French, B., Thomas, L.H., Baker, P., Burton, C.R., Pennington, L., & Roddam, H. (2009). What can management theories offer evidence-based practice? A comparative analysis of measurement tools for organisational context. *Implementation Science, 4*, Item 28. Retrieved from http://implementationscience.com/content/4/1/28

Fuld, L.M. (2003). *Intelligence software report 2003: Leveraging the web* (Private report). Fuld & Company, Boston, MA.

Fuller-Love, N. (2006). Management development in small firms. *International Journal of Management Reviews, 8*, 175–190.

Gib, A., & Gooding, R. (1998, April). *CI tool time: What's missing from your toolbag?* Paper presented at the International conference of the Society of Competitive Intelligence Professionals, Chicago, IL.

Gilad, B. (1994). *Business blindspots: Replacing your company's entrenched and outdated myths, beliefs, and assumptions with the realities of today's markets.* Chicago, IL: Probus.

Gilad, B. (2004). *Early warning.* New York: Amacom.

Goncaloa, J.A., & Duguid, M.M. (2008). Hidden consequences of the group-serving bias: Causal attributions and the quality of group decision making. *Organizational Behavior and Human Decision Processes, 107*, 219–233.

Grewal, R., & Slotegraaf, R. (2007). Embeddedness of organizational capabilities. *Decision Sciences, 38*, 450–488.

Griseri, P. (2002). Emotion and cognition in business ethics teaching. *Teaching Business Ethics, 6*, 371–391.

Herrmann, P. (2005). Evolution of strategic management: The need for new dominant designs. *International Journal of Management Reviews*, *7*, 111–130.

Heuer, J.R., Jr. (1999). *The psychology of intelligence analysis*. Washington, DC: Center for the Study of Intelligence.

Heuer, J.R., Jr. (2005). Limits of intelligence analysis. *Orbis*, *49*(1), 75–94.

Hines, T. (1987). Left brain/right brain mythology and implications for management and training. *Academy of Management Review*, *12*, 600–606.

Hogarth, R.M., & Karelaia, N. (2008). *Entrepreneurial success and failure: Confidence and fallible judgement* (Economics and Business Working Papers Series No. 1130). Department d'Economia i Empresa, Universitat Pompeu Fabra. Retrieved from http://hdl.handle.net/2072/14545

Hooley, G., Piercy, N.F., & Nicouloud, B. (2008). *Marketing strategy and competitive positioning* (4th ed.). Harlow, UK: Prentice Hall.

Johnston, R. (2005). *Analytic culture in the U.S. intelligence community*. Washington, DC: The Center for the Study of Intelligence.

Jordan, S., Messner, M., & Becker, A. (2009). Reflection and mindfulness in organizations: Rationales and possibilities for integration. *Management Learning*, *40*, 465–473.

Kavanagh, M.H., & Drennan, L. (2008). What skills and attributes does an accounting graduate need? Evidence from student perceptions and employer expectations. *Accounting and Finance*, *48*, 279–300.

Keil, M., Depledge, G., & Rai, A. (2007). Escalation: The role of problem recognition and cognitive bias. *Decision Sciences*, *38*, 391–421.

Kim, K.I. (2006). A cultural artefact 'show and tell': A pedagogic tool for teaching cross-cultural management. *Journal of Business Innovation and Research*, *1*, 144–148.

Klingberg, T. (2009). *The overflowing brain: Information overload and the limits of working memory*. Oxford: Oxford University Press.

Koopman, S.J., & Lucas, A. (2005). Business and default cycles for credit risk. *Journal of Applied Econometrics*, *20*, 311–323.

Langley, A. (1995). Between paralysis by analysis and extinction by instinct. *Sloan Management Review*, *36*(3), 63–76.

Locke, E.A. (2006). Business ethics: A way out of the morass. *Academy of Management Learning and Education*, *5*, 324–332.

Loviscky, G.E., Treviño, L.K., & Jacobs, R.R. (2007). Assessing managers' ethical decision-making: An objective measure of managerial moral judgment. *Journal of Business Ethics*, *73*, 263–285.

Lundberg, C.G. (2007). Models of emerging contexts in risky and complex decision settings. *European Journal of Operational Research*, *177*, 1363–1374.

Lynch, J. (2007, July). *The creation of the new marketer – are we getting it right?* Paper presented at the Academy of Marketing Conference, Royal Holloway, London, UK.

Magnusson, C. (2010). Improving competitive analysis with temporal text visualization. *Marketing Intelligence & Planning*, *28*, 571–581.

Manassea, P., & Roubini, N. (2009). Rules of thumb for sovereign debt crises. *Journal of International Economics*, *78*, 192–205.

Marr, B. (2006). *Strategic performance management: Leveraging and measuring your intangible value drivers*. Amsterdam: Butterworth-Heinemann.

Marrin, S., & Clemente, J. (2005). Improving intelligence analysis by looking to the medical profession. *International Journal of Intelligence and Counterintelligence*, *18*, 707–729.

Marteniuk, J. (2003). How do companies find the best balance between the technical and personal in effective Competitive Intelligence systems? In C.S. Fleisher & D.L. Blenkhorn (Eds.), *Controversies in Competitive Intelligence: The enduring issues* (pp. 176–189). Westport, CT: Praeger.

McMullen, J.S., Shepherd, D.A., & Patzelt, H. (2009). Managerial (in)attention to competitive threats. *Journal of Management Studies*, *46*, 157–181.

Militello, L.G., Bowers, D.M., Boehnlein, T.R., Olding, R.B., & Ambrose, K. (2009, June). Visualizations: From complex analyses to actionable findings. In *Proceedings of the 9th International Conference on Naturalistic Decision Making* (pp. 255–256). London: British Computer Society.

Miller, C.C., & Ireland, R.D. (2005). Intuition in strategic decision making: Friend or foe in the fast paced 21st century. *Academy of Management*, *19*(1), 19–30.

Miller, G.A. (1956). The magical number seven, plus or minus two: Some limits on our capacity for processing information. *Psychological Review*, *63*(2), 81–97.

Mintzberg, H., & Westley, F. (2010). Decision making: It's not what you think. In P.C. Nutt & D.C. Wilson (Eds.), *Handbook of decision making* (pp. 73–82). Chichester: Wiley-Blackwell. (First published in 2001, *Sloan Management Review*, *42*(3), 89–93)

Morecroft, J.D. (2006). The feedback view of business policy and strategy. *Systems Dynamics Review*, *1*(1), 4–19.

Morse, J.M., & Mitcham, C. (2002). Exploring qualitatively-derived concepts: Inductive-deductive pitfalls. *International Journal of Qualitative Methods*, *1*(4), 28–35.

Nabi, G.R. (2003). Graduate employment and underemployment: Opportunity for skill use and career experiences amongst recent business graduates. *Education+Training*, *45*, 371–381.

Nielsen, B.B., & Michailova, S. (2007). Knowledge management systems in multinational corporations: Typology and transitional dynamics. *Long Range Planning*, *40*, 314–340.

Palmer, M., Simmons, G., & deKervenoael, R. (2010). Brilliant mistake! Essays on incidents of management mistakes and *mea culpa*. *International Journal of Retail & Distribution Management*, *38*, 234–257.

Pansiri, J., & Temtime, Z.T. (2008). Assessing managerial skills in SMEs for capacity building. *Journal of Management Development*, *27*, 251–260.

Pawelski, J.O. (2006). Teaching pragmatism pragmatically: A promising approach to the cultivation of character. *Contemporary Pragmatism*, *3*(1), 127–143.

Pink, D.H. (2005). *A whole new mind: Moving from the information age to the conceptual age*. New York: Riverhead.

Raybould, J., & Sheedy, V. (2005). Are graduates equipped with the right skills in the employability stakes? *Industrial and Commercial Training*, *37*, 259–263.

Rhee, K.S., & Honeycutt Sigler, T. (2010). Developing enlightened leaders for industry and community: Executive education and service-learning. *Journal of Management Education*, *34*(1), 163–181.

Rigby, D.K. (2001). Putting the tools to the test: Senior executives rate 25 top management tools. *Strategy & Leadership*, *29*(3), 4–12.

Rigby, D.K. (2003). *Management tools 2003* (White Paper). Boston, MA: Bain & Co.

Rigby, D.K. (2009). *Management tools 2009: An executive's guide* (White Paper). Boston, MA: Bain & Co.

Rigby, D., & Bilodeau, B. (2007). Bain's global 2007 management tools and trends survey. *Strategy & Leadership*, *3*(5), 9–16.

Rowlinson, M., Booth, C., Clark, P., Delahaye, A., & Procter, S. (2010). Social remembering and organizational memory. *Organization Studies*, *31*(1), 69–87.

Saaty, T.L. (2008). Decision making with the analytic hierarchy process. *International Journal of Services Sciences*, *1*(1), 83–98.

Saaty, T.L., & Shih, H.-S. (2009). Structures in decision making: On the subjective geometry of hierarchies and networks. *European Journal of Operational Research*, *199*, 867–872.

Sadler-Smith, E., & Sparrow, P.R. (2007). *Intuition in organisational decision making* (Lancaster University Management School Centre for Performance-led HR Working Paper, No. 2007-03). Retrieved from http://www.lums.lancs.ac.uk/research/centres/hr/

Sawyer, D.C. (1999). *Getting it right: Avoiding the high cost of wrong decisions*. Boca Raton, FL: St Lucie Press.

Schmidlin, W.G. (1993). *Zen and the art of intelligence analysis* (MSSI thesis). Washington, DC: Joint Military Intelligence College.

Schmidt-Wilk, J. (2009). Teaching to the levels of the mind. *Journal of Management Education*, *33*, 655–658.

Schum, D.A. (1987). *Evidence and inference for the intelligence analyst*. Lanham, MD: Rowman & Littlefield.

Self, K. (2003). Why do so many firms fail at Competitive Intelligence? In C.S. Fleisher & D.L. Blenkhorn (Eds.), *Controversies in Competitive Intelligence: The enduring issues* (pp. 190–202). Westport, CT: Praeger.

Shacham, M., Cutlip, M.B., & Brauner, N. (2008). What is in and what is out in engineering problem solving. In B. Braunschweig & X. Joulia (Eds.), *18th European symposium on computer aided process engineering* (pp. 1187–1192). Amsterdam: Elsevier.

Short, J.C., Ketchen, D.J., Jr, Palmer, T.B., & Hult, F.T.M. (2007). Firm, strategic group, and industry influences on performance. *Strategic Management Journal, 28*, 147–167.

Sinclair, M., & Ashkanasy, N.M. (2005). Intuition: Myth or a decision making tool. *Management Learning, 36*, 353–370.

Smith, J.A., Flowers, P., & Larkin, M. (2009). *Interpretative Phenomenological Analysis: Theory, method and research*. London: Sage.

Snævarr, S. (2007). Pragmatism and popular culture: Shusterman, popular art, and the challenge of visuality. *Journal of Aesthetic Education, 41*(4), 1–11.

Sousa, D.A. (2009). *How the gifted brain learns* (2nd ed.). London: Sage.

Spens, K.M., & Kovács, G. (2006). A content analysis of research approaches in logistics research. *International Journal of Physical Distribution & Logistics Management, 36*, 374–390.

Spreng, R.N., & Grady, C.L. (2010). Patterns of brain activity supporting autobiographical memory, prospection and theory of mind, and their relationship to the default mode network. *Journal of Cognitive Neuroscience, 22*, 1112–1123.

Stanton, P., & Tweed, D. (2009). Evaluation of small business failure and the framing problem. *International Journal of Economics and Business Research, 1*, 438–453.

Stepanovich, P.L. (2009). The lobster tale: An exercise in critical thinking. *Journal of Management Education, 33*, 725–746.

Sutcliffe, A. (2010). Juxtaposing design representations for creativity. *Human Technology, 6*(1), 38–54. Retrieved from www.humantechnology.jyu.fi

Swanson, R.A. (2007). *Analysis for improving performance: Tools for diagnosing organizations and documenting workplace expertise*. San Francisco, CA: Berrett-Koehler.

Thom, L.H., Reichert, M., Chiao, C.M., Iochpe, C., & Hess, G.N. (2008). Inventing less, reusing more, and adding intelligence to business process modeling. *Database and Expert Systems Applications, 5181*, 837–850.

Tokarczyk, J., Hansen, E., Green, M., & Down, J. (2007). A resource-based view and market orientation theory examination of the role of 'familiness' in family business success. *Family Business Review, 20*(1), 17–31.

Tversky, A., & Kahneman, D. (1986). Rational choice and the framing of decisions. *Journal of Business, 59*, 251–294.

Tynjälä, P., Slotte, V., Nieminen, J., Lonka, K., & Olkinuora, E. (2006). From university to working life: Graduates' workplace skills in practice. In P. Tynjälä, J. Valimaa, & G. Boulton-Lewis (Eds.), *Higher education and working life, collaborations, confrontations and challenges* (pp. 73–88). Oxford: Elsevier.

Underwood, J. (2006). Making the break: From competitive analysis to strategic intelligence. *Competitive Intelligence Review, 6*(1), 15–21.

Van Raan, A.F.J. (2004). Measuring science: Capita selecta of current main issues. In H.F. Moed, W. Glänzel, & U. Schmoch (Eds.), *Handbook of quantitative science and technology research* (pp. 19–50). Dordrecht: Kluwer.

Vibert, C. (2001). Leveraging technology: CI in an electronic classroom teaching environment. *Competitive Intelligence Review, 12*(1), 48–58.

Wallenius, J., Dyer, J.S., Fishburn, P.C., Steuer, R.E., Zionts, S., & Deb, K. (2008). Multiple criteria decision making, multi attribute utility theory: Recent accomplishments and what lies ahead. *Management Science, 54*, 1336–1349.

Westney, R., Fort, J., Lucas, J.R., Messier, L.J., Vardeman, D., & Renfro, K. (2009, May). *When failure is not an option: Managing mega projects in the current environment*. Paper no. 20303-MS, Proceedings of the Offshore Technology Conference, Houston, Texas.

Wright, S., & Calof, J.L. (2006). The quest for competitive, business and marketing intelligence: A country comparison of current practices. *European Journal of Marketing, 40*, 453–465.

Wright, S., & Pickton, D.W. (1995, September). *What marketers can learn from photography*. Paper presented at the Marketing Eschatology Conference, University of Ulster, Belfast.

Zangoueinezhad, A., & Moshabaki, A. (2009). The role of structural capital on Competitive Intelligence. *Industrial Management & Data Systems, 109*, 262–280.

Is loyalty driving growth for the brand in front? A two-purchase analysis of car category dynamics in Thailand

Dag Bennett and Charles Graham

The Ehrenberg Centre for Research in Marketing, London South Bank University, 103 Borough Road, London, SE1 0AA, UK

Marketers are often exhorted to grow brand share through increased loyalty. To investigate this proposition, we report on an extension of the two-purchase analysis technique to a dynamic category of infrequently bought goods, new cars in Thailand. This analysis captures market structure quite well, and reveals that brand-share growth comes not from unusually high loyalty but from first time customers attracted to large brands in line with the duplication of purchase law.

Introduction

Analysis of two consecutive purchase records, easily collected from a simple survey, has been shown to reveal many of the well-known brand buying patterns found in consumer panel data (Bennett, 2003a, 2008; Bennett, Ehrenberg, & Goodhardt, 2000). The technique, although still relatively new, is useful in markets where full datasets are hard to come by, or where a diagnostic test is required quickly. In this paper we extend the technique from frequently purchased stable categories to two conditions suggested in Bennett et al. (2000), an infrequently bought item in a dynamic market context.

From 2007 to 2009 the market for new cars in Thailand was volatile. It first expanded by over 34%, and then stalled dramatically in 2009 with the global financial crisis (GFC). Toyota, the biggest brand throughout, reported, in the face of intensifying competition, a 39% share of the market in January 2008 and 45% in October 2009 (Toyota Motor Thailand, 2010). This performance raises some important questions for practitioners. For example, did growth result from customer retention or customer acquisition? Aaker and McLoughlin (2007, p. 177) have described Toyota's brand loyalty as 'legendary', implying a special ability to attract committed customers who refuse to defect through thick and thin. On the other hand, a year into the thin times of the GFC, Art Spinella, president of CNW Research in the USA was quoted in the *New York Times* as saying: 'The days when people bought a Toyota car or a General Motors product for 25 years are over. There really isn't any brand loyalty anymore' (Vlasic, 2009, p. B1).

In the recent academic literature the assertion of the death of loyalty at the hands of the downturn has been given weight by Piercy, Cravens, and Lane (2010) who suggested that one effect of the GFC was the emergence of a 'smart shopper' prepared to look harder at value, and prepared also to defer purchase. Raggio and Leone (2009, p. 85) agreed, citing the successful US launch of the Hyundai Genesis as evidence that many are being forced to re-evaluate familiar brands, switching to those 'that surpass ... performance thresholds at a value price'. Tellis and Tellis (2009) too, in a meta-analysis of research on advertising in recession, reported results on the sensitivities of brand versus private-label shares, and indicated increased switching to 'better' value alternatives during economic slowdown. On the other hand, Tikoo and Ebrahim (2010) have suggested that during a downturn, firms that strengthen intangible brand assets with increased advertising perform better than those focusing on new product development. Toyota is not a budget brand, but remained a mass-market, quality marque. It grew share over the period and so, in examining the Thai market, observers might expect to see evidence of exceptional brand loyalty countering the effects of recession. Lessons from this current study may therefore be of interest to marketing strategists wishing to evaluate the performance of brands of various positions across categories and economic situations.

Regular patterns in consumer behaviour

In analysing the data, findings were benchmarked against the established patterns of consumer behaviour described in the NBD-Dirichlet model (Dirichlet) of purchase incidence and brand choice (Goodhardt, Ehrenberg, & Chatfield, 1984). This parsimonious model has repeatedly been shown to capture closely near-stationary market structure, replicating across widely varied goods and services categories (Ehrenberg, 1988; Ehrenberg, Uncles, & Goodhardt, 2004; Sharp, 2010), subscription markets such as insurance and medical prescriptions (Sharp, Wright, & Goodhardt, 2002), business to business buying (Pickford & Goodhardt, 2000) and in other consumer behaviours such as TV channel choice. Regularities in television viewing were first noted in studies published in the 1960s (Goodhardt, 1966), which have been replicated and extended subsequently (Barwise & Ehrenberg, 1987). The main behavioural metrics are all described in the Dirichlet; how many people buy each brand, how often they do so and which other brands they buy. The fundamental pattern observed is that all brand performance measures vary together according to brand size (Ehrenberg, 1988).

This is easily seen in loyalty measures such as repeat purchase and brand switching that are dependent upon brand share rather than any particular brand attribute or customer segmentation (Kennedy & Ehrenberg, 2001). Big brands tend to score higher and small brands lower on these metrics. Loyalty is therefore not specific to any particular brand or differentiated positioning: rather, brands of similar size in any category normally attract similar loyalty (Ehrenberg, Barnard, & Scriven, 1997).

In addition, loyalty is usually split between brands. Most consumers buy from a portfolio of established choices over a series of purchases, favouring one over another, but buying each regularly if infrequently (Banelis, 2008). Sometimes they may switch away from a particular brand, add a new one or downgrade a former favourite, but few customers are 100% loyal and those that are tend to be the lightest category buyers (Uncles, Ehrenberg, & Hammond, 1995).

Empirical generalization and the NBD-Dirichlet model

Regular patterns of repeat-buying have important implications for marketing strategy. They have been observed in over 50 years of study, and the empirical generalizations developed from them have become the few laws of marketing. These laws provide benchmarks against which achievable objectives can be set and performance can be evaluated, and they subsequently led to the development of the Dirichlet (Goodhardt et al., 1984). Dirichlet benchmarking is extensively reviewed in Ehrenberg et al. (2004) and the model development in Driesener (2005).

The research approach in this body of work has been based on study-replications under varied conditions of time, market categories, countries and business conditions in which it has been possible to see whether findings recurred (or not). The approach does not attempt to build a new model or to create the 'best fit' of one model to a single set of data, but to find a 'generally good fit' for a single model across many sets of data. The understanding of behavioural norms and benchmarks established in this way therefore reliably informs marketing science and it continues to assist practitioners in the planning and evaluation of marketing strategies.

'Compared with what?'

For managers to interpret readily available data, benchmarks are needed that go far beyond 'this time last year'. Is it, for example, 'only 35%' or 'as many as 35%' of the brand's customers who bought a brand again in the past year? Is 35% 'normal' for the category? How does it compare with other brands of the same size, or positioning or price level? Without benchmarks the answers to such questions are meaningless. When looked at systematically, most brand performance measures are just about normal most of the time. To see that this is so, one must know what the patterns are.

To illustrate, Table 1 shows a selection of annual brand performance measures (BPMs) in the UK Laundry Detergent category that compares observed measures (O), with the theoretical output (T) of the Dirichlet. The measures are arranged by those that describe brand size, brand loyalty and brand switching, and the eight brands themselves are ordered from top to bottom by market share (to make pattern spotting easier). The averages show that the fit of the model output to the data is generally good, while the table clearly reveals four regular 'Dirichlet' patterns of consumer behaviour that have determined each brand's sales over the year.

Four Dirichlet patterns

Brand share is defined by the law of Double Jeopardy

Under this law, small brands are punished twice. Compared with bigger brands they have fewer buyers, and those buyers buy that brand slightly less often. In Table 1, market shares and penetrations are very closely correlated, and although they vary considerably (there are big brands and tiny brands, based on the number of people who buy them) share and penetration metrics decline together (*Persil* is four times the size of *ASDA*, and has around four times as many buyers). On the other hand, purchase frequency is very similar across all brands in the table, although it is slightly above average for bigger brands, and slightly below average for smaller brands. This implies that penetration, the number of customers that a brand has, is far more important in determining brand size than how loyal those customers are, a measure which hardly varies between large and small competitors.

The Double Jeopardy phenomenon was first recognized by the sociologist William McPhee (1963), but has many useful applications in marketing since the relationship between penetration (b) and purchase frequency (w) for brands in any near-stationary category is approximately constant (Ehrenberg, Goodhardt, & Barwise, 1990), described as $w(1 - b)$. In other words, a marketer with knowledge of basic brand performance measures

Table 1. A comparison of observed and theoretical annual BPMs for eight laundry detergent brands (2006/2007).

Brands (by share)	Brand size					Loyalty related measures (annual)								Switching (annual)					
	Market share %	Percent buying		Purchases per buyer		Percent buying 5 + times		Category purchases per buyer		100% loyal				Percentage who also bought….					
										Percent buying		Purchases		Persil		Ariel		Fairy	
		O	T	O	T	O	T	O	T	O	T	O	T	O	T	O	T	O	T
Persil	19	38	37	3.7	3.8	24	27	9	10	21	14	5.8	4.0	–	–	34	25	17	14
Bold	12	24	26	3.8	3.5	25	24	10	10	18	12	5.5	3.7	42	36	33	25	11	14
Ariel	12	25	25	3.5	3.5	21	24	10	10	17	12	5.7	3.7	51	36	–	–	17	14
Tesco	10	21	22	3.6	3.4	23	23	10	10	15	12	4.7	3.6	39	36	25	25	11	14
Daz	8	17	18	3.7	3.4	23	23	11	10	15	11	5.6	3.5	37	36	29	25	10	14
Surf	8	18	18	3.2	3.4	18	22	11	10	9	11	5.8	3.5	43	36	28	25	10	14
Fairy	7	13	15	3.7	3.3	26	22	9	10	21	11	6.1	3.5	47	36	32	25	–	–
ASDA	5	11	12	3.6	3.2	22	21	11	10	10	10	6.3	3.4	39	36	22	25	11	14
Average	*10*	*21*	*22*	*3.6*	*3.4*	*23*	*23*	*10*	*10*	*16*	*12*	*5.7*	*3.6*	*38**	*36*	*24**	*25*	*12**	*14*

O = Observed, T = Theoretical.
*Averages calculated over 20 brands.
52 weeks to July 15th 2007.
Source: Kantar WorldPanel.

in a category should be able to see whether any particular brand is performing as expected, or not.

Your buyers are the buyers of other brands who occasionally buy you

Table 1 shows that although the average *Persil* consumer bought nine packs of detergent in the year (Category purchases per buyer), only around a third of those purchases were *Persil*. This pattern of polygamous loyalty is entirely normal, if unexpected. It has been observed in categories from soup to soap in data from across the world, and long ago cast doubt on the worth of loyalty schemes (Dowling & Uncles, 1997). The reason is that in frequently purchased categories such as laundry detergent, consumers are experienced and buy habitually from their established portfolio of two or three acceptable brands, often choosing the brand on deal on any single occasion (Ehrenberg, Hammond, & Goodhardt, 1994).

Hard-core loyalty exists, but mostly among light buyers

While the marketing literature has long argued that increasing loyalty brings increased customer lifetime value through higher sales, profitability and recommendation (Reichheld & Sasser, 1990) in practice, it is hardly the marketer's golden key. Table 1 showed that about 16% of consumers over the course of a year were sole brand buyers, meaning that 84% were switchers. These few 100% loyal buyers bought at only half the average category purchase rate, which is a typical pattern. They may well have remained loyal simply because they had fewer opportunities to switch. Note also that the Dirichlet often under represents 100% loyal purchasing by a couple of packs, but this and one or two other systematic deviations from empirical data are more fully described in Ehrenberg et al. (2004).

Duplication of purchase is in line with brand penetration

In Table 1, four in ten buyers of *Bold* also bought *Persil*, the largest brand. This proportion is much the same across all the competing brands, so that an average of 38% of *any* brand's buyers also bought *Persil*. For *Fairy* the proportion was far lower, with just over one in ten of any brand's buyers also buying it. The reason is that *Fairy* is a far smaller brand (Scriven & Danenberg, 2010).

Most markets share customers between brands fairly evenly without any partitioning (groups of brands that compete with each other more closely than with the category) but there are sometimes exceptions. *Persil* and *Ariel* buyers duplicated together far beyond predicted levels, suggesting a closer than normal brand substitutability. In addition, both brands over-duplicated with Fairy, indicating that it was an *additional* purchase. Here, as elsewhere in these examples, the known patterns of normal consumer behaviour give a benchmark against which exceptions can be interpreted and competitive structure more closely identified.

One last pattern concerns brand share growth. Permanent share increase is exceptional in steady-state markets (Dekimpe & Hanssens, 1995; Graham, 2009) yet the retention marketing literature has argued that improved loyalty brings more sales (Aaker, 2002; Aaker & McLoughlin, 2007; Reichheld & Sasser, 1990). Strong empirical evidence from established markets over many years (Baldinger, Blair, & Echambi, 2002; East, Hammond, & Gendall, 2006) has cast doubt on this. Anschuetz (2002) for example, demonstrated how brand share is both built by increased penetration and governed by the law of Double Jeopardy, although little empirical research has as yet examined these patterns in dynamic markets.

Procedure: two-purchase analysis

The structure of the paper is as follows: in this section the procedure and data are described. The analysis and findings are subsequently presented and finally their implications discussed.

A two-purchase analysis identifies the distribution of two consecutive brand choices over a sample of buyers (including new buyers). Switching and duplication measures can therefore be derived that reveal the patterns supporting share increase in stable or growing categories.

On occasion, for example for a quick assessment of an unfolding strategy, there may not always be enough data available to calibrate the full Dirichlet. Data from a two-purchase survey may then be used to construct a duplication table (in effect a conditional probability matrix of brand choice), which can be interpreted in comparison with the benchmarks. Data for this study were collected in 2009 from a survey of visitors to a motor fair in Bangkok, which included the questions (in translation) 'What make of car do you currently own?' and 'What make of car did you own before?' It was considered likely that respondents could recall these facts accurately, even over a number of years. The survey produced 171 usable responses and frequencies were calculated to establish brand shares, which were then compared with published data from Toyota Motor Thailand Co. (Toyota Motor Thailand, 2010).

As might be expected from such a sample, the fit was close for the biggest brands (the Toyota share was within a point of the published average quarterly share in this period), but contained anomalies as brand size decreased. To compensate for sampling error, the smallest brands were thus combined in the analysis as 'Other'. The data showed an 18% market volume increase from new buyers. Given that the published average annual market growth rate was 17.5% between 2007 and 2009 this was a good fit.

From the data, which included both repeating and new buyers, simple frequency counts then established total purchases, brand penetrations and 'closing' market shares defined as brand shares of current rather than previous cars owned. Then, having isolated the repeating buyers, Table 2 was constructed in order to establish loyalty (on the diagonal) and switching levels between brands.

Even in this raw form, the emergence of the Double Jeopardy pattern in the diagonal repeat-percentages was clear to see. Bigger brands had higher repeat rates. In addition,

Table 2. Duplication of car purchasing in Thailand.

Previous car	Current car					
	Toyota %	Other %	Honda %	Nissan %	BMW %	Mitsubishi %
Toyota	**56**	16	11	13	2	3
Other	31	**47**	11	3	8	0
Honda	38	8	**31**	8	8	8
Nissan	33	17	8	**33**	8	0
BMW	20	10	20	10	**30**	10
Mitsubishi	29	14	0	29	0	**29**
Average	*31*	*13*	*11*	*13*	*6*	*4*

Sample size: $N = 171$.

regular switching patterns were discerned in comparison with average duplication values calculated at the base of the table. Further analysis of repeat-purchase behaviour was then possible using the norms previously described and starting with an estimation of market structure.

Market structure

Table 3 shows summary performance measures calculated from the two-purchase data. It was clear from the table that despite category dynamics, this market still conformed to the repeat-buying norms previously discussed. The market share and market penetration measures varied together as expected, and were closely correlated. The loyalty measure of repeat purchase varied little between the smaller brands, each of which appeared to retain around a third of their customers on a second purchase.

On the other hand, the largest brands, Toyota and 'Others' achieved slightly over-average loyalty with about half their customers choosing to repeat on a second purchase. This was in line with repeat rates in car buying in Western Europe and the USA (Bennett, 2003b; Sharp, 2009), and also reflected a characteristic Double Jeopardy pattern. Smaller brands in Thailand, just as elsewhere, suffered twice in having fewer buyers who showed slightly lower loyalty. The appearance of this pattern so clearly was confirmation of the face validity of the data. It also demonstrated that, other than size there was no particular brand attribute here (for example German engineering, or local manufacture), which attracted exceptional loyalty. Big brands just scored higher.

Once having observed that market structure appeared normal, a more detailed analysis of loyalty and penetration growth was undertaken. From two-purchase data it is possible to investigate loyalty and switching rather more closely using a duplication of purchase analysis, and to detect market partitioning (evidence of exceptional patterns of loyalty) if it is occurring. This is a simple matter in steady state categories, but here the market had both repeat purchasers and a large proportion of new buyers and so these classes of consumers were first separated in order to reveal the patterns of growth present in the data.

Table 3. Brand performance measures: two-purchase analysis of the Thai car market.

Brand	Market share %	Market penetration %	Repeat purchase %
Toyota	46	61	56
Other	24	32	47
Honda	10	18	31
Nissan	8	15	33
BMW	7	9	30
Mitsubishi	5	10	29
Average	*17*	*24*	*38*

Sample size: $N = 171$.

Duplication of purchase

To calculate purchase duplication, the distribution of choices was analysed between each pair of brands. Table 4 shows the percentage of buyers of each of the brands in the left hand column whose second purchase choice switched to the brands listed across the top of table. It was possible to conclude earlier from Table 3 that 30% of BMW owners remained loyal to their brand. Table 4 indicates that another 20% switched to Toyota, 10% to Nissan

Table 4. Duplication of purchase in the Thai car market.

			...whose next purchase was a ...			
Percentage of the owners of a ...	Toyota %	Other %	Honda %	Nissan %	BMW %	Mitsubishi %
Toyota	*	16	11	13	2	3
Other	50	*	18	5	14	0
Honda	38	8	*	8	8	8
Nissan	33	17	8	*	8	0
BMW	20	10	20	10	*	10
Mitsubishi	29	14	0	29	0	*
Avg. switching %	31	13	11	13	6	4
Penetration (b) %	61	32	18	15	9	10
Switching (T) = D × Pen (*Category D* = .55)	33	18	10	8	5	5

Note: Sample of repeating buyers only: $N = 141$.

and so on. The diagonal shows loyalty but is omitted from Table 4 for clarity. At the base three further variables show, for each brand, its average switching percentage, penetration (taken from Table 3) and a theoretical switching value (T) predicted from the category duplication coefficient.

It can be seen that in this market, brand switching generally declines in line with brand penetration. At the second purchase Toyota has drawn around a third of the buyers of each of the other brands, while Honda, a smaller brand, has only attracted about a tenth from each. This is a typical pattern in Dirichlet markets; bigger brands attract more switching buyers. The regularity is captured in the duplication of purchase law (Ehrenberg & Goodhardt, 1970):

$$b_{y|x} = Db_y$$

where $b_{y|x}$ is the proportion of brand x purchasers who bought y on the second purchase, b_y the proportion of the population which bought y on the second occasion and $D = a$ proportionality coefficient, in this case .55, which is approximately constant across the brands in the category.

Table 4 can be interpreted in the light of this law and any exceptional patterns identified. Toyota, Honda and BMW all performed in line with the predicted (T) levels (using D times penetration), attracting switchers in line with brand size. On the other hand, Mitsubishi and 'Others' were slightly out of line, but this can be explained. 'Others' is an aggregation of small brands. The penetration is a total for every included brand while the switching is the *mean* of each included brand's value. Individually these values are low, so the mean switching is lower than the penetration and Double Jeopardy might indicate. Mitsubishi appears to have drawn disproportionately from BMW and Honda, but the discrepancy may be a function of a small sample size.

The picture from Table 4 (which represents only repeating buyers) is by and large that of a normal market. Car brands in Thailand have attracted new buyers in line with their market share in this study just as in the many other and varied categories previously examined (enumerated recently in Sharp, 2010). Toyota exhibited no exceptional loyalty at the category level (see Table 3) or in the rate it attracted switchers at the repeat-buyer level, so neither has been driving its growth.

Share of purchase among new buyers

Since switching and loyalty measures were no more nor less than expected for Toyota, where has growth come from? The answer of course was from new buyers, those who had only ever bought one car. In this case new buyers are 18% of the sample, which is the annual growth rate of the market. Table 5 shows the proportion of new buyers drawn to each brand and compares this with each brand's observed switching levels. Three points are illustrated in this table.

First, it can be seen that the brand choices of new buyers were clearly related to all other brand performance measures, declining approximately in line with share and

Table 5. Observed switching and share of new buyers.

	Toyota	Other	Honda	Nissan	BMW	Mitsubishi
Switching % (O)	31	13	11	13	6	4
Share of new buyers (%)	57	14	14	4	4	7

penetration. Second, switching is a good indicator of a brand's size and attractiveness to both repeat buyers and to first time buyers. Third, the clear exception of Toyota emphasises the extent to which Toyota outperformed the market and the means by which it did so. The increase in share was due only to an increase in buyer numbers, and not to any particular loyalty. The implications of these findings and the replication of the two-purchase technique will now be discussed.

Implications for strategic marketers

These findings have implications for the further use of the two-purchase technique, and for the development of marketing and brand strategies. The main finding is that brand growth is constrained by known patterns of repeat-purchase behaviour, even in a non-stationary category, and during an economic downturn. The leading brand, as expected, has drawn more switchers and retained slightly more existing customers, but only in line with its share. Over half its buyers still defected on a second purchase, yet Toyota was growing because it attracted many more new category buyers than the smaller brands. The analysis described this market structure quite well, and clearly showed brand loyalty to be unexceptional, mostly in line with levels seen in established, near-stationary markets around the world.

Two-purchase analysis

Analysis of just two purchases can provide surprisingly detailed insight into brand performance against competitors and benchmarks in a dynamic category. Two-purchase data have some limitations though, when compared with commercial panel data. They cannot differentiate between heavy and light buyers, nor generate commonly used loyalty measures such as share of category requirements (SCR). In this survey, the date of either purchase was unclear, although it could be included in the question specification in future replications in order to define the period of analysis more closely.

Nevertheless, the two-purchase analysis even of a small sample gave useful diagnostic results in a timely manner in an evolving category. Just two questions in omnibus research or as here, included in another survey revealed much about patterns and exceptions in market structure, for example that consumers are generally switchers (not loyal), and tend to switch to higher share brands. These results are consistent with those from other durables markets such as televisions (Bennett, 2008). In all respects repeat-buying in this market appeared normal and much like that in established categories on other continents.

Implications for loyalty and brand growth

The major new finding of this study is that brand-share growth for Toyota in this dynamic market came not from unexpectedly high retention rates but from first-time buyers. In steady-state categories there are very few new buyers, so brand growth can only be at the expense of established competitors that will react quickly to threats of all sorts. Brand shares consequently tend to remain remarkably stable over the long term with switching related to penetration. In developing markets by contrast, the structure is being defined as new buyers come in. While this might seem like the best ever chance for a small brand to get bigger, this study has shown that the duplication of purchase law governs new buyers too: they simply make a first purchase in line with brand penetrations and sign up mostly to the bigger brands. Using this new benchmark, it was possible to see that Toyota appeared to be attracting more than its expected share of the new car-owners, even during a recession, as if it had a sort of super-premium. This phenomenon has been noted for very large brands in other categories (Fader & Schmittlein, 1993).

Growth through penetration rather than retention may run counter to most of the established literature, but as Sharp (2009) points out, the benefits of retention loyalty can only ever be quite limited. In the data presented here, Nissan had an 8% market share and a 33% customer retention rate. In other words while the brand lost two-thirds of its buyers in this period, it also attracted new ones to replace them; but even if Nissan's marketers had succeeded in retaining *all* of their defecting buyers (and brand loyalty at this level has simply *never* been seen), the possible market share increase is constrained to just five points, not enough to get close to Toyota. On the other hand, the data showed that over 60% of *all* Thai car-buyers switched brands, so there was a possible 60 points of market share available to Nissan, plus new buyers entering the market. Brand growth through penetration was therefore almost unrestricted, so that Nissan, in theory, might have significantly altered category structure and achieved a stronger competitive position against Toyota with successful customer attraction strategies. As with laundry detergent, so with cars: loyalty is polygamous, even towards the very largest brands. In any period over half the buyers in the market will be in transition. Since this is the normal order, all marketers would be well advised to concentrate on both attraction and retention strategies. To focus on only one approach is to court disaster, which implies that growth is most likely to be the result of maintaining normal levels of loyalty while increasing penetration.

Implications for marketing strategy

A brand the size of Toyota, with a 47% share of the market, remains constantly salient. Almost every other car in Thailand is a Toyota, and the effects of the law of Double Jeopardy on switching, loyalty and new customer attraction have accounted for its continued success. In practical terms, the brand has better distribution, more dealerships, advertises more and is made locally. In the USA, as Sharp (2009) noted, General Motors is easier to buy and has far higher salience than competitors. In Thailand, Toyota has benefited from the same virtuous marketing circle. As penetration built, so did mental and physical availability, and loyalty followed in proportion, all of which in combination have driven further increases in brand share.

Epilogue

For Toyota, success might have come with a high price tag. A recall crisis in 2009 and 2010 dented sales in their markets around the world and was attributed directly to the speed at which the brand had been expanding. Referring to the pursuit of volume over product safety and quality, Akiyo Toyoda admitted to a US House of Representatives committee: 'I fear the pace at which we have grown may have been too quick' (Frean & Lewis, 2010). While there are now clear signs that Toyota will recover (Buerk, 2010), the crisis has been a reminder that brand growth, despite being an almost universal marketing objective, brings its own particular challenges.

Implications for future research

Important questions for further research have been raised in the light of global media attention in 2010 on Toyota and subsequently BP. Two-purchase analysis highlights changes associated with decline as well as growth in brand share, and studies would give valuable insights into the short and long-term influence of reputational damage on consumer retention and acquisition, an overriding concern for marketing strategists shepherding brand value.

We have demonstrated here how two-purchase analysis identified sources of growth from readily accessible survey data. Further work is now needed to replicate the technique with more substantial samples and in other dynamic markets. Replication studies under varied conditions should examine the relationship between brand growth and changes in penetration and loyalty in order to ascertain if it becomes routinely predictable. This is the point at which 'mere data regularities' become an empirical generalization (Ehrenberg, 1995; Wright & Kearns, 1998). Such a relationship may then lead to the development of a theory to explain scientifically the true contribution of loyalty to brand growth.

Acknowledgements

The authors would like to thank Bawornphan Phaisarnsirintkoon for his invaluable help in compiling the sampling frame and collecting the data used in this research.

References

Aaker, D. (2002). *Building strong brands*. London: Simon & Schuster.

Aaker, D., & McLoughlin, D. (2007). *Strategic market management*. Chichester: John Wiley.

Anschuetz, N. (2002). Why a brand's most valuable customer is the next one it adds. *Journal of Advertising Research, 42*(1), 15–21.

Baldinger, A., Blair, E., & Echambi, R. (2002). Why brands grow. *Journal of Advertising Research, 42*(1), 7–14.

Banelis, M. (2008). *Understanding consumers' repertoire sizes* (Doctoral dissertation). Retrieved from the UNISA website: http://arrow.unisa.edu.au/vital/access/manager/Repository/unisa:36817

Barwise, P., & Ehrenberg, A. (1987). The liking and viewing of regular TV series. *Journal of Consumer Research, 14*(1), 63–70.

Bennett, D. (2003a, December). *Two lunches show the Taiwanese are just like the Australians*. Paper presented at the Australian and New Zealand Marketing Academy Conference, Adelaide, Australia.

Bennett, D. (2003b). *Two-purchase analysis of automotive survey data* (R&D Initiative working paper). London: London South Bank University.

Bennett, D. (2008). Brand loyalty dynamics: China's television brands come of age. *Australasian Marketing Journal, 16*(2), 39–50.

Bennett, D., Ehrenberg, A., & Goodhardt, G. (2000, November). *Two-purchase analysis of brand loyalty among petrol buyers*. Paper presented at the Australian and New Zealand Marketing Academy Conference, Griffith University, Queensland, Australia.

Buerk, R. (2010, August 4). Toyota profits up as sales recover. *BBC News Online*. Retrieved from http://www.bbc.co.uk/news/business-10863077

Dekimpe, M., & Hanssens, D. (1995). The persistence of marketing effects on sales. *Marketing Science, 14*(1), 1–21.

Dowling, G., & Uncles, M. (1997). Do customer loyalty programs really work? *Sloan Management Review, 38*(4), 71–82.

Driesener, C. (2005). *Empirical generalizations in the parameter values of the Dirichlet model: An examination across 50 categories* (Doctoral dissertation). Retrieved from the UNISA website: http://arrow.unisa.edu.au:8081/1959.8/82916

East, R., Hammond, K., & Gendall, P. (2006). Fact and fallacy in retention marketing. *Journal of Marketing Management, 22*(1/2), 5–23.

Ehrenberg, A. (1988). *Repeat buying* (2nd ed.). London: Charles Griffin.

Ehrenberg, A. (1995). Empirical generalisations, theory and method. *Marketing Science, 14*(3), G20–G28.

Ehrenberg, A., Barnard, N., & Scriven, J. (1997). Differentiation or salience. *Journal of Advertising Research, 37*(6), 7–14.

Ehrenberg, A., & Goodhardt, G. (1970). A model of multibrand buying. *Journal of Marketing Research*, *7*(1), 77–84.

Ehrenberg, A., Goodhardt, G., & Barwise, P. (1990). Double Jeopardy revisited. *Journal of Marketing*, *54*(3), 82–91.

Ehrenberg, A., Hammond, K., & Goodhardt, G. (1994). The after-effects of price related consumer promotions. *Journal of Advertising Research*, *34*(4), 11–21.

Ehrenberg, A., Uncles, M., & Goodhardt, G. (2004). Understanding brand performance measures: Using Dirichlet benchmarks. *Journal of Business Research*, *57*, 1307–1325.

Fader, P., & Schmittlein, D. (1993). Triple jeopardy: Excess behavioral loyalty experienced by high-share brands. *Journal of Marketing Research*, *30*, 478–493.

Frean, A., & Lewis, L. (2010, February 24). We grew too fast, priorities became confused. *The Times Online*. Retrieved from http://business.timesonline.co.uk/tol/business/industry_sectors/engineering/article7038470.ece

Goodhardt, G. (1966). The constant in duplicated television viewing. *Nature*, *212*, 1616.

Goodhardt, G., Ehrenberg, A., & Chatfield, C. (1984). The Dirichlet: A comprehensive model of buying behaviour. *Journal of the Statistical Society, A*, *147*, 621–655.

Graham, C. (2009). What's the point of marketing anyway? *Journal of Marketing Management*, *25*, 867–874.

Kennedy, R., & Ehrenberg, A. (2001). There is *no* brand segmentation. *Marketing Research*, *13*(1), 4–7.

McPhee, W. (1963). *Formal theories of mass behavior*. New York: Free Press.

Pickford, C., & Goodhardt, G. (2000, July). *An empirical study of buying behaviour in an industrial market*. Paper presented at the Academy of Marketing Conference, University of Derby, East Midlands, UK.

Piercy, N., Cravens, D., & Lane, N. (2010). Marketing out of the recession: Recovery is coming, but things will never be the same again. *Marketing Review*, *10*(1), 3–23.

Raggio, R., & Leone, R. (2009). Postscript: Preserving (and growing) brand value in a downturn. *Brand Management*, *17*(1), 84–89.

Reichheld, F., & Sasser, W. (1990). Zero defections: Quality comes to services. *Harvard Business Review*, *68*(5), 105–111.

Scriven, J., & Danenberg, N. (2010). *Understanding how brands compete: A guide to duplication of purchase analysis* (Ehrenberg-Bass Institute for Marketing Science, report 53 for corporate members). Adelaide, Australia: University of South Australia.

Sharp, B. (2009). Detroit's real problem: It's customer acquisition, not loyalty. *Marketing Research*, *21*(1), 26–27.

Sharp, B. (2010). *How brands grow: What marketers don't know*. South Melbourne: Oxford University Press.

Sharp, B., Wright, M., & Goodhardt, G. (2002). Purchase loyalty is polarized into either repertoire or subscription patterns. *Australasian Marketing Journal*, *10*(3), 7–20.

Tellis, G., & Tellis, K. (2009). Research on advertising in a recession: A critical review and synthesis. *Journal of Advertising Research*, *49*, 304–327.

Tikoo, S., & Ebrahim, A. (2010). Financial markets and marketing: The tradeoff between R&D and advertising during an economic downturn. *Journal of Advertising Research*, *50*(1), 50–56.

Toyota Motor Thailand. (2010). *Toyota sales volume*. Retrieved August 20, 2010 from: http://www.toyota.co.th/en/sale_volum.asp

Uncles, M., Ehrenberg, A., & Hammond, K. (1995). Patterns of buyer behavior: Regularities, models and extensions. *Marketing Science*, *14*(3), G71–G78.

Vlasic, B. (2009, October 21). For car buyers the brand romance is gone. *New York Times* (New York edition), p. B1.

Wright, M., & Kearns, F. (1998). Progress in marketing knowledge. *Journal of Empirical Generalisations in Marketing Science*, *3*(1), 1–21.

Modeling customer churn in a non-contractual setting: the case of telecommunications service providers

Ali Tamaddoni Jahromi, Mohammad Mehdi Sepehri, Babak Teimourpour and Sarvenaz Choobdar

Department of Industrial Engineering, Tarbiat Modares University, Tehran, I.R. Iran

The telecommunications industry with an approximate annual churn rate of 30% can nowadays be considered as one of the top sectors on the list of those suffering from customer churn. Although different studies have focused on developing a predictive model for customer churn under contractual settings, the mobile telecommunications industry, performing in a non-contractual setting in which customer churn is not easy to define and trace, has always been neglected in such investigations. In this study, we have developed a dual-step computer-assisted model in which a clustering model and a classification model are employed for defining and predicting customer churn. Results indicate the promising performance of the proposed models in identifying future churners.

Introduction

As markets become increasingly saturated, companies have acknowledged that their business strategies should focus on identifying those customers who are likely to churn (Hadden, Tiwari, Roy, & Ruta, 2005). While acquiring new customers is the first step for any business to start growing, the importance of customer retention should not be overlooked. Reinartz, Thomas, and Kumar (2005) showed that insufficient allocation to customer retention efforts would have a greater negative impact on long-term customer profitability as compared to insufficient allocation to customer-acquisition efforts. One of the most significant ways of increasing customers' value is to keep them for longer periods of time. In other words, retained customers produce higher revenues and profit margins than the new ones (Reichheld & Sasser, 1990). Since the net return on investments for retention strategies is higher than that for acquisitions, it is claimed that companies first spend their marketing resources to keep the existing customers rather than to attract new ones (Mozer, Wolniewicz, Grimes, Johnson, & Kaushansky, 2000; Rust & Zahorik, 1993). However, because of the emergence of e-commerce, retaining the existing customers is not as easy as it used to be. Peppard (2000) maintains that the Internet channel has empowered those customers who are no longer stuck with the decisions of a single company and has led to exacerbation of the competition. While competitors are only one 'click away', customer empowerment is likely to amplify the attrition rate of a company's customers (Lejeune, 2001).

Consequently, retaining customers by avoiding their defection has become an important issue for Customer Relationship Management (CRM) managers (Bucknix & van den Poel, 2005). Thus, companies should be equipped and armed with the most efficient and effective methods to examine their clients' behavior and predict their possible future failure.

Model building for churn prediction becomes more complicated when dealing with the non-contractual setting, where customers have the opportunity to continuously change their purchase behavior without informing the company about it. In other words, since there have not been any contracts between the customer and the company, tracking and predicting the churn, in this setting, has been an issue of high complexity (Bucknix & van den Poel, 2005). This is exactly what pre-paid telecommunications service providers suffer from. In such a market segment, because of the fact that customers do not experience any switching costs when changing their supplier, 'churn' is a common and invisible phenomenon.

The present study aims to develop a predictive model for customer churn in '*pre-paid mobile telephony companies*'. Such a model enables the companies to identify the customers who are likely to churn in the near future so that they can be targeted by incentives and convinced to stay. The first step is to develop a sensible definition of churn in such companies, on the basis of which, a predictive model can be constructed.

Review of literature

Integrating customer relationship management and data mining

Eagerness toward Customer Relationship Management (CRM) began to grow in the 1990s (Ling & Yen, 2001; Xu, Yen, Lin, & Chou, 2002). Despite the fact that CRM has become widely recognized, there is no comprehensive and universally accepted definition of CRM and experts have defined it in different ways (Bose, 2002; Kincaid, 2003; Kotler & Keller, 2006; Richards & Jones, 2008; Swift, 2001).

A glimpse at the definitions of CRM given by the above-mentioned authors gives one the understanding that they have all emphasized CRM as a comprehensive strategy and a process of acquiring, retaining, and partnering with selective customers to create superior value for the company and the customer. It involves the integration of marketing, sales, customer service, and supply-chain functions of the organization to achieve greater efficiencies and effectiveness in delivering customer value (Parvatiyar & Sheth, 2001).

Different categories of approaches exist toward CRM (He, Xu, Huang, & Deng, 2004; Ngai, 2005; Teo, Devadoss, & Pan, 2006; Xu et al., 2002). From an architectural point of view, the CRM framework can be divided into the operational and analytical (He et al., 2004; Teo et al., 2006). While operational CRM refers to the automation of business process, the analytical CRM refers to the analysis of customer characteristics and attitudes in order to support the organization's customer management strategies. Thus, it can help the company in more effective allocation of its resources (Ngai, Xiu, & Chau, 2009).

Today's variety of tastes and preferences among customers has made it impossible for companies to group them into large homogenous populations to develop appropriate marketing strategies. In fact, firms are faced with customers who want to be served according to their individual and unique needs (Shaw, Subramaniam, Tan, & Welge, 2001). This requirement brought IT and knowledge management into the field of Customer Relationship Management. In fact, CRM can be broadly presented in the form of customer management which requires the collection and treatment of a significant amount of data that enable companies to exploit them in acquisition, retention, extension, and also selection of their customers (Komenar, 1997).

In the realm of IT, CRM means an enterprise wide integration of technologies such as data warehouse, website, intranet/extranet, and so on (Bose, 2002). In fact, CRM utilizes information technology and information systems (IS) to gather data which can be used to develop the information required for creating a one-to-one interaction with the customers (Bose, 2002; Ngai, 2005).

Recent researches have pointed out that a major portion of the research in the CRM field is related to the application of IT and IS in CRM (Ngai, 2005; Ngai et al., 2009). Furthermore, the first role in IT and IS fields is played by data mining (Ngai, 2005; Ngai et al., 2009).

The application of data mining tools in CRM is an emerging trend in the global economy. With large volumes of data generated in CRM, data mining plays a leading role in the overall CRM task (Shaw et al., 2001). Since most companies try to analyze and understand their customers' behavior and characteristics for developing a competitive CRM strategy, data mining tools have become highly popular (Ngai et al., 2009).

Moreover, a review of the literature from 2000 to 2006 shows that 54 out of 87 papers (62%) in the field of data mining and CRM focused on customer retention aspects of CRM. Besides, the authors have identified an increasing trend toward this area of research which would suggest that more publications will appear in the field (Ngai et al., 2009).

One can conclude that data mining has a fundamental and critical role to play in CRM (Rygielski, Wang, & Yen, 2002) and that it enables the transformation of customer data into useful information and knowledge that can be exploited to identify valuable customers, predict future behavior, and make proactive and knowledge-based decisions (Rygielski et al., 2002). In the CRM context, data mining can be seen as a business driven process aimed at discovery and consistent use of knowledge from organizational data (Ling & Yen, 2001).

From an expert point of view, data mining is the process of selecting, exploring, and modeling large amounts of data to uncover previously unknown data patterns for business advantage (SAS Institute, 2000). It can also be defined as: the exploration and analysis of large quantities of data in order to discover meaningful patterns and rules (Berry & Linoff, 2004). What data mining tools do is take data and construct a model as a representation of reality. The derived model describes the patterns and relationships present in the data (Rygielski et al., 2002).

Customer churn

The propensity of customers to cease doing business with a company in a given time period can be defined as customer churn (Chandar, Laha, & Krishna, 2006).

Nowadays, customer churn has become the main concern for firms in all industries (Neslin, Gupta, Kamakura, Lu, & Mason, 2006), and regardless of the industry they are active in, companies are being challenged to deal with this issue. Customer churn can blemish a company by decreasing profit levels, losing a great deal of price premium, and losing referrals from continuing service customers (Reichheld & Sasser, 1990). Research by Reichheld (1996) revealed that an increase of 5% in customer retention rate can increase the average net present value of customers by 35% for software companies and 95% for advertising agencies.

Two basic approaches exist for managing customer churn: 'untargeted approaches' which rely on superior product and mass advertising to increase brand loyalty and retain customers, and 'targeted approaches' which rely on identifying customers who are likely to churn, and then either provide them with a direct incentive or customize a service plan to stay (Burez & van den Poel, 2007).

The targeted approaches fall in two categories: reactive and proactive. Adopting a reactive approach, a company waits until customers contact the company to cancel their (service) relationship. The company then offers the customer an incentive, for example a rebate, to stay. Adopting the proactive approach, the company tries to identify customers who are likely to churn at some later date in advance. The company then targets these customers with special programs or incentives to keep the customer from churning. Targeted proactive programs have potential advantages of having lower incentive costs (because the incentive may not have to be as high as when the customer has to be 'bribed' not to leave at the last minute) and because customers are not trained to negotiate for better deals under the threat of churning. However, these systems would be wasteful if churn predictions are inaccurate, because then companies are wasting incentive money on customers who would have stayed anyway (Coussement & van den Poel, 2008a; Neslin et al., 2006).

Studies considering customer churn in different industries can be divided into descriptive and predictive studies. While descriptive studies aim at extracting the underlying factors of customer churn (Ahn, Han, & Lee, 2006; Gerpott, Rams, & Schindler, 2001; Kim & Yoon, 2004; Seo, Ranganathan, & Babad, 2008), the predictive ones try to build a predictive model to identify the future churners before they churn (Burez & van den Poel, 2009; Coussement & van den Poel, 2008a, 2009; Hung, Yen, & Wang, 2006; Pendharkar, 2009; Wei & Chiu, 2002; Xie, Li, Ngai, & Ying, 2009; Zhao, Li, Li, Liu, & Ren, 2005).

Reviewing the existing studies regarding customer churn, one can find that a great number of them are in the contractual setting, in which it is easy to observe when defection occurs. In other words, most studies have focused on cases in which the customer notifies their intention to churn by terminating their contract (contractual telecommunications services, newspaper publishers) or closes their account (banking) (see Table 1). Thus, more studies seem to be required which focus on predicting customer churn in the non-contractual setting in order to gain those deeper insights necessary for defining the concept of 'churn' and its predictor variables in this segment.

Furthermore, as can be seen from Table 1, despite the broad continuum of sectors which have been the target of customer defection studies, the *pre-paid mobile telephony* sector has been deprived of academic notice.

Working data

The raw data used in this study to construct the churn predictive model included the call record data (date of call, time of call, duration of call, type of call, and cost) of 34,504 users of a mobile telecommunications service provider company in Iran over the period from 1 November 2007 to 30 April 2008.

Methodology and results

The first hurdle faced in the initial steps of model construction was the problem of 'churn definition'. In almost all the above-mentioned computer-assisted studies, the customers were subscribers to the service provider who had a contract with the company. Consequently, 'churn' in such conditions could be defined as the termination of contract from the customer's side or not renewing it after its expiry date, but circumstances would be different with pre-paid telecommunications service providers. In such companies, there is no contract between the company and the clients which expires or terminates. In other words, churn in such cases happens with no tracking point such as terminating the contract or not renewing, complicating its recognition.

As an illustration, imagine a database consisting of a number of customers with different calling behaviors, some using their cell phone every day and others using it

Table 1. Modeling customer churn: review of literature.

Researches on modeling customer churn	Non-contractual setting	Contractual setting	Sector Telecom	Finance	Newspaper publisher	Retail	Pure-click retailing	Pay TV	Other service
Hung et al. (2006)		X	X						
Burez and van den Poel (2008)		X						X	
Coussement and van den Poel (2008a)		X			X				
Burez and van den Poel (2009)		X	X	X	X	X		X	X
Madden, Savage, and Coble-Neal (1999)		X							
Gerpott et al. (2001)		X	X						
Seo et al. (2008)		X	X						
Xie et al. (2009)		X		X					
Pendharkar (2009)		X	X						
Van den Poel and Lariviere (2004)		X		X					
Chu, Tsai, and Ho (2007)		X	X						
Burez and van den Poel (2007)		X						X	
Athanassopoulos (2000)		X		X					
Kim and Yoon (2004)		X	X						
Ahn et al. (2006)		X	X						
Wei and Chiu (2002)		X	X						
Coussement and van den Poel (2008b)		X			X				X
Neslin et al. (2006)		X				X			
Buckinx and van den Poel (2005)	X					X			
This study	X		X						

haphazardly. If we define a churner as 'persons who have not used their cell phone for seven days', a considerable part of customers who used their cell phones occasionally would be mistakenly considered as churners. On the other hand, if a longer time span is considered and a churner is defined as 'persons who have not used their cell phone for 25 days' our model may suffer from the inability to recognize the real churners.

These wrong signaling measures would increase the number of False Negatives (FN) and False Positives (FP) in our predictive model and, consequently, lower the accuracy of the model.

In order to resolve this problem, our model construction process was broken into two phases.

(1) The clustering phase in order to arrive at definition for the concept of 'churn'.
(2) The classification phase to predict customer churn.

The relevant features were extracted from the raw data available and drawing upon the results from previous studies in this area (Ansari, Kohavi, Mason, & Zheng, 2000; Hung et al., 2006). The following features were extracted to be used in the clustering phase:

(1) *Call Ratio*: proportion of calls made by each customer with more than one day time distance to their total number of calls;
(2) *Average Call Distance*: the average time distance between one's calls;
(3) *Max Date*: the last date in our observed time period in which a call was made by a specific customer;
(4) *Min Date*: the first date in our observed time period in which a call was made by a specific customer;
(5) *Life*: the period of time in our observed time span in which each customer was active;
(6) *Max-Distance*: the maximum time distance between two calls by a specific person in the study period;
(7) *No-of-Days*: the number of days a specific customer made or received a call;
(8) *Total-No-In*: the total number of incoming calls for each customer over the study period;
(9) *Total-No-Out*: the total number of outgoing calls for each customer over the study period;
(10) *Total-Cost*: the total money that each customer was charged for using the services over the study period;
(11) *Total-Duration-In*: the total duration of incoming calls for a specific customer over the study period;
(12) *Total-Duration-Out*: the total duration of outgoing calls for a specific customer over the study period.

The above-mentioned 12 Recency, Frequency, and Monetary (RFM)-related features were used to divide the customer base up into four individual clusters. Drawing upon the findings of Wei and Chiu (2002), the Two-Step Cluster technique was used (SPSS Inc., 2007) with different Max-Distances, the 'Prediction Period' length was assumed to be twice the 'Max-Distance', resulting in the four sets of Observation, Retention, and Prediction periods for the four extracted clusters (Table 2).

Using two sub-periods of fifteen days in the observation period of each cluster, it was possible to construct the following features for every single cluster based on Wei and Chiu's (2002) study and based on the call record data of the observation period:

Table 2. Prediction, retention, and observation period for each extracted cluster of customers.

Cluster no.	Observation length	Retention length	Prediction length	Cluster's Max-Distance
1	18 March to 16 April (30 days)	17 April to 23 April (7 days)	24 to 30 April (7 days)	3.88 days
2	14 March to 12 April (30 days)	13 to 19 April (7 days)	20 to 30 April (11 days)	5.66 days
3	21 February to 22 March (30 days)	23 to 29 March (7 days)	30 March to 30 April (32 days)	16.33 days
4	4 February to 5 March (30 days)	6 to 12 March (7 days)	13 March to 30 April (49 days)	24.88 days

(1) *IMOU*$_{initial}$: incoming MOU of a customer in the first sub-period;
(2) *IFOU*$_{initial}$: incoming FOU of a customer in the first sub-period;
(3) *OMOU*$_{initial}$: outgoing MOU of a customer in the first sub-period;
(4) *OFOU*$_{initial}$: outgoing FOU of a customer in the first sub-period;
(5) $\Delta IMOU_2$: the change in IMOU of a customer between the sub-period 1 and 2;
(6) $\Delta IFOU_2$: the change in IFOU of a customer between the sub-period 1 and 2;
(7) $\Delta OMOU_2$: the change in OMOU of a customer between the sub-period 1 and 2;
(8) $\Delta OFOU_2$: the change in OFOU of a customer between the sub-period 1 and 2;
(9) **Churn:** the binary churn labels for each customer according to their churn status in the prediction period. According to this, a churner is a person who does not have a call record in the prediction period; otherwise, they would be considered as a non-churner.

Utilizing these new features and considering a hit ratio of 1:2 (churner: non-churner), the predictive model was developed using the Decision Tree technique (CART algorithm) for every single cluster.

Table 3 depicts the performance of the proposed churn predictive models for each cluster based on 'gain measure'.

While the gain factor of random sampling was 20% for the top 20% of the customer base in all clusters, Table 2 shows that the model developed here is capable of assigning gain factors of 77.8%, 66.7%, 30%, and 45.5% for the top 20% of the customer base of the four clusters, respectively. This implies that by applying the proposed predictive model, a sample size of only 20% representing each cluster in the customer base will suffice to identify 77.8%, 66.7%, 30%, and 45.5% of the total number of churners in each of the four clusters, respectively.

Furthermore, because of the nature of the data set which suffered from class imbalance, the effect of cost-sensitive learning methods on the performance of the proposed models was also tested. The results presented in Table 4 confirm the positive effect of cost-sensitive learning on the performance of the models.

Table 3. Performance of developed predictive models based on gain measure.

Cluster no.	% Gain for percentile = 10	% Gain for percentile = 20	% Gain for percentile = 30
1	46.3	77.8	80
2	54	66.7	66.7
3	15	30	47
4	17	45.5	81

Table 4. Performance of cost-sensitive predictive models based on gain measure.

Cluster no.	% Gain for percentile = 10	% Gain for percentile = 20	% Gain for percentile = 30
1	56.1	77.8	80
2	54	66.7	66.7
3	15	30	47
4	36	63	90

Figures 1–4 illustrate the performance of both simple and cost-sensitive models developed for each of the four clusters.

Based on these Figures, both simple and cost-sensitive predictive models have a considerably better performance than the random sampling one (diagonal line). Additionally, the cost-sensitive learning method has been shown to outperform the simple model and to play a considerable role in model building with imbalanced data.

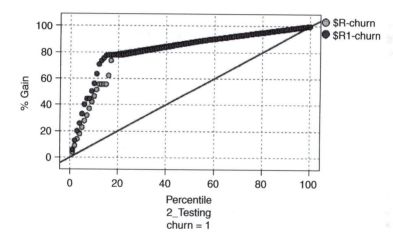

Figure 1. Gain chart of simple (light points) and cost-sensitive (dark points) models for cluster 1.

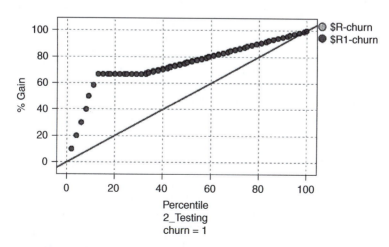

Figure 2. Gain chart of simple (light points) and cost-sensitive (dark points) models for cluster 2.

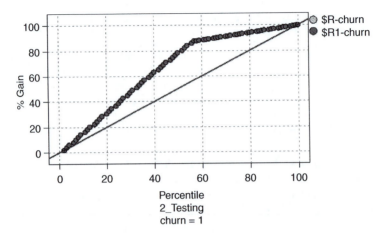

Figure 3.   Gain chart of simple (light points) and cost-sensitive (dark points) models for cluster 3.

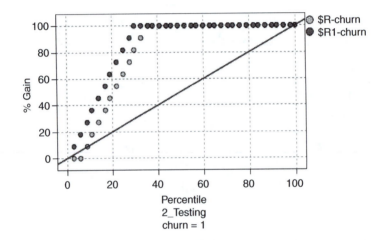

Figure 4.   Gain chart of simple (light points) and cost-sensitive (dark points) models for cluster 4.

By extracting the determinant features for model building in each cluster, we found $\Delta IFOU_2$, $\Delta IFOU_{initial}$, $OFOU_{initial}$, and $\Delta IMOU_2$ to be the most determinant features in model building for churn prediction in the mobile telephony market (Table 5).

The results show that changes in incoming call frequncy and also minutes of use of a customer in addition to the initial frequency of outgoing and incoming calls can serve as deteminant features distinguishing churners from non-churners.

Table 5.   Determinant features for model building in each cluster.

Cluster no.	Determinant features
1	$\Delta IFOU_2$, $\Delta OMOU_2$, $IMOU_{initial}$
2	$IFOU_{initial}$, $OFOU_{initial}$, $\Delta IMOU_2$
3	$IFOU_{initial}$, $OFOU_{initial}$, $\Delta IFOU_2$
4	$OFOU_{initial}$, $\Delta IMOU_2$

Conclusion

In this study, a predictive model for customer churn in pre-paid mobile telephony companies was constructed. Handling the problem of churn definition in the non-contractual (pre-paid) setting, a clustering phase was proposed prior to the model building phase. Thus, the customer base was initially divided into four clusters based on their RFM-related features in order to develop churn definitions for each cluster which were then used in the model building phase. Based on gain charts, the results confirm the satisfactory performance of the proposed models.

Furthermore, dealing with an imbalanced dataset, the cost-sensitive learning method proposed by Weiss (2004) was tested and the effectiveness of his proposed solution was confirmed. While it is likely that this learning method would be of limited use to the adopted technique (Decision Tree), it is essential to test different data mining algorithms with the cost-sensitive learning method in order to generalize the findings of this study.

Finally, the features that can be used to serve as churn indicators among pre-paid mobile telephony customers were extracted. We believe that, in the absence of features other than those constructed for our model building, the deteminant feature(s) extracted here can yield a model with a satisfactory accuracy and the capability to identify likely churners.

Managerial implications

The objective of this research was to develop a predictive model for customer churn in the pre-paid mobile telephony market which would be able to distinguish between customers who are likely to churn in the near future and the ones who are likely to stay with the company. The contribution of such a model for the company lies in the prevention of wasted expenditure due to mass marketing approaches and it enables companies to target the real churners by extracting those customers with the highest probability of churn.

The findings of this research have significant application for companies that are active in the mobile telecommunications market (especially pre-paid). Besides, the idea of developing a dual-step model for extracting the churn definition prior to the model building phase can also be applied in other companies active in non-contractual settings such as pure click online stores.

Research limitations

The major limitation of this research was data classification and data confidentiality in the company under study. This, quite rightly, prevented access to customers' data such as billing and credit data. This forced us to calculate the monetary features manually and deprived us from involving the credit features into our model building. Lack of demographic data of customers was also another other limitation in conducting this research. Because of this fact such factors were unable to be integrated into the clustering phase which would have potentially improved the accuracy and also interpretability of clusters.

It seems obvious that by having unrestricted access to a data base which included all necessary fields, the rigor and reliability of the constructed model would increase which can be the case of future research.

References

Ahn, J., Han, S., & Lee, Y. (2006). Customer churn analysis: Churn determinants and mediation effects of partial defection in the Korean mobile telecommunications service industry. *Telecommunications Policy, 30*, 552–568.

Ansari, S., Kohavi, R., Mason, L., & Zheng, Z. (2000, July). *Integrating e-commerce and data mining: Architecture and challenges*. Paper presented at the First IEEE International Conference on Data Mining, San Jose, CA.

Athanassopoulos, A. (2000). Customer satisfaction cues to support market segmentation and explain switching behavior. *Journal of Business Research, 47*, 191–207.

Berry, M., & Linoff, G. (2004). *Data mining techniques for marketing, sales, and customer relationship management*. Indianapolis: Wiley Publishing.

Bose, R. (2002). Customer relationship management: Key components for IT success. *Industrial Management & Data Systems, 102*(2), 89–97.

Bucknix, W., & van den Poel, D. (2005). Customer base analysis: Partial defection of behaviourally loyal clients in a non-contractual FMCG retail setting. *European Journal of Operational Research, 164*, 252–268.

Burez, J., & van den Poel, D. (2007). CRM at a pay-TV company: Using analytical models to reduce customer attrition by targeted marketing for subscription services. *Expert Systems with Application, 164*, 277–288.

Burez, J., & van den Poel, D. (2008). Separating financial from commercial customer churn: A modeling step towards resolving the conflict between sales and credit department. *Expert Systems with Applications, 35*, 497–514.

Burez, J., & van den Poel, D. (2009). Handling class imbalance in customer churn prediction. *Expert Systems with Applications, 36*, 4626–4636.

Chandar, M., Laha, A., & Krishna, P. (2006, March). *Modeling churn behavior of bank customers using predictive data mining techniques*. Paper presented at the National Conference in Soft Computing Techniques for Engineering Applications (SCT-2006), Rourkela, India.

Chu, B., Tsai, M., & Ho, C. (2007). Toward a hybrid data mining model for customer retention. *Knowledge-Based Systems, 20*, 703–718.

Coussement, K., & van den Poel, D. (2008a). Integrating the voice of customers through call center emails into a decision support system for churn prediction. *Information & Management, 45*, 164–174.

Coussement, K., & van den Poel, D. (2008b). Churn prediction in subscription services: An application of support vector machines while comparing two parameter-selection techniques. *Expert Systems with Applications, 34*, 313–327.

Coussement, K., & van den Poel, D. (2009). Improving customer attrition prediction by integrating emotions from client/company interaction emails and evaluating multiple classifiers. *Expert Systems with Applications, 36*, 6127–6134.

Gerpott, T., Rams, W., & Schindler, A. (2001). Customer retention, loyalty, and satisfaction in the German mobile cellular telecommunications market. *Telecommunications Policy, 25*, 249–269.

Hadden, J., Tiwari, A., Roy, R., & Ruta, D. (2005). Computer assisted customer churn management: State-of-the-art and future trends. *Computers & Operations Research, 34*, 2902–2917.

He, Z., Xu, X., Huang, J., & Deng, S. (2004). Mining class outliers: Concepts, algorithms and applications in CRM. *Expert Systems with Applications, 27*, 681–697.

Hung, S., Yen, D., & Wang, H. (2006). Applying data mining to telecom churn management. *Expert Systems with Applications, 31*, 515–524.

Kim, H., & Yoon, C. (2004). Determinants of subscriber churn and customer loyalty in Korean mobile telephony market. *Telecommunications Policy, 2*, 751–765.

Kincaid, J. (2003). *Customer relationship management: Getting it right*. New Jersey: Prentice-Hall.

Komenar, M. (1997). *Electronic marketing*. New York: Wiley.

Kotler, P., & Keller, L. (2006). *Marketing management*. New Jersey: Pearson/Prentice Hall.

Lejeune, M. (2001). Measuring the impact of data mining on churn management. *Internet Research: Electronic Networking Applications and policy, 11*, 375–387.

Ling, R., & Yen, D. (2001). Customer relationship management: An analysis framework and implementation strategies. *Journal of Computer Information Systems, 41*, 82–97.

Madden, G., Savage, S., & Coble-Neal, G. (1999). Subscriber churn in the Australian ISP market. *Information Economics and Policy, 11*, 195–207.

Mozer, M., Wolniewicz, R., Grimes, D., Johnson, E., & Kaushansky, H. (2000). Predicting subscriber dissatisfaction and improving retention in the wireless telecommunications industry. *IEEE Transactions and Neural Networks, 11*, 690–696.

Neslin, S., Gupta, S., Kamakura, W., Lu, J., & Mason, C. (2006). Defection detection: Measuring and understanding the predictive accuracy of customer churn models. *Journal of Marketing Research, XLIII*, 204–211.

Ngai, E. (2005). Customer relationship management research (1992–2002): An academic literature review and classification. *Marketing Intelligence & Planning, 23*, 582–605.

Ngai, E., Xiu, L., & Chau, D. (2009). Application of data mining techniques in customer relationship management: A literature review and classification. *Expert Systems with Applications, 36*, 2592–2602.

Parvatiyar, A., & Sheth, J. (2001). Customer relationship management: Emerging practice, process and discipline. *Journal of Economic & Social Research, 3*(2), 1–34.

Pendharkar, P. (2009). Genetic algorithm based neural network approaches for predicting churn in cellular wireless networks service. *Expert Systems with Applications, 36*, 6714–6720.

Peppard, J. (2000). Customer relationship management (CRM) in financial services. *European Management Journal, 18*, 312–327.

Reichheld, F. (1996). *The loyalty effect: The hidden force behind growth, profits and lasting value*. Cambridge, MA: Harvard Business School Press.

Reichheld, F., & Sasser, W. (1990). Zero defection: Quality comes to services. *Harvard Business Review, 68*(5), 105–111.

Reinartz, W., Thomas, J., & Kumar, V. (2005). Balancing acquisition and retention resources to maximize profitability. *Journal of Marketing, 69*(1), 63–79.

Richards, K.A., & Jones, E. (2008). Customer relationship management: Finding value drivers. *Industrial Marketing Management, 37*, 120–130.

Rust, R., & Zahorik, A. (1993). Customer satisfaction, customer retention, and market share. *Journal of Retailing, 69*, 193–215.

Rygielski, C., Wang, J., & Yen, D. (2002). Data mining techniques for customer relationship management. *Technology in Society, 24*, 483–502.

SAS Institute. (2000). *Best practice in churn prediction* (White Paper). Cary, NC: SAS Institute.

Seo, D., Ranganathan, C., & Babad, Y. (2008). Two-level model of customer retention in the US mobile telecommunications service market. *Telecommunications Policy, 32*, 182–196.

Shaw, M., Subramaniam, C., Tan, G., & Welge, M. (2001). Knowledge management and datamining for marketing. *Decision Support Systems, 31*, 127–137.

SPSS Inc. (2007). *Clementine 11.1 algorithms guide*. USA: Integral Solutions Limited.

Swift, R. (2001). *Accelerating customer relationships using CRM and relationship technologies*. Upper Saddle River, NJ: Prentice-Hall.

Teo, T., Devadoss, P., & Pan, S. (2006). Towards a holistic perspective of customer relationship management implementation: A case study of the housing and development board singapore. *Decision Support Systems, 42*, 1613–1627.

Van den Poel, D., & Lariviere, B. (2004). Customer attrition analysis for financial services using proportional hazard models. *European Journal of Operational Research, 157*, 196–217.

Wei, C., & Chiu, I. (2002). Turning telecommunications call details to churn prediction: A data mining approach. *Expert Systems with Applications, 23*, 103–112.

Weiss, G. (2004). Mining with rarity: A unifying framework. *SIGKDD Explorations, 6*(1), 7–19.

Xie, Y., Li, X., Ngai, E., & Ying, W. (2009). Customer churn prediction using improved balanced random forests. *Expert Systems with Applications, 36*, 5445–5449.

Xu, Y., Yen, D., Lin, B., & Chou, D. (2002). Adopting customer relationship management technology. *Industrial Managemenet and Data Systems, 102*, 442–452.

Zhao, Y., Li, B., Li, X., Liu, W., & Ren, S. (2005). Customer churn prediction using improved one-class support vector machine. *Lecture Notes in Computer Science, 3584*, 300–306.

Part III: Competitive Strategy

Protecting the Olympic brand: winners and losers

Trevor Hartland[a] and Nicola Williams-Burnett[b]

[a]Business School, University of Glamorgan, Treforest, South Wales, Pontypridd, UK; [b]Cardiff Metropolitan University, Cardiff, South Wales, UK

This paper considers the measures that have been put in place to protect brands and official sponsors of the London 2012 Olympic Games in an attempt to drive out the practice of ambush marketing. London's original bid to host the Games included measures to prevent ambush marketing and once awarded, passed legislation that made it illegal for companies that are not official sponsors to link their products with the Games. Through examination of the London Olympic and Paralympic Games Act 2006, together with case studies from previous Games, this paper questions the potential implications for other organisations should the letter of the law be applied. It is proposed that the Act goes far beyond its valid remit of preventing ambush marketing and is likely to restrict severely companies and other event organisers from pursuing their legitimate business practices. Exploratory research revealed a colossal 2,284,414 potential infringements of the Act. And while this may mean a win for the London Organising Committee for the Olympic Games (LOCOG), it could potentially mean that other organisations become losers as they will be prevented from using specified terms and images without fear of falling foul of the law.

Introduction

Sandler and Shani (1989, p. 10) describe ambush marketing as 'a planned effort by an organisation to associate themselves indirectly with an event in order to gain at least some of the recognition and benefits that are associated with being an official sponsor'. The concept of ambush marketing, also described as parasite and guerrilla marketing (Mullin, Hardy, & Sutton, 2000) and vigilante marketing (Kolah, 2003) is, however, not new and Smith and Zook (2011) suggest that it has been around almost as long as sponsorship itself. It has, nevertheless, been referred to as 'one of the most disquieting developments in sponsorship' (Meenaghan, 1998, p. 20). The 1984 Los Angeles Olympic Games has been identified as the first event to be targeted by ambush marketing, since which time it has become a 'major issue for the sponsoring industry' (Meenaghan, 1998, p. 21).

The aim of this paper is to consider the measures that have been put in place to protect event brands and events' official sponsors in an attempt to drive out the practice of ambush marketing. While a number of previously ambushed events and resultant protectionist measures will be considered, this paper will focus on both the ambushing and protection of the Olympic Games brand, with a focus on the measures being put in place to protect the brand of the Olympic Games taking place in London in 2012. In doing so, this paper questions the potential implications for a range of stakeholders that could be brought about should the letter of the law relating to the protection of this brand be applied.

Effectiveness of ambush marketing

An abundance of empirical evidence exists that illustrates the effectiveness of ambush marketing (Garrahan, 2000; Meenaghan, 1994; Sandler & Shani, 1989) against a range of sport event settings. Vodaphone's six-year deal sponsoring the Wallabies for the 2003 rugby World Cup was sidelined after archrival Telstra signed up as the official tournament sponsor. Vodaphone responded by deploying a team of look-alike players named 'The Vodaphone Wannabies' to tour the country. An independent poll revealed that Vodaphone ranked ahead of Telstra in a list of the event's 'sponsors' (Media Asia, 2004). At the 1994 Winter Olympics in Lillehammer, Norway, in response to official-sponsor Visa's claims that American Express would not be accepted in the Olympic Village, American Express created an advertising campaign playing on two different connotations of the word *visa*, 'claiming (correctly) that Americans do not need "visas" to travel to Norway' (Sauer, 2002). During the 1996 Atlanta Olympic Games, Nike embarked upon an ambush campaign by prominently displaying its logo on the building directly opposite the Olympic stadium. Although not an official Olympic sponsor, this promotion inextricably tied Nike to the city and to the event (Sauer, 2002). Adidas, although not an official sponsor of the 2000 Sydney Olympic Games, was cited as the seventh most recognised 'sponsor' of the Games (Garrahan, 2000). This was due largely to the publicity surrounding the Adidas body suits worn by the Australian swimming team that prominently displayed the organisation's logo throughout the event. A more recent event occurred during the 2010 FIFA World Cup when Dutch brewery, Bavaria, handed out orange mini dresses prior to the Netherlands game. Since orange is the corporate colour of Bavaria, it was deemed to be an ambush stunt by FIFA and over 30 women were removed from the match as a result of wearing the orange clothing despite it not incorporating any brand identity. Under the sponsorship agreement that FIFA had with Budweiser, no other beer company would be permitted to advertise in association with the event. The Bavaria example was therefore seen to be contravening this agreement and the Dutch brewery were taken to court by FIFA. No ruling was made, however, due to insufficient proof that it was a deliberate act.

The legal battle

As the practice of ambush marketing is increasing, and appearing to be highly effective for certain brands, organisers of major sporting events have been forced to put preventative measures in place to minimise or attempt to eradicate this practice. To date, however, legislation has proved to be less than effective as evidenced by Hartland and Skinner (2005). The Sydney 2000 Act which was passed for the purpose of protecting the official sponsors of the 2000 Olympics from those very issues of most concern, failed to achieve what it set out to deliver. The organising committee for the Sydney 2000 Olympic Games was successful in lobbying for new legal protection measures to prevent ambush marketing and as a result the Sydney 2000 Games (Indicia & Images) Protection Act 1996 was passed. Fundamentally, the Act was designed to prevent the use of, or association with, any words, sounds or images that could be commonly recognised as having a direct connection with the Olympics. However, as subsequent court decisions show, the deterrent laws may be considered difficult to interpret:

It is interesting to note that the Bill singles out the use of the stand-alone references to the words 'Olympic' and 'Sydney 2000' when the Senate Committee report only proposed that those phrases be protected when used in conjunction with others. (Curthoys & Kendall, 2001, p. 15)

Whatever form the ambush may take however, the end result will ultimately lead to what Meenaghan (1996, p. 106) describes as 'consumer confusion [which in turn will] deny the legitimate sponsor clear recognition for its sponsorship role'. This then 'damages the integrity and financial basis of an event' (Hoek & Gendall, 2002, p. 384) for which the sponsors have paid dearly. Nonetheless as Lagae (2005, p. 218) identifies, 'the legal battle against ambushers is not straightforward [because ambushers operate in a] grey zone'. The more adroit ambushers avoid using official identifiers and will instead often create alternative devices that relate to the event or team without actually breaching registered trademarks. For example, Hoek (1997) cites the New Zealand 'Ring Ring' case where the imaginative use of a visual device clearly referred to the Olympic Rings symbol when read closely. Indeed, the fact that some ambushing could be regarded as being legal only serves to highlight the need for sponsors and event organisers to plug as many potential ambushing loopholes as possible. Europe currently has very few legal precedents with regard to ambush marketing, but as Hartland and Skinner (2005) point out, this situation could soon be changing.

Protecting London 2012 against ambush marketers

Part of London's original bid to host the 2012 Olympic Games included measures to prevent ambush marketing. Sherwood and Owen (2005, p. 21) reported that in its bid, legislation is to be passed that 'would make it illegal for companies that are not official sponsors to try to link their products with the [London] Olympics'. Sherwood and Owen (2005, p. 21) further noted that Tessa Jowell, the British Culture Secretary of the day, was said to be determined to introduce legislation that would 'make it unlawful for people to associate themselves, their products or their services with the Games for any commercial benefit, unless they have been authorised to do so'. Upon being awarded the 2012 Olympic and Paralympic Games, London was immediately required to enter into the 'Host City Contract'. Obligations under this contract meant fulfilling all commitments made in the bidding process including protection for the official sponsors. As a result, the UK government brought into force the London Olympic and Paralympic Games Act 2006 (Intellectual Property Office, 2009). The Act essentially grants the London Organising Committee for the Olympic Games (LOCOG) the rights to prevent any unauthorised representations or associations with the Games (a much wider right than available under normal intellectual property rights) and LOCOG has made it clear that it will do everything in its power to stop unlawful use. *Representation* is described as being 'any image, graphic design, sound or word of any kind which is likely to suggest to the public an association between a person, goods or services and the London Olympics', while *associations* are defined as being 'any kind of contractual or commercial relationship, corporate or structural connection; or the provision of financial or other support' (Macfarlanes, 2010). Infringement of the Act, therefore, is not restricted to the use of Olympic-specific words or symbols. Furthermore, the 2006 Act provides no limitations on what may or may not create an 'association'. Whilst there are certain key terms that the 2006 Act provides that the Court may take into particular account when considering whether there is an association, the Secretary of State is free to add to this list. For the London Olympic Games in 2012, the use of two words from list A or one word from list

A and one from list B together will in effect create a potential infringement of the Act (Table 1).

Protecting the Olympic brand – a step too far?

LOCOG, however, has also stressed that the absence of these words will not prevent infringement. It is therefore proposed in this paper that the Act goes a step too far and could severely restrict businesses and planned events in the London area from promoting and conducting their legal, day-to-day activities. Take, for example, the London Tourist Board who may wish to use the phrase 'visit London in 2012', or a local school wanting to promote its 2012 Summer Sports Day. Using these words in their promotions would, according to the letter of the law, be an infringement under the measures taken to protect the Olympic brand, and yet would not be an attempt (deliberate or otherwise) to ambush the Olympic brand.

It would appear that this argument is echoed by the UK's Chartered Institute of Marketing who contend that the Act goes far beyond its 'valid remit of preventing ambush marketing and preserving investment value for official sponsors', further pointing out that it 'fails to give allowance to the (by Olympic standards) minuscule efforts of small and medium-sized companies to gain some benefit from the presence of the Games', and that since the majority of marketers are unaware of the provisions of the Act, they are 'likely to get a rude awakening' when they discover that a planned activity could contravene it (Thorp, 2008).

Iconic buildings and the marketing of destinations

Each geographic location has a distinctive culture, history and unique selling point differentiating one location from another (Morgan & Pritchard, 2002). Tourist destinations and cities are being branded to ensure that they do not blend into the background within the competitive market place (Keller, 2008). Moreover, tourist destinations are no longer being viewed as just places, but are increasingly being viewed as at least part of the actual product that is consumed (Ashworth & Voogd, 1990). Ritchie and Ritchie (1998) propose that destination branding occurs when a destination differentiates itself but is also distinguished through a number of elements such as logo, name or symbol. With the combination of these elements it is said to convey the promise of a memorable travel experience that is uniquely associated with the destination, can also serve to consolidate and reinforce the recollection of memorable destination experiences. Skinner (2010) believes that further consideration of the uniqueness of a place also involves understanding what comprises the *genius loci*, the essence, or spirit of an individual place, proposing that this needs to include a consideration of the unique architecture that

Table 1. Key terms that may form 'associations' with the 2012 Olympic Games.

A	B
Games	Gold
2012	Silver
Twenty Twelve	Bronze
Two Thousand and Twelve	London
	Medals
	Sponsors
	Summer

contributes to the overall physical environment, as well as other experiential aspects in order to understand what constitutes the unique offering of one destination over another. This perspective therefore shows the importance of the destination brand itself in being able to align its promotions with the place's iconic buildings that contribute to its unique identity. With 15 million tourists visiting the capital annually (Bremmer, 2010), London is the most visited city in the world, topping Euromonitor International's list of Top City Destinations in 2008. When considering what London has to offer as its unique destination proposition, both the English Tourist Board website and Visit London website include Westminster Abbey, the Houses of Parliament, Buckingham Palace (Online Enjoy England, 2010), the London Eye and the Tower of London (Online Visit London, 2010) in their 'top 10 places to visit' in London. All of these places are synonymous with London, are instantly recognisable and are iconic land marks within the city of London. But what is it that makes these buildings so iconic? Firstly, the above buildings and many other places in London are famous in their own right and secondly, they are symbolic to the English culture and aesthetic to the eye (Sklair, 2006). Sklair (2006) further suggests that iconic buildings have the ability to transform skylines and be identifiable across the globe. The iconic buildings and landmarks in London therefore form part of London's destination product, are the unique selling points that help to create a large part of the experience for the tourist, and also entice the tourist to visit the destination. However, according to the letter of the law, the use of London's iconic buildings in promotional activities, or even representation of the London skyline could indeed cause an infringement of the regulations set out by the London Olympic Association Right (LOAR).

As one example shows, although not directly connected to the Olympics, a recent publicity stunt by the Australian cricket team in October 2010 saw pictures of the team's captain and vice captain beamed onto Big Ben with the caption 'Don't forget to pack the urn' (Scott, 2010). As a result, Westminster City Council threatened to take legal action claiming that the stunt constituted a criminal offence as Big Ben is classed as a world heritage site (Scott, 2010). Prior to this, Westminster City Council had not taken any legal action against other parties who had undertaken similar promotional activities (Scott, 2010). For example, no action was taken when, in 1999, FHM magazine projected a naked image of Gail Porter onto the Houses of Parliament (Cunning, 2010). This particular campaign captured public attention, created a vast amount of publicity within the media and made many headlines in front page newspapers and on television programmes (Fry, 1999). Scott (2010) suggests that with the 2012 London Olympics approaching, if Westminster City Council did take action against companies that flaunt the law, they could fear an increase in 'guerrilla advertising'. Even though the Australian cricket team escaped prosecution (Online BBC, 2010) and the image projected onto Big Ben contained none of the words or images restricted by LOCOG, the team were still made an example of to the rest of the world as a direct result of the forthcoming 2012 Olympics. Whilst it is acknowledged that within the guidelines of the Olympic handbook there is no mention or restriction in using iconic buildings of London either as a place to advertise or to use within promotional material, it nevertheless leads to questions in relation to Westminster City Council's responses to the actions of the Australian cricket team.

The images of London are used by countless companies, schools and other institutions and the buildings and icons are a fundamental part of the tourist industry and figure prominently on the sightseeing tours (see, for example, http://www.themustardagency. com/education.php?sub=education_prospectuses and http://www.theoriginaltour.com/ tour_information/page_109.html). Upon closer inspection of LOCOG's Brand Protection guidelines (http://www.london2012.com), along with a consideration of the protected words in columns A and B in Table 1, it can be easily foreseen that a large amount of all promotional activities undertaken in 2012 could come under scrutiny. With these strict guidelines in mind, how can the marketer or proprietor ensure that they are free from prosecution and do not inadvertently launch a campaign only to find out that they are accused of ambush marketing? Furthermore, with so many people using the London skyline, buildings and icons in their promotional materials, how can such restrictive brand protection be enforced, and if it is, to whose cost?

Most of the venues that will be used for the London Olympic Games are iconic city buildings and landmarks (http://www.london2012.com/map.php). Moreover, in addition to the list of potential associations caused by using the words in columns A and B in Table 1, there is an additional list in the Brand Protection handbook (LOCOG, 2010, p. 37) that, according to Mommas (2003) would be the type of symbols, logos, words and graphics generally used to brand a destination, but which, if used in promotional materials by companies who are not official sponsors of the event could constitute an infringement of the rights of LOCOG to protect the Olympic brand. This list includes 'images of venues to be used for, and closely associated with, the 2012 Games', and 'words which capture the essence of the 2012 Games and/or qualities associated with Olympism, (eg: "Spirit"; "Endeavour"; "Friendship"; "Winning"; "Determination")' (LOCOG, 2010). While LOCOG stresses that it

is NOT suggesting that use of the items listed below will immediately create an association with the 2012 Games, but they may well be relevant. The more of these items that are used, the more likely it is that an association with the 2012 Games will be created. (LOCOG, 2010)

Whilst the LOAR allows the screening of events in public houses and entertainment venues and the use of such terms as 'Watch the Olympic Games Here' or 'Live Coverage of the 2012 Games Here' would not be classed as an infringement of the act, *per se* (Mcfarlanes, 2010), it is clearly outlined in section 4.6.3. of the Act that if the venue uses such statements displayed within or on other items that include other brands, this would then be classed as an infringement (LOCOG, 2010). Many public houses and entertainment establishments advertise their upcoming events and promotions using promotional boards, blackboards, posters and such like, that may already display a number of brand logos. Is the LOAR suggesting that all establishments screening Olympic Games events remove ALL other promotional materials within the establishment in the run up and during the Games that may be adjacent to the promotion of the Olympic Games (even though these may be permanent fixtures), or that the venues in question buy in new non-branded promotional boards solely for the use of promoting the Olympic Games? With this in mind, where does the LOAR draw the line as to what is classed as an infringement on the promotion of the 2012 Olympics?

Also of concern is that LOCOG decided to use the iconic London red Routemaster Bus in the closing ceremony of the previous Olympic Games in Beijing (http://www. london2012.com/games/ceremonies/index.php). Does this use therefore mean that, because LOCOG has already associated this 'icon of England' (http://www.icons.org. uk/theicons/collection/view?mode=list) with the London 2012 Olympic Games, that they could include this image as a potential Olympic association if used by a potential ambush marketer?

Methodology

The aim of this research was to highlight the possible ramifications of marketing activity for all organisations alike in the run up to and during the forthcoming London 2012

Olympic and Paralympics Games as a result of the measures that have been put into place to protect the brands and the official sponsors.

In order to achieve a greater understanding of the paper's aim, a descriptive research approach was implemented. The primary objectives of this method are not only to describe events but also to count the effects that will contribute to building up a picture and counting the possible infringements that could occur in 2012 (McGivern, 2003).

The very nature of this research aim naturally lends itself to a quantitative data collection method, which is an approach that can determine and quantify data collected for this research (Hussey & Hussey, 1997). By implementing this approach it will hopefully highlight the possible future effect and risk that organisations may face in 2012 *if* they use the restricted terms as outlined by LOGOC and consequently infringe the Act.

Content analysis was utilised and is defined by Berelson (1952, p. 18) as 'a research technique for the objective, systematic, and quantitative description of the manifest content of communication'. This research method has the ability to condense text into more manageable smaller groupings (Krippendorff, 1980) making the task of analysing significant amounts of data more manageable (US General Accounting Office, 1996) and produces valid inferences from the data collected (Krippendorff, 1980). Content analysis is increasingly effective in studying trends and relationships which allow the researcher to replicate the data collection as a result of coding (Stemler, 2001) and by definition is a quantitative method (Hansen, Cottle, Negrine, & Newbold, 1998). In utilising a quasi-quantitative approach it permitted the researchers to gather a broad-spectrum of the possible effects of likely outcomes for 2012 and undertake data collection on an event that is yet to happen. Hansen et al. (1998) identify that content analysis can be divided into definable stages. This study implemented Hansen et al.'s (1998, p. 98) key steps of content analysis that involve six stages:

(1) Definition of the research problem.
(2) Selection of media and sample.
(3) Defining analytical categories.
(4) Constructing a coding schedule.
(5) Piloting the coding schedule and checking reliability.
(6) Data preparation and analysis.

Definition of the research problem

The possible effect on marketing activity for organisations in the run up and during the Olympic and Paralympics Games 2012 as a result of the 2006 Act set in place to protect the brand and its official sponsors.

Selection of media and sample

The authors acknowledge that to analyse all the various media types surrounding this issue for the entire United Kingdom would be unmanageable and virtually impossible. For this reason, data were collected by using the internet and in particular the search engine, Google. Although it is noted that the internet lacks the ability to produce a complete answer, it can and has in this study, highlighted areas where further research is needed (Malhotra & Birks, 2007). Statistically, of all the search engines available in the United Kingdom, Google UK is the most popular and widely used site and accounted for 76.7% of all visits for the week ending 9 July 2011. In contrast, Google.com accounted for 8.13% and Bing accounted for 4.46% respectively (Hitwise, 2011). When undertaking a search,

Google routinely looks for documents that include all of the search terms entered and unlike other search engines that display the first few lines from a document on their page, Google will highlight and present the words that are applicable to the search (O'Dochartaigh, 2002). All searches were conducted using Google Advanced, which allowed the researchers to limit their search by domain, exact phrase, language and country, and to exclude certain words and content (O'Dochartaigh, 2002).

The search term parameters employed were:

- *The exact wording or phrase*: This included a combination of the restricted terms surrounded by quotation marks.
- *Unwanted/excluded words*: Olympics was excluded within the searches to ensure that only non-Olympic sites were displayed.
- *Region*: United Kingdom.

In order that the scale of the data could be kept manageable, the search criteria were restricted to the United Kingdom and only the first page of search results was included in the data collection. Recent research has revealed that 95.8% of non-branded traffic is as of a direct result of individuals clicking on the first page of a search engine's results page, whereas only 2.5% of traffic comes from the second page (Cornwell, 2010).

Data collection was undertaken on 27 July 2011; a year to the date of the London Olympics opening ceremony. This date was considered to be of most relevance in relation to the Olympic calendar in 2012 and on reflection generated large amounts of media attention.

Defining analytical categories

Although there are a variety of possible avenues which could result in a business being in breach of the Act (use of images, essence words and a combination of the restricted terms from list A and/or B), for the purposes of this research, key words were taken from the restricted terms listed in Table 1 as outlined by LOCOG.

Constructing a coding schedule

In line with LOCOG's Act relating to the restricted use of the terms in Table 1, the researchers combined all words from list A followed by one word from list A and one word from list B. In total, 40 unique searches were conducted through the use of Google Advanced using the parameters previously outlined in Step Two.

Piloting the coding schedule and checking reliability

During the preliminary stages of the research, the authors conducted a pilot of the proposed coding to identify any inconsistencies. As a result, the following amendments were made:

- The excluding of the word 'Olympics' from the search.
- The exclusion of images and essence words from the search.
- Limiting the word combinations to only those terms from list A and one word from list A with one from list B.

These exclusions were specified so as to avoid capturing the large number of search results displaying hits for the official Olympic and Paralympics sites and sponsors.

Table 2.   Results of search for 'associated' terms.

Key terms	Hits	Industry	Examples
List A			
Games 2012	53,200	Community Sports Games	Abriachan Highland Games
			London Youth Games (CP)
		Stationers	Desk top calendar
Games Twenty Twelve	8	Sustainable energy	Wind turbine manufacturers
Games Two Thousand and Twelve	2	Marketing	Direct mail
2012 Games	480,000	Travel	Trains & bus (travel to the Games)
		Local councils	Watching the Games
		Theatre	Christian theatre groups
2012 Twenty Twelve	7080	Entertainment	Music recommendation site, Orange TV blog
		Graphic design	Print design (promotional materials)
		Stationers	Calendar
2012 Two Thousand and Twelve	65	Forums	2012 pronunciation
		Photographers	Imagery stockists
Twenty Twelve Games	324	Sports	X Games
		Gaming	X Box live
		Forums	2012 pronunciation
		Media company	Media 2012 (official)
Twenty Twelve 2012	11,200	Business listing site	Business called 'Twenty Twelve 2012'
		Auction site	Ebay
		Graphic design	Print design (promotional material)
Twenty Twelve Two Thousand and Twelve	1	Student community website	The student room
Two Thousand and Twelve Games	1	News	Reuter blog
Two Thousand and Twelve 2012	8	Marketing	Direct mail
		News	BBC
Two Thousand and Twelve Twenty Twelve	1	Local council website	
Lists A and B			
2012 Gold	25,900	News	BBC, Metro
		Sport	World professional darts
		Charity	Stroke
		Bike manufacturer	Goldwing, Mongoose
2012 Silver	13,000	Tourism	Cruises
		Jewellers	Watches
		Bike manufacturers	Bike stockists
		Online shopping	Amazon
		Industry event	Security
2012 Bronze	703	Sport	Badminton & Squash club
		Activity	Duke of Edinburgh
		Retail	Antiques
		Entertainment	What's on calendar
		Education	Archaeological course

(continued)

Table 2. (*Continued*).

Key terms	Hits	Industry	Examples
2012 London	586,000	Entertainment	NYE London
		Industry event	Education trade fair Oceanology International Conference Gas Tech
		Activist group	Playfair, workers' rights for 2012
		Charity	Pride
2012 Medals	912	News	Online media
		Community programmes	Youth scheme
2012 Sponsors	3090	Film	Film company
		Sport	Manchester marathon
		Industry news	Sports business
		Blog	Venture Yorkshire
		Industry event	Mining, travel awards
2012 Summer	180,000	Tourism	Customer review sites
		Retail: Holiday	Major players in travel industry
		Entertainment	Film guide
		Institution blog	Psychopharmcology
Games Gold	232,000	Sport	Commonwealth Games Asian Games
Games Silver	101,000	Extreme sports	X Games-snowboarding
		Community Games	Croydon Youth Games
Games Bronze	26,400	Sport	Commonwealth Games
		Online gaming	Lumberjack Games
Games London	312,000	Community games	London Youth Games
		Games software supplier	Raven Games London
Games Medals	18,100	Sport	Commonwealth Games
		Regional Games	Island Games
Games Sponsors	4410	Regional Games	Killin Highland Games
		Entertainment	Heart Radio
Games Summer	229,000	Online gaming	Microsoft – Indie Games Summer
		Online shopping	Amazon
Twenty Twelve Gold	0	N/A	N/A
Twenty Twelve Silver	1	Online shopping	Zazzle.co.uk
Twenty Twelve Bronze	0	N/A	N/A
Twenty Twelve London	7	Online directory	Useyourlocal.com
Twenty Twelve Medals	0	N/A	N/A
Twenty Twelve Sponsors	0	N/A	N/A
Twenty Twelve Summer	0	N/A	N/A
Two Thousand and Twelve Gold	0	N/A	N/A
Two Thousand and Twelve Silver	0	N/A	N/A
Two Thousand and Twelve Bronze	0	N/A	N/A
Two Thousand and Twelve London	1	Tourism	This is Nottingham
Two Thousand and Twelve Medals	0	N/A	N/A

(*continued*)

Table 2. (*Continued*).

Key terms	Hits	Industry	Examples
Two Thousand and Twelve Sponsors	0	N/A	N/A
Two Thousand and Twelve Summer	0	N/A	N/A
Total	*2,284,414*		

Data preparation and analysis

Due to the data collected for this research being relatively small and simplistic, analysis was conducted manually and did not employ the use of any analytical software package.

Results and implications

Table 2 contains the results of the content analysis regarding potential infringements of the London Olympic and Paralympic Games Act 2006 when compared with the listed terms identified in Table 1.

The search, which was conducted on 27 July 2011 (exactly 12 months ahead of the commencement of the 2012 Olympic Games), revealed no fewer than 2,284,414 matches which if they were to be 'live' a year on, would be contravening the London Olympic and Paralympic Games Act 2006 and therefore likely to attract legal action by LOCOG. Although it is acknowledged that the figure of 2,284,414 matches does not allow for the possibility for some of the hits to contain multiple results from the same organisation and thereby reducing the total, it is nonetheless a staggering statistic and is regarded to be of considerable concern for those companies who today are going about the legitimate business of promoting their organisations, but would be in breach of the Act were they to be employing these promotional messages 12 months later. Furthermore, it must also be acknowledged that a significant number, if not most organisations will not yet be engaged in promoting their 2012 activities and therefore this current figure is most likely to be considerably less than it will be during 2012. It can also be assumed that had searches been conducted to include two or more of the list B terms, the number of 'matches' would have further increased. In addition, of the 60 plus examples provided in Table 2, the majority of them are either small and medium enterprises or not-for-profit organisations who would be much more greatly affected by any fines levied upon them for contravening the Act than those multi-national enterprises found to be in the same position.

And whilst the significance of the potential number of organisations revealed by the search is of considerable concern, more worryingly, perhaps, is the lack of awareness for the potential to contravene the law by these companies as previously outlined by Thorp (2008). Furthermore, since the Act provides no limitations on what may or may not create an association, together with the additional caveat of permitting the Secretary of State to add to the list, the potential for organisations to fall foul of the law is immense.

A closer analysis of the results reveals a large number of industries that could be affected were they to continue to include the restricted terms in their promotional material. These include: tourism; entertainment (film, music and television); event organisations (industry and public events); graphic designers; stationers; and charities to name but a few. Unsurprisingly, sporting events ranked highly in many of the results pages. These events ranged from local community games such as the Abriachan Highland Games, Killin Highland Games and Croydon Youth Games, to larger sporting events that attract competitors, spectators and sponsors alike, and not just from the United Kingdom such as the Manchester Marathon, but also from other countries around the world, for example, the Commonwealth Games and X Games (Extreme sports games). When reflecting upon the results that have identified other world famous events that are currently in possible breach of LOCOG's regulations, this raises the issue as to whether these events will be made an example of in a similar way to the Australian cricket team, who, although were not in breach of LOCOG's regulations unlike the events mentioned above, nevertheless attracted the threat of legal action, or will they simply be 'brushed under the carpet' so to speak.

Different word combinations entered into Google's Advanced search from the restricted terms in lists A and B yielded different results, as was expected. Some of the combinations produced fewer than 10 results, and in some case no matches whatsoever. These outcomes were usually associated when the list 'A' terms 'Twenty Twelve' and 'Two Thousand and Twelve' were entered as the search criteria. The top five largest search results came from the combinations '2012 London' 586,000, '2012 Games' 480,000, 'Games London' 312,000, 'Games Gold' 232,000 and 'Games Summer' 229,000. This result not only highlights the significance of utilising specific terminology, but also the number of organisations that are at risk of falling foul of LOCOG's regulations.

Conclusion

It is not the purpose of this paper to suggest that attempts at minimising the practice of ambush marketing should not be pursued by LOCOG. What is being proposed, however, is that any planned measures, especially those that could bring attendant legal redress, should not go too far in attempting to protect the Olympic brand. We suggest that the measures put in place to protect the brand of the forthcoming 2012 London Olympic Games are indeed a step too far and the 2,284,414 potential infringements of the London Olympic and Paralympic Games Act 2006 revealed by our research clearly support this view.

Whilst it is acknowledged that the measures that have been taken to protect the Olympic brand may mean a win against ambush marketing for LOCOG, these very same measures, however, could potentially result in other organisations becoming the losers as they may unwittingly use restricted terms, images and/or expressions in their marketing communications and consequently be in breach of the law. Moreover, for those businesses that are aware of the Act, restricting their usage of the listed terms, images or expressions is likely to handicap their marketing strategies by not being permitted to communicate their business activities to their fullest potential.

Although these restrictions are likely to deter some businesses from entering into illegal practice, the Act itself may not discourage all from attempting to jump on to the Olympic 'brand wagon' as some may enter into some form of ambush marketing campaign given that previous events have fallen foul to such practice. Examples, as outlined in the literature review such as Nike during the 1996 Atlanta Olympic Games (Sauer, 2002) and Adidas during the 2000 Sydney Olympic Games (Garrahan, 2000) have proved to be very successful in promoting their organisation as a recognised associated brand with the Olympic Games even when not official Olympic sponsors. After all, raising brand awareness and achieving consumer recognition are two of the many tasks that the marketing department seeks to fulfil within the organisation. While sponsors continue to pay high premiums to be correctly associated with events, there will always be competing organisations who continue to circumvent all attempts to prevent ambush attacks.

Future research could be undertaken to track legal actions by LOCOG in pursuit of the protection of the Olympic brand, and also a content analysis of promotional materials utilising brand icons of London and words forming potential Olympic associations.

References

Ashworth, G., & Voogd, H. (1990). Can places be sold for tourism. In G. Ashworth & B. Goodall (Eds.), *Marketing tourism places* (pp. 1–9). London: Routledge.

Berelson, B. (1952). *Content analysis in communication research.* Glencoe, IL: Free Press.

Bremmer, C. (2010). *Euromonitor International's top city destination ranking.* Retrieved December 15, 2010, from http://www.euromonitor.com/Euromonitor_Internationals_Top_City_Destination_Ranking

Cornwell, S. (2010). *The importance of page-one visibility: Keywords queries and natural search trends for non-branded key words.* Retrieved July 31, 2011, from http://www.icrossing.com/research/the-importance-of-page-one-visibility.php

Curthoys, J., & Kendall, C. (2001). Ambush marketing and the Sydney 2000 Games (Indicia and Images) Protection Act: A retrospective. *Murdoch University Electronic Journal of Law, 8.* Retrieved December 12, 2010, from http://www.murdoch.edu.au/elaw/issues/v8n2/kendall82.html

Fry, A. (1999). *Marketing, surprise strategy catches attention – according to clients, the bigger and more unusual the media, the better.* Retrieved December 15, 2010, from http://www.marketingmagazine.co.uk/news/69880/MEDIA-Surprise-strategy-catches-attention---According-clients-bigger-unusual-media-better-Andy-Fry/?DCMP=ILC-SEARCH

Garrahan, M. (2000, September 16). Stringent measures taken to prevent ambush marketing. *Financial Times,* p. 8.

Hansen, A., Cottle, S., Negrine, R., & Newbold, C. (1998). *Mass communication research methods.* Basingstoke: Macmillan.

Hartland, T., & Skinner, H. (2005). What is being done to deter ambush marketing, and are these attempts working? *International Journal of Sports Marketing and Sponsorship, 6,* 231–241.

Hitwise. (2011). Retrieved July 28, 2011, from http://www.hitwise.com/uk/datacentre/main/dashboard-7323.html

Hoek, J. (1997). Ring Ring: Visual pun or passing off? *Asia-Australia Marketing Journal, 5,* 33–44.

Hoek, J., & Gendall, P. (2002). When do ex-sponsors become ambush marketers? *International Journal of Sports Marketing and Sponsorship, 3,* 383–401.

Hussey, J., & Hussey, R. (1997). *Business research: A practical guide for undergraduate and postgraduate student.* London: Macmillan Press.

Intellectual Property Office. (2009). Retrieved January 18, 2011, from http://www.ipo.gov.uk/pro-types/pro-tm/t-policy/t-policy-ambush.htm

Keller, K.L. (2008). *Strategic brand management: Building measuring and managing brand equity.* Essex: Pearson Education.

Kolah, A. (2003). *Maximising the value of sponsorship.* London: SportBusiness Group.

Krippendorff, K. (1980). *Content analysis: An introduction to its methodology.* Newbury Park, CA: Sage.

Lagae, W. (2005). *Sports sponsorship and marketing communications – a European perspective.* Harlow: FT Prentice Hall.

London Organising Committee of the Olympic Games (LOCOG). (2010). *London 2012's UK statutory marketing rights, brand protection.* Retrieved December 15, 2010, from http://www.london2012.com/documents/brand-guidelines/statutory-marketing-rights.pdf

Macfarlanes, IP. (2010). Retrieved January 18, 2011, from http://ecomms.macfarlanes.com/ve/ZZ65j00978370LY8584m85/VT=0/page=1

Malhotra, N.K., & Birks, D.F. (2007). *Marketing research: An applied approach* (3rd European ed.). Harlow: FT Prentice Hall.

McGivern, Y. (2003). *The practice of market and social research: An introduction.* Harlow: FT Prentice Hall.

Media Asia. (2004, November 19). *Specialist & technique – promotional activity.* Asia Pacific Awards, p. 23. Retrieved February 21, 2005, from http://web.ebscohost.com/ehost/detail?hid=9&sid=1d44ad85-cce6-440d-aa1b-5a046ce78a5a%40sessionmgr12&vid=4&bdata=JnNpdGU9ZWhvc3QtbGl2ZQ%3d%3d#db=buh&AN=15358197

Meenaghan, T. (1994). Point of view: Ambush marketing: Immoral or imaginative practice. *Journal of Advertising Research, 34*(5), 77–88.

Meenaghan, T. (1996). Ambush marketing – a threat to corporate sponsorship. *Sloan Management Review, 38*, 103–113.

Meenaghan, T. (1998). Current developments & future directions in sponsorship. *International Journal of Advertising, 17*, 3–28.

Mommas, H. (2003). *City branding*. Rotterdam, The Netherlands: NAI Publishers.

Morgan, N., & Pritchard, A. (2002). Contextualising destination branding. In N. Morgan, A. Pritchard, & K. Pride (Eds.), *Destination branding, creating the unique destination proposition* (pp. 11–42). Oxford: Butterworth-Heinemann.

Mullin, B., Hardy, S., & Sutton, W. (2000). *Sport marketing*. Champaign, IL: Human Kinetics.

O'Dochartaigh, N. (2002). *The internet research handbook: A practical guide for students and researchers in the social sciences*. London: Sage.

Online BBC. (2010). Retrieved December 15, 2010, from http://www.bbc.co.uk/news/uk-england-london-11840048

Online Cunning. (2010). Retrieved December 15, 2010, from http://www.cunning.com/upload/pdf/cf3875b0c4df5cd93fa72ad94f15b817_FHM%20Case%20Study.pdf

Online Enjoy England. (2010). Retrieved December 15, 2010, from http://www.enjoyengland.com/Images/London-travel-itinerary_tcm21-186171.pdf

Online Visit London. (2010). Retrieved December 15, 2010, from http://www.visitlondon.com/attractions/culture/top-ten-attractions

Ritchie, J.R.B., & Ritchie, R.J.B. (1998). The branding of tourism destinations: Past achievements and future challenges. In P. Keller (Ed.), *Proceedings of the 1998 Annual Congress of the International Association of Scientific Experts in Tourism, Destination Marketing: Scopes and limitations* (pp. 89–116). Marrakech, Morocco: International Association of Scientific Experts in Tourism.

Sandler, D.M., & Shani, D. (1989). Olympic sponsorship vs. 'ambush' marketing: Who gets the gold? *Journal of Advertising Research, 29*(4), 9–14.

Sauer, A.D. (2002). Ambush marketing: Steals the show. *Brandchannel*. Retrieved December 2, 2010, from http://www.brandchannel.com/features_effect.asp?pf_id=98#more

Scott, M. (2010, October 29). Big Ben Ashes stunt may land Australia in legal action. *Guardian*. Retrieved December 15, 2010, from http://www.guardian.co.uk/sport/2010/oct/29/england-australia-ashes-big-ben

Sherwood, B., & Owen, D. (2005, February 7). London Olympics would trigger ad curbs. *Financial Times*, p. 21.

Skinner, H. (2010, July). *In search of the genius loci - the essence of a place brand*. Paper presented at the Academy of Marketing annual conference, Coventry, UK.

Sklair, L. (2006). Iconic architecture and capitalist globalization. *City, 10*, 21–47.

Smith, P.R., & Zook, Z. (2011). *Marketing communications*. London: Kogan Page.

Stemler, S. (2001). An overview of content analysis. *Practical Assessment, Research & Evaluation, 7*. Retrieved July 31, 2011, from http://PAREonline.net/getvn.asp?v=7&n=17

Thorp, D. (2008). The event that dare not speak its name: Marketing and the Olympics. *Shape the Agenda*, (14). Retrieved December 12, 2010, from http://www.cim.co.uk/filestore/resources/agendapapers/marketingandtheolympics.pdf

US General Accounting Office. (1996). *Content analysis: A methodology for structuring and analyzing written material*. Retrieved July 31, 2011, from http://archive.gao.gov/f0102/157490.pdf

Moving closer to the customers: effects of vertical integration in the Swedish commercial printing industry

Thomas Mejtoft

Department of Applied Physics and Electronics, Umeå University, Umeå, SE-90187, Sweden

This paper reports on a study regarding how vertical integration is used to increase customer relations in the printing industry and illustrates the competitive consequences with vertical integration towards customers. Results show that since direct customers are perceived as more loyal and profitable than advertising agencies and/or print brokers, integration of content creation is common to increase relations with direct customers. However, as direct customers' part of total production is still very small, integration of content creation gives rise to a potentially competitive situation between printing firms and advertising agencies. Printing firms recognized this problem as they try to avoid this competition. Two different approaches to the problem are illustrated. Printing firms either focus on simple jobs that are not of advertising agencies' interest or they isolate these services in a separate firm, and consequently can compete for direct customers and still be a printing firm to advertising agencies.

Introduction

Having good relations with customers is important in most areas of business. Through close customer contact and involvement of customers in the development of new products or services, it is possible to identify better the needs and expectations of those buying the firm's products (Buttle, 2009). Gummesson (2002, p. 67) expresses this as 'we can talk about interactive marketing, but also about interactive service development, production and delivery. The provider and the customer create value together.' Consequently, having good customer relations can have a positive impact on a firm's production costs and revenues (Buttle, 2009) and be a source of competitive advantage (Langlois, 1992). The classic Five Forces Framework (Porter, 1979, 1980) illustrates the fundamental forces that should be considered when determining the level of competition in an industry – *existing industry competition, customers, suppliers, new competitors* and *competition from substitutes*. In this framework the competition from suppliers and customers is emphasized, even though suppliers and customers are often not regarded as competitors. However, customers can often bypass a firm and buy from its supplier and a firm can go directly to the customers' customer with their products or services. This can, potentially, create a competitive situation between suppliers and customers. According to Sawyer (1996, p. 91) vertical integration is a 'common route over which the customer–competitor transition takes place'. The concept of vertical integration has been discussed and researched for a long time and an early definition by Adelman (1949, p. 27) states that a firm is vertically integrated whenever it 'transmits from one of its departments to another a good or service which could, without major adaptation, be sold in the market'. Consequently, vertical integration occurs when a firm integrates activities in the value chain to produce its own inputs and/or take care of its own outputs (Adelman, 1949, 1955; D'Aveni & Ilinitch, 1992; Harrigan, 1983b; Hirsch, 1950; Jarillo, 1993; Mahoney, 1992; Perry, 1989; Porter, 1985).

Even though print is still an important marketing channel, the technological advancements in the media industry constantly change the competitive landscape. Because of changes in the structure of the media industry during the 1900s and the increase in the number of competing marketing channels (Kotler, Wong, Saunders, & Armstrong, 2005), the printing industry has shifted from a predominant position in mass marketing to having quite a low bargaining power over other actors in the value chain for media creation and communication. This situation, along with changed business strategies and customer demands, has required the commercial printing industry to integrate vertically and become full service firms for print media (Mejtoft, 2008). Having loyal customers is, in general, strongly influenced by a supplier satisfying the needs of their buyers (Yang & Peterson, 2004). Previous research investigating how customers' needs affect loyalty in print purchase has illustrated that direct customers to printing firms (customers whose core business is not within the graphic arts industry and that could otherwise be customers to advertising agencies) have a tendency to strive towards having close relations with their printing firms (Mejtoft, 2006). Advertising agencies (customers with great knowledge within the graphic arts industry), on the other hand, try to take advantage of the competition in the commercial printing industry by using their knowledge, primarily, to find good deals on print.

Through vertical integration many firms within the commercial printing industry have incorporated backward related activities in the media value chain and started to act like an advertising agency. Consequently, they make parts of the input to the printing activity internally (Mejtoft, 2008; Packmohr & Mejtoft, 2008). By integrating activities in connection with content creation, the potential for close contact with the final customer increases. However, this integration also creates a potentially competitive situation between printing firms and their primary customers, the advertising agencies. This study investigates how vertical integration is used to achieve close customer contact and increase customer relations in the printing industry. The study explores and illustrates the competitive consequences of vertical integration towards certain customer segments.

Industry structure

Historically, the printing industry has consisted of many privately owned small and medium-sized firms. Even though the situation is constantly changing with mergers and bankruptcies, the fragmentation in the industry is still high. Because of over-capacity and strong internal industry competition, there have been continuous price reductions (Birkenshaw, 2004; Gilboa, 2002; Intergraf, 2007; Kipphan, 2001; Mejtoft & Viström, 2007; Smyth, 2006). According to studies by Pira International (Smyth, 2006) and Caslon and Company (2005), about 90% of the European printing firms employ less than 15 people and digital printing firms in the USA have a median of 16 employees. The fragmentation and situation of the Swedish commercial printing industry is very similar to these conditions.

Theoretical framework

In the beginning of the 1980s, Michael Porter popularized the concept of the value chain, and showed how it could be used to understand potential sources of competitive advantage at the firm level. In general, a producing firm performs different types of activities that add value to its products or services (the word *product* will be used from now on to cover both *products* and *services*). The added value constitutes how much a specific firm or activity contributes to the value of a product (Porter, 1985). In many cases all activities in a value chain are not necessarily produced by a single firm but can be performed by different firms. Behind every decision regarding value adding activities, managers have to ask themselves whether the activities should be (1) purchased on the market (market transaction), (2) performed by a partner (co-operation) or (3) performed internally within the firm (vertical integration) (Child, Faulkner, & Tallman, 2005; Faulkner, 1995; Gulati, 2007; Gulati, Nohria, & Zaheer, 2000; Harrigan, 1983b; Jarillo, 1988; Williamson, 1975, 1985). All of these strategies have their advantages and disadvantages. Specializing in a certain task can be successful, especially in those cases when the industry benefits from cost advantages in large scale production (Faulkner, 1995). However, when specializing, it is most often necessary to interact with other firms to be able to produce the final product. Because of their importance, buyer–supplier relationships have been extensively studied in the literature over a long period of time (Batt & Purchase, 2004; Dyer & Singh, 1998; Grönroos, 1996; Morgan & Hunt, 1994; Zaheer, McEvily, & Perrone, 1998). To explain why firms make or buy, the concept of transaction costs was introduced in the literature by Coase (1937) in his seminal work 'The nature of the firm' and has further been developed since then by Williamson (1971, 1975, 1985, 1991a, 1996). Transaction costs are costs that occur when an economic exchange is made and are the costs involved in managing a relationship. These are costs not for the actual production per se, but for the 'problems' that are connected with procurement of activities from an external firm. To lower transaction costs or to expand the business (Chandler, 1977), a firm can choose to incorporate an activity such as vertical integration.

Vertical integration

There are many definitions of vertical integration and whether a firm is to be regarded as vertically integrated or not. Nevertheless, vertical integration arises when a firm integrates activities to produce its own inputs and/or take care of its own outputs, in order to increase its power in the marketplace (Adelman, 1955; D'Aveni & Ilinitch, 1992; Harrigan, 1983b; Hirsch, 1950; Jarillo, 1993; Mahoney, 1992; Perry, 1989; Porter, 1985). Vertical integration plays a major role in strengthening a firm's position to obtain competitive advantage in the market and makes it possible to exploit some of the benefits gained by performing more value added services and broadening the firm's value chain (Porter, 1985). As identified by Harrigan (1984), a firm may benefit from reduced costs by avoiding time-consuming tasks, improving co-ordination between activities, differentiating products and assuring supply. Gaining access to the end-user by integration is a way for new products to penetrate a mature market since it is possible, for a producer, to show the products' superiority (Harrigan, 1985). Vertical integration is an important part of corporate strategy since it is a frequently adopted growth strategy (Chandler, 1977).

There are also many possible negative consequences that may strike firms that choose a strategic path of vertical integration. Common in the literature are: increased internal and fixed costs which raise the exit barriers, and decreased flexibility (Christensen, Raynor, & Verliden, 2001; D'Aveni & Ravenscraft, 1994; Harrigan, 1985; Porter, 1980). How costs and profits are allocated along the value chain might also become unclear when vertical integration becomes more common (Gadiesh & Gilbert, 1998). Williamson (1991b, p. 83) suggests a conservative approach to vertical integration as this is the 'organization form, not of first, but of last resort – to be adopted when all else fails. Try markets, try long-term contracts and other hybrid modes, and revert to hierarchy only for compelling reasons.'

As suggested by Perry (1989), a firm can engage in backward and/or forward vertical integration into neighbouring activities in the value creation process and turn these activities into new internal business units (Figure 1).

Nevertheless, being vertically integrated does not necessarily mean a total transfer between all integrated stages in the value chain (Harrigan, 1983a, 1984, 1985; MacDonald, 1985; Perry, 1989). There can be differences in both the number of integrated stages and the degree of internal transfer in each stage. When firms are integrating backwards and/or forward but still rely on other firms for portions of their supply and distribution, they are adopting an approach denoted *taper integration* (Harrigan, 1983a, 1984, 1985; Kessler & Stern, 1959; Porter, 1980). According to Porter (1980, p. 319) tapered integration can 'yield many of the benefits of integration . . . while reducing some of the costs'. Packmohr and Mejtoft (2008), Parmigiani (2007) and Rothaermel, Hitt, and Jobe (2006) have found indications of positive effects on firms when combining vertical integration with outsourcing and co-operation with partners. However, a negative consequence of taper integration is the competitive situation that might arise towards suppliers and customers when performing similar activities (Sawyer, 1996).

Opportunistic behaviour in relationships

A combination of a buyer–supplier and a competitor relationship makes concepts of trust and commitment important. Trust, described by Moorman, Zaltman, and Deshpandé (1992, p. 315) as 'a willingness to rely on an exchange partner in whom one has confidence', is very important for a long-term buyer–supplier relationship (Lynch, 1990; Morgan & Hunt, 1994), especially when customer data are exchanged between partners. Damaging the trust that has been built in a relationship, by a partner engaging in opportunistic behaviour may have a severe impact on the existence of the partnership (Child et al., 2005; Gulati et al., 2000; Jarillo, 1988; Morgan & Hunt, 1994). Opportunism (Williamson, 1975, 1985) is a result of uncertainties that exist in transactions between different firms and accordingly opportunistic behaviour refers to 'a lack of candor or honesty in transactions, to include self-interest seeking with guile' (Williamson, 1975, p. 9). When a part in a relationship experiences that another part has engaged in opportunistic behaviour, it can have different impacts on a co-operation and is usually dependent on the time span of the relationship (Das, 2004). Gnyawali and Madhavan (2001) point out that in a strong co-operative relationship, a partner taking a competitive

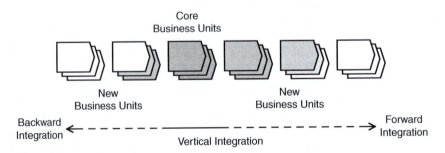

Figure 1. Backward and forward vertical integration into neighbouring activities in the value creation process.

action against another is most likely to experience an immediate response. Nevertheless, since feelings regarding deceit are deeply imbedded in human emotion, the long-term effect of opportunistic behaviour can be 'costly because the damage to one's reputation can influence not just the specific alliance in which one behaved opportunistically, but all other current and potential alliance partners' (Gulati et al., 2000, p. 209).

Research methodology

To capture the advantages with both quantitative and qualitative research approaches, this paper is based on two inter-connected studies. A quantitative survey study regarding the integration of content creation and project management activities in the value chain of print media was first conducted. These data were based on a subset from a survey of 136 Swedish commercial printing firms carried out during 2006 (Mejtoft & Viström, 2006). The questionnaire was sent out by letter to 300 randomly selected Swedish commercial printing firms. The population used was the members list of the Swedish Graphic Companies Federation (GFF). Even though this members list does not include all commercial printing firms in Sweden, the list included firms covering at least 80% of invoiced sales of printed commercial products in Sweden (K. Flick, GFF, personal communication, 25 January 2007). Hence, it is the author's belief that compared to other sources, this list constituted a good basis for this research study. From a total selection of 300 firms, 46 were found to be ineligible because they had either recently declared bankruptcy, sold their printing units or, because of other reasons, did not currently own any printing equipment, despite retaining membership of GFF. Since the purpose of the study was to investigate active printing firms, these firms were excluded. The case firms were mostly small and medium-sized printing firms. Because of the importance of the top management in setting the strategic plan for the firm (Beal & Yasai-Ardekani, 2000; Collis & Montgomery, 2005; Harrigan, 1985; Porter, 1996; Schein, 1983), the managing director, marketing director, sales manager or equivalent were also selected as respondents for the qualitative study. Consequently, 136 eligible firms responded, which constituted a total response rate of 54%. The response rate was calculated in accordance with the requirements of the Council of American Survey Research Organizations (CASRO, 1982; Wiseman & Billington, 1984). The results indicated that 82% of the respondents were managing directors or vice managing directors at the target firms. The remaining respondents were employees responsible for marketing, production or logistics.

To gain a deeper knowledge of the studied problem and get insight into how vertical integration increased customer contact for firms within the commercial printing industry, an additional multiple qualitative case study (Robson, 2002; Saunders, Lewis, & Thornhill, 2007; Yin, 2003) with five vertically integrated Swedish commercial printing firms was also conducted. The findings from this qualitative study were analysed using pattern matching techniques (Campbell, 1975; Yin, 2003). The case study firms were first analysed separately, and then matching patterns between firms were identified.

Results and discussion

The results from the quantitative survey study give indications on how common it is for printing firms to integrate activities that, in an ordinary value network with specialized firms, usually are performed by advertising agencies. The two activities regarded in this study were content creation and project management. The latter is an important activity to offer full service solutions to customers and, thus, more seriously compete with advertising agencies.

The results from the initial survey study showed that the integration into content creation is widespread in the Swedish commercial printing industry (Table 1).

It can be seen from the quantitative study that 78.7% of Swedish commercial printing firms offered services connected with content creation for their customers. This, however, does not necessarily mean that all these firms had complete departments for content creation, but rather that activities at these firms ranged from small services for creating very simple printed matters to full blown internal advertising agencies. Regarding project management in the value creation process of print media, a much smaller part of the industry has integrated this activity as only 17.6% of the printing firms offered this service to their customers. Nevertheless, these results, with about three-quarters of the firms working with content creation, show that the potential competitive situation between printing firms and one of their primary customers, the advertising agencies, might be strong. This further strengthens the need for managers within the media industry to consider this situation.

Competition with advertising agencies

The results from the quantitative survey study were further strengthened by the respondents during the interviews in the qualitative study. The results from both these studies suggest that there is a risk of a competitive situation between printing firms and the advertising agencies. A conceptual illustration of the competitive situation in this particular part of the value chain is therefore proposed. Figure 2a exemplifies the ordinary value chain with specialized firms for the different activities. The specialized printing firm receives jobs from the advertising agency, which makes the competitive situation between the printing firm and the advertising agencies weak as the printing firm can be regarded as a supplier to the advertising agency or vice versa. In this value chain there exists a buyer–supplier relationship between the two firms. On the other hand, in Figure 2b the printing firm has integrated activities that make them able to act as an advertising agency. This, consequently, means that there simultaneously might exist both a competitor and a buyer–supplier relationship between the firms. Hence, in this scenario there can arise competitive tendencies between the printing firm and the advertising agencies that are also their customers.

The results from the interviews showed that it is usually only a small part of the total production, approximately 2 to 15%, except for Printing Firm 5 which reported approximately 50%, where content creation was undertaken internally by the printing firm and sold to direct customers. This implies that the firms are taper integrated. According to the respondents, the greater part of the print production is sold to advertising agencies, print brokers or the in-house marketing departments in the case of larger firms. Even though the general opinion is that the share of direct customers is increasing, it is still a rather small part of the total production. Consequently, the advertising agencies are acknowledged as an important customer segment. Because of the large proportion of jobs which still come from advertising agencies, a potential competitive situation between the printing firm and its customers (the advertising agencies) arises when printing firms strive

Table 1. Result of backward vertical integration into services connected to the content creation.

Service	Number of firms[a]
Project management	24 (17.6%)
Content creation	107 (78.7%)

[a] A total of 136 firms in the study.

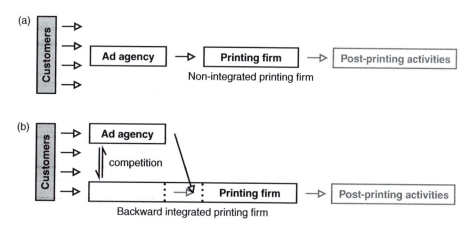

Figure 2(a) and 2(b). Conceptual illustration of (a) the value chain for print production with specialized firms and (b) the potential competitive situation between an integrated printing firm and part of its customers.

to increase the number of direct customers. As a result, working close with direct customers by integrating content creation activities, gives, according to the respondents, a competitive situation between the printing firms and the advertising agencies.

Many direct customers to printing firms are small firms with limited needs and, consequently, customers that advertising agencies have a limited interest in. According to the respondents, conflict over this category of customers is generally not a problem. However, since many other direct customers to the printing firms are firms that are potential customers to advertising agencies, direct conflict over these customers is an issue that may arise. Because of the sensitive nature of establishing a competitive situation with firms that also are customers (the advertising agencies), a competitive situation regarding direct customers is often avoided by the printing firms. This is typically done to stay away from hostile situations with advertising agencies and a potential loss of them as customers. Consequently, as Printing Firm 1 described it, 'we say "no thanks" if their [the advertising agencies] customers come to us directly'. This is a common attitude regarding how to handle customers' customers.

The qualitative case study illustrated two different ways of handling the competition problem with advertising agency customers. Printing Firms 1, 3, 4 and 5 have chosen to be loyal to the advertising agencies they work closely with and consequently do not contract or work with the advertising agencies' customers directly (Figure 3a). These four firms mainly perform simpler jobs where the potential competitive situation is weak. Printing Firm 2 on the other hand does recognize the competition problem as a serious threat towards their print business and has chosen to put all their activities regarding content creation in a separate firm (a sister firm within the same group of firms) (Figure 3b). By this arrangement Printing Firm 2 believes that it is possible both to compete with advertising agencies for the direct customers and still not lose credibility in being a printing firm. According to the respondent at Printing Firm 2, they consider the opinion among the advertising agencies they work with to be that 'we [the printing firm] should print and nothing else'. With this arrangement it is possible to function as such a firm.

Integration to capture profits

During the 1900s, technological innovation increased the number of potential channels for spreading messages and the amount of information that reaches each individual is massive.

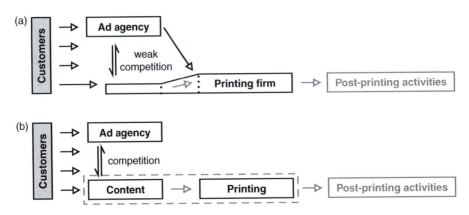

Figure 3(a) and 3(b).   Illustration of two different ways of handling the problem with competition that may arise with advertising agency customers.

These are just two reasons why, today, the actual content is the most important part of the print production input supply chain (Cost, 2005). Accordingly, there is a belief among the respondents that working with content creation is important to satisfy customers' request for a supplier that can provide complete solutions for print production. This one-stop-shopping among buyers of printed matters has become increasingly popular and is today very common. The respondents believe that either they can be a provider of a complete service or they can be a subcontractor to another firm that provides this concept. Nevertheless, the main reason to integrate content creation, mentioned by all respondents, is the need to capture the profits from this activity. There is a general opinion in the commercial printing industry that the profitability of print is very low, even declining, and by integrating content creation it is, according to the respondents, possible to increase profitability. Consequently, by capturing profits from one or several adjacent activities in the value chain it is possible to maintain or even increase a printing firm's profit margin and total profit. Furthermore, by having control over the content creation, jobs suitable for the firm's production equipment can be created and consequently generate a cost-effective workflow with shorter lead times. These are also driving forces for engaging in content creation.

Despite the importance of satisfying the need for providing a complete print solution and capturing profits from additional activities, working close to advertising agencies is necessary in order to achieve high print volume and avoid low utilization of capacity. These results are similar to other research results which propose close relationships between manufacturers and suppliers to improve the quality of the offered service (Srivastava & Singh, 2010). As mentioned earlier, it should be noted that most often only a small part of the total print volume comes from internally created jobs, the major part is delivered by advertising agencies and print brokers. Consequently, printing firms are usually very dependent on keeping good relations with advertising agencies.

Loyalty and customer relations

According to the results from the interviews, there are differences in the perceived loyalty between different types of customers. The respondents believed that direct customers are more loyal and recognize a value in creating a relationship with a printing firm. Brokers and advertising agencies, on the other hand, tend to 'shop around' for the best deal on print. This is not a surprising result because of the nature of content creation compared to printing.

When collaborating with a printing firm for content creation, more time and effort is needed to make a satisfying final product than only working with a commodity product like print. Consequently, the actual price of print is often more important for a printing firm when working with advertising agencies than direct customers. These results are in accordance with research by Chatain (2010), which suggests that working with a client in several different areas decreases the probability of the buyer–supplier relationship ending and, hence, increases the loyalty.

Because of a general desire in the commercial printing industry to escape the fierce price competition, the respondents stated that they were acting to increase their share of direct customers. This is done not only to increase the loyalty among their customers, but also to capture better profits through the provision of more services to these customers.

Even though there is a trend of more printing firms collaborating in networks and other types of alliances to increase their national competitive advantage, the printing industry is, in general, a local and regional business. This is also the general opinion among the respondents as the interviewed printing firms acted mostly in a local or regional market. This strong local and regional connection, with the limited number of customers, has made the firms' reputation among its customers important for a successful business. The printing firms believe that performing a good job and providing services that the customers appreciate are the most important things to focus on in order to achieve good customer relations. The geographic closeness creates a stronger tie to the customers and builds loyalty that works both ways. This is another reason for the solutions illustrated above to the problematic situation with the competitive situation that arises among the printing firms and the advertising agencies that are their customers. The local and regional connections between all the firms mean that individual reputation is very important for future collaboration and accruing new customers.

Nevertheless, even though this paper discusses the idea of building close relations with customers and increasing customer loyalty to avoid fierce price competition, price remains a very important element. As the commercial printing industry is under heavy price pressure, it should be noted that loyalty among direct customers is based on the mutual understanding that they automatically get a competitive price. The respondents believed that loyalty alone was not a means to raise prices but to create a mutual understanding about the value of different services.

Conclusions

This study concludes that it is common in the Swedish commercial printing industry to integrate content creation, as roughly three-quarters of the industry offer these services to their customers. This is primarily done because of two reasons: (1) to increase relations with direct customers and to some extent bypass advertising agencies in the print media value chain; and (2) to capture profits from the content creation stage in the value chain (which is perceived as more profitable than printing) and streamline the workflow. Consequently, direct customers are perceived as more loyal and profitable than advertising agencies and print brokers. However, since usually only a small part of the printing firm's total production is delivered to direct customers, advertising agencies are a very important customer segment.

The integration of content creation gives rise to a potentially competitive situation within the advertising agency customer segment. This problem is recognized by commercial printing firms as they try to avoid competition with these customers and reduce the risk of losing them as customers. The results illustrate two possible ways to work with direct customers and still avoid creating a harmful competitive situation with advertising agencies: (1) printing firms perform only simpler jobs that advertising agencies are not interested in and refuse to take on jobs that are offered from customers' customers and (2) printing firms isolate content creation in a separate firm and consequently can both compete with advertising agencies and still be a printing firm to these customers.

Managerial implications

This study has some important implications for practice. It is illustrated, as has been suggested in the theory (Sawyer, 1996), that vertical integration leads to a possible scenario where a buyer–supplier relationship may change into a competitive situation. Nevertheless, by being humble to the situation it is possible to walk the fine line between being a supplier and a competitor. The study's contribution to management can be seen in the findings on the handling of the competitive situation in the buyer–supplier relationship. Because of the limited competitive advantage of the printing industry today, managers strive to increase revenues and increase profitability by vertical integration. However, small and medium sized firms have a limited ability to lose advertising agencies as their customers because of the large revenues this customer segment constitutes. This delicate situation makes it important to balance the backward integration into content creation and project management, areas that might seem as competitive towards advertising agencies by choosing segments of direct customers that are not attractive to advertising agencies.

Larger printing firms or firms with a strategic intent to grow within content creation activities might have a need, and a better opportunity, to engage in head-on competition with advertising agencies. However, since this customer segment is still very important for a firm's long-term survival, it is important to choose a strategic path to avoid a hostile competitive situation. Consequently, separating services that might be regarded as competitive from the printing firm and creating a subsidiary firm is a solution for making the competitive situation appear less obvious between the printing firm and the advertising agencies. As a result, the competition appears to be between the subsidiary firm and the advertising agencies.

Since the printing industry is highly integrated into content creation today it is also important not to forget the potential consequences with the gradual increase in volumes and complexity of these services, which is the usual trend in organic growth of vertical integration. This might lead to a slow, but sure, change to the buyer–supplier relationship. Even so, a printing firm should not avoid integration because of the threat of losing adverting agencies as customers but should instead carefully choose a strategic path that makes them avoid being perceived as opportunistic. In this case the printing industry is a declining industry trying to re-gain some power and profitability. The situation had probably been easier to handle for a weak, but growing, sub-part of an industry experiencing similar problems. The printing and the media industry are not unique isolated cases, and the problem illustrated in this study could probably translate to other industries with similar conditions.

Limitations and potential for further research

In research it is important to ensure high reliability and validity and one way that is often used is triangulation, 'the combination of methodologies in the study of the same phenomena' (Denzin, 1989, p. 234). Even though the results in this study are based on two different methodologies, there are some limitations and these should be kept in mind. The members list used in the quantitative survey study does not include all commercial printing firms in Sweden, which limits the possibilities to generalize the results to the industry. Nevertheless, because of the importance of being a member of the industry association, the vast majority of commercial printing firms in Sweden are members of the industry association (K. Flick, GFF, personal communication, 25 January 2007). It is the author's opinion that there is no other directory better suited for such study. In the qualitative study, the case firms have not been chosen randomly. They have been chosen to conform to certain predefined criteria and be representative to the case. However, 'the purpose of a case report is not to represent the world, but to represent the case' (Stake, 2005, p. 460).

Furthermore, to be able to draw more general conclusions on the competitive situation between suppliers and customers in the commercial printing industry, interviews should be performed with both advertising agencies and direct customers to printing firms. Since only Swedish firms are represented in this study, further research should involve firms from other markets. Because of constant changes of the competitive landscape and industry structure in the media industry, longitudinal studies are also of great importance.

Acknowledgements

I thank the editor for this issue, Sheila Wright, for her detailed feedback and suggestions that helped to significantly improve the paper. I would also like to show my respect to my colleague Dr Magnus Viström, Packaging Mid Sweden, for his collaboration on our quantitative survey study. The financial support of the Kempe Foundations and Grafiska Företagens Stipendiestiftelse is gratefully acknowledged.

References

Adelman, M.A. (1949). Integration and antitrust policy. *Harvard Law Review, 63,* 27–77.

Adelman, M.A. (1955). Concept and statistical measurement of vertical integration. In G.J. Stigler (Ed.), *Business concentration and price policy: A conference of the Universities – National Bureau Committee for Economic Research* (pp. 281–330). Princeton, NJ: Princeton University Press.

Batt, P.J., & Purchase, S. (2004). Managing collaboration within networks and relationships. *Industrial Marketing Management, 33,* 169–174.

Beal, R.M., & Yasai-Ardekani, M. (2000). Performance implications of aligning CEO functional experiences with competitive strategies. *Journal of Management, 26,* 733–762.

Birkenshaw, J. (2004). *The future of print on paper.* Prepress and print technology, Pira International. Retrieved from http://pira.atalink.co.uk/pulp-and-paper/163.html

Buttle, F. (2009). *Customer relationship management: Concepts and technologies* (2nd ed.). Amsterdam: Butterworth-Heinemann.

Campbell, D.T. (1975). 'Degrees of freedom' and the case study. *Comparative Political Studies, 8,* 178–193.

Caslon & Company. (2005). *Digital printers: Growth leaders of the printing market.* Rochester, NY: Caslon & Company.

CASRO. (1982). *On the definition of response rates.* A special report of the CASRO Task Force on completion rates. Retrieved from http://www.casro.org/resprates.cfm

Chandler, A.D. (1977). *The visible hand: The managerial revolution in American business.* Cambridge, MA: Belknap Press.

Chatain, O. (2010). Value creation, competition, and performance in buyer–supplier relationships. *Strategic Management Journal.* Advance online publication. doi:10.1002/smj.864

Child, J., Faulkner, D., & Tallman, S. (2005). *Cooperative strategy: Managing alliances, network and joint ventures* (2nd ed.). Oxford: Oxford University Press.

Christensen, C.M., Raynor, M., & Verliden, M. (2001). Skate to where the money will be. *Harvard Business Review, 79*(10), 73–81.

Coase, R.H. (1937). The nature of the firm. *Economica, 4,* 386–405.

Collis, D.J., & Montgomery, C.A. (2005). *Corporate strategy: A resource-based approach* (2nd ed.). Boston, MA: McGraw-Hill/Irwin.

Cost, F. (2005). *The new medium of print: Material communication in the Internet age.* Rochester, NY: RIT Cary Graphic Arts Press.

D'Aveni, R.A., & Ilinitch, A.Y. (1992). Complex patterns of vertical integration in the forest products industry: Systematic and bankruptcy risks. *Academy of Management Journal, 35,* 596–625.

D'Aveni, R.A., & Ravenscraft, D.J. (1994). Economies of integration versus bureaucracy costs: Does vertical integration improve performance? *Academy of Management Journal, 37,* 1167–1197.

Das, T.K. (2004). Time-span and risk of partner opportunism in strategic alliances. *Journal of Managerial Psychology, 19,* 744–759.

Denzin, N.K. (1989). *The research act: A theoretical introduction to sociological methods* (3rd ed.). Englewood Cliffs, NJ: Prentice Hall.

Dyer, J.H., & Singh, H. (1998). The relational view: Cooperative strategy and sources of interorganizational competitive advantage. *Academy of Management Review, 23,* 660–679.

Faulkner, D. (1995). *International strategic alliances: Co-operating to compete.* London: McGraw-Hill.

Gadiesh, O., & Gilbert, J.L. (1998). How to map your industry's profit pool. *Harvard Business Review, 76*(3), 149–162.

Gilboa, R. (2002). The production digital printing market: Opportunities and trends. *Proceedings from IS&T's NIP18,* 134–138.

Gnyawali, D.R., & Madhavan, R. (2001). Cooperative networks and competitive dynamics: A structural embeddedness perspective. *Academy of Management Review, 26,* 431–445.

Grönroos, C. (1996). Relationship marketing: Strategic and tactical implications. *Management Decision, 34*(3), 5–14.

Gulati, R. (2007). *Managing network resources, alliances, affiliations and other relational assets.* New York: Oxford University Press.

Gulati, R., Nohria, N., & Zaheer, A. (2000). Strategic networks. *Strategic Management Journal, 21,* 203–215.

Gummesson, E. (2002). *Total relationship marketing* (2nd ed.). Oxford: Butterworth-Heinemann.

Harrigan, K.R. (1983a). A framework for looking at vertical integration. *Journal of Business Strategy, 3,* 30–37.

Harrigan, K.R. (1983b). *Vertical integration, outsourcing, and corporate strategy.* Washington, DC: BeardBooks.

Harrigan, K.R. (1984). Formulating vertical integration strategies. *Academy of Management Review, 9,* 638–652.

Harrigan, K.R. (1985). Vertical integration and corporate strategy. *Academy of Management Journal, 9,* 397–425.

Hirsch, W.Z. (1950). Toward a definition of integration. *Southern Economic Journal, 17,* 159–165.

Intergraf. (2007). *Competitiveness of the European graphic industry.* Brussels: European Commission, Enterprise and Industry Directorate-General.

Jarillo, J.C. (1988). On strategic networks. *Strategic Management Journal, 9,* 31–41.

Jarillo, J.C. (1993). *Strategic networks: Creating the borderless organization.* Oxford: Butterworth-Heinemann.

Kessler, F., & Stern, R.H. (1959). Competition, contract, and vertical integration. *Yale Law Journal, 69,* 1–129.

Kipphan, H. (2001). *Handbook of print media: Technologies and production methods.* Berlin: Springer.

Kotler, P., Wong, V., Saunders, J., & Armstrong, G. (2005). *Principles of marketing* (4th European ed.). Harlow: Prentice Hall.

Langlois, R.N. (1992). External economies and economic progress: The case of the microcomputer industry. *Business History Review, 66,* 1–50.

Lynch, R.P. (1990). Building alliances to penetrate European markets. *Journal of Business Strategy, 11*(2), 4–8.

MacDonald, J.M. (1985). Market exchange or vertical integration: An empirical analysis. *Review of Economics and Statistics, 67,* 327–331.

Mahoney, J.T. (1992). The choice of organizational form: Vertical financial ownership versus other methods of vertical integration. *Strategic Management Journal, 13,* 559–584.

Mejtoft, T. (2006). Perceived satisfaction by customers in the digital printing value system. In *Taga 2006 Proceedings* (pp. 486–511). Sewickley, PA: TAGA Office.

Mejtoft, T. (2008). *Institutional arrangements and competitive posture: Effects of company structures in the commercial printing industry* (Doctoral dissertation). Royal Institute of Technology, Sweden.

Mejtoft, T., & Viström, M. (2006). Commercial and packaging printing firm survey study in Sweden [Data set]. Unpublished raw data.

Mejtoft, T., & Viström, M. (2007). Positioning in the printing industry: Differentiation in terms of price, lead time, print quality and flexibility. In N. Enlund & M. Lovreček (Eds.), *Advances in printing and media technology* (Vol. XXXIV, pp. 327–336). Zagreb: Acta Graphica Publishers.

Moorman, C., Zaltman, G., & Deshpandé, R. (1992). Relationship between providers and users of market research: The dynamics of trust within and between organizations. *Journal of Marketing Research, 29*, 314–328.

Morgan, R.M., & Hunt, S.D. (1994). The commitment–trust theory of relationship marketing. *Journal of Marketing, 58*(3), 20–38.

Packmohr, S., & Mejtoft, T. (2008). Transaction costs and their influence on institutional arrangements: A comparison between the Swedish and the German printing industry. In N. Enlund & M. Lovreček (Eds.), *Advances in printing and media technology* (Vol. XXXV, pp. 55–66). Darmstadt: International Association of Research Organizations for the Information, Media and Graphic Industries.

Parmigiani, A. (2007). Why do firms both make and buy? An investigation of concurrent sourcing. *Strategic Management Journal, 28*, 285–311.

Perry, M.K. (1989). Vertical integration: Determinants and effects. In R. Schmalensee & R.D. Willig (Eds.), *Handbook of industrial organization* (Vol. 1, pp. 183–255). Amsterdam: North-Holland.

Porter, M.E. (1979). How competitive forces shape strategy? *Harvard Business Review, 57*(2), 137–145.

Porter, M.E. (1980). *Competitive strategy*. New York: Free Press.

Porter, M.E. (1985). *Competitive advantage*. New York: Free Press.

Porter, M.E. (1996). What is strategy? *Harvard Business Review, 74*(6), 61–79.

Robson, C. (2002). *Real world research* (2nd ed.). Oxford: Blackwell Publishing.

Rothaermel, F.T., Hitt, M.A., & Jobe, L.A. (2006). Balancing vertical integration and strategic outsourcing: Effects on product portfolio, product success, and firm performance. *Strategic Management Journal, 27*, 1033–1056.

Saunders, M., Lewis, P., & Thornhill, A. (2007). *Research methods for business students* (4th ed.). Harlow: Prentice Hall.

Sawyer, D.C. (1996). Customers as competitors. *Competitive Intelligence Review, 7*(1), 90–91.

Schein, E.H. (1983). The role of the founder in creating organizational culture. *Organizational Dynamics, 12*, 13–28.

Smyth, S. (2006). *The future of European printing to 2011*. Leatherhead, Surrey: Pira International.

Srivastava, V., & Singh, T. (2010). Value creation through relationship closeness. *Journal of Strategic Marketing, 18*, 3–17.

Stake, R.E. (2005). Qualitative case studies. In N.K. Denzin & Y.S. Lincoln (Eds.), *The Sage handbook of qualitative research* (3rd ed.) (pp. 443–466). Thousand Oaks, CA: SAGE.

Williamson, O.E. (1971). The vertical integration of production: Market failure considerations. *American Economic Review, 61*(2), 112–123.

Williamson, O.E. (1975). *Markets and hierarchies: Analysis and antitrust implications*. New York: Free Press.

Williamson, O.E. (1985). *The economic institutions of capitalism: Firms, markets, relational contracting*. New York: Free Press.

Williamson, O.E. (1991a). Comparative economic organization: The analysis of discrete structural alternatives. *Administrative Science Quarterly, 36*, 269–296.

Williamson, O.E. (1991b). Strategizing, economizing, and economic organization. *Strategic Management Journal, 12*, 75–94.

Williamson, O.E. (1996). *The mechanism of governance*. New York: Oxford University Press.

Wiseman, F., & Billington, M. (1984). Comment on a standard definition of response rates. *Journal of Marketing, 21*, 336–338.

Yang, Z., & Peterson, R.T. (2004). Customer perceived value, satisfaction, and loyalty: The role of switching costs. *Psychology & Marketing, 21*, 799–822.

Yin, R.K. (2003). *Case study research, design and methods* (3rd ed.). Thousand Oaks, CA: SAGE.

Zaheer, A., McEvily, B., & Perrone, V. (1998). Does trust matter? Exploring the effects of interorganizational and interpersonal trust on performance. *Organization Science, 9*, 141–159.

Market orientation in nonprofit organizations: innovativeness, resource scarcity, and performance

Pratik Modi

Institute of Rural Management, Anand, India

The theory of market orientation, emerging from the context of for-profit organizations, has potential application and use in the nonprofit sector. This research proposes links between market orientation, innovativeness, resource scarcity, funding source, and performance related variables in the nonprofit context. Based on the empirical data from 579 nonprofit organizations in India engaged in service delivery to beneficiaries, the study shows that market orientation in nonprofit organizations improves peer reputation, beneficiary satisfaction, and innovativeness. However, market orientation alone is not enough. Innovativeness is the missing link that mediates the market orientation and effectiveness relationship. The study shows that market orientation does not help in attracting resources in the Indian context, a finding which runs counter to the evidences from previous studies carried out in the context of developed countries. The study finds that resource scarcity and funding sources do not moderate the market orientation and performance relationship. The implications for practitioners are discussed.

The choice facing those who manage nonbusiness organizations is not whether to market or not to market; for no organization can avoid marketing. The choice is whether to do it well or poorly, and on this necessity the case for organizational marketing is basically founded. (Kotler & Levy, 1969, p. 15)

Introduction

Nonprofit organizations deliver services to the section of society that governments fail to reach and markets choose to ignore (Salamon & Anheier, 1998). While for-profit organizations continue to thrive and benefit from developing a market orientation, nonprofit organizations remain skeptical of adopting it. This reluctance may partly be ascribed to their lack of appreciation of the relevance of market orientation in nonprofit organizations. Lack of market orientation in nonprofit organizations often results in their programs and services meeting partial successes at best, or outright failures in several cases. Family planning initiative in India, for example, met with limited success because the program design and implementation had ignored the needs of an Indian population (Dholakia, 1984). Similarly, literacy programs, vaccination drives, and many such initiatives in India could not reach their potential impact because of two reasons: (1) these programs were designed top–down rather than bottom–up; and (2) these initiatives could not fully understand the requirements of their customers or targeted beneficiaries. Kotler and Andreasen (1996) reported that a majority of nonprofit organizations (referred to as NPOs hereafter) were sales oriented in their approach and lacked focus on their customers.

The theory of market orientation is an important knowledge domain in marketing that has potential applications in the nonprofit sector (Kotler & Andreasen, 1996). Several scholars (e.g. Andreasen, 1994; Andreasen, Goodstein, & Wilson, 2005) advocate inter-sectoral transfer of marketing knowledge from the for-profit sector to the nonprofit sector. This paper seeks to adapt and test the theory of market orientation for use and application in NPOs. Toward this objective, this research makes several contributions. First, the study investigates the influence of market orientation on several performance outcomes and examines the role of innovativeness in NPOs. Second, the study explores whether two major funding sources – public and private funding – moderate the market orientation and performance relationship in NPOs. By implication, the study covers only those NPOs that depend on third party funding, partially or fully, for meeting their resources needs. Third, the nonprofit sector all over the world, particularly in India, has witnessed a huge increase in the number of NPOs in recent decades (Mishra, Biswas, & Roy, 2005); however, there is no commensurate increase in the available resources to them. Thus, a large number of NPOs are facing resource scarcity in varying degrees (Balabanis, Stables, & Phillips, 1997). The research explores how market orientation is useful to NPOs facing a resource scarce environment. Finally, this study adds empirical weight to the unresolved issue of whether size and age of an NPO have any bearing on its level of market orientation.

Theoretical framework

The research stream on market orientation has its genesis in the marketing concept (Kohli & Jaworski, 1990) which emphasizes identifying the customer needs before satisfying them better than any other competitor (Kotler, 2000, p. 19). The subsequent studies conceptualized market orientation as: (a) generation, dissemination of market intelligence, and responsiveness to it (Kohli & Jaworski, 1990); (b) a set of culturally supported behaviors (Narver & Slater, 1990); (c) an organizational culture (Deshpande, Farley, & Webster, 1993); and (d) a set of market-sensing and customer-linking capabilities (Day, 1994). Jaworski and Kohli (1996) note that despite the differences in the conceptualizations of market orientation, they share a common core with respect to the external orientation and customer focus elements. Several studies (e.g. Deng & Dart, 1994; Gebhardt, Carpenter, & Sherry, 2006; Gray, Matear, Boshoff, & Matheson, 1998; Oczkowski & Farrell, 1998; Pelham & Wilson, 1996; Ruekert, 1992) and a few meta-analyses (e.g. Cano, Carrillat, & Jaramillo 2004; Kirca, Jayachandran, & Bearden, 2005) have established the positive influence of market orientation on business performance.

In the nonprofit context, the past studies have viewed market orientation as generation and dissemination of and response to the market intelligence on donors (e.g. Balabanis et al., 1997) environmental factors (e.g. Wood, Bhuian, & Kiecker, 2000), and beneficiaries and donors (e.g. Gainer & Padanyi, 2005; Macedo & Pinho, 2006; Morris, Coombes, Schindehutte, & Allen, 2007; Vazquez, Alvarez, & Santos, 2002). However, the market intelligence perspective is narrowly focused on information gathering and dissemination (Oczkowski & Farrell, 1998; Pelham, 1993). Many NPOs working in developing countries may not find the market intelligence perspective relevant as these organizations often lack formal information gathering and dissemination mechanisms (Modi & Mishra, 2010). Synthesizing the dual target-customer perspective for NPOs

(Shapiro, 1973) and the Narver and Slater (1990) perspective on market orientation, Modi and Mishra (2010) proposed a four-component view of market orientation in nonprofit organizations (referred to as MONPO hereafter) and defined it as an the coordinated outward focus of an organization on its key stakeholder. These four components are beneficiary orientation, donor orientation, peer orientation, and interfunctional coordination. This research adopts this view of market orientation due to its inherent advantages such as relevance to nonprofit practitioners and applicability in a developing country context.

In the nonprofit context, the small body of extant research shows that market orientation improves performance of a variety of NPOs including universities (Caruana, Ramaseshan, & Ewing, 1998; Flavián & Lozano, 2006), public service organizations (Caruana, Ramaseshan, & Ewing, 1997, 1999; Cervera, Molla, & Sanchez, 2001), charities (Balabanis et al., 1997; Bennett, 1998; Kara, Spillan, & DeShields, 2004; Macedo & Pinho, 2006; Modi & Mishra, 2010; Morris et al., 2007; Vazquez et al., 2002), cultural organizations (Gainer & Padanyi, 2002, 2005; Voss & Voss, 2000), and hospitals (Wood et al., 2000). However, the role of innovativeness, resource scarcity, and funding source in a market oriented nonprofit organization remains unexplored so far. The following sections explore these relationships.

MONPO and performance outcomes

A market oriented NPO develops coordinated focus on its key external stakeholders – donors, beneficiaries, and peers. Such an NPO tries to understand latent as well as explicit needs of both its customers – beneficiaries and donors. It designs its programs to meet the customers' needs, and shows willingness to make necessary modifications in the programs based on their feedback. This consistent focus on understanding and fulfilling the beneficiaries' needs improves the beneficiaries' satisfaction with the NPO and its programs (Gainer & Padanyi, 2002; Wood et al., 2000). The consistent focus on understanding and meeting the donors' expectations and remaining accountable to them attracts resource commitments from the donors (Vazquez et al., 2002; White & Simas, 2008).

H1:   Market orientation in nonprofit organizations improves beneficiary satisfaction.

H2:   Market oriented nonprofit organizations attract more resources from their donors.

For a market oriented NPO, its peer organizations are important stakeholders as they are working toward the same larger social goals. The organizational focus restricted to beneficiaries and donors, to the exclusion of one's peer organizations is a sign of an underdeveloped MONPO. A market oriented NPO will simultaneously focus on the peers, beneficiaries, and donors. It will be willing to collaborate with its peers to complement each other's strengths and weaknesses to better serve their beneficiaries. As a result, a market oriented NPO would command respect of its peers (Gainer & Padanyi, 2002).

H3:   Market oriented nonprofit organizations will create a reputation amongst their peer NPOs.

Market orientation in an NPO helps it develop a seamless focus on its beneficiaries, donors, and peers. This organization-wide focus gives it a better understanding of the needs and wants of the key external stakeholders, which is crucial in improving effectiveness or mission achievement of an NPO (Balabanis et al., 1997; Vazquez et al., 2002).

H4:   Market orientation in NPOs enhances their effectiveness or mission achievement.

Innovativeness and performance

Innovativeness has been viewed as an aspect of organizational culture (Hurley & Hult, 1998) and a dynamic capability (Menguc & Auh, 2006) that creates capacity for successful innovations. Market orientation is an important antecedent of innovativeness (Hult, Hurley, & Knight, 2004; Kirca et al., 2005; Menguc & Auh, 2006). A market oriented NPO stays close to its beneficiaries, donors, and peers. This closeness helps it develop better understanding of their needs and requirements, which engenders innovativeness in the organization (Atuahene-Gima, 1995; Hult et al., 2004).

H5:   Market orientation in nonprofit organizations enhances their innovativeness.

The research in the for-profit context shows innovativeness as a partial mediator of the market orientation and performance relationship (e.g. Han, Kim, & Srivastava, 1998; Hult et al., 2004; Kirca et al., 2005). However, the role of innovativeness in the nonprofit context is not studied so far. It is argued here that market orientation in NPOs nurtures innovativeness which generates program design and delivery related innovations, which in turn, increases beneficiary satisfaction and helps the NPO in mission achievement.

H6:   Innovativeness mediates the relationships between market orientation and beneficiary satisfaction.
H7:   Innovativeness mediates the relationships between market orientation and effectiveness.

An NPO cannot successfully achieve its mission objectives if it is not able to satisfy the beneficiaries' needs. Satisfied beneficiaries show more involvement, participation, and enthusiasm in an NPO's activities, which is crucial to improving the overall effectiveness of the organization. An NPO that is able to achieve a higher level of beneficiary satisfaction also receives the appreciation of its peers (Gainer & Padanyi, 2002).

H8:   Beneficiary satisfaction enhances effectiveness of NPOs.
H9:   Beneficiary satisfaction enhances peer reputation of NPOs.

As an NPO establishes its reputation amongst its peers, it attracts donors who are willing to fund its programs and activities (Gainer & Padanyi, 2002). The organization, then, with adequate resources at its disposal can work unencumbered toward its mission achievement.

H10:   Peer reputation increases resource attraction.
H11:   Resource attraction increases effectiveness.

Resource scarcity

Several studies in the for-profit context have explored the influence of environmental complexity on market orientation. A few of them report that environmental complexity does not alter the market orientation and performance relationship (e.g. Jaworski & Kohli, 1993; Subramanian & Gopalakrishna, 2001; Tay & Morgan, 2002). At the same time, many other report evidences of the moderation effect of environmental complexity on the market orientation and performance link (e.g. Harris, 2001; Kumar, Subramanian, & Yauger, 1998; Slater & Narver, 1994). So far, the issue remains inconclusive. In the non-profit context, however, the past studies have ignored the influence of environmental complexity on the MONPO and performance relationship. The past literature does not propose any conceptualization or operationalization of the environmental complexity construct. From the in-depth discussions with senior practitioners, it emerged that resource scarcity is an important external environmental condition facing NPOs in India. Market orientation in NPOs becomes a valuable resource (Hult & Ketchen, 2001), particularly under a resource scarce environment, when the ability to maintain their mission related activities is under threat (Palmer & Randall, 2002). The market orientated NPOs are likely to perform better than their less market oriented peer NPOs under such a hostile environmental condition.

H12:   Resource scarcity moderates the relationship between market orientation and effectiveness.

Source of funding

An NPO may get funding from two broad groups of donors: (1) the public sector, which includes funding sources such as government and its various agencies; (2) the private sector, which includes funding sources such as individual donors, for-profit organizations, and donor NPOs. It is likely that NPOs would acquire the attributes of their funders through mimetic processes (DiMaggio & Powell, 1983). Hence, it is expected that the funding source will moderate the market orientation and performance relationship in such a way that the strength of the relationship will be higher for NPOs funded by the private sector. No previous research was available; hence, I approached this question in an exploratory manner. I wrote to the members of an online forum – Voluntary Sector Studies Network (http://www.vssn.org.uk) – requesting them to provide their views, leads, or references to any past literature on the matter. A number of responses informed us that they were unaware of any past reference to the issue; however, several members intuitively agreed with our hypothesis.

H13:   Funding source moderates the market orientation and performance relationship.

Size and age of an NPO and its market orientation

Seymour, Gilbert, and Kolsaker (2006) found positive correlation between market orientation and size of charities. A few studies also reported a negative correlation between market orientation and size of NPOs (e.g. Balabanis et al., 1997; Cervera et al., 2001). Modi and Mishra (2010) in their exploratory work found that market orientation correlates neither with size nor age of NPOs. The issue remains unresolved. Intuitively, size and age of an NPO should not have any bearing on its market orientation.

H14:   Market orientation and size and age of NPOs have positive correlations.

Methodology

The research was carried out in two phases. The initial exploratory phase of the research comprised free flowing in-depth discussions with 10 senior executives from various NPOs. The way market orientation was understood in the business context was first explained to the practitioners. They were invited then to discuss the relevance and application of the theory of market orientation in their organizations. They also discussed issues such as what should be the meaning of market orientation in the nonprofit context, what kind of behaviors and practice a market oriented NPO would exhibit, and what consequences such an orientation would have for an NPO. These discussions informed the theoretical framework along with the past literature. The next phase of the research was quantitative seeking to test the hypotheses.

Data collection procedures

The interest population comprised those NPOs in India that met three selection criteria: (1) NPOs should depend on some third party funding for meeting the large part of their resource needs; (2) NPOs are registered under the Societies Registration Act 1860, or the Indian Trusts Act 1882, or the Charitable & Religious Trusts Act 1920; the section 25 charitable companies of the Companies Act 1956 are excluded from the study; (3) NPOs are engaged in service provision/delivery. Two directories – the ninth edition of *Environmental NGOs in India 2008–09* compiled by the World Wide Fund for Nature, India and the Charity Aid Foundation 2008 charity profiles, India – were used as a sampling frame for the study from which 2000 NPOs were randomly selected for data collection.

The questionnaire was prepared in both Hindi and English using the back-to-back scale translation technique (Behling & Law, 2000). Mail-packs, each containing the structured close-ended questionnaire, a cover-letter, and a self-addressed stamped return envelope, were addressed to the chief executive officers of these NPOs. About 100 mail-packs were returned undelivered as the addresses were not found. In all, 783 responses representing 25 Indian states were received, which meant an effective response rate of 41.2%. The final sample comprised 579 NPOs after many responses were discarded due to several inadequacies in them. Comparison of the early with late respondents showed that nonresponse was not a serious problem for the study (Armstrong & Overton, 1977). The missing data were imputed using the mean value of the person's responses to the other items of the same scale (Roth, Switzer, & Switzer, 1999). The overall distribution of the data was multivariate non-normal.

Ensuring high quality of data was a big concern, and a number of steps were taken to deal with the common method bias. Any response from a person who did not belong either to the top management or have at least two years of experience within the organization was removed from the dataset (Kumar, Stem, & Anderson, 1993). We also randomly checked with 10% of the responding organizations to verify the details which did not show any misrepresentation. The predictor items were listed first in the questionnaire followed by the criterion items so as not to artificially inflate the inter-construct correlations (Podsakoff, MacKenzie, Lee, & Podsakoff, 2003). Finally as a curative step, the Fischer and Fick (1993) version of the Crowne and Marlowe (1960) social desirability scale was embedded in the questionnaire so that the social desirability bias on the results was taken into account.

Measures

Performance

Measuring performance in NPOs is not easy as they have multiple and sometimes competing objectives to pursue. For the purpose of this research, the Padanyi and Gainer (2004) multi-item measure of performance was adopted, which included beneficiary satisfaction, resource attraction, and peer reputation components. Confirmatory factor analyses (CFA) of the three performance components showed adequate fit with the data. The peer reputation scale ($X^2 = 14.5$, d.f. $= 2$, *p Value* $= .001$, CFI $= 0.99$, TLI $= 0.96$, GFI $= 0.99$) and the resource attraction scale ($X^2 = 31.7$, d.f. $= 2$, *p Value* $= .000$, CFI $= 0.97$, TLI $= 0.97$, GFI $= 0.98$) showed good fit indices. The beneficiary satisfaction scale could not be put through CFA as it had only three indicators (just-identified model and zero degree of freedom). Hence, the tau-equivalence constraint was added on the scale, and the result showed non-significant chi-square value.

Effectiveness

Effectiveness or the extent of mission achievement of an NPO is an important performance criterion (Balabanis et al., 1997; Kotler & Andreasen, 1996; Lamb & Crompton, 1990). One more item was added to the Balabanis et al. (1997) two-item scale to create a measure for effectiveness. Tau-equivalence constraint on the scale produced an acceptable fit ($X^2 = 31.9$, d.f. $= 2$, p Value $= .000$, CFI $= 0.95$, TLI $= 0.92$, GFI $= 0.97$).

Social desirability

Social desirability is a major source of common method bias (Podsakoff et al., 2003). If left unmeasured, social desirability may suppress, enhance, or moderate the true relationship between constructs (Ganster, Hennessey, & Luthans, 1983). No previous studies on market orientation in the nonprofit context have factored in the impact of social desirability on their results. The Fischer and Fick (1993) version of the social desirability scale (Crowne & Marlowe, 1960) was embedded in the questionnaire to measure and partial out the influence of social desirability. In agreement with the previous works (e.g. Millham, 1974; Ramanaiah & Martin, 1980; Ramanaiah, Schill, & Leung, 1977), the two factor CFA model produced an acceptable fit ($X^2 = 40.7$, d.f. $= 13$, p Value $= .000$, CFI $= 0.94$, TLI $= 0.91$, GFI $= 0.98$).

Innovativeness

Innovativeness was measured with the Hurley and Hult (1998) scale after minor adaptations in its wordings to suit the nonprofit context. One negatively worded item was dropped from the scale based on the feedback from the pilot study. The four-item innovativeness CFA model produced a non-significant chi-square value indicating good fit with the data ($X^2 = 0.34$, d.f. $= 2$, p Value $= .84$).

Resource scarcity

No scale was currently available to measure resource scarcity. Based on the discussions with practitioners, three important indicators of resource scarcity were identified. These were first content validated by other practitioners and later extensively pretested. The chi-square value under the tau-equivalence test was non-significant at $p < .01$ and the fit indices were acceptable ($X^2 = 8.7$, d.f. $= 2$, p Value $= .013$, CFI $= 0.98$, TLI $= 0.98$, GFI $= 0.99$).

Size and age

Size of an NPO was measured by the number of full-time employees on the payroll, and age by the number of years since the organization was formally registered as an NPO.

Market orientation in nonprofit organizations

This study used the refined MONPO scale (Modi & Mishra, 2010). The final 14 items of the MONPO scale showed good fit with the data ($X^2 = 124$, d.f. $= 73$, p Value $= .000$, CFI $= 0.98$, TLI $= 0.97$, GFI $= 0.97$, RMSEA $= 0.035$).

Structural model evaluation and results

The hypotheses were tested using structural equation modeling (maximum likelihood estimation method). The result showed a good fit of the proposed model with the data ($X^2 = 726.7$, d.f. $= 390$, p $Value = .000$, CFI $= 0.95$, TLI $= 0.95$, GFI $= 0.92$). The 90% confidence interval around the RMSEA value was between 0.034 and 0.043, well below the recommended cut-off level 0.05 (Hu & Bentler, 1999). The Expected Cross-Validation Index (ECVI) and Akaike Information Criterion (AIC) indices for the default model were smaller than those for the saturated and independence models. However, the model chi-square value was still significant. This may be due to the non-normal distribution of the data which was inflating the chi-square value (West, Finch, & Curran, 1995). To ascertain this suspicion, the Bollen-Stine bootstrap in AMOS 16.0 was run on 2000 samples drawn with replacement. The result produced non-significant chi-square (p .06), which shows that there is no difference between the model and data implied covariance. Thus, the data empirically support the proposed theoretical model. Figure 1 depicts the hypothesized relationships and the standardized path coefficients are inserted in it.

Of the first 11 hypotheses, the paths between MONPO $\rightarrow$ effectiveness and MONPO $\rightarrow$ resource attraction were non-significant, which is counterintuitive. All the other hypothesized paths in the structural model were supported as argued in the theoretical framework section. The lack of association between market orientation and effectiveness is explained by the role of innovativeness as a mediator of the relationship. The market orientation $\rightarrow$ effectiveness path, which is non-significant in the presence of the mediator, turns significant if the mediator is removed from the structural model. The direct effect of market orientation on effectiveness, in that case, is significant and positive (path coefficient 0.27; $p = .000$). Thus, innovativeness fully mediates the influence of market orientation on effectiveness. Innovativeness is the missing link between market orientation and

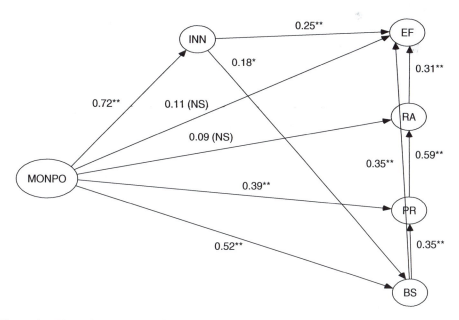

Figure 1. Theoretical model and path coefficients. Note: MONPO = Market orientation in nonprofit organizations; INN = Innovativeness; EF = Effectiveness; RA = Resource attraction; PR = Peer reputation; BS = Beneficiary satisfaction. **$p = .01$; *$p = .05$; NS = Not significant.

effectiveness (Han et al., 1998). At the same time, innovativeness partially mediates the influence of market orientation on beneficiary satisfaction.

To verify if social desirability had biased the results, it was loaded on the structural model ($X^2 = 1233.1$, d.f. $= 612$, p $Value = .000$, CFI $= 0.92$, TLI $= 0.91$, GFI $= 0.90$, RMSEA $= 0.042$). All the fit indices and the RMSEA value worsened with the introduction of social desirability factors. The ECVI and AIC indices reported much smaller values for the theoretical model than for the social desirability plus theoretical model. This shows that the theoretical model has better chances of getting replicated than the one with the social desirability influence. Essentially, it indicates that social desirability does not have a worrisome impact on the results of this research.

Does resource scarcity moderate the market orientation and effectiveness link?

Resource scarcity is an important environmental condition facing NPOs. To explore whether resource scarcity moderated the market orientation and performance relationship, a latent interaction factor was created by multiplying each of the four first-order indicators of MONPO (Modi & Mishra, 2010) with the three indicators of the resource scarcity factor. The indicators were orthogonalized (mean-centred) before creating the product terms to avoid multicollinearity (Little, Bovaird, & Widaman, 2006). The interaction latent loaded onto the structural model showed absence of the hypothesized moderation effect (standardized regression weight 0.034, p .336). The overall fit of the model worsened significantly as proved by the chi-square difference test. This proves that the strength of the MONPO and performance link does not vary across the different degrees of resource scarcity faced by NPOs. Thus, market oriented NPOs would be more effective even during the times of relatively high resource scarcity. Market orientation could prove to be an effective strategic response of NPOs in dealing with a resource scarce environment. The finding assumes greater significance given the current economic conditions world over, which have led to substantial cuts in the available funding globally.

Do the sources of the fund moderate the market orientation and performance link?

The path invariance test for two groups in AMOS 16.0 was used to explore this hypothesis. The first group contained NPOs primarily funded through private donation and the second group contained NPOs funded from public money. The path invariance condition on all the structural paths did not worsen the fit compared to that of the base model (X^2 difference $= 17.2$, d.f. difference $= 12$). The result showed that the structural paths in the model were invariant across the two groups of NPOs as the funding sources did not moderate the strength of the hypothesized relationships. This is an interesting and counterintuitive finding because it was expected that the NPOs funded through private sources would show stronger relationships.

Do size and age of NPOs have any bearing on their levels of market orientation?

The size and age were added as observed exogenous variables in the structural model with direct structural paths on the MONPO latent. The result showed non-significant path coefficients. It means that both age and size neither hinder nor help in developing a market orientation.

Conclusions and implications

Nonprofit organizations occupy an important space in our society as they provide services where the State or markets fail to reach. In fact, Weisbrod (1977) argues that market and state failure provides impetus for the establishment of NPOs. The objective of this research was to study the links between market orientation, innovativeness, resource scarcity, funding source, and performance in the nonprofit context. By doing so, the research aimed at exhibiting the benefits of developing a market orientation to nonprofit practitioners. The results prove that market orientation in an NPO not only increases beneficiaries' satisfaction level but also enhances reputation amongst its peer NPOs. Market orientation also enhances innovation capabilities in an NPO, which could produce program design and delivery related innovations on a consistent basis. However, market orientation alone is not sufficient in improving effectiveness or mission achievement of an NPO. *Innovativeness is the missing link* between market orientation and effectiveness (Han et al., 1998). Innovativeness also partially mediates the market orientation and beneficiary satisfaction link. The implication of the result for practitioners is that they should not focus merely on developing a market orientation to the exclusion of developing innovation capabilities. Both should be simultaneously attempted.

The past studies in the developed country context have shown that market oriented NPOs are able to attract higher resources from their donors (e.g. Gainer & Padanyi, 2002; Morris et al., 2007; Vazquez et al., 2002; White & Simas, 2008). A similar finding was also expected from this research. However, this hypothesis was not supported by the data. I suspected the presence of some moderator or mediator variable, specific to the developing country context, which was suppressing the relationship. I discussed this curious finding with practitioners who believed that networking with donors mattered a great deal in attracting resources. This could form an interesting hypothesis for future research.

The finding that the funding sources do not moderate the market orientation and performance relationships is an interesting one. It was also expected that the NPOs funded primarily through private money would exhibit a higher level of market orientation than the NPOs funded through public money. However, the result showed that their market orientation levels are not significantly different from each other. This means that funding source has no role in development of market orientation in NPOs. Any NPO, funded by public or private money, can develop market focus. This finding has implications for policy makers in India where huge sums of money from various government sponsored welfare schemes (such as National Rural Employment Guarantee Scheme, National Rural Health Mission, etc.) are currently being channeled through a large number of NPOs. The performance of a market oriented NPO does not get affected by the public or private nature of its funders. The policy makers in India can use an NPO's level of market orientation as one of the criteria for empaneling NPOs as partners in service provision or program delivery. If an NPO is market oriented then its performance is not affected by whether it is funded through public or private money. In future research, it would be interesting to see if the finding is replicated in the developed country context.

Limitations

The research has several limitations and the results must be read in light of them. The interest population of the research is limited to those NPOs that depend on third party funding. Future research should try and replicate the findings for self-sufficient NPOs. The cross-sectional design of the research is inadequate in testing the causal claims of the theory. This limitation could be addressed by a future longitudinal study. The data were collected from single, albeit key respondents. Future research may collect data from multiple respondents.

References

Andreasen, A. (1994). Social marketing: Its definition and domain. *Journal of Public Policy & Marketing, 13*, 108–114.

Andreasen, A., Goodstein, R., & Wilson, J. (2005). Transferring 'marketing knowledge' to the nonprofit sector. *California Management Review, 47*(4), 46–67.

Armstrong, J.S., & Overton, T.S. (1977). Estimating nonresponse bias in mail surveys. *Journal of Marketing Research, 14*, 396–402.

Atuahene-Gima, K. (1995). An exploratory analysis of the impact of market orientation on new product performance. *Journal of Product Innovation Management, 12*, 275–293.

Balabanis, G., Stables, R., & Phillips, H. (1997). Market orientation in the top 200 British charity organizations and its impact on their performance. *European Journal of Marketing, 31*, 583–603.

Behling, O., & Law, K. (2000). *Translating questionnaires and other research instruments: Problems and Solutions*. New Delhi: Sage.

Bennett, R. (1998). Market orientation among small to medium sized UK charitable organizations: Implications for fund-raising performance. *Journal of Nonprofit & Public Sector Marketing, 6*, 31–45.

Cano, C.R., Carrillat, F.A., & Jaramillo, F. (2004). A meta-analysis of the relationship between market orientation and business performance: Evidence from five continents. *International Journal of Research in Marketing, 21*, 179–200.

Caruana, A., Ramaseshan, B., & Ewing, M.T. (1997). Market orientation and organizational commitment in the Australian public sector. *International Journal of Public Sector Management, 10*, 294–303.

Caruana, A., Ramaseshan, B., & Ewing, M.T. (1998). Do universities that are more market oriented perform better? *International Journal of Public Sector Management, 11*, 55–70.

Caruana, A., Ramaseshan, B., & Ewing, M.T. (1999). Market orientation and performance in the public sector: The role of organizational commitment. *Journal of Global Marketing, 12*(3), 59–79.

Cervera, A., Molla, A., & Sanchez, M. (2001). Antecedents and consequences of market orientation in public organizations. *European Journal of Marketing, 35*, 1259–1286.

Crowne, D., & Marlowe, D. (1960). A new scale of social desirability independent of psychopathology. *Journal of Consulting Psychology, 24*, 349–354.

Day, G. (1994). The capabilities of market-driven organizations. *Journal of Marketing, 58*(4), 37–52.

Deng, S., & Dart, J. (1994). Measuring market orientation: A multi-factor, multi-item approach. *Journal of Marketing Management, 10*, 725–742.

Deshpande, R., Farley, J., & Webster, F. (1993). Corporate culture, customer orientation, and innovativeness in Japanese firms: A quadrad analysis. *Journal of Marketing, 57*(1), 23–37.

Dholakia, R. (1984). A macromarketing perspective on social marketing: The case of family planning in India. *Journal of Macromarketing, 4*, 53–61.

DiMaggio, P., & Powell, W. (1983). The iron cage revisited: Institutional isomorphism and collective rationality in organizational fields. *American Sociological Review, 48*, 147–160.

Fischer, D.G., & Fick, C. (1993). Measuring social desirability: Short forms of the Marlowe-Crowne social desirability scale. *Educational and Psychological Measurement, 53*, 417–424.

Flavián, C., & Lozano, J. (2006). Organizational antecedents of market orientation in the public university system. *International Journal of Public Sector Management, 19*, 447–467.

Gainer, B., & Padanyi, P. (2002). Applying the marketing concept to cultural organisations: An empirical study of the relationship between market orientation and performance. *International Journal of Nonprofit and Voluntary Sector Marketing, 7*, 182–193.

Gainer, B., & Padanyi, P. (2005). The relationship between market-oriented activities and market-oriented culture: Implications for the development of market orientation in nonprofit service organizations. *Journal of Business Research, 58*, 854–862.

Ganster, D., Hennessey, H., & Luthans, F. (1983). Social desirability response effects: Three alternative models. *Academy of Management Journal, 26*, 321–331.

Gebhardt, G., Carpenter, G., & Sherry, J. (2006). Creating a market orientation: A longitudinal, multifirm, grounded analysis of cultural transformation. *Journal of Marketing*, *70*(4), 37–55.

Gray, B., Matear, S., Boshoff, C., & Matheson, P. (1998). Developing a better measure of market orientation. *European Journal of Marketing*, *32*, 884–903.

Han, J., Kim, N., & Srivastava, R. (1998). Market orientation and organizational performance: Is innovation a missing link? *Journal of Marketing*, *62*(4), 30–45.

Harris, L. (2001). Market orientation and performance: Objective and subjective empirical evidence from UK companies. *Journal of Management Studies*, *38*(1), 17–43.

Hu, L.-T., & Bentler, P. (1999). Cutoff criteria for fit indexes in covariance structure analysis: Conventional criteria versus new alternatives. *Structural Equation Modeling*, *6*, 1–55.

Hult, G.T.M., Hurley, R., & Knight, G. (2004). Innovativeness: Its antecedents and impact on business performance. *Industrial Marketing Management*, *33*, 429–438.

Hult, G.T.M., & Ketchen, D.J. Jr. (2001). Does market orientation matter? A test of the relationship between positional advantage and performance. *Strategic Management Journal*, *22*, 899–906.

Hurley, R., & Hult, G.T.M. (1998). Innovation, market orientation, and organizational learning: An integration and empirical examination. *Journal of Marketing*, *62*(3), 42–54.

Jaworski, B., & Kohli, A. (1993). Market orientation: Antecedents and consequences. *Journal of Marketing*, *57*(3), 53–70.

Jaworski, B., & Kohli, A. (1996). Market orientation: Review, refinement, and roadmap. *Journal of Market-Focused Management*, *1*, 119–135.

Kara, A., Spillan, J., & DeShields, O. (2004). An empirical investigation of the link between market orientation and business performance in non-profit service providers. *Journal of Marketing Theory and Practice*, *12*(2), 59–72.

Kirca, A., Jayachandran, S., & Bearden, W. (2005). Market orientation: A meta-analytic review and assessment of its antecedents and impact on performance. *Journal of Marketing*, *69*(2), 24–41.

Kohli, A., & Jaworski, B. (1990). Market orientation: The construct, research propositions, and managerial implications. *Journal of Marketing*, *54*(2), 1–18.

Kotler, P. (2000). *Marketing management*. Upper Saddle River, NJ: Prentice-Hall.

Kotler, P., & Andreasen, A. (1996). *Strategic marketing for nonprofit organizations*. Upper Saddle River, NJ: Prentice-Hall.

Kotler, P., & Levy, S. (1969). Broadening the concept of marketing. *Journal of Marketing*, *33*(1), 10–15.

Kumar, K., Subramanian, R., & Yauger, C. (1998). Examining the market orientation–performance relationship: A context-specific study. *Journal of Management*, *24*, 201–233.

Kumar, N., Stem, L., & Anderson, J. (1993). Conducting interorganisational research using key informants. *Academy of Management Journal*, *36*, 1633–1651.

Lamb, C.W.Jr., & Crompton, J.L. (1990). Analysing marketing performance. In S.H. Fine (Ed.), *Social marketing: Promoting the causes of public and nonprofit agencies* (pp. 173–194). Needham Heights, MA: Allyn & Bacon.

Little, T., Bovaird, J., & Widaman, K. (2006). On the merits of orthogonalizing powered and product terms: Implications for modeling interactions among latent variables. *Structural Equation Modeling*, *13*, 497–519.

Macedo, I., & Pinho, J. (2006). The relationship between resource dependence and market orientation: The specific case of non-profit organizations. *European Journal of Marketing*, *40*, 533–553.

Menguc, B., & Auh, S. (2006). Creating a firm-level dynamic capability through capitalizing on market orientation and innovativeness. *Academy of Marketing Science Journal*, *34*, 63–73.

Millham, J. (1974). Two components of need for approval score and their relationships to cheating following success and failure. *Journal of Research in Personality*, *8*, 378–392.

Mishra, D., Biswas, S., & Roy, S. (2005). Governance of NGOs: Contextualizing in the Indian experience. *International Journal of Rural Management*, *1*, 185–201.

Modi, P., & Mishra, D. (2010). Conceptualising market orientation in non-profit organisations: Definition, performance, and preliminary construction of a scale. *Journal of Marketing Management*, *26*, 548–569.

Morris, M., Coombes, S., Schindehutte, M., & Allen, J. (2007). Antecedents and outcomes of entrepreneurial and market orientations in a non-profit context: Theoretical and empirical insights. *Journal of Leadership & Organizational Studies*, *13*(4), 12–39.

Narver, J., & Slater, S. (1990). The effect of a market orientation on business profitability. *Journal of Marketing, 54*(2), 20–35.

Oczkowski, E., & Farrell, M. (1998). Discriminating between measurement scales using non-nested tests and two-stage least squares: The case of market orientation. *International Journal of Research in Marketing, 15*, 349–366.

Padanyi, P., & Gainer, B. (2004). Market orientation in the nonprofit sector: Taking multiple constituencies into consideration. *Journal of Marketing Theory and Practice, 12*(2), 43–58.

Palmer, R., & Randall, A. (2002). *Financial management in the voluntary sector*. London: Routledge.

Pelham, A. (1993). *Mediating and moderating influences on the relationship between market orientation and performance* (Unpublished doctoral dissertation). Pennsylvania State University.

Pelham, A., & Wilson, D. (1996). A longitudinal study of the impact of market structure, firm structure, strategy, and market orientation culture on dimensions of small-firm performance. *Journal of the Academy of Marketing Science, 24*, 27–43.

Podsakoff, P., MacKenzie, S., Lee, J., & Podsakoff, N. (2003). Common method biases in behavioral research: A critical review of the literature and recommended remedies. *Journal of Applied Psychology, 88*, 879–903.

Ramanaiah, N., & Martin, H. (1980). On the two-dimensional nature of the Marlowe-Crowne social desirability scale. *Journal of Personality Assessment, 44*, 507–514.

Ramanaiah, N., Schill, T., & Leung, L. (1977). A test of the hypothesis about the two dimensional nature of the Marlowe-Crowne social desirability scale. *Journal of Research in Personality, 11*, 251–259.

Roth, P., Switzer, F., & Switzer, D. (1999). Missing data in multiple item scales: A Monte-Carlo analysis of missing data techniques. *Organizational Research Methods, 2*, 211–232.

Ruekert, R. (1992). Developing a market orientation: An organizational strategy perspective. *International Journal of Research in Marketing, 9*, 225–245.

Salamon, L., & Anheier, H. (1998). Social origins of civil society: Explaining the nonprofit sector cross-nationally. *Voluntas: International Journal of Voluntary and Nonprofit Organizations, 9*, 213–248.

Seymour, T., Gilbert, D., & Kolsaker, A. (2006). Aspects of market orientation of English and Welsh charities. *Journal of Nonprofit & Public Sector Marketing, 16*, 151–169.

Shapiro, B. (1973). Marketing for nonprofit organizations. *Harvard Business Review, 51*, 223–232.

Slater, S., & Narver, J. (1994). Does competitive environment moderate the market orientation–performance relationship? *Journal of Marketing, 58*(1), 46–55.

Subramanian, R., & Gopalakrishna, P. (2001). The market orientation–performance relationship in the context of a developing economy: An empirical analysis. *Journal of Business Research, 53*, 1–13.

Tay, L., & Morgan, N. (2002). Antecedents and consequences of market orientation in chartered surveying firms. *Construction Management and Economics, 20*, 331–341.

Vazquez, R., Alvarez, L., & Santos, M. (2002). Market orientation and social services in private non-profit organizations. *European Journal of Marketing, 36*, 1022–1046.

Voss, G., & Voss, Z. (2000). Strategic orientation and firm performance in an artistic environment. *Journal of Marketing, 64*(1), 67–83.

Weisbrod, B.A. (1977). *The voluntary non-profit sector*. Lexington, DC: Heath and Company.

West, S., Finch, J., & Curran, P. (1995). Structural equations with non-normal variables: Problems and remedies. In R.H. Hoyle (Ed.), *Structural equation modeling: Issues and applications* (pp. 56–75). Newbury Park, CA: Sage.

White, D., & Simas, C. (2008). An empirical investigation of the link between market orientation and church performance. *International Journal of Nonprofit and Voluntary Sector Marketing, 13*, 153–165.

Wood, V., Bhuian, S., & Kiecker, P. (2000). Market orientation and organizational performance in nonprofit hospitals. *Journal of Business Research, 48*, 213–226.

Bridging virtual and real worlds: enhancing outlying clustered value creations

Daniel D. Bretonès[a], Bernard Quinio[b,c] and Gilbert Reveillon[b]

[a]Département Management, Stratégie, et Systèmes, Université Centre Val de Loire/ESCEM, 11, rue de l'Ancienne Comédie, Poitiers, 86001, France; [b]Département Gestion, Université Paris Ouest, 200, avenue de la République, Nanterre, 92001, France; [c]Département Information, Opérations Management, ESCP EUROPE, 79 avenue de la République, Paris, France

Virtual worlds and virtual social networks provide real opportunities for companies to implement research in management dealing with immersive environment, interaction and co-creation of values (artefact, process, knowledge). New capabilities and new tools are emerging. The observations drawn from experiments allow categorizing them. We then propose an approach that could help companies to start activities inside these new environments of collaborative work. The cross fertilizing insights between the virtual and the real world are shown and introduced as the bridge. The 3D economy process is based on shorter cycles of decision making processes. The 'bridge model' integrates the added value chain and goes beyond it with the creation of outlying clustered values. The bridge mechanism shows a spectrum from low potential to high potential areas – of fulfillments. A company strategy may explain a positioning on one or the other limits of the spectrum.

Introduction

The three dimensional economy (3D) illustrated through virtual worlds (VW) and virtual social networks (VSN) provide real opportunities for companies in the fields of immersion, interaction and value co-creation. VW without at least one individual member of a VSN, being linked synchronously or asynchronously due to persistence characteristics of the online world, is an empty space out of our scope. For practical reasons, when 'VW' is mentioned in this document it means 'VW and 3D VSN' including serious games and Massively Multiplayer Online Role Playing Games (MMORPG). Inputs coming from R&D and management practices suggest that between the digital environment and the reality there is a mutual enrichment process. 3D economy process relies on reducing decision making cycles and their persistent capabilities (e.g. with rehearsal/simulation functionalities) to provide a safer workplace and collaborative environment. This may be understood through the 'bridge model' which not only integrates but surpasses the value chain model and the associated silos. This bridge model lets value creation rise out in new distributed dimensions coming from innovative practices, achievements and tangible outcomes.

Business cases were made, from those virtual worlds defined by Limayen, Hendaoui, and Thompson (2008). They aim at defining the technical, organizational and functional systems used. The goal of this paper is to understand how companies can use those 3D applications and VSN to create value. Those virtual worlds and VSN are first classified and defined. A double stage approach is then introduced to help companies find out what virtualization is. The first stage deals with the strategic position aimed at. The second one deals with the selection of the strategic operations which can be 'virtualized' through the activity theory framework and the transition from reality to 'virtual reality' enhanced with the bridge model. This approach has been tested over a 3-year period and 56 case studies coming from the international Intraverse awards. The Intraverse awards competition was created in 2007 (Quinio & Réveillon, 2008). It gathers, through an international competition process, the world best usage of 3D virtual worlds within organizations as presented in the Intraverse awards (2010). Four issues of the Intraverse awards were held from 2007 to 2010. The 2009 Intraverse London ceremony awards can be viewed on a multimedia support (Réveillon, 2009). A practical study coming from the selected cases in 2009, the case of Michelin, is presented in the last section of this paper.

Virtual social networks and organizations

State of the art

The technical dimension of those VW originates in the industrial applications. According to Fuchs, Arnaldi, and Moreau (2006), the virtual reality allows users, via their avatar, to change the time, the place(s) and interact with a new world and others' avatars. First applications of virtual reality came from the technical field (Arnaldi & Gerbault, 2009). Interactions between world users, as changes are carried out, make the virtual world constantly on the move, and this evolution seems to be improvised (Ortiz de Gortari, 2007).

There exists today more than 300 VW listed in the world with an estimated 700 million web users and more than 150 million users with mobile phones. The most important ones are located in Asia (*QQ* with 1 billion multi-media registered accounts) and *Cyworld* in the USA (*Penguin Club* and *Neopets*). Some of those VW are clearly dedicated to a young public (teenagers) or opened to a wide public (*Second Life* and *Facebook* with 500 million registered users using extensively 3D applications such as *Scene Caster* or the online game *Farmville* with 80 million registered accounts) and their in world and real world (RW) communities. These worlds allow new experiments where users can be free from time, space and gravity constraints. Social relations are regulated by the in world or the social network behavioural practice code and habit called community management.

Those 3D immersive VW allow the final user to get involved in the upstream design process. So they make easier the products and services customization by the companies. The user may form new virtual objects (content) but also change the world environment (context) and develop new communities and new linkages within VW. Companies try to capture the users' generated content and context through those 3D platforms, and must identify, listen and adapt their offers to what these communities say about them within these VW. A consumer is not viewed as an isolated individual but as an influential force in an online community. A clothes manufacturer may observe avatars trying its range of products in the virtual world, study the collections which are the most successful and propose customizations for marketing in tangible shops. Virtual worlds are closed, and for this reason each company selects an environment which may disappear. A possible solution could be found in the outcome of the 3D Metaverse worlds (METAVERSE Roadmaps, 2010) that is to say a set of virtual worlds communicating between themselves; another solution is the development of virtual world standards (Sivan, 2009). VW are increasingly perceived as an opportunity for business activity and some typologies of VW have already been proposed to promote studies and applications (Kim, Lyons, & Cunningham, 2008; Messinger, Stroulia, & Lyons, 2008). But these typologies generally do not include technology within social or business contexts.

Definition and classification of VW

In order to define and classify VW, a study was made on 60 international VW (Quinio & Réveillon, 2008). This study was made through direct observations among the following VW (*QQ*, *Second Life*, *Entropia* and *Facebook*) enhancing online communities management such as what is happening through the usage of VSN, MMORPG and serious games. This study is different from the 56 case studies obtained from the Intraverse awards competitions from 2007 to 2010.

A VW is defined as a 3D and persistent environment linking up a human community through avatars. Each avatar may interact directly and freely with the other ones within the virtual social networks generated as it can make it on the virtual environment (objects and or contexts creation and changes).

In this survey of 60 VW, the following characteristics were used:

- communication analysis (dialog tool via chat, voice through IP);
- pictures analysis and graphics tool because the quality of a virtual world is partly assessed through the immersion process;
- consumer analysis (understand how the VW is used and by whom);
- VW analysis (dealing with the world and categories of actions related to the virtual environment).

The results distinguished three main VW categories:

(1) the scenario worlds: this category relies on a basic scenario from which all the actions carried out in this world have to be modelled such as serious games and MMORPG;
(2) the worlds relying on chats: the main goal of a visit is to allow the Internet users having subscribed to chat and interact within virtual communities;
(3) the worlds with parallel reality: this category is quite close to the present web. Users may go shopping, meet and wander around in the scenery without having goals to reach.

From those virtual environments *Second Life* was selected as it best illustrated the transition from the value chain concept to what we call the 'outlying clustered value creations'. Despite the fact that Linden labs, the founder of *Second Life*, implemented a major downsizing in the organization in June 2010, this VW seems to offer great opportunities for companies.

Firms can create value

The study of value creation in VW was made using case studies in a scientific approach (Yin, 1989). A survey was conducted on 56 companies from 2008 to 2010. The associated business cases were coming from the Intraverse award competitions (Intraverse awards, 2010). These cases were assessed by the Intraverse assessment committee. This committee is made up of academic experts and professionals. It ranks the proposed cases according to a list of criteria as shown in Table 1.

The cases received for the Intraverse awards competition may belong to seven categories: small and medium companies; big business; territorial communities; R&D; education; project; serious games.

Table 1. Intraverse case studies assessment matrix.

Marks by group of criteria	Case studies selection criteria
30	**Topic of the 3D virtual world/serious game** Level of innovation Concerned audience and relative importance Strategic importance of the project (not yet online versus operating) International scope Stakeholders engagement
20	**Attitude 2.0** Number of exchanges done over the 3D platform Importance of the contributions as value creation Hierarchy levels concerned within the organization
15	**Quality of the intangible asset (island, building, 3D object)** Clear graphics, ergonomics Interaction Multimedia Update
20	**Feedback of the platform content** Audience measures (traditional media, Internet, blog, wiki) ROI (level of allocated resources versus measured return) Strategic alignment of the organization versus 3D
10	**General quality of the application file**
5	**Media impact obtained further to awarding it**
100	

First stage: strategic positioning

The results of the Intraverse awards from 2008 to 2010 are presented in Intraverse awards (2009) and Le blog des managers 2.0 (2008); and completed by a literature survey (Chang et al., 2008; Chen, Slau, & Nah, 2008; Ives & Junglas, 2008; Lee, 2008) which allowed studying the first experiments. All the categories of organizations have been scrutinized, from small to large companies, associations and administrations. The business models may be internal to a VW (for instance a real estate agency selling virtual islands to virtual residents in *Second Life*) or located at the real world border (a real estate agency selling real properties having had them first visited in a virtual way). The experiments described are relying on Porter's (1985) value chain (see Figure 1).

The targets of using those strategic tools may be internal (company employees) or external (customers and partners) within communities being on or off line. In Figure 1, the character's

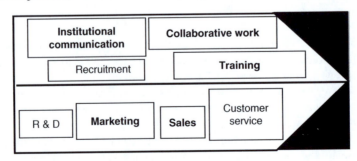

Figure 1. Organizations' experiments characteristics.

size specifies the importance in volume of the experiments in the portfolio of 56 case studies. A few lessons can be drawn from the virtualization introduction inside the companies' activities. The initial investment to provide a presence, even imperfect, is limited and it allows the acquisition of a real knowledge of those new environments within which the immersion and the persistency are implemented in new managerial dimensions. Design risks may be limited having recourse to the 3D simulation. 3D immersive tools bring in a real added value for specific activities, such as training and marketing for instance. The crucial point for the companies is to select the adequate business activities and have the good ideas necessary to obtain productivity gains, stress reductions or build a competitive advantage. Two tracks may be outlined. The first one shows an external direction towards the institutional communication and then a marketing orientation to product co-creation and sales. The second one is internally oriented towards innovation, training and collaborative work. In this case, the goal is to save and protect resources and to increase the creativity. Some authors have proposed a classification of strategic attitudes for organizations that have a virtual and a real business (Goel & Prokopec, 2009). Companies may have a specific virtual strategy, a virtual strategy parallel with a real one, a mirroring strategy and finally a virtual strategy linked with a real one.

To go beyond the classical value chain, showing the silos characterizing organizations, the expression 'outlying clusters value creations' (OCVC) was created. In a VW actors may co-operate and co-produce in multidimensional ways and generate OCVC. In Figure 1, the black area at the chain's tip shows the value creation area. The latter originates from the outlying clustered value creations obtained by the decompartmentalization of the organizations' traditional silos. The 'outlying clusters value creations' concept was first designed and tested from the Intraverse awards cases studied. The mechanism shows a spectrum from low potential to high potential value creation. In Figure 2, the graphic corresponds to a world leading continental European bank. The positioning of two businesses is presented. The company strategy may explain a positioning on one or the other limit of the spectrum; fostering value creation for stakeholders being inside and/or outside virtual communities. The initial presence of this bank in *Second Life* with its virtual building and the first avatars of the participating team members can be analysed as a mirror effect of the real world. Media coverage benefits can be related to a communication strategy and to an increased awareness for the brand on specific targets. The bank archipelago (including a selection of business units) in *Second Life* was developed later with a few virtual buildings and a strong customization of the participants' avatars. In this model, we distinguished a 'low added value creation area' bridge defined by the duplication of the real world activities and or the brand communication channels like in the tangible economy (Figure 2).

We also can notice a 'high added value creation area' bridge where the OCVC translate the synergies coming from the overall system. It formalizes the bridges between the RW and the VW in the framework of strategically managed activities (Quinio & Réveillon, 2008). In addition to that, if the VW developments last as expected, the company will find in the VW, new collaborative work spaces and milestones.

This first stage of the approach allows the definition of a global positioning of the organization, and then leveraged activities, which can be virtualized and transcended, may be chosen.

Analysing activities: the activity theory

The activity theory analyses the human practices in a social context and in relation with tools (Leontiev, 1981; Vygotsky, 1978). It focuses on work and learning and defining activity as an essential component (Marciniak, 2009). An activity is a relationship between

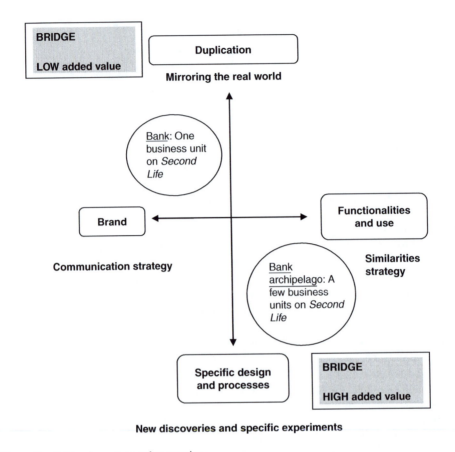

Figure 2.   Bridge impact on value creation.

a subject (individual or group) and its environment through an object. This theory has been used in the studies on collective work (Hasan, 2003; Lorino, 2006). Observing activities allow understanding of the tools evolution and how they influence knowledge and social groups practices. Once the knowledge is assimilated, it is integrated in the tool to enrich it. In the most recent developments (Quinio, Marciniak, & Réveillon, 2009), the triad subject/tool/object is studied within the organization context in VW (Figure 3).

The relationship between the subject and the goal is used not only by the tools but also the community which defines the rules, the organization and the context in which the subject or the subjects act. The global model (Figure 4) allows the representation of

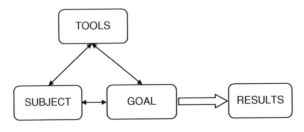

Figure 3.   The activity theory triad.

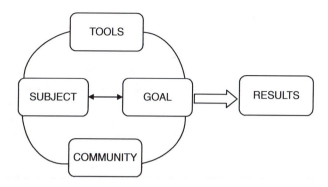

Figure 4. The activity theory global model.

activity systems or activities networks. For instance, the tool component of an activity may result from another design and achievement activity from a technical team. In addition, an activity may evolve towards a more complex activity. In the case of a system of activities, a main activity is determined, upon which are connected support or related activities.

The activity (level 1) is related to the goal. It is achieved through a run of actions (level 2) which define a part of the 'how to do it'. Actions are composed of operations (level 3) which define the 'how to do it' in specific conditions. The following example is proposed from the literature (Hasan, 2003). A designer wants to lay out a product (activity) to be marketed (goal). Among the activities to achieve, he has to manufacture the product (action) which will make use of data acquisition, implemented with specific engineering tools (operations) (Figure 5).

The goal is to compare the activity taking place in the real world and the one going off in a virtual world (in world). Every time that the VW possibilities allow for a real action to be turned into a virtual operation embedded in the tool, participants may face more complex actions. With this point of view on activity in a VW, it is possible to identify which activity can create value for the organization. In Figure 5, the descending direction corresponds to a simplification of the studied practice. The increase in the number of operations and the decrease in the number of actions allow to automate a part of the work and to free some time to tackle more complex activities. The knowledge really acquired is grafted therefore in the tool during operations. Then, the knowledge is made re-usable in another action or in another activity. Relying on developments obtained from the activity theory, one may assume that the components transferred from the VW to the RW constitute the knowledge embedded in the tool (including the avatar itself) through the virtualized activities. Thus company borders are changed as the VW and the RW fit in.

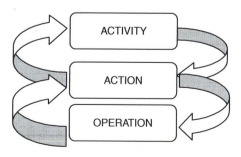

Figure 5. The three activity levels.

Studying the transition points: the bridge model

The VW practice for a company requires necessarily shifting at a certain time from the real world to the VW. It requires going over activities in the VW then to return in the RW. The process analysis (Hammer & Champy, 1993) allows specifying when and where the transition to the virtual world may happen and when and where the return to the real world takes place. In our approach, virtualization is not opposed to reality but understood as a space opening new opportunities (Quinio et al., 2009). Virtualization is an unrivalled environment to experience milestone achievements (including experiential marketing for brands). The key questions are dealing with the transition points between the VW and the RW. This can be shown peculiarly in the consumption of virtual goods which can never be totally substituted to the consumption of tangible goods such as described by Siddiqui and Turley (2006). Knowledge management and value creation are placed at the interface between the RW and the VW. Some activities happening in the RW may not be held in the VW and some activities can be achieved only inside the immersive 3D environment. On the other hand, a significant number of activities are improved with this cross fertilization system dealing with the following stages: design integration; achievement; and discrepancies reduction in both worlds.

Business case: a training centre for the enterprise architecture

This case study introduced by Michelin comes from the London Intraverse awards competition in 2009 (Intraverse awards, 2009). In the course of 2007 this European industrial tyre and rubber group was facing strong rivalry from its world competitors in Asia and in North America. This company is one of the leading players in the global tyres and rubber world market value approaching US$115 billion in 2009 (Table 2).

More than 94% of this market is distributed on three continents: Asia; Europe; and North America (Table 3). Among decisions made to foster the firm's global services development, the Board of Directors wished to improve the firm's productivity and an enhanced creative team work approach on a worldwide basis. This orientation supported the goals to grow the base of global customers and to accelerate the products and services delivery cycles. In this context, the firm wanted to develop Enterprise Architecture projects and to improve the effectiveness of training on this complex topic. For the understanding of this case, we also rely on a case study of Forrester (Driver, 2008).

All traditional teaching slides based approaches were not satisfactory

The chief information officer and the enterprise architecture (EA) IT teams were assigned a major role in promoting the new global teaching environment relying on an innovative collaborative and immersive solution (Le blog des managers 2.0). All traditional slide based

Table 2. Global tyres and rubber market value: 2005–2009.

Years 2005–2009	Market value: US$ billion
2005	110
2006	118
2007	130
2008	120
2009	115

Source: Datamonitor, March 2010.

Table 3.   Global tyres and rubber market segmentation.

Territory	% share, by value, 2009
Asia Pacific	34.4
Europe	26.5
North America	33.6
Rest of the World	5.5

Source: Datamonitor, March 2010.

approaches were unsatisfactory as they appeared to be too conceptual and too complex. The challenge was to train, in a first period, 163 IT people in North America, Europe and Asia to understand the EA, so that they would design and deliver global applications based on EA.

A virtual and totally interactive training centre was established with the support of an IT agency in March 2008. The EA group within the IT division launched a private two island region in *Second Life* designed to train the IT professionals on architecture concepts. The total training package was redesigned and simplified. It was then made virtual to be accessible from anywhere, without requiring a change of location. This virtual environment allowed teaching complex concepts in new ways. Trainees used interactive teaching materials built into the environment which helped them work on business concepts, process management, functional blocks and business services relying on service oriented architecture. The importance of the IT governance was stressed by placing a space dedicated to teaching and learning about governance at the geographical centre of the region. The training sessions were under the supervision of a coach trainer, but they were also designed for self-training.

To introduce some fun, the participants, who completed the exercises, are allowed to race against their peers in virtual go-karts around a track, where the centrepiece was a giant company logo. This conveys within the company an image of EA as something new and exciting (Driver, 2008).

Costs assessment

A virtual world development agency was hired to build the *Second Life* region. It took about two months and the cost was close to €60,000, which is more or less the same as what was spent for the traditional classroom training. In this first stage the traditional classroom cost is increased by the *Second Life* training cost. However reducing the training cost was not the firm's main objective. In the future, training within the virtual environment could replace part of the traditional training methods (Driver, 2008). Thus the global training cost per employee might be reduced. Nevertheless, specific training actions which require face to face situations will not disappear, despite the virtual training environment take off. During this experiment, significant time and budget savings were made on transport and meeting place costs.

The pedagogical approach

Training was based on a mix of PowerPoint presentations and interactive lessons where trainees manipulated objects. Training the IT professionals on the basic navigation skills, how to move an avatar in their new *Second Life* environment, takes only few minutes. Trainees attend sessions using their avatars, sit in an audience with the avatars of their peers and listen to a presentation. Trainees visit a variety of interactive sessions where they can learn to build a road map. IT projects are represented by circles with related costs. The trainees may click on them and then match the cost of the project with the company's goals and business priorities.

A good or bad answer turns the clicked circle green or red. Trainees are taught to build business processes which fit with the company's strategic options. They can also learn how to turn the business processes into business services delivered across activities as shown by Driver (2008).

Simulation is a complementary part of this training. It involves employees in virtual situations where they can gain experience which will benefit the company later. The trainees were asked to express their satisfaction level on the EA methodology implemented and on their *Second Life* immersive environment perception. The 163 trainees answered a basic questionnaire, the results are shown in Table 4.

These results are considered as promising by the EA group. The EA management believe virtual worlds are a great way to present, to train and to interact. It allows the unleashing of group members' creativity but it also requires a careful preparation prior to being implemented.

Additional benefits

Training the IT professionals to use the *Second Life* virtual environment was the first stage in an ambitious programme within the Michelin group. The positive results obtained by the IT professionals triggered off the scheduling of more training sessions within the group.

The firm aims at training more than 2000 executives in both the conceptual and functional aspects of EA. Islands were used for internal events such as communication of the 2009 objectives. They are now used to set up meetings and conferences. The firm is investigating other opportunities to use the virtual worlds for training in other areas.

Confrontation with our model

The firm's strategic position was obviously in the 'high value area' of Figure 2. The VW platform did not propose only the duplication of a traditional learning platform but additional functionalities. The 3D environment allowed shifting a traditional teaching environment to a new learning concept. By using the capacity of the VW (3D and immersion) the participants were able to integrate their new knowledge in the tool. The trainees were not only reading, but were also manipulating, complex concepts via their avatar. The outcome of the satisfaction survey in Table 4 shows that participants have transferred their knowledge from the VW to the RW.

Conclusion

In this paper, the theoretical input relies mostly on the activity theory and on the concept of outlying cluster value creations observed and measured from our 56 case studies carried out over a 3-year period. The cases studied dealt with the positioning of one, or a few,

Table 4. EA methodology understanding and immersive environment satisfaction.

	I understand the EA methodology (%)	*Second Life* appropriate to learn about EA (%)
Very true	61	59
True	35	38
Somewhat true	4	3
Not true	0	0

Source: Intraverse awards (2009).

strategic selections of business units and activities in the virtual world. Once the activities are selected, the way in which an optimal value can be co-produced in one or a few selections of communities, has to be thought through the framework of an open innovation process. As we saw, companies may have a specific virtual strategy, a virtual strategy parallel with a real one, a mirroring strategy and/or a virtual strategy linked with a real one (Goel & Prokopec, 2009).

Training implications

Integrating the 3D environments in the teaching and training solutions is possible. It brings new and innovative aspects in the field of training. Trainees may learn quickly to manipulate objects and concepts. They are able to redesign processes and business roadmaps. They can also assess the services delivery quality and relevance within their organizations. These 3D immersive solutions may be mixed with traditional training formulas. From the Intraverse experiences, it can be suggested that academic institutions and organizations could take advantage to enhance the role of 3D environments in their teaching and training activities. Promoting the 3D training might become a differentiation criterion between organizations in the future.

Managerial implications

From a managerial perspective, integrating the 3D immersive environment in a strategic approach requires a few pre-requisites. Management has to be aware of the potential value creations that can be repatriated from the VW to the RW. Manager awareness is one thing, but a potential value creation has to be turned into a project showing the many possibilities proposed by the 3D environments. With the EA project, it has been shown that the new functionalities integrated in the tools allowed for the manipulation of objects in a new and creative way. Experiences acquired and integrated in the tools allow firms to identify the outlying clustered value creations which will position the company strategy in the 'high value area' of Figure 2. The integration of the OCVC opportunities in a company strategy requires an adequate testing, prior to the strategy implementation. Once new OCVC have been identified and tested, it is necessary to assess their potential in terms of additional revenues for the company. In addition to that, the transfer to the RW from concepts tested in the VW may affect significantly the company organization and its managerial practices. The strategic integration of the OCVC potential requires managers to show a forerunner profile as well as business developers' skills, supported with a strong taste for assessing innovative outcomes.

What is at stake for a company is to be able to differentiate from its competitors and to reinforce its strategic position. This can be done through something like the EA project depicted above which can be prepared and structured before being tested in a programme. It is also possible to imagine that a small innovation entity, related to the corporate management, might test the 3D environments and their subsequent new positioning for related potentialities. Recommendations could then be made to the management, whose responsibility would be to choose to commit investment in those 3D immersive ventures, or not.

Taking into account the major developments of the 3D environments, it seems difficult for companies to do without them. The 3D environments could be used to support the creation of blue ocean market segments as introduced by Kim and Mauborgne (2005). One of the possible uses of these 3D environments would be to make easier the achievement of new strategic options. It seems difficult for managers not to get involved in what turns out to be a possible source of value creation. Business schools should also be tasked with integrating these immersive tools into their educational programmes for both current and future managers, not only to stimulate their intellectual contribution in the development of strategy, but to open up their eyes to strategic capabilities.

3D environments technical limits

This research has to be reinforced with new cases, showing details of technological environments. On a technical point, solutions such as the *Second Life* environment are proprietary ones. There is a strong demand from companies which want to implement these solutions to move to non-proprietary '3D' standards. Companies may invest in proprietary solutions, only if they are maintained on the medium/long term. They want to secure their 3D investment. A real 3D market development seems to be dependent on the outcome of non-proprietary standards shared by a large group of the software developer community.

Limitations and future research orientations

The 3D cases, studied within the Intraverse awards competitions, are limited to a small number. A more extended period of survey would allow a better understanding of the way the VW work and their relationships with the RW. This research has to be reinforced with new cases showing details on the technological environments. Scientific analysis, applied to the new 3D solutions, will play a major role in the coming years. The R&D investigators in this field will have to test and assess the innovative solutions proposed and their related benefits. Their analysis will orientate the possible growth of the 3D immersive markets in the coming years. The main direction of the research is to study in depth the cases identified in the Intraverse competitions. It is also planned to develop a serious game as a complementary field of expertise. Ultimately, this study describes the new capabilities proposed to the management in terms of knowledge urbanization with 3D, within strategically evolving organizations.

References

Arnaldi, B., & Gerbault, S. (2009). Humains virtuels et collaboration dans un environnement virtuel de formation. *Techniques et sciences informatiques, 28*, 741–766.

Chang, K.T.T., Koh, A.T.T., Low, B.Y.Y., Santos Onghanseng, D.J., Tanoto, K., & Thuong-Thuong, T.S. (2008). *Why I love this on line game: The MMORPG stickiness factor*. International Conference on Information Systems (ICIS) 2008 proceedings. Paper 88. Retrieved from http://aisel.aisnet.org/icis2008/88

Chen, X.F., Slau, K., & Nah, F.F.H. (2008). *Adoption of 3-D virtual worlds for education*. International Conference on Information Systems (ICIS) 2008 proceedings. Paper 113. Retrieved from http://aisel.aisnet.org/icis2008/113

Driver, E. (2008). *Michelin uses Second Life for enterprise architecture training*. Retrieved from http://www.forrester.com/rb/Research/case_study_michelin_uses_second_life_for/q/id/46085/t/2

Fuchs, O., Arnaldi, B., & Moreau, G. (2006). *Le traité de la réalité virtuelle, volume 4: Les applications de la réalité virtuelle*. Paris: Les Presses – Mines Paris (Science, Mathématiques & Informatique).

Goel, L., & Prokopec, S. (2009). If you build it will they come? An empirical investigation of consumer perceptions and strategy in virtual worlds. *Electron Commerce Research, 9*, 115–134.

Hammer, M., & Champy, J. (1993). *Le reengineering: Réinventer l'entreprise pour une amélioration spectaculaire de ses performances*. Paris: Editions Dunod.

Hasan, H. (2003, January 6–9). *An activity-based model of collective knowledge*. Proceedings of the 36th Hawaii International Conference on System Sciences, Big Island, HI.

Intraverse awards. (2009, May 9). Re: Intraverse 2009-Liste des lauréats. Retrieved from http://www.intraverse.eu/news/intraverse-awards-2009-laureats

Intraverse awards. (2010, January 10). Re: International Intraverse awards 2010. Retrieved from http://www.intraverse.eu/

Ives, B., & Junglas, I. (2008). APC forum: Business implications of virtual world and serious game. *MIS Quarterly Executive*, *7*(3), 151–155.

Kim, H.M., Lyons, K., & Cunningham, M.A. (2008). Towards a theoretically-grounded framework for evaluating immersive business models and applications: Analysis of ventures in Second Life. *Journal of Virtual Worlds Research: Past, Present and Future*, *1*(1), 1–19.

Kim, W.C., & Mauborgne, R. (2005). *The blue ocean strategy: How to create uncontested market space and make the competition irrelevant*. Boston, MA: Harvard Business School Press.

Le blog des managers 2.0. (2008, June 5). Re: Résultats du prix Intraverse. Retrieved from http://b-r-ent.com/news/resultats-du-prix-intraverse-2008

Le blog des managers 2.0. (2009, July 6). Re: La vidéo du Chief Architecture Officer de Michelin [Video file]. Retrieved from http://b-r-ent.com/news/world-intraverse-awards-london-7-mai-09-live-second-life-et-trophees-loov#comment_14

Lee, P.D. (2008, March 29). *Do supply chains exist in virtual worlds?* Paper presented at the 2008 Northeast Decision Sciences Institute Conference, School of Business, Rutgers, Camden, Brooklyn, USA.

Leontiev, A.N. (1981). *Problems of the development of mind*. Moscow: Progress.

Limayen, M., Hendaoui, A., & Thompson, C.W. (2008). 3D social virtual worlds research issues and challenges. *IEEE International Computing*, *12*(1), 88–92.

Lorino, P. (2006, September). *La notion de processus en gestion comme première approche des activités coopératives complexes*. Paper presented at the Cerisy Conference on Des pratiques coopératives: Constitution des agents, constitution des œuvres, Cerisy, France.

Marciniak, R. (2009). *Coordination, théorie de l'activité et théories des organisations*. Paris: Editions Presses Universitaires Paris Ouest Nanterre La Défense.

Messinger, P., Stroulia, E., & Lyons, K. (2008). A typology of virtual worlds, historical overview and future directions. *Virtual Worlds Research*, *1*(1), 1–18.

METAVERSE Roadmaps. (2010). *Pathways to the 3D web*. Retrieved from http://www.metaverseroadmap.org/

Ortiz de Gortari, A. (2007, September). *Second Life survey: User profile for psychological engagement & gambling*. Paper presented at the Virtual 2007 Conference, Stockholm, Sweden.

Porter, M. (1985). *Competitive advantage*. New York: Free Press.

Quinio, B., Marciniak, R., & Réveillon, G. (2009, June 10–12). *La recherche sur les univers virtuels une proposition de démarche fondée sur l'activité*. Paper presented at the meeting of AIM, Marrakech, Morocco.

Quinio, B., & Réveillon, G. (2008). Economie 3D et intégration des univers virtuels. *Vie & Sciences Economiques*, *179–180*, 76–93.

Réveillon, G. (2009, May 18). 2009-Wiva-Intraverse-awards-Apply-London-New3S [Video file]. Retrieved from http://www.youtube.com/watch?v=5MK-10dCMzs

Siddiqui, S., & Turley, D. (2006). Extending the self in a virtual world. *Advances in Consumer Research*, *33*, 647–648.

Sivan, Y. (2009). Overview: State of virtual worlds standards in 2009. *Journal of Virtual Worlds Research*, *2*(3), 3–18.

Vygotsky, L.S. (1978). *Mind and society*. Cambridge, MA: Harvard University Press.

Yin, R.K. (1989). *Case study research: Design and methods* (2nd ed.). Newbury Park, CA: Sage.

Index

Page numbers in *Italics* represent tables.
Page numbers in **Bold** represent figures.
Page numbers followed by a represent appendix.